TOWARD A SUSTAINABLE WATER FUTURE

VISIONS FOR 2050

SPONSORED BY
Emerging and Innovative Technology Committee

Environmental and Water Resources Institute (EWRI)
of the American Society of Civil Engineers

EDITED BY
Walter M. Grayman, Ph.D., P.E., D.WRE
Daniel P. Loucks, Ph.D.
Laurel Saito, Ph.D., P.E.

Published by the American Society of Civil Engineers

Library of Congress Cataloging-in-Publication Data

Toward a sustainable water future : visions for 2050 / sponsored by Emerging and
Innovative Technology Committee, Environmental and Water Resources Institute (EWRI)
of the American Society of Civil Engineers; edited by Walter M. Grayman, Daniel P.
Loucks, Laurel Saito.
    p. cm.
  Includes bibliographical references and index.
  ISBN 978-0-7844-1207-7 (pbk.) — ISBN 978-0-7844-7675-8 (ebook)
  1. Water resources development. 2. Watershed management. 3. Environmental protection.
4. Sustainable engineering. I. Grayman, W. M. II. Loucks, Daniel P. III. Saito, Laurel. IV.
Environmental and Water Resources Institute (U.S.) Emerging and Innovative Technology
Committee.
  TC411.T69 2012
  333.79—dc23

                                                                    2011052534

Published by American Society of Civil Engineers
1801 Alexander Bell Drive
Reston, Virginia, 20191-4400
www.asce.org/pubs

Contents

V: Conclusions

Foreword

Toward a Sustainable Water Future: Visions for 2050 comes at a very opportune time. The need to go out of "the water box" is greater than ever, as underlined from the third edition of the World Water Development Report series in 2009. The external forces that are impacting the state, use and management of water resources are not only accelerating, but the interactions among them are becoming more complex, be it the growth and mobility of populations, changes in the diets and consumption patterns, the impacts of economic development and the fluctuations in the international markets. The picture is further exacerbated by climate change, the growing and expanding quest for energy and the various incentives and disincentives that nations and supranational bodies implement in support of their various policies. And all these happen in the foreground of continuing crises, economic, financial, food and energy-related and sometimes political. Inequalities also continue to exist and the collective wisdom of the nations is yet to make the collective goals of the humanity materialize in appreciable proportions.

This is also an era in which attempts to move forward and deal with such global issues as poverty, underdevelopment, climate change, environmental degradation, trade and security are taking place, driven by the nations, which make up the international community.

Water is one of the very few, if not the unique, component in this complex picture that cuts across the entire spectrum and link sectors, issues, crises and responses. A possible response to food shortage can link to environmental degradation via decreased water availability for ecosystem needs and increased pollution. Increased storage to respond to climate change can link to increased social and environmental pressures through water and the neglect of the need for water infrastructure and better management can lead to a deepening of poverty and inequalities.

Those in a position to manage water or influence water management operate within a framework established by the decision makers in governments, civil society and private sector, who may not be aware of these interlinkages. Their responses may be limited to the narrow boundaries of the sectors that they operate in while the impacts typically go way beyond.

Toward a Sustainable Water Future: Visions for 2050 will serve as a valuable tool for those inside "the water box" not only to improve the management of our water resources but, and perhaps more importantly, to properly inform those who are making the decisions and hence creating constraints (and opportunities) for them to operate within. Those outside the water box will also benefit from this book by learning from some of the best experts and scientists in the sector what a not too distant horizon may look like and how best they can tune their decisions for the collective good of our planet.

Olcay Ünver
Coordinator
United Nations World Water Assessment Programme
Director
Programme Office for Global Water Assessment
Division of Water Sciences, UNESCO

Foreword

This book is a milestone contribution to the literature on water resources management. It is composed of a rich mixture of science and imagination with flashes of well-placed humor. It demonstrates in a qualitative manner how developments in water sciences and engineering might be combined with those of biotechnology, nanotechnology, neurotechnology, and information communications technology to ensure that, in future generations, all will have reliable access to the socioeconomic benefits that only water can provide.

Although the future is ill-defined and impossible to predict, actions today will influence it, for better or worse. The authors start from the often demonstrated premises that all living matter and everything constructed, manufactured, and used require water (precious little, if anything, in our environment can be created without water) and that from a global perspective there is plenty of renewable water on this planet. It just is not always available in the desired amounts or qualities when and where locally needed and at acceptable costs. They proceed to clearly present a wealth of technological information and ideas that chart a path for water scientists and engineers. Undoubtedly, these will be used by others in building qualitative and quantitative scenarios of possible futures for the planet that will inform decision-makers for years to come.

World Water Vision: Making Water Everybody's Business, which was published by the World Water Council in 2000, examined three scenarios qualitatively and quantitatively: business as usual; moving forward relying on technological advances, economics and the private sector; and changes in values and lifestyles. 'Business as usual' will lead to disaster. Under neither of the other scenarios could a sustainable future be achieved by 2025. However, a participatory process involving 15,000 people, right down to the village level in some cases, led to a vision of a healthy, hunger-free world with a sustainable environment.

As is correctly assessed in this book, some progress has been made toward achieving the World Water Vision for 2025, such as building new water infrastructure so that a greater proportion of the world population has access to improved drinking water. However, little progress has been made on other aspects, and accelerating change, including the impacts of climate change, have made the challenges greater while at the same time generating opportunities, including those described in these visions for 2050.

The dedicated authors of this book care about the future and water, because they care about assuring good health, adequate food and energy supplies, employment, and other development needs, while sustaining the environment—for our children and grandchildren. They recognize that the decisions on trade-offs and the setting of priorities to provide these benefits to the population are most often made 'outside the water box' and, until now, without consideration of the essential role that water plays. They recognize too that popular desire for change must overcome natural bureaucratic inertia and precede the creation of political will to act.

The World Water Vision report described a qualitative scenario in which it was possible to achieve that vision, but only if there was a combination of change in values and behaviors as well as changes in technology and a new approach to economics. I am optimistic that the visions for 2050 described in this book can be achieved. The financial crisis through which we are passing as this book goes to press can well lead leaders in government and the private sector to understand that 'business as usual' is not financially and economically sustainable, thus creating an opportunity for discussion of new ways forward. At the same time, communications technology is creating shared knowledge and wisdom and facilitating collective, sometime spontaneous, popular action. The combination of leadership and a bottom-up movement will increase the opportunities to adopt the approaches proposed in the authors' visions.

The authors point out that there are some four decades to achieve their visions of an ideal 2050. Even given a positive scenario for social and cultural change, the extent to which the vision for 2050 is realized depends on how well professionals from a range of disciplines can effectively work together to transmit the vision and how it can be achieved to the public and decision-makers. They note the difficulties to be faced in the United States. These will be compounded in reaching out to the rest of the world. But it can be done.

This book should be required reading for all students in all disciplines of engineering as well as the water sciences. Members of the Emerging and Innovative Technology Committee should quickly involve other ASCE members in spreading the visions. Some members are outside of the United States. Using networks and new communications technology, water scientists and engineers throughout the world can share their visions, among themselves and with the public and government and private sector decision-makers. Ultimately they can participate in the decision-making process with the other stakeholders. I echo the authors' conclusion: "What could be more useful as well as enjoyable?"

William J. Cosgrove
Co-author
World Water Vision: Making Water Everybody's Business
Honorary President
World Water Council

Preface

This book is a product of the 2050 Vision Initiative undertaken by the Emerging and Innovative Technology Committee (EITC) of the Environmental and Water Resources Institute (EWRI) of the American Society of Civil Engineers (ASCE). The Committee's mission is *to pay watchful attention for emerging and innovative technologies, both within and outside of Civil Engineering research areas, which have the potential to benefit environmental and water resource programs. It is the objective of the Committee to effectively disseminate this information to the appropriate technical areas within EWRI.*

In most of its activities, the Committee has generally worked on the "edge" of emerging technology that applied to the water resources and environmental field. As a consequence, there was an ongoing discussion as to when a technology evolves from being innovative and emerging to being a well-accepted technology that is approaching mainstream usage within the field. As an example, in the early 1990s the committee played a large role in publicizing the emerging internet technology within ASCE and educating engineers in its usage. As most will agree, that technology moved very rapidly from an emerging technology to a technology that was widely embraced by all segments of society.

At its annual meeting in 2005, the Committee discussed the concept of expanding its focus from just the "edge of technology" to looking at a time frame that extended further into the future. This focus would put the committee in the position to identify longer term trends and, more importantly, to define what our field could and should look like in the future. A time frame covering the period from the present to 2050 was chosen and the term "2050 Vision Initiative" was selected as the title for this direction.

The choice of 2050 as our target year was both methodical and arbitrary. At the time that the initiative was proposed, 2050 was 45 years in the future. While this period can be expected to see much evolutionary change, it is not bound by the policies that are in place today. At the same time, it is a short enough duration that revolutionary scientific changes (e.g., discovery and full implementation of cold fusion) or widespread revolutionary political or social changes (e.g., all nations at peace with each other) are unlikely.

The basic concept that was proposed by the Committee was to develop a vision based on an optimistic, futurist look at environmental/water resources issues in the year 2050 and to define a general pathway that could lead to fulfilling that optimistic view. A path toward developing a futurist view includes both an examination of how water resources and environmental planning has changed over the past about 40 years (i.e., equal to the approximate duration from the present to 2050) and then attempting to look over the horizon at what water resources and environmental engineering will look like 40 years from now.

This book consists of invited chapters written by a wide range of professionals in the broad field of water and the environment. Each chapter was peer reviewed by members of the EITC and further reviewed and edited by the book editors. The introductory chapters and concluding chapter were written by the editors. The opinions expressed are those of the authors of each chapter.

The editors would like to express their appreciation to the following for their critical and thoughtful reviews: Sajjad Ahmad, Lily Baldwin, Dominic Boccelli, Amy Chan-Hilton, Bob Clark, Barbara Cosins, Zoran Kapelan, Mohammad Karamouz, Karl Lambert, Yu-Feng Lin, Hugo Loaiciga, Stephanie Luster-Teasley, Richard Males, Morris Maslia, Sean McKenna, Rob Montgomery, Nur Muhammad, Emmanuel Nzewi, Lindell Ormsbee, Sri Panguluri, Craig Patterson, Rajib Sinha, Aditya Tyagi, Richard Vogel, and Rob Wallace.

The editors would also like to thank Angela Liu, our illustrator extraordinaire. During the preparation of this book Ms Liu was a civil engineering student at Cornell University. We are convinced that the world will see more of her illustrations in the future.

I INTRODUCTION

Chapter 1

Background

"Now that we're done with 2010,
can you see the path to 2050?"

A VISION FOR THE BOOK

This book is about the future. It is also about our environment and water. It focuses on the future state of our environment and water resource systems. When considering the future, it seems we have two choices: we can passively let the future happen and react to it, or alternatively we can actively shape the future by taking specific steps that will beneficially impact the state of the world and the resources available to those living in the future. We benefit, or suffer, today from the decisions made by our ancestors who preceded us. Our descendents will say the same, but they will be referring to us. Hence we who are here today should be thinking about satisfying not only our own demands, but also those of future generations as well. This book has been created in an attempt to identify just what we can and should do now to shape the future we (or at least our children and their children) would like to see and live in, say in the year 2050.

In this book we speculate on what the desired condition of various aspects of this water world should be like some 40 years from now. Our goal is to motivate some thinking about how we as a society want to achieve this more perfect water world. This theme fits in with the current interest in sustainability. No matter how it is defined, the notion of sustainability forces us to think about the long-term future. How do we develop and manage our natural and cultural resources in ways that benefit both our and future generations living on this earth? If they could, just what would future generations tell us today about how we today should develop and manage our water resources and environment so that they, then, will be better able to meet their needs, achieve their goals, and improve the quality of their lives? And what will their needs and goals be, and what demands will they place on the environment and water resources? Of course it is impossible to know, but here we, the writers of this book, make our attempts to guess what will be desired then, and given those desires, what is needed to make them happen.

> *This book has been created in an attempt to identify just what we can and should do now to shape the future we (or at least our children and their children) would like to see and live in, say in the year 2050.*

This chapter introduces this book. Each of us who contributed to this book has chosen a particular aspect of our water resources and environmental profession and created a scenario of what we would like to see (if we could live that long) in the year 2050. In addition each author was asked to identify ways of achieving such a vision. These scenarios are not intended to be predictions, but rather visions to make us think about what we might be doing today and in the coming decades to achieve a better world in the more distant future, at least with respect to our environment and water resources. This process included elements of both futurology and visioning.

In this introductory chapter, we briefly describe the uniqueness of water in our lives and society, ask how much we will need in the future, how clean it should be, how likely the lack of it will result in conflict, how population shifts to urban environments will impact its management, and just how we can achieve a more sustainable water future.

FUTUROLOGY AND VISIONING

Futurology and *visioning* are two concepts that are inherent in the 2050 Vision Initiative and this book. Futurology is the study of postulating possible, probable, and preferable futures (http://en.wikipedia.org/wiki/Futurology) and visioning is the process of identifying, developing and documenting vision and values, leading towards strategy and tactics (http://www.tetradian.com/Glossary).

Past efforts in futurology have run the gamut from fanciful novels such as those written by Jules Verne in the 19th century to scholarly books such as *The Year 2000: A Framework for Speculation on the Next Thirty-Three Years* (Kahn and Wiener

1967) that made a serious attempt to look at what advances would be likely or possible in the years 1967 to 2000, and the *Limits of Growth* (Meadows et al. 1972), a controversial book that used mathematical modeling to examine how the interaction of population, food production, industrialization, pollution and nonrenewable natural resources may limit growth through the 21st century. However, futurism has not been widely applied within the water resources and environmental field. An occasional paper will appear in journals or presentations made at conferences discussing likely advances in the relatively near term. Unlike some other fields such as medicine and physics that devote some portion of their budgets to research that may not have direct benefits for decades into the future, most water resources and environmental research is expected to result in products that will come to the market within a 5- to 10-year (or less) time frame. In large part, the water resources and environmental fields have not been as supportive of more innovative research aimed at long-range solutions, products or methodologies as we believe they should be.

Though visioning includes elements that are related to futurology, visioning is a more directed and proactive process. A vision generally includes a positive and sometimes inspirational image of where the authors want their area of concern or purview to advance towards. Visioning usually involves a group of people and frequently uses structured methods to elicit a consensus vision.

A recent example of visioning was carried out by the American Society of Civil Engineers (ASCE). A diverse group of civil engineering and other leaders gathered in 2006 to actively participate in the Summit on the Future of Civil Engineering (ASCE 2007). Their purpose was to articulate a future vision for all levels and facets of the civil engineering community. The visioning process was subsequently followed by a second group process involving volunteer members of ASCE with the aim of sketching a roadmap to transform that vision into concrete action (ASCE 2009a).

THE CURRENT STATE OF WATER AND THE ENVIRONMENT

While the focus of this book is on the future, it seems appropriate to reflect some on the current state of our environment and water resource systems. Given this current state, what needs changing? To answer this question it seems reasonable to take a brief look at what is making the headlines in today's world, and why.

Water: A Unique Resource
Before reading further, we challenge you to look around and identify anything you see that did NOT require water. All living matter and everything we construct, manufacture and use require water. Water is even needed to generate the electricity needed for the light you may be using to see this text more clearly. Precious little (if anything) in our environment can be created without water. While from a global perspective there is plenty of water on this planet, it is not always in the desired amounts or qualities when and where locally needed, and at acceptable costs. This imbalance between where the water is and where we want it to be, and how clean it is and how clean and inexpensive we would like it, is precisely why this indispensable

resource needs managing. In part because it is so essential for just about every activity humans undertake, to effectively and efficiently manage it requires expertise in a multitude of disciplines such as communication, ecology, economics, engineering, geography, governance, hydrology, law, planning, policy sciences, and more.

Many, especially in developing regions, consider water as common to all, needed by all, and hence it should be free to all. However, as discussed in more detail later, water certainly has economic value and that value depends in part on its demand and use. Furthermore, it costs money to make it available when and where needed in the desired amount and quality.

But water is more than just an economic good. For many, it has a sacred or mystical quality that one can appreciate by observing those using the Ganges and Jordan Rivers, for example. Water makes up a large percentage of the human body, and many believe it is also in the human soul. Water has provided not just life and food and fiber, but it also has been a home for fish and other aquatic animals, a medium for cleaning, cooking, swimming, skating, sailing, transporting cargo and assimilating sewage, and a thing of beauty to provide inspiration, to gaze upon and enjoy, even if only coming out of fountains in city landscapes. The fact that water impacts so many people in so many ways makes it a complex resource to manage. It is little wonder that water management typically involves so many water management agencies even though this fragmentation doesn't make it any easier to take an integrated approach.

How Much Do We Need?

"Americans use about 100 gallons (380 liters) of water at home each day. In Florida 3,000 gallons are used to water the grass for each golf game played. US swimming pools lose 150 billion gallons to evaporation every year. Millions of the world's poorest subsist on fewer than 5 gallons [per capita per day]. Forty six percent of people on earth do not have water piped to their homes. Women in developing countries walk an average of 3.7 miles (6 km) [each day] to get water. In 15 years, 1.8 billion people will live in regions of severe water scarcity" (National Geographic 2010).

Statements such as these are typically found in the popular press concerning water use. While one can argue over the precision of these average values, the general message is clear and true. We in the developed world have little appreciation of what it is like to live with water that we have to spend much of our day carrying even if drinking it will make us sick.

The amount of water we use to satisfy demands depends in part on how much is available and its cost. In areas where there is a lot of water compared to its demand, we tend to have little concern about efficient water use. In many regions, agriculture is the dominant consumptive water user, and the extent to which that sector has learned to grow more crops "with less drops" depends on its need to implement conservation measures. Although farming demands the majority of the water consumed, industry generates about 70 times as much value from water (WWAP 2009), and thus industry takes a much larger share of water in wealthier regions as compared to poorer areas. However, in all cases the ratio of water use per unit economic output has declined in recent decades, suggesting that industry can use water more efficiently if it can make money doing so, or if it is forced to because of water shortages or regulations.

In the US, total withdrawals of water for farming remained steady between 1985 and 2000, but groundwater withdrawal rose by 14%. Europe too increasingly relies on groundwater, as does the Middle East. Much of the groundwater used in the Middle East is non-renewable (Foster and Loucks 2006). Up to 95% of Libya's water demands are being met from non-renewable groundwater sources, mostly coming from under the Sahara Desert (Great Man-made River Authority, personal communication, 2008). The tripling of groundwater use in India since 1965 has provided some temporary prosperity to mainly agriculture users, but also has substantially depleted groundwater supplies. This in turn has resulted in decreasing yields, increasing energy costs, debt, and unemployment, crime, suicides and other adverse social as well as economic impacts (Associated Press 2009; Sainath 2010).

How Clean Does Our Water Need to Be?
Having enough water, whatever that amount is, is not enough. It also has to be clean enough to safely use, whether for agriculture, industry, or domestic purposes. Dirty water and poor sanitation are public health issues. Contaminated water results in the daily deaths of over five thousand children in the poorer regions of the world. It is the direct cause of diarrheal diseases and respiratory infections, and consequently the indirect cause of malnutrition. These ailments are also a real constraint to achieving full economic productivity and prosperity. It is one thing to report that a quarter to half of the people living in Addis Ababa and Lagos have no access to decent sanitation or piped clean water, or that no city in India can supply water for domestic use 24 hours per day, but even in the US, 40% of the sewer systems illegally discharged raw sewage or other contaminants into rivers or lakes, and over 40% of the nation's lakes and rivers were considered polluted based on their intended use in 2007-2009. Sickness resulting from contaminated water impacts over 20 million Americans each year (Economist 2010a,b).

As the oil spills off the Louisiana shore and in Prince William Sound of Alaska have so aptly demonstrated, it is not only direct human health that can suffer from contaminated water. The oil has adversely impacted the ecosystem and we will not know the full extent of the damage for years or decades. It has also had severe economic impacts and job loss, especially in the seafood and tourism industries.

Water and Conflict
When the word "water" is mentioned in the news media these days, it is almost certain the word "crisis" follows it. Water is a resource that has long been mismanaged and increasing demands for it cannot be met in many parts of the world. A major reason for the overthrow of the president of Madagascar in March of 2009

was due to the lack of sufficient water, not in Madagascar, but in South Korea. More than half of the arable land in Madagascar was being leased by South Korea to hedge against food shortages in South Korea, bringing little benefit to the local Malagasies. Fish stocks in the world's lakes and rivers have fallen about 30% in the past 40 years, a bigger decrease than animals in any other large ecosystem (Economist 2009). Water shortages spanning multiple years in California, Australia, Brazil and South Africa have caused repeated rationing and brownouts because of insufficient water for power production and cooling. Water levels in aquifers are falling, glaciers are vanishing, reservoirs are drying up, and rivers as large as the Indus, Rio Grande, Colorado, Murray-Darling and Yellow no longer continually discharge water into the sea. Rivers without water cannot support aquatic plants or animals that live in them. "Wars are about to break out between countries squabbling over [water]. If the apocalypse is still a little way off, it is only because the four horsemen and their steeds have stopped to search for something to drink" (Economist 2010a). Some of the reasons for the decisions taken, or not taken, that have caused all this alarming rhetoric are discussed in Chapter 3 on stressors.

> *If there is a perceived or real "water crisis," we should not allow it to go to waste. It can be an opportunity to do big and important things we might otherwise not have the opportunity to do to achieve a more perfect "water world."*

While leaders of major international organizations are often quoted as predicting that future major conflicts will not be over oil, but over water, so far there have been no major water wars. However, there have been disputes, and these will certainly continue as supplies diminish, demands increase, climate changes, and social unrest leads to migrations, crime, and other adverse impacts. While the South-North Water Transfer Project in China can increase the availability and reliability of water supplies in the north of China, many people living in areas from where that water originates are not at all happy. Similar water transfer and sharing projects in India bring mixed feelings – some people will benefit, others will not. Disputes over well water abstractions and use such as in Yemen are common and the long-running civil war in Darfur was at least partly due to the chronic scarcity of water in western Sudan.

Many water disputes can become international. For example, the damming and use of water of the Tigris and Euphrates Rivers in Turkey in order to double their irrigated farmland is decreasing water availability to the downstream countries of Syria and Iraq. When water disputes become international, the threat of major conflict increases. International river basins extend across the borders of some 145 countries, while about 280 aquifers also cross national borders (Economist 2010b). In North America, a Canadian-US organization called the International Joint Commission (IJC) was established in 1909 to deal with potential issues of dispute over waters that cross and form the border between Canada and the US. This commission likes to say that over the past century its existence has successfully prevented wars between these two countries. Nothing like the IJC exists in the Tigris and Euphrates basins, but river basin authorities or commissions exist in many other basins such as the Congo,

Danube, Mekong, Niger, Nile, Rhine and Zambezi, where many countries share their waters and thus the potential for conflict is present. These organizations help avoid open military conflicts over the sharing of the benefits of water resources development in different countries. Examples include the resolution of conflicts between India and Pakistan in the Indus Basin and its tributaries, between Ethiopia and Egypt in the Nile Basin, between China and many downstream countries in the Mekong Basin, and among Mali, Senegal, Guinea and Mauritania in the Senegal Basin, to name a few (Economist 2010b).

If indeed there is a perceived or real "water crisis," we should not allow it to go to waste. It can be an opportunity to do big and important things we might otherwise not have the opportunity to do to achieve a more perfect "water world."

Managing Water in an Increasingly Urban Environment
In an assessment of the future world population, the United Nations Population Fund (UNFPA) made the following observation (UNFPA 2007):
> *"In 2008, the world reaches an invisible but momentous milestone: For the first time in history, more than half its human population, 3.3 billion people, will be living in urban areas. By 2030, this is expected to swell to almost 5 billion. Many of the new urbanites will be poor. Their future, the future of cities in developing countries, the future of humanity itself, all depend very much on decisions made now in preparation for this growth."*

Increasing urbanization puts an ever-increasing burden on water management. Water must be delivered greater distances from sources to concentrated population areas. Wastewater generated by the concentrated population must be more highly treated or moved further from population centers so as not to unduly impact the environment. In the US, insufficient amounts of money are budgeted to keep up with deteriorating urban water and wastewater infrastructure (ASCE 2009b). Throughout the world, urban centers with tens of millions of people struggle to build adequate water and wastewater infrastructures. The issue of how can this type of development be sustainable is often discussed but we are far from an acceptable solution.

OBJECTIVES AND ORGANIZATION OF THIS BOOK

The primary objective of this book is quite simple – to paint a picture of what the water resources and environmental landscape could (or should) look like in 2050 and identify what the water resources/environmental profession and our society needs to do to achieve this vision. One would not and should not expect that there can be unanimity on what that vision will look like. Frequently professionals in our field cannot even agree on decisions as mundane as the most appropriate modeling methods or appropriate policy statements, but that is okay. It is the debate over these disagreements that is most valuable.

To develop a set of possible 2050 visions, the editors of the book enlisted the talents of a diverse set of highly respected professionals in the water resources and environmental fields. These prominent professionals hold positions in academic, governmental, non-governmental, and private organizations. They have a variety of experiences and backgrounds. They were asked to prepare their 2050 visions of specific areas within the water resources and environmental spectrum and then speculate on what should be done to achieve those desired visions. Few constraints (other than the maximum length of their chapters) were placed on them. The resulting chapters were peer-reviewed and then edited to improve clarity and maintain the desired scope and focus. The final draft of each chapter has been approved by each author.

> *Frequently professionals in our field cannot agree on decisions or appropriate policy statements, but that is okay. It is the debate over these disagreements that is most valuable.*

The book is divided into five sections. The first section is composed of three chapters, including this one, written by the editors. This first chapter introduces the subject and the objectives of the book. The next chapter looks back about 40 years or so to examine where the water resources and environmental fields were at a time interval in the past that is roughly equivalent to the future time interval between the present and the year 2050. The question addressed in that chapter is whether the state of today's environment and water resources was predicted or predictable some 40 years ago, and could they have been better managed to reduce some of the problems and issues we face today. The third chapter is an examination of the likely stressors that may impact the water resources and environment fields in the coming 40 years.

The second through fourth sections of this book contain individual chapters written by our diverse set of contributing authors grouped in three areas: Planning and Policy, Education, and Science and Technology. Each chapter can be viewed as a brief scenario that represents what the author(s) sees or would like to see in 2050, and how to get there. The final section of the book contains a single chapter that attempts to synthesize an overall ideal vision for 2050 and offer some suggestions on how to begin to achieve it.

REFERENCES

American Society of Civil Engineers (ASCE). (2007). *The vision for civil engineering in 2025*, prepared by the ASCE Steering Committee to Plan a Summit on the Future of the Civil Engineering Profession in 2025, American Society of Civil Engineers, Reston, VA.

American Society of Civil Engineers (ASCE). (2009a). *Achieving the vision for civil engineering in 2025*, prepared by the ASCE Task Committee to Achieve the Vision for Civil Engineering in 2025 Profession in 2025, American Society of Civil Engineers, Reston, VA.

American Society of Civil Engineers (ASCE). (2009b). "Report card 2009 grades." *Report card for America's infrastructure*, American Society of Civil Engineers, <http://www.asce.org/reportcard/2009/grades.cfm> (Oct, 2010).

Associated Press. (2009). "Indian farmers faced with debt and drought turn to suicide, leaving families helpless in the fields." *NYDailyNews.com*, August 28, 2009, <http://www.nydailynews.com/news/world/2009/08/28/2009-08-28_indian_farmers_faced_with_debt_and_drought_turn_to_suicide_leaving_families_help.html> (Nov, 2010).

Kahn H., and Wiener, A. J. (1967). *The year 2000: a framework for speculation on the next thirty-three years*, The Macmillan Company, New York, NY.

Economist. (2009). "Sin aqua non." *Economist*, 390 (8626), 59-61.

Economist. (2010a). "For want of a drink." *Economist*, 395(8683), 3-5.

Economist. (2010b). "To the last drop." *Economist*, 395(8683), 17-19.

Foster, S., and Loucks, D. P., eds. (2006). Nonrenewable Groundwater Resources: A Guidebook on Socially Sustainable Management for Water-Policy Makers, Paris: United Nations Educational, Scientific and Cultural Organization (IHP-VI series on groundwater 10). <http://unesdoc.unesco.org/images/0014/001469/146997e.pdf> (Nov, 2010)

Meadows, D. H., Meadows, D. L., Randers, J., and Behrens III, W. W. (1972). *The Limits of Growth*, Universe Books, New York, NY.

National Geographic. (2010). *Water, our thirsty world, National Geographic*, 217(4), 56, 150.

Sainath P. (2010). "Nearly 2 lakh farm suicides since 1997." *India Together*, January 25, 2010, <http://indiatogether.org/2010/jan/psa-suicides.htm> (Nov, 2010).

United Nations Population Fund (UNFPA). (2007). *State of the world population 2007, unleashing the potential of urban growth,* United Nations Population Fund. New York, NY, http://www.unfpa.org/swp/2007/english/introduction.html (November 2010) <http://www.unfpa.org/swp/2007/presskit/pdf/sowp2007_eng.pdf> (Oct, 2010).

World Water Assessment Programme (WWAP). (2009). *The United Nations world water development report 3: water in a changing world*, United Nations Educational, Scientific, and Cultural Organization, Paris, France, <http://www.unesco.org/water/wwap/wwdr/wwdr3/> (Oct, 2010).

Chapter 2

Looking Into the Next 40 Years – 40 Years Ago

ABSTRACT

Here we look into the past to see if leading water resource economists, engineers and planners some 40 to 50 years ago were successful in identifying the issues we face today and whether they addressed those issues when making their decisions in the water resources and environmental areas. This gives us some idea about how well we today may be able to do the same with regard to the future some 40 years from now. A review of some of the papers written by leaders in water resources planning, development and management some 40 to 50 years ago suggests most professionals at that time were concentrating on better ways to address their immediate or near-term water management challenges, perhaps so that we, living today, would not have to deal with those issues. Some writers did indeed foresee some of the challenges we are addressing today, and advocated approaches for meeting those challenges. Some of their decisions are benefiting us today. Some of their decisions are not, mainly because some of our goals and objectives differ from those they considered important. For example, we are far more concerned about ecosystem rehabilitation and environmental quality than were those making decisions 40 to 50 years ago. What becomes evident is that our decisions today can indeed affect the conditions of those living and managing the environment and water 40 to 50 years from now. Forecasting the long-term impacts of our decisions was, and continues to be, a difficult task, but it is a task worth taking if we wish to achieve those visions, however uncertain they may be.

"I hope our grandkids won't have the same problems we do."

INTRODUCTION

This chapter stems from the thought that maybe we can look more clearly into the future if we first put ourselves in the shoes of those who preceded us some 40 years ago. Did our predecessors predict what issues we would be facing today, and if so, did they do anything about it? What were their decisions that in fact have resulted in what is available to us today? What could they have done differently that might have reduced, if not prevented, some of the adversities we face today? Would we have wanted them to make different decisions on our behalf with respect to water resources infrastructure, management institutions and environmental stewardship?

Obviously (or hopefully) water and environmental management issues some 40 years ago were addressed in ways considered beneficial to society living at that time. But as the next section discusses, with few exceptions, there seemed to be little thought about preventing many of the adverse impacts resulting from further economic and technological development that we face today. Our predecessors' objectives and concerns (e.g., reliable water supply and quality, and flood control) did not include many of the ecological and social objectives we currently consider important. No doubt future generations will have different goals and needs than ours today, and this will present new challenges for them. All we can do today is to try to think about what those needs and goals might be, and then try to identify the tradeoffs, if any, between what we wish to do today to further our current objectives and what future generations may wish us to do to further enhance theirs (ASCE 1998). This objective is consistent with many of the principles associated with sustainability – a term and concept that was not widely thought about some 40 years ago.

LOOKING BACK

Looking back about 40 years ago puts us at the end of the tumultuous 1960s decade – a truly transitional period in the history of the US. In the political realm, there were assassinations, racial discord, a cold war and a very divisive hot war. Science was greatly influenced by the launch of the Sputnik satellite in 1957, the rapidly emerging influence of computers and the decade-long rush to put a man on the moon. Rachel Carson's 1962 book, *Silent Spring,* helped to launch the environmental movement. Alvin Toffler's 1970 book *Future Shock* predicted a rapidly changing future influenced by technology and other drivers and how people may or may not cope with the resulting changes.

A time span of 40 years can be viewed from many perspectives. For a teenager or young professional, 1970 may seem a long time ago. For older generations, 1970 may represent the start of their professional career and feel like "just yesterday." From a perspective of electronic computer-based technology, the period since 1970 has seen phenomenal growth and revolutionary development. For more mature technologies such as hydropower, sewerage and water supply, changes over that same 40 years have been gradual and evolutionary. Within the context of the natural ecosystem, the perception in 1970 would have been that 40 years represents only a "blink of the eye" and a general expectation existed that any human impacts on the natural environment would take much longer than 40 years.

> *Our predecessors' objectives and concerns (e.g., reliable water supply and quality, and flood control) did not include many of the ecological and social objectives we currently consider important.*

In 1970, the fields of water resources management and environmental management were far less intertwined than they are today. Water resources management was a relatively mature field with a significant presence at the federal level and primary emphasis on issues related to water quantity rather than water quality. Environmental management was in its infancy with no centralized presence in the federal government. There was an increasing overlap in the area of water quality but in 1970 these were generally two disparate fields.

Water Resources Management
Reading many of the documents written 40 to 50 years ago by leaders in water resources development and management, or published by governmental agencies responsible for water resources planning and development, one gets the impression that there wasn't much thought given to long-term planning. Certainly reservoirs and canals were built to last a long time, but large-scale building projects were coming to an end. In the US, water quality improvement was becoming the big issue – and the big cost. With the notable exception of California, plans for large water transfer schemes, e.g., from Canada to the US, or from one river basin to another within the US, were beginning to lose their attraction, both from an economic as well as political perspective. Increasing concern was evident for meeting water demands for irrigation and water quality control (dilution). Industrial and irrigation water use efficiency was stressed, but not always practiced. Flood damage risk reduction on floodplains was also talked about, but, as today, not always practiced. Diversions of increasing amounts of water for agricultural, municipal and industrial uses and changes in land cover concerned some who made predictions such as L'vovich (1979):

> *"In the coming decades it is most likely that the Northern Hemisphere will experience a general decline in the wetness of the land area and in the volume of flow of the rivers, which will create unfavorable prerequisites for implementing water-management programs under future conditions."*

Multi-purpose planning and infrastructure design was advocated over single-purpose projects. Taking a world-wide, if not US, perspective L'vovich (1979) suggested:

> *"Reservoirs are needed for hydropower as well as irrigation and sources of water supply and flood control. They need to be multiple purpose reservoirs... Diversions should be the last resort option. Resources are adequate to meet all needs only if water use efficiency and conservation and sewage reuse measures are taken. This will require at least 2 to 3 decades, during which a comprehensive package of purposive measures would be carried out. Only then can humanity look into the future with full optimism in the belief that men*

and their economic activity will always be furnished with water in the necessary amount and proper quality. The water component of man's natural environment will not only be successfully preserved, but will also be rid of the adverse features that have already occurred in it and will be made more conducive to human life – not only in places for recreation and tourism, in rural localities, but, which is perhaps the most important, also in cities where the destruction of the environment has been most substantial and where a considerable part of humanity lives."

The final report to the President and Congress by the US National Water Commission (NWC; NWC 1973) contained recommendations on policies for the efficient, equitable and environmentally responsible management of the nation's water resources. The writers of that report recognized water resources management objectives were changing. Water quality was replacing past objectives of regional development in the west, and providing for water navigation. Cleaning up the nation's rivers was predicted to cost more than all the navigation, flood control, hydropower, and irrigation projects undertaken by the Federal Government since the formation of the Union.

The NWC (1973) report also stressed the need for institutional changes for more effective coordination and decision-making at all levels. Improved planning and coordination was the explicit reason for the establishment of the US Water Resources Council (WRC) in 1965. Its job was to encourage the conservation, development, and use of water and related land resources on a coordinated basis by the Federal Government, the states, localities, and private enterprises. It also coordinated and reviewed river basin and regional plans. It clearly foresaw the decrease in Federal funding of major water supply projects while at the same time projecting increases in total withdrawals (~200%) and total consumptive use (~50%) through 2020 (WRC 1968). The Council was terminated in 1982. By that time Federal support for basin-wide planning and coordination had essentially ended. This resulted in the dissolution of many river basin commissions that could coordinate and consider basin-wide impacts of particular water projects.

Wollman and Bonem (1971) foresaw the possibility that future planning might have to be based on other than just the statistics of past historical records due to changes in watershed conditions such as land cover and use. However, no mention was made of other possible causes such as climate change. Water quality was a concern, especially dissolved oxygen and heat. They acknowledged the need for environmental flows, especially in estuaries, but admitted such requirements were not yet well-defined. They also recognized the tradeoffs involving storage for dilution and wastewater treatment for waste discharge reduction.

Kneese and Smith (1966) provided a review of events in the 1950s and 1960s that changed how we conduct our economic policy research and analyses today, but offered no projections of what the management issues might be today and how relevant those tools and approaches might be for addressing today's issues. Six years later Brubaker (1972) suggested a key to human survival is population control, and that alterations in climate, extreme degradation of water or air quality, nuclear contamination, or impairment of life supporting ecosystems could be other possible destructors of us: "An irreducible product of combustion is carbon dioxide, whose mounting concentration in the atmosphere will, it is feared, have a significant effect on climate" (Brubaker 1972).

After the historic mid-1960s drought in the northeastern US, drought planning was undertaken for the entire North Atlantic region. This Federal North Atlantic Regional study (USACE 1972) began after New York City stopped releasing water from its Delaware River Basin reservoirs into the Delaware River. Without freshwater flowing down the Delaware from those reservoirs into the Atlantic Ocean, Atlantic salt water might have been introduced into the Philadelphia drinking water system. The lessons learned in the North Atlantic Study were later encoded in the Federal "Principles and Standards for Planning Water and Related Land Resources" (NWC 1973) often shortened to the "P&S." The P&S were used in the design and justification of proposed federal water projects. A modified version of these P&S is in use by the Corps today (WRC 1983). Economic criteria remain the drivers of P&S, subject to environmental quality constraints as defined by environmental regulations. Leonard Dworsky summed up the general feeling at that time by writing (Hitchcock 1967):

> *"The major task is to better manage available water supplies. Science and technology are adequate to support proper water management schemes for the foreseeable future. The major problems blocking proper management are in the political environment."*

> **Science and technology are adequate to support proper water management schemes for the foreseeable future. The major problems blocking proper management are in the political environment.**

Other important developments in the area of water resources in the 1960s were the publication of the book *Design of Water-Resource Systems* (Maass et al. 1962) by the Harvard Water Program, the formation of the Office of Water Resources Research (OWRR) in 1964 as part of the Water Resources Research Act of 1964, the establishment of a new journal by the American Geophysical Union (AGU) called *Water Resources Research* (WRR) in 1965, and the formation of the American Water Resources Association (AWRA) in 1964. The American Society of Civil Engineers (ASCE) followed suit in 1971 with the formation of the Technical Council on Water Resources Planning and Management, transitioning a few years later to the Water Resources Planning and Management Division and the inauguration of a journal by the same name.

The Harvard Water Program is best known for its integration of water resource systems, economic engineering and government analysis. Many of the concepts and techniques that were developed a half century ago by this group are still widely accepted and in use today. OWRR is most noted for funding a robust and far reaching research program in water resources and as the administrator of the State Water Resources Research Institutes Program (Burton 1986).

Many of the policy papers published in the early issues of WRR, as well as in other water resources planning and management journals, did not conceive of terms like shared vision planning and stakeholder involvement. No one at that time speculated on the decision support technology we enjoy today that facilitates shared vision planning and stakeholder involvement in planning and decision-making. Authors of these early WRR papers did, however, recognize the increasing concentration of people in urban areas, and the need to consider water reuse sometime in the foreseeable future.

One of the leading scholars of his time was Gilbert White. In his book on *Strategies of American Water Management*, White (1969) saw "parching drought, stinking streams, and muddy floods" all as indications of the need for improved water management. He did not think that serious economic dislocations would result from shortages of water quantity: "It is more likely that human welfare in the US will be impaired through degradation of water quality or through inept management than from a physical scarcity of water" (White 1969). Quantity seemed to him manageable in the foreseeable future, but not without difficulties. He was not a fan of the excessive amount of concrete being used to tame nature (i.e., manage our water resources) nor of the idea that national economic efficiency should be the sole criterion for water resources development. He saw integrated multipurpose watershed and river basin planning as a better way of achieving social aims or objectives. He believed that examining how people make decisions in managing water would lead to better understanding of the process of water management and thereby aid in finding more suitable ways of managing the natural water system. He argued for more sensitivity to human needs for spiritual and aesthetic expression.

When he wrote his 1969 book, White saw two prevailing attitudes with respect to water management: either conquering nature or living harmoniously with her. Whether man the conqueror or man the cooperator, by the late 1960s humans had dug millions of wells, hacked out 19,000 kilometers (12,000 miles) of waterways, irrigated 12 million hectares (30 million acres) of land, drained an even larger area, curbed the frequency of overbank flows of several thousand streams, and harnessed more than 30 million kilowatts of electric power capacity. Now at the peak of a massive construction program, White had the feeling that all was not well with the national water budget as modified by man. He believed that major channel and streamflow regulation would not be the primary means and foundation of water management in the future. The prevailing methods of water management that lead to such decisions were in his view ill-suited to the changing conditions he saw of both water supply and its use. He saw the need for a more integrative regional approach involving multiple inputs from many disciplines, including planners, economists, engineers, ecologists, sociologists and political scientists.

Environmental Management

The past 40 years has seen the emergence of the environmental field as a widely accepted and integral part of our society. It has progressed from a perception forty years ago of environmentalism as a fringe group of "tree huggers" to mainstream acceptance today. During that period, the Green Movement, concepts of sustainability and widespread (though certainly not total) acceptance of climate change have been key elements associated with the environmental field.

> *The past 40 years has seen the emergence of the environmental field as a widely accepted and integral part of our society. It has progressed from a perception forty years ago of environmentalism as a fringe group of "tree huggers" to mainstream acceptance today.*

Forty years ago, the field of environmental management in the US was in a major state of flux, transitioning from an informal amalgam of many disparate interests to a focused federal program. The publication of *Silent Spring* by Rachel Carson in 1962 is frequently credited as the start of the environmental movement. The book documented the effects of pesticides on the environment resulting in widespread public concerns. In the engineering field, the relatively narrow bounds of sanitary engineering were morphing into the broader field of environmental engineering.

In 1970, the field of environmental management and regulation took several giant steps to establish itself in the US. On January 1, 1970, President Nixon signed the National Environmental Policy Act (NEPA) with the following stated purposes (Lewis 1985):

- *"To declare a national policy which will encourage productive and enjoyable harmony between man and his environment.*
- *To promote efforts which will prevent or eliminate damage to the environment and biosphere and stimulate the health and welfare of man.*
- *To enrich our understanding of the ecological systems and natural resources important to the Nation."*

On 22 April 1970, Earth Day marked the beginning of the modern environmental movement. Approximately 20 million Americans participated, with a goal of a healthy, clean environment. Earth Day included massive coast-to-coast rallies, organized protests at colleges and universities against the deterioration of the environment, and participation by groups that had been fighting against oil spills, polluting factories and power plants, raw sewage, toxic dumps, pesticides, freeways, the loss of wilderness, and the extinction of wildlife. A shared vision and a shared common value for the environment immediately emerged from this one-day event. The newly-formed Council on Environmental Quality declared that (CEQ 1970):

> *"1970 marks the beginning of a new emphasis on the environment – a turning point, a year when the quality of life has become more than a phrase; environment and pollution have become everyday words; and ecology has*

become almost a religion to some of the young. Environmental problems, standing for many years on the threshold of national prominence, are now at the center of nationwide concern. Action to improve the environment has been launched by government at all levels. And private groups, industry, and individuals have joined the attack. "

LOOKING FORWARD

Given both the successes and failures of our predecessors some 40 years ago in taking actions that have affected how we manage water and the environment today, can we expect any greater success in predicting and acting so as to reduce the challenges water managers will be facing 30, 40 or 50 years from now? Our forecasting abilities are made no easier given the increasing rates of change in populations (especially urban populations), scientific knowledge, technology and world events (such as the current economic and political difficulties throughout the world), all of which will shape the environment of those managing water in 2050.

In this book, the authors were not asked to forecast, rather they were asked to express what they would like to see in the year 2050, and suggest ways of getting to that vision. This exercise is based on the premise that if we know where we want to go, and act accordingly, we have a much better chance of getting there, than if we just react over time to events that might otherwise take place. This goal is similar to ASCE's 2025 "Future of Civil Engineering" visioning project (ASCE 2007), but focused only on environmental and water management rather than addressing all levels and facets of the civil engineering community.

Any forward-looking visioning exercise for water and the environment will be influenced by factors and decisions made by individuals who are not environmental and water managers. These factors and decisions are uncertain, as are their impacts by the year 2050. Our world confronts rapid and potentially profound transitions driven by social, economic, environmental, and technological change. Advances in computational technology together with increased knowledge and understandings in the physical and social sciences may radically transform our ability to reason systematically about the long-term future (Lempert et al. 2003). Changes in regional economic development and the world's commerce, environmental protection, the spread of diseases and terrorism, the development and use of new biological and genetic materials, improved sensor and computer technologies, to mention a few drivers, can all impact our decisions about how we manage our natural resources. This includes the ability of future generations to enjoy reliable and sufficient amounts of water of sufficient quality at reasonable costs to meet their needs as well as for sustaining a quality environment. Clearly achieving this vision will be among the goals of any generation, present and future.

Having a long-term vision of the goals we want to accomplish, even if it is uncertain, can increase the efficiency and effectiveness of public spending aimed at achieving that vision. Of course, that collective vision will change over time. Adaptation strategies can and need to be developed in the face of substantial future uncertainties and changes in public attitudes and goals (Jansen et al. 2009; Walker et al. 2001).

CONCLUSIONS

Assessing how today's actions affect the long-term future is critical to long-term planning and impact analyses. Across most sectors of society, near-term impacts of decisions are often emphasized. However, our greatest potential influence for shaping the future may often be precisely over those time scales where our sight is most dim. By its nature, where the short term is more predictable and subject to forces we can identify and quantify, we may have little effect. Where the future is ill-defined, hardest to see, and full of possibilities and opportunities, our actions today may well have their largest influence in shaping it. In an era of radical and rapid change, immense possibilities, and great risks, it is time to help shape the long-term future, especially for managing a unique resource – water – that impacts all sectors of our economy and is critical to human health and welfare.

Looking into the past to see if leading water resource economists, engineers and planners some 40 to 50 years ago were successful in considering the long-term impacts of their decisions suggests that most professionals at that time were concentrating on better ways to address their immediate or near-term water management challenges. Some did indeed foresee some of the challenges we are addressing today, and advocated approaches for meeting those challenges. What becomes evident is that our decisions today can indeed affect the conditions of those living and managing water 40 to 50 years from now. Forecasting these impacts was, and continues to be, a difficult task. In spite of this uncertainty, and the likelihood of changes in our environment, in our economy, and in our society that we cannot predict, we must try if we have any hope of achieving the visions we wish to observe when we (or our descendents) reach 2050!

REFERENCES

American Society of Civil Engineers (ASCE). (1998). *Sustainability criteria for water resource systems*, Task Committee on Sustainability Criteria, Water Resources Planning and Management Division, ASCE and the Working Group of UNESCO/IHP IV Project M-4.3, ASCE Press, Reston, VA, 253 p.

American Society of Civil Engineers (ASCE). (2007). *The vision for civil engineering in 2025*, prepared by the ASCE Steering Committee to Plan a Summit on the Future of the Civil Engineering Profession in 2025, American Society of Civil Engineers, Reston, VA.

Brubaker, S. (1972). *To live on Earth: man and his environment in perspective*, Resources for the Future, Johns-Hopkins Press, Baltimore, MD.

Burton, J. S. (1986). "History of the Federal-State cooperative water resources research institute." *J. Am. Water Resour. As.*, 22(4), 637-647.

Carson, R. (1962). *Silent spring*, Houghton-Mifflin, Boston, MA.

Council on Environmental Quality (CEQ). (1970). *Environmental quality: the first annual report of the Council on Environmental Quality*, Washington DC.

Hitchcock, L., ed. (1967). *The fresh water of New York State and its conservation and use*, Wm. C. Brown Book Co., Dubuque, IA.

Jansen, G. J., van Lier Lels, M. E., Ruijgh-van der Ploeg, M. P. M.,Toonen, T. A. J., Vreeman, R. L., Westdijk, N. J., and Verkooijen, H. J. M. (2009). *Witte zwanen, zwarte zwanen: advies over proactieve adaptatie aan klimaatverandering*, Raad voor Verkeer en Waterstaat, (ISBN/EAN: 978-90-77323-17-5), Den Haag, The Netherlands..

Kneese, A. V., and Smith, S. C. (1966). *Water research*, Resources for the Future, John-Hopkins Press, Baltimore, MD.

Lempert, R. J., Popper, S. W., Bankes, S. C. (2003). *Shaping the next one hundred years: new methods for quantitative, long-term policy analysis*, Rand Corporation, Santa Monica, CA.

Lewis, J. (1985). "The Birth of EPA." *EPA Journal*, November 1985, <http://www.epa.gov/history/topics/epa/15c.htm> (Oct, 2010).

L'vovich, M. I. (1979). *World water resources and their future*, American Geophysical Union, Washington, DC, translation of L'vovich, M. I. (1974). *World water resources and their future*, Mysl'P. H., Moscow.

Maass, A., Hufschmidt, M., Dorfman, R., Thomas, H., Marglin, S., and Fair, G. (1962). *The design of water resource systems*, Harvard University Press, Cambridge, MA.

US Army Corps of Engineers (USACE). (1972). *North Atlantic regional water resources study*, US Army Corps of Engineers, North Atlantic Division.

US National Water Commission (NWC). (1973). *Water policies for the future*, Final Report to the President and Congress, Washington, DC.

US Water Resources Council (WRC). (1968). *The nation's water resources*, Part 1, Washington, DC.

US Water Resources Council (WRC). (1983). *Economic and environmental principles and guidelines for water and related land resources implementation studies*, Government Printing Office, Washington, DC.

Walker, W. E., Rahman, S. A., and Cave, J. (2001). "Adaptive policies, policy analysis, and policy-making." *Eur. J. Oper. Res.*, 128, 282-289.

White, G. F. (1969). *Strategies of American water management*, The University of Michigan Press, Ann Arbor, MI.

Wollman, N., and Bonem, G. W. (1971). *The outlook for water quality, quantity, and national growth*, Resources for the Future, Johns-Hopkins Press, Baltimore, MD.

Chapter 3

Stressors Influencing Our Future Visions

ABSTRACT

Natural events and human activities and processes of all types can stress our water resources and environment. In addition, many of these "stressors" can affect each other. In this chapter we examine six groups of stressors and their impacts over time in an attempt to set the stage for creating future visions of particular features of water systems and their management, and for identifying what is needed to achieve those visions. The six groups include 1) natural and climate-related stressors; 2) demographic and social stressors; 3) economic stressors; 4) technological, infrastructure and security stressors; 5) governance stressors including institutions, policies, laws and finance; and 6) environmental, public health and sustainability stressors. While each group is discussed separately, interactions among these six groups of stressors pose the real challenges for decision-makers as they try to identify and implement plans and policies that will lead to beneficial outcomes. Their job is to reduce or adapt to the stresses imposed by all these six stressor groups without causing more stress from any single group.

INTRODUCTION

Future changes in the distributions of water quantities and qualities will depend on both natural events and human activities. These natural events and human activities are the primary forces or "stressors" affecting the state or condition of our planet's environmental and water systems. We define stressors broadly as activities, events, or other stimuli that change the world we live in and that influence what we can and want to do. This chapter focuses on these stressors and their interactions as they may affect or impact our future environmental and water resources systems. Understanding these stressors and their effects helps us not only to think more clearly about what we would like to see in 2050, but more importantly it helps us identify decisions and actions that may be needed to achieve those future visions.

To make this task manageable we have grouped our stressors into six categories, namely:
- natural (including climate related and anthropogenic-induced),
- demographic and social,
- economic,
- technological including infrastructure and security,
- governance (institutions, policies, laws and finance), and
- environmental, public health and sustainability.

These categories include stressors that are external as well as internal to the water/environmental 'box', yet directly or indirectly codetermine the evolution of natural and constructed water and environmental systems.

These six categories of stressors can also be viewed as six components of our individual, and hence society's, welfare. It is the interactions among these six components that pose real challenges for decision-makers as they try to identify and implement plans and policies that will lead to an increase in our collective welfare.

NATURAL STRESSORS

Many natural geological, hydrological and meteorological processes cause changes in our water and environmental systems, directly and indirectly. However, it is not only nature's extreme events, including droughts, floods, storms, tsunamis, fires, earthquakes, hurricanes, landslides, and tornados, that can change landscapes and what inhabits them. Natural events and their impacts may be exacerbated or even triggered by human actions. The anthropogenic influences of climate change and development in floodplains are examples of the interaction between natural events and human activities. A warmer climate can affect the metabolism of aquatic organisms. Excessive biological production due to higher temperatures or non-point nutrient loadings from agricultural and urban lands can degrade water quality, which in turn can adversely impact aquatic animal life, including fish, thereby reducing commercial and recreational benefits, and hence the economies of local communities.

Water and environmental managers are accustomed to managing naturally occurring variability with respect to both water supply and water demand. Climate can directly affect the hydrologic cycle and, through it, the timing, intensity, seasonality and spatial distribution of precipitation and hence the quantity and quality of water resources and the environment. It can lower minimum flows in rivers, affecting water availability and quality for its flora and fauna and for drinking water intakes, energy production (hydropower), thermal plant cooling and navigation. Climate can also directly affect demand for both agricultural and urban water supplies.

Climate change threatens to make this variability greater, shifting and intensifying the extremes, and introducing greater uncertainty in the quantity and quality of supply over the long term (IPCC 2007). Potential impacts of climate change on water resources and the environment include perturbation of stressed ecosystems; destabilization of natural biological controls of pests and pathogens; more sediment and polluted runoff to surface waters and less infiltration to replenish aquifers; increased wildfires; reservoir eutrophication; and an increase in the risk of coastal flooding and salinity in coastal aquifers (Buchberger et al. 2008; Cromwell et al. 2007; Levin et al. 2002; Miller and Yates 2006).

All of these possible climate change impacts suggest the need to continually re-evaluate water resource infrastructure development policies and adaptive management strategies at basin-wide levels as well as at the levels of local utilities that are responsible for building, maintaining and operating community water supply and wastewater systems. Periodic re-evaluation is needed of the entire utility portfolio from source to tap with respect to adaptation strategies.

The relationships between natural and climate-related stressors and the other stressors resulting from demographic processes, economic growth, social change, technological innovation and policies, laws and finance are complex and interwoven. Nevertheless they all involve water and occur through water. All of the potential impacts of climate-related disasters, including economic losses, health problems and environmental disruptions, affect, and are affected by, water.

> *Over the long term, the effects of climate change are likely to influence decisions affecting ecosystems, energy and food security and land use. All of these decisions impact water resources and environmental sustainability.*

As we proceed toward 2050, a pressing challenge of climate change will be to reduce the economic and social vulnerability of humans to extreme hydrologic events. Over the long term, the effects of climate change are likely to influence decisions affecting ecosystems, energy and food security and land use. All of these decisions impact water resources and environmental sustainability.

DEMOGRAPHIC AND SOCIAL STRESSORS

People are the ultimate stressors of change on a global scale, through both their needs (their requirements for survival) and their wants (their desires for products and services that enhance safety, comfort and well-being). Whatever goods and services people need or want, each will require water to produce them. The continued growth of populations of people in desert environments and in urban and coastal areas where water supplies are already the most stressed will force water managers to look beyond augmenting water supplies to find solutions for meeting water demands (UN 2004; US Census Bureau 2005).

Trends in population and demographic shifts are viewed by our water utility industry as among the top ten major stressors that will affect how the water industry operates in coming decades (Means et al. 2005). Communities with burgeoning populations will need to find resources to fund new facilities for water, wastewater and other infrastructure. Areas with static or shrinking populations face the challenge of a diminishing customer base, resulting in reduced revenues needed to maintain under-used, or to replace aging, infrastructure. Other demographic aspects that may impact water utility management include an aging customer base, a more educated population, ethnic shifts in population, changes in diets and lifestyles, and increasing income gaps. The question of utility asset management in a dynamic population environment within the service time of a built environment deserves better understanding.

Water scarcity and flooding, and their adverse impacts on local ecosystems as well as on humans and their infrastructure, can trigger migration decisions. The social, economic and political contexts under which such water stresses occur will influence the migration response. If the natural environment becomes sufficiently degraded, people will be motivated to move to other areas where the quality of their lives may be improved. Once people move, their places of destination must provide them with water resources, which can lead to further environmental stresses.

Social stressors on water resource systems are influenced by poverty, education, cultures and value systems (including religious beliefs), and lifestyles and consumption patterns. Social perceptions and attitudes about the environment and water resources can result in stresses that impact water demands and uses.

ECONOMIC STRESSORS

Once people's survival needs are met, their wants usually focus on increasing human comfort and convenience. This in turn is generally associated with rising consumption of material goods and non-essential services such as travel and leisure. The desire for a better lifestyle is arguably one of the most powerful human motivations, and the rapid global rise in living standards, combined with population growth, poses a major threat to the sustainability of water resources and the environment. The production of goods to satisfy these growing human wants is often not possible without the overuse of natural resources. Further, it is accompanied by the production of wastes and other non-useful by-products. Unrestrained fulfillment of the desire for a better lifestyle will be accompanied by environmental stresses, many of them unprecedented.

A major challenge is to reconcile human needs and human wants with the ability of nature to provide or replenish the resources needed to produce them. Society must address the dual goal of enhancing human well-being and lifestyles while ensuring the sustainability of the ecosystems and environmental conditions that provide the desired goods and services. Achieving this goal will prove impossible unless we humans recognize and better understand the links between their actions and the condition and sustainability of the natural environment. Raising awareness to bring about behavioral change is one approach, but still an elusive goal.

Economic growth is affected by a wide range of policy decisions, from international trade to education and public health. The potential rate of economic growth can be affected by demographic variables such as population distribution (local workforce availability) and social characteristics (workforce capacity) and by the availability of new technologies. There is significant uncertainty in the impacts of future economic development because of increasing trends towards globalization, shifts in agricultural water practices, and the possible effects of technological change. Technological change could foster further development that could increase the strain on the water resources infrastructure or, more optimistically, could provide methods for mitigating the impacts of development (Daigger 2007). Adequate investments in water management, infrastructure and services can yield a high economic return by reducing the risks of floods and water shortages, water contamination, and hazards to public and ecosystem health.

TECHNOLOGICAL STRESSORS

Technology has provided humanity with the means to reshape the structure and functioning of the natural and built environment, and thus to alter possibilities and provide opportunities for future development. In many cases, technological changes have been (and in the future will be) a positive mechanism for improving society. In other cases, it acts as a stressor that can negatively impact society and the environment.

> *Technology has provided humanity with the means to reshape the structure and functioning of the natural and built environment, and thus to alter possibilities and provide opportunities for future development.*

In the water sector, the expansion of scientific knowledge and technological applications is changing the way water is monitored, managed, used, cleaned, and increasingly reused, to meet human, economic and environmental needs (ASCE 2009b). Industries are investing in new technologies and processes that reduce water use and wastewater discharges. Household consumers are being offered water-saving technologies such as low-flush toilets, low-flow showers and faucet aerators. Agricultural productivity is being leveraged by drip irrigation and maintained by soil fertility and conservation techniques. Water supplies are being enhanced through innovative wastewater treatment and reuse techniques. Advances in technologies and energy efficiency in the past decade have made desalination an economic option for water supplies in coastal cities.

Technological advances that address human wants and needs are major reasons why many people enjoy the standard of living they do, one that at a minimum includes access to safe drinking water and adequate sanitation. The sad fact that so many humans still do not have access to safe water supplies and adequate sanitation is certainly not because of a lack of existing technology, but rather because of a lack of access to it.

While these basic water supply and sanitation needs are generally met in the US, the technological infrastructure improvements of the past century or so have not been adequately maintained. As a result, we have a problem of aging infrastructure that impacts our ability to treat water, distribute it, and to collect and treat wastewater. According to the American Society of Civil Engineers (ASCE 2009a), the nation's infrastructure needs an investment of $2.2 trillion over a five-year period to bring it to a good condition. The report gives grades of D- to both water supply and wastewater infrastructure, marks indicating the failing condition of these infrastructures and the urgency for immediate repair, rehabilitation and replacement. Looking toward 2050, perhaps we should be thinking of more innovative ways of meeting the demands currently provided by our decaying water pipes and sewers, since people seem unwilling to pay for digging them up and replacing them.

Technology development in the water sector both drives and is driven by demands for cheaper and more reliable supplies and better water management. Technologies can have positive benefits by reducing water demand and increasing water availability (for example, rainwater harvesting), while others can increase water demands (such as using crops to produce bioenergy). Technological innovations can create both positive and negative pressures on not only water quantities, but also on their qualities as well. Some innovations reduce environmental pressures (e.g., by lowering emissions or using water resources more efficiently), while others increase them (e.g., by increasing water demands for their production). The green revolution of the 1970s and 1980s and genetically modified organisms for agricultural applications are examples of technological advances that may also induce stresses on the environment. Environmental regulations that motivate industries and other water users to develop technology that address water availability and water quality problems can result in improvements to society and the environment, but they may also be counterproductive because incentives to engage in further technology development may dissipate once required standards are met.

"Son, you should be ashamed of yourself.
You'll never be successful unless you get better grades."

There is a strong linkage between the water and energy sectors since water is required to produce and use energy, and energy is used to clean, transport and use water (Gleick 2006). Since renewable energy resources alone are not sufficient to meet the predicted dramatic increase in energy demands through 2050, fossil fuel extraction and development of nuclear energy (at least in many countries) will continue to increase, as will their impacts on water resources and the environment. There have been significant increases in water use in parts of the country to accommodate agriculture and processing costs associated with bio fuels. Increasing energy costs may force water and wastewater utilities to achieve greater energy efficiency in order to offset these costs (Alliance to Save Energy 2002). However new energy-intensive treatment technologies may not achieve their expected potential despite their advantages (Means et al. 2005).

Water and wastewater utilities have historically been concerned with security issues such as accidental pollution spills, and vandalism or other criminal activities resulting in damage to equipment. In addition, there is increasing concern over intentional acts directed against water and wastewater utilities designed to harm if not kill people. These include physical damage to utility facilities and purposeful contamination of the water supply (Means et al. 2005). This motivates the need for new technologies for reducing such risks and vulnerabilities, and mediating their impacts if such an attack should occur.

GOVERNANCE STRESSORS

Effective policy and legal frameworks are necessary to develop, implement and enforce rules and regulations for controlling water uses. Although policy and law go hand in hand, they are fundamentally different. Policy serves mainly as a guide for decision-makers. Law provides a set of enforceable rules. The legal system within which water law operates can be a strong instrument of change, or an impediment to progress. Typically the legal system usually functions as the latter. Water law sets the framework for stakeholders' use of water resources and responds (often slowly) to demographic, economic and social stressors.

Policy and laws that do not directly address water issues can nevertheless affect management of the water environment. These include land use planning, environmental assessment, nature conservation and environmental law. Public health laws influence the supply of water and sanitation, as does land tenure reform. Conflicts and regional instability (or stability) can influence water demand and use, particularly in water-scarce regions.

> *Legitimate, transparent and participatory processes can effectively mobilize input for designing and implementing water resources policy in response to numerous and conflicting stressors.*

Water resources development and management in the interests of national development objectives require effective policy and legal frameworks that also respect deeply rooted customary practices. Participatory processes that take account of the social, economic and cultural characteristics of the country or community will make a significant contribution to meeting this challenge (Gleick 2006). However, a greater challenge is to ensure that such laws and the regulations that support them are effectively administered and enforced. Conflicting water resources and environmental regulations can lead to inefficient or insufficient management of resources.

Other governance issues include privatization of water systems, customer expectations concerning the safety and reliability of their water supplies, communications of information to water customers, water as a human right, valuation of water, and creative partnerships between water/wastewater utilities and other sectors.

ENVIRONMENTAL STRESSORS

Sustainability

The report of the Brundtland Commission, formally the World Commission on Environment and Development (WCED), *Our Common Future*, defines sustainable development as "development that meets the needs of the present without compromising the ability of future generations to meet their own needs" (Brundtland 1987). It recognizes that land, water, air, and minerals are all essential but finite natural resources that contribute to a healthy planet and society. UNESCO (2006) established a goal to ensure environmental sustainability and recognized that "healthy ecosystems are essential for the maintenance of biodiversity and human well-being" and that "we depend upon them for our drinking water, food security and a wide range of environmental goods and services." It sets a target to "integrate the principles of sustainable development into country policies and programmes and reverse the loss of environmental resources."

Water professionals have an obligation to manage their resources in such a way that they meet, to the maximum extent possible, the demands of not only the current generation but those of future generations as well. If water systems are managed to do that, in spite of the uncertainties of future supplies and demands, while maintaining their hydrologic, ecologic and cultural integrities, they can be called sustainable (Loucks and Gladwell 1999).

Pollution

There are many pathways by which our water resources and environment can be compromised through excessive contamination, or in popular terms, pollution. These pathways include deposition from the air, point and nonpoint source runoff, saltwater intrusion into existing aquifers, and others. "Pollution of water bodies alters the chemistry and ecology of rivers, lakes and wetlands; greenhouse gas emissions can alter runoff and rainfall patterns" (UNESCO 2006).

As we proceed toward 2050, groundwater will likely be used more and more to meet water demands and, hence, it should be protected against depletion and contamination, especially from nonpoint sources (Bouwer 2002). A significant nonpoint source of groundwater pollution is agriculture, with its use of fertilizers, pesticides, and salt-containing irrigation water that contaminates the drainage water as it moves from the root zone to the underlying groundwater. The problem can be expected to get worse in the future as agriculture attempts to keep up with the demands for more food and fiber by increasing populations and per capita demands.

Saltwater intrusion is a natural process that occurs in coastal aquifers where there is hydraulic connectivity between the aquifer and the seawater. The rate of saltwater intrusion can increase or decrease depending on the imbalance between freshwater aquifer and sea water levels. Increasing groundwater withdrawals from the freshwater aquifers can cause further lateral and vertical intrusion of surrounding saltwater. Similarly, sea level rises due to climate change, as previously mentioned, can result in increased saltwater intrusion. The impacts of saltwater intrusion include more intensive water treatment requirements and/or decreased availability of fresh water for various uses including agriculture.

Public health
During the 19th and 20th centuries public health was the primary stressor in the US for establishing both public drinking water supplies and municipal sewer systems and treatment plants. The result was the virtual elimination of the most serious waterborne diseases such as cholera and typhoid. However, waterborne infectious diseases are still a significant concern in the US (Levin et al. 2002). In many less developed countries, waterborne diseases are still rampant, killing millions of people per year.

Specific public health concerns for those managing water on into the future include:
- the identification of potential impacts and removal of endocrine disruptors, persistent organic pollutants and pharmaceuticals in the environment and in raw drinking water sources, along with the wide range of disinfection by-products resulting from chlorination that may be carcinogenic and have other possible health effects.
- the removal of common waterborne pathogens (e.g., *Giardia, Cryptosporidium*, and some viruses), including waterborne pathogens that have developed resistance to antibiotics or increased in virulence.

CONCLUSIONS

We cannot perfectly predict the state of our water resource systems in 2050, but we know their states will be influenced by a sequence of human decisions in response to a wide variety of stressors between now and 2050. These stressors may interact and at times, the responses to individual stressors may conflict. Hence, it is essential that water resources be viewed and managed holistically, considering both their natural states and the need to balance competing demands – domestic, agricultural, industrial and environmental – to ensure sustainability. This is no small task, but knowledge of the effects or impacts of each stressor and their combined effects can lead to more informed decisions about how to respond to them.

Sustainable management of water resources requires systematic, integrated decision-making that recognizes the interdependence of decisions. Decisions about land use can affect the availability and condition of water resources, while decisions about water resources can also affect the environment and land use. Decisions about economic and social futures can affect hydrology and ecosystems that in turn will impact economic and social futures. The global rise in living standards, combined with population growth, create pressures on freshwater resources through increased water demands and pollution. Growing international trade in goods and services can aggravate water stress in some countries while relieving it in others through flows of "virtual water," particularly in the form of imported agricultural commodities. Technological innovation is one of the most unpredictable stressors and can create both positive and negative pressures, sometimes simultaneously, resulting in increased or decreased water demand, supply and quality.

The challenge is to get decision-makers inside and outside the environmental and water management profession to adopt appropriate measures to reduce the negative pressures on environmental and water systems and increase the positive pressures. Most decision-makers would admit to wanting to do this, but are not sure of how best to do it. The interdependencies among various stressors makes their job challenging. Legitimate, transparent and participatory processes can effectively mobilize input for designing and implementing water resources policy in response to these multiple and often conflicting stressors (World Water Assessment Programme 2009).

REFERENCES

Alliance to Save Energy. (2002). *Watergy: taking advantage of untapped energy and water efficiency opportunities in municipal water systems,* Alliance to Save Energy and USAID, Washington, DC, <http://technologies.ew.eea.europa.eu/technologies/resourc_mngt/water_use/watergy.pdf/> (Oct, 2010).

American Society of Civil Engineers (ASCE). (2009a). "Report card 2009 grades." *Report card for America's infrastructure,* American Society of Civil Engineers, <http://www.asce.org/reportcard/2009/grades.cfm> (Oct, 2010).

ASCE (2009b). The Role of Technology in Water Resources Planning and Management, by Elizabeth M. Perez, P.E., (editor) and Warren Viessman, Jr., P.E., (editors) *Reston, VA: ASCE / EWRI,* 978-0-7844-1028-8, 2009, 134 pp. (Barcode: 585806897)

Bouwer, H. (2002). "Integrated water management for the 21st century: problems and solutions." *J. Irrig. Drain. E.-ASCE,* 128(4), 193-203.

Brundtland, G., ed. (1987). *Our common future: the world commission on environment and development,* Oxford University Press, Oxford, UK.

Buchberger, S. G., Clark, R. M. Grayman, W. M., Li, Z., Tong, S., and Yang, Y. J. (2008). "Impacts of global change on municipal water distribution systems." *Proc., 2008 International Symposium on WDSA,* Kruger Park, South Africa.

Cromwell III, J. E., Smith, J. B., and Raucher, R. S. (2007). "No doubt about climate change and its implications for water suppliers." *J. Am. Water Works As.,* 99(9), 112-117.

Daigger, G. T. (2007). "Wastewater management in the 21st century." *J. Environ. Eng.-ASCE,* 133(7), 671-680.

Gleick, P. (2006). *The world's water, 2006-2007: the biennial report on freshwater resources,* Island Press, Washington, DC.

Intergovernmental Panel on Climate Change (IPCC). (2007). *Climate change 2007 - the physical science basis, contribution of working group I to the fourth assessment report of the Intergovernmental Panel on Climate Change* [S. Solomon, D. Qin, M. Manning, Z. Chen, M. Marquis, K. B. Averyt, M. Tignor, and H. L. Miller (eds.)], Cambridge University Press, New York, NY, 996 p.

Levin, R. B., Epstein, P. R., Ford, T. E., Harrington, W., Olson, E., and Reichard, E. G. (2002). "U.S. drinking water challenges in the twenty-first century." *Environ. Health Persp.*, 110, 43-52.

Loucks, D. P., and Gladwell, J. S., eds. (1999). *Sustainability criteria for water resource systems*, UNESCO, Cambridge University Press, Cambridge, UK.

Means III, E. G., Ospina, L., and Patrick, R. (2005). "Ten primary trends and their implications for water utilities." *J. Am. Water Works As.*, 97(7), 64-77.

Miller, K. A., and Yates, D. N. (2006). *Climate change and water resources : a primer for municipal water providers*, AWWA Research Foundation, American Water Works Association, IWA Pub., Denver, CO.

UNESCO. (2006). *Water a shared responsibility - the United Nations world water development report 2,* UN-WATER/WWAP/2006/3, UNESCO, <http://unesdoc.unesco.org/images/0014/001444/144409E.pdf> (Oct, 2010).

United Nations (UN). (2004). *World population to 2300,* New York, NY, <http://www.un.org/esa/population/publications/longrange2/WorldPop2300final.pdf> (Oct, 2010).

US Census Bureau. (2005). "U.S. population projections." *U.S. Census Bureau*, <http://www.census.gov/population/www/projections/popproj.html> (Oct, 2010).

World Water Assessment Programme. (2009). *The United Nations world water development report 3: water in a changing world*, United Nations Educational, Scientific, and Cultural Organization, Paris, France, <http://www.unesco.org/water/wwap/wwdr/wwdr3/> (Oct, 2010).

II PLANNING AND POLICY

Chapter 4

Water Management in 2050

Uri Shamir and Charles D.D. Howard

ABSTRACT

Local, national, and international water resources management encompasses a broad range of activities from flood control to providing adequate supplies of clean water for domestic use. As populations shift and expand, it will become increasingly difficult to meet consumer demands for reliable water of high quality. Future flood damages, already nature's greatest source of destruction, will likely become even greater as riparian populations increase and property values rise. The focus of this chapter is on *timely adaptation* to change. The water management tools for this approach are policies, means and actions. Ideally water systems planning, design and operations should evolve to rely more on science and technology and less on arbitrary political decisions. Realistically, the challenge for adaptation is to recognize changes in advance and to appropriately modify or invent new technologies, rules, regulations, and institutional and political arrangements. The perspective of this chapter is that of developed countries with the hope that, with proper commitment, improvements to water management practices wherever made will also find their way to less developed countries.

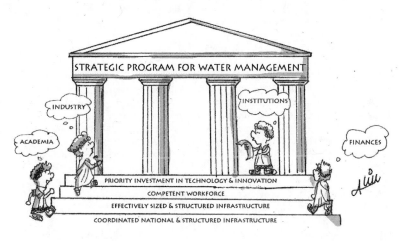

INTRODUCTION

Water resources management has a long history of notable water engineering achievements. Among the most famous are Hezekiah's tunnel that delivered water to Jerusalem, the qanats of Persia, aqueducts of Rome, and the Grand Canal and the Dujiangyuan River diversion in China. These major projects are lasting symbols of the planning and engineering organizations that identified the opportunities and funding, undertook the surveys, developed designs, assembled the contractors, supervised construction, and managed financing and operation of the facilities. Since 1850 the US government has responded to problems by passing several national water planning acts and initiatives to modify policies and plans for management of irrigation, water quality, hydroelectric power, navigation, and flood control. Other nations and international political alliances have followed similar paths (e.g., Australian Government National Water Commission (2009), European Union Water Framework Directive (2000)). There can be no doubt that underlying issues of water management will continue to evolve to 2050 and beyond, accentuated by the expansion of populations and changes in the availability of water.

As competition for water grows and floodplains became more densely populated, especially in urban areas, water management will become more difficult and complex. Physical and institutional challenges to serve and protect consumer sectors will stem from a variety of reasons:
- declining availability of good quality natural water;
- higher variability of supplies driven by climate change;
- rising costs of securing water quality;
- population pressures;
- affordable potable water treatment for developing countries;
- sustaining agriculture and the public services it provides;
- increasing public demand to sustain and protect the environment with its diverse ecology and ever-expanding services;
- continuous evolution of technology; and
- evolution of national and international structures, laws and regulations.

Much can and must be done to *mitigate* diminishing access to supplies, declining water quality, and the increasing threats of flood damage through supply side management by developing new infrastructure and through watershed protection. *Mitigating* change offers possibilities, for example by reducing pollution of sources, but introduces heightened uncertainties and high costs. A better approach is *adaptation* to change through demand side management. Demand side management emphasizes priorities on robust planning to *adapt* water management to the expected changes in supplies. While both supply and demand side management offer possible solutions on their own, policies and actions with a rational balance of supply and demand are the most effective way to achieve safety and reliability of water services.

The lack of coincidence between political and physical water boundaries generates difficulties in rational management. Difficulties arise through incomplete scientific information, real or seemingly conflicting objectives (e.g., local economic development versus national environmental quality), and political mandates. The greatest obstacle to rational management of water stems today from the lack of cooperative agreements among political jurisdictions.

> *The greatest obstacle to rational management of water stems from failures of governance and lack of coordination among political jurisdictions.*

Water resources and water control systems are managed over a range of political levels: local, urban, national, regional, and international. Within each level and in coordination with the other levels, decisions depend on the issues being addressed and the specific interacting political and institutional systems. The pressures of scarcity and the threats of future flood damage create incentives for cooperative actions to overcome political/institutional/legal constraints on effective physical and economical management of water resources.

Modalities for water management vary widely among countries, but universal key priorities are to avoid over-exploitation and pollution of natural sources and to provide flood management. In the developing world, water management is far from maturity, whereas in the developed world it is more sophisticated, but still less than perfect. The 3rd World Water Development Report provides, through its chapters and case studies, a water management panorama with considerable emphasis on developing countries (WWAP 2009, see especially Part 4: Responses and choices).

FUTURE TECHNOLOGIES FOR ADAPTING TO CHANGE

Monitoring: Before water can be managed, it must be known in quality and quantity with methods for predicting its future behavior in time and space. The 21st century is a breakthrough century for remote sensing, distributed monitoring and control of water facilities. Remote sensing technologies provide diagnostic measurements as a means for compensating for the reduction in land-based monitoring systems, and for expanding into data sparse regions, in particular in the developing world. These techniques are already being used to detect changes in soil moisture, water stored in snow, river and lake levels (Committee on Earth Science and Applications from Space 2007). New sensors and algorithms will extend these measurements on local to continental scales to estimate river discharges, and groundwater and snow water changes. Improved near-real-time estimates of precipitation will be available widely for any location on earth. In the next few years these technologies will be perfected to provide more accurate and more frequent updates of data for controlling systems that manage floods, predict drought and distribute water to fields and cities.

Reduction of water losses: Benefits of improved water management based on better data will include reduced evaporation losses from reservoirs, reduced leakage from distribution systems, and more effective management of surface and groundwater reservoirs.

Reduced water use in home and city without lowering the quality-of-life: Technology will provide on-site disposal of human and household waste with little or no water usage. Household appliances will use less water or none at all. Recycled water for special uses will become more widely used and accepted, and localized treatment will become a viable option to the costs and waste of centralized water pumping and transport. Sewerage systems and wastewater treatment plants will be upgraded to accommodate lower flows, higher concentrations and a wider range of pollutants.

Efficient irrigation technologies: Optimized application of irrigation will continue to develop by using new sensors and remotely sensed monitoring of site specific plant stress in agriculture, parks and gardens. Precision and automated agricultural practices based on local feedback systems and space platforms will provide a huge leap forward in an industry that is the largest consumer of water (Committee on Earth Science and Applications from Space 2007).

Stress resistant crops and plants: Widespread planting of engineered species will generate the same or better crops with lower quantity and lesser quality of water.

Systems approach to integrated uses and non-potable water treatment: Systems will include desalination of sea-water and brackish groundwater, treatment of sewage for irrigation and domestic use, and membrane technologies for removal of trace pollutants. Parallel multi-quality and blended-quality supply systems will increase the flexibility of developing and operating distribution networks.

Targeted water treatment for natural, recycled and manufactured water: Treatment and transport systems will produce and deliver customized product streams that meet quality requirements for specific uses.

Point-of-Use (POU) water treatment technologies: While public urban water supply systems must be obligated to deliver potable water quality, there are opportunities and good reasons to advance in parallel with POU technologies. These range from simple and cheap devices suitable for rural and urban communities in developing countries (Clearinghouse 2009; Doocy and Burnham 2006; NSF International 2009) to reverse osmosis and ultraviolet-based systems that can be used in homes, public buildings, restaurants and mass feeding establishments. For example, LifeStraw is a simple hand-held filter device that can filter up to 700 liters of water to remove dirt and kill bacteria, viruses and parasitic organisms ($3-5/unit), and ceramic filters (from 1-10 liter/hr, useful life 6 months to 10 years, $2.25-3.50/unit) can remove biological contaminants. POU can improve public health in poor communities, address accidental or intentional contamination events in distribution systems, and reduce the serious negative environmental consequences of bottled water. There is great potential for POU innovations, including low-cost devices and innovative use of nanotechnology materials.

Water Sensitive Planning (WSP) of the built environment: Water considerations will be integrated into planning and maintenance of land uses and land cover at all spatial levels from yard and neighborhood to the entire watershed. Such initiatives will minimize the loss of usable runoff water, reduce flooding, improve streamflow regimes, reduce downstream pollution and enhance the built environment by judicious placement of built and open spaces, landscaping, and use of best management practices for direct use and/or infiltration of runoff and regulation of flows (Carmon and Shamir 2010; USEPA 2007).

Watershed management: Planning and operation of water supply, water quality and flood protection schemes will be based on a watershed framework, the natural and necessary unit for rational water management.

Models and systems to support decision making: Improved models will be developed for supply and flood forecasting and for chemistry and biology in rivers, water bodies, groundwater, wetlands and other ecological systems. Efficient and effective optimization methods will support management decisions under uncertainty.

Methodologies for formulation of water management policies, strategies and master plans, comprising: (1) definition of the physical, organizational and institutional water system and its division into logical subsystems; (2) identification of the boundaries with other systems, and the "boundary conditions;" (3) identification of the system's objectives, and their organization into a hierarchy; (4) definition of the measures by which the attainment of these objectives is to be evaluated; (5) identification of all policy areas, and for each of its components; (6) identification of all "reasonable" alternatives for each component; (7) identification and analysis of the effects of each alternative on all measures; (8) construction of candidate comprehensive policies, for one policy area, for a group of areas, or for all of the areas, by selecting one alternative for each component; (9) evaluation of these policies according to their effects on the measures, and thus on the objectives, using multi-objective evaluation methods; (10) interaction with decision-makers, interest groups, and experts throughout the above activities to aid in decision-making; and (11) continuous monitoring and evaluation of changing conditions and of the effectiveness of implemented policies that are reported to the decision-makers and that provide feedback on all phases of the analysis. This approach has been applied in the past (Shamir et al. 1985) and is currently being used for the Israeli Water Sector.

WATER ECONOMICS

Pricing alone pays for water but does not capture its value. The value of water has three components (Howard 2003): (1) Existence value; (2) Aesthetic and environmental value; and (3) Economic value. Water provides common goods that are difficult to measure. It must also maintain equity among users and can be a motive for political agreement. In addition, for sustainable water infrastructure and rational management, it is necessary for social policy adjustments to support cost-based pricing for all sectors.

Water supplies, like other commodities, only have economic value in relation to their scarcity. Thus, the value of water is related to the reliability of its supply. Also, like some other resources, the value stems from water's role in the production of other goods and services. As a result, estimates of the economic value of water, and its pricing, must include measures of both its reliability and its impact on economic and social activity.

> *Estimates of the economic value of water and its pricing must include measures of both reliability and the impact on economic and social activity.*

Demand management and temporary curtailment of water supplies during drought have an effect that is much broader than water pricing. They affect the regional economy and imply the use of devices and operating strategies that affect one or more parameters of the criteria for management of supply systems. Together the intersection of water supply and demand define the reliability of a system and managers must be skilled in both. Engineers will become participants and partners with politicians and citizens in the process of effective and equitable balancing of both aspects to develop appropriate water supply management criteria.

INSTITUTIONAL, POLITICAL AND INTERNATIONAL ARRANGEMENTS

Politicians view water as a strategic resource, a life-giving element that cannot be given up or even shared. But while water is essential to support life (its "existence value") it also has aesthetic, environmental and economic values that are created jointly with other inputs, including land, labor, technologies, and investments. Even the "existence value" of water should be placed in an economic context because where supply can be augmented, the value of water cannot be greater than the cost of producing it (Fisher et al. 2005).

A paradigm shift will be required to move policies, agreements and plans from simply *allocation* of water to *sharing its benefits* in combination with other inputs. Benefits can be focused to represent the parties' priorities and preferences (Fisher et al. 2005; Jenkins et al. 2004; Kronaveter and Shamir 2009a,b).

The share of water supplies and services by public-private partnerships has risen dramatically over the last few decades. Past successes and failures indicate that with a degree of caution, and without the state relinquishing its overall responsibility, the relative advantages of the public and private sectors can be combined to create a more effective water management framework. Public-civic partnerships, with civil society mobilized to participate more fully in policy and management decisions, are also gaining an increasing role in water management. Civil society's involvement is essential for successful demand management, and acceptance of temporary curtailment of consumption during droughts.

International coordinated or cooperative water management of shared water resources can yield substantial benefits (Kronaveter and Shamir 2009a,b). Contrary to some publicized statements that "water will be the cause of future wars," there is ample evidence of cooperation among neighboring countries and of stable water agreements that survive even in times of political strain and conflict (Wolf 2007). Because water has values beyond its "existence value," it is possible to base international arrangements on sharing the benefits created by water rather than the water itself.

SUMMARY

As water issues become more pressing, merely waiting and expecting that progress is inevitable will not serve society. Improvements in water management will come through innovation fueled by individual curiosity, dedicated effort, and opportunities within a strategic program supported by national and international agencies, universities and industries.

Four foundational elements are critical to a purposeful, effective, strategic program for advancement in water management, science and engineering:

1. *Coordinated national and international strategies* - implementing national water policy coherently across all agencies in support of national needs and priorities and aligning attention to regional and international shared interests for efficient management of water resources;
2. *A competent technical workforce* - developing expertise sufficient in number, talent, breadth of perspective and experience to address difficult and pressing challenges;
3. *An effectively sized and structured infrastructure* - realizing synergy from the public and private sectors and from international partnerships; and
4. *A priority investment in technology and innovation* - strengthening and sustaining the capacity to meet national and international needs through major support for research that can provide transformational advances.

This century continues to present age-old water management problems in unpalatable packages of population pressure, political changes and climate change. A well-defined broad path for future investment in science and technology will present unparalleled opportunities for advancing the quality of life throughout the world.

REFERENCES

Australian Government National Water Commission. (2009). "Troubled waters: Australian water reform 2009 (Second biennial assessment of progress in implementation of the National Water Initiative." <http://www.nwc.gov.au/www/html/147-introduction---2009-biennial-assessments.asp?intSiteID=1> (Dec, 2009).

Carmon, N., and Shamir, U. (2010). "Water-sensitive planning: integrating water considerations into urban and regional planning." *Water Environ. J.*, 24(3), 181-191, DOI: 10.1111/j.1747-6593.2009.00172.x.

Clearinghouse. (2009). "Low-cost water security technologies for developing countries." <http://www.jalmandir.com/filtration/life/life-straw.html> (Dec, 2009).

Committee on Earth Science and Applications from Space. (2007). *Earth science and applications from space: national imperatives for the next decade and beyond.* Committee on Earth Science and Applications from Space, National Research Council, Washington, DC, 456 p. <http://www.nap.edu/catalog/11820.html> (Dec, 2009).

Doocy, S., and Burnham, G. (2006). "Point-of-use water treatment and diarrhoea reduction in the emergency context: an effectiveness trial in Liberia." *Trop. Med. Int. Health,* 11(10), 1542-1552.

European Union Water Framework Directive. (2000). "The EU Water Framework Directive - integrated river basin management for Europe." European Commission-Environment-Water <http://ec.europa.eu/environment/water/water-framework/index_en.html> (Dec, 2009)

Fisher, F. M., Huber-Lee, A., Amir, I., Arlosoroff, S., Eckstein, Z., Haddadin, M. J., Hamati, S. G., Jarrar, A. M., Jayyusi, A. F., Shamir, U., and Wesseling, H. (2005) *Liquid assets: an economic approach for water management and conflict resolution in the Middle East and beyond.* Resources for the Future, Washington, DC.

Howard, C. D. D. (2003). "The economic value of water." *Proc., Mountains as Water Towers*, Banff, Canada.

Jenkins, M. W., Lund, R. J., and Howitt, R. E. (2004). "Optimization of California's water supply system: results and insights." *J. Water Res. Pl.-ASCE*, 130(4), 271-280.

Kronaveter, L., and Shamir, U. (2009a). "Negotiation support for cooperative allocation of a shared water resource: methodology." *J. Water Res. Pl.-ASCE*, 135(2), 60-69.

Kronaveter, L., and Shamir, U. (2009b). "Negotiation support for cooperative allocation of a shared water resource: application." *J. Water Res. Pl.-ASCE*, 135(2), 70-79.

NSF International. (2009). "Home water treatment devices." <http://www.nsf.org/consumer/drinking_water/dw_treatment.asp> (Dec, 2009).

Shamir, U., Bear, J., Arad, N., Gal-Noor, Y., Selbst, N., and Vardi, Y. (1985). "National water policy: a methodology and its application to Israel." *Scientific basis for water resources management*, M. Diskin, ed., IAHS Publication No. 153, 369-379.

United States Environmental Protection Agency (USEPA). (2007). *Reducing stormwater costs through low impact development (LID) strategies and practices*, EPA 841-F-07-006. Washington, DC.

Wolf, A. T. (2007). "Shared waters: conflict and cooperation." *Annu. Rev. Env. Resour.*, 32, 3.1-3.29.
World Water Assessment Programme (WWAP). (2009). *Water in a changing world.* World Water Development Report 3, UNESCO Publishing. <http://www.unesco.org/water/wwap/wwdr/wwdr3/> (Dec, 2009).

AUTHOR INFORMATION

Uri Shamir is Professor Emeritus at the Faculty of Civil and Environmental Engineering, and Founding Director of the Stephen and Nancy Grand Water Research Institute at the Technion – Israel Institute of Technology. He holds a BS from the Technion and a PhD from MIT. For over four decades he has taught, conducted research and consulted to national and local authorities and companies in Israel and other countries on hydrology and water resources management, and has been visiting professor at various universities in the US and Canada. He is Fellow of AGU, Life Member of ASCE, recipient of the IAHS-UNESCO-WMO International Hydrology Prize in 2000 and the ASCE Hinds Award in 2003. He was President of the International Association of Hydrological Sciences (1991-1995), President of the International Unions of Geodesy and Geophysics (2003-2007) and is currently (2005-2011) Member of the Executive Board of the International Council of Science (ICSU). Email: Shamir@technion.ac.il

Charles D. D. Howard is an independent consulting engineer in water resources management, hydraulic engineering and development of innovative water management software. He provided senior level technical advice to water and power utilities, provincial, state, and federal governments in Canada and the US, and in many countries under the United Nations Development Program and for the World Bank. He served on many committees of the US National Academy of Sciences (National Research Council) and as an external examiner for the US National Science Foundation's research program on semi-arid hydrology. He received the 1998 Julian Hinds Award of ASCE for leadership and technical achievement in advancing the state of the art in water resources management. He is a registered engineer in British Columbia and Washington, and holds civil engineering degrees from University of Alberta (BS and MS) and from Massachusetts Institute of Technology (MS). Email: CddHoward@shaw.ca

Chapter 5

Transboundary Water Sharing:
Confronting the Challenge of Growing Water Scarcity

Stephen E. Draper

ABSTRACT

Water scarcity poses a significant challenge for the 21st century. This growing scarcity is not only due to increased demand for water, but is also magnified by a potentially significant reduction in accessible water due to global climate change. This challenge is most daunting for shared use of transboundary water resources. Most of the world's useable freshwater resources are shared in some fashion by two or more governments. Conflict between and among those governments will grow as the scarcity of accessible freshwater grows. Only cooperative management that engages government, quasi-government and non-state actors can ensure that adequate supplies of quality water will be available in 2050 to support economic growth and a meaningful quality of life. Central to meeting the challenge is the need to create, implement and enforce effective water sharing agreements between and among riparian governments. Certain principles of negotiation are essential for creation of these agreements. Strategies that have historically demonstrated their effectiveness must be integrated into administrative and institutional frameworks that assure efficient implementation of feasible and effective agreements.

"Sharing transboundary waters"

INTRODUCTION

The critical natural resources challenge for the 21st century, arguably equal in importance to developing renewable energy, is the effective and equitable sharing of scarce freshwater from the world's rivers, lakes and aquifers. The core issue is, in economic terms, a question of supply and demand. When supply of accessible freshwater is greater than demand, no conflict exists among those seeking to use the water resource. When demand begins to approach or exceed the supply of water, water scarcity emerges which can lead to conflict. This issue is most evident and becomes even more complex when transboundary water resources are involved.

THE EXTENT OF TRANSBOUNDARY WATER SHARING

The transboundary water scarcity issue is formidable. Shared surface and underground water comprise a significant part of the world's freshwater. These transboundary waters must be shared between and among riparian states and/or nations, each with their own set of water policies, laws and regulations, setting the stage for possible conflict.

In the continental United States, over 90% of rivers greater than 560 km (350 mi) in length are shared by two or more states and/or with other countries. When the water resources of underground aquifers as well as significant surface water bodies such as the Great Lakes are also considered, over 90% of the population in the continental US depends on waters that are shared between states (Draper 2002). The potential for conflict is enormous (Draper 2002; Oregon State University 2005).

Worldwide, over 93% of major rivers are shared between or among two or more nations. Over fifty rivers are shared by three or more nations, with the Danube shared by 13 riparian countries. The watersheds of these rivers cover almost two-thirds of the global landmass. Forty percent of the world's population depends on these shared river basins for the water they need (Draper 2002; Oregon State University 2005). When aquifers and large water bodies such as Lake Victoria are considered, the percentage increases significantly.

THE GROWING THREAT OF WATER SCARCITY

Lack of adequate freshwater is found today in many places around the globe. This water scarcity is spreading as developing countries struggle to find water needed to expand their economies. Inadequate freshwater to meet a growing demand is now a major obstacle to improving the standard of living for many nations and cultures.

In 2009, the burdens of increasing water scarcity are linked primarily to the increasing demand for reliable and consistent supplies of clean water. The world's population is expanding dramatically, led by developing nations. At the same time, the per capita demand for water increases significantly, again led by the developing nations. When no comparable increase in freshwater exists to meet this growing demand, conflict can arise. The challenge for governments and their water managers today is to maximize their use of transboundary waters while minimizing the effects of conflicts that may arise.

CHALLENGES FOR SHARED USE OF TRANSBOUNDARY WATERS IN 2050

By 2050, the challenge will be significantly aggravated, not only because of increased demand but also because the supply of accessible water will shrink as climate change disrupts the pattern and distribution of water available for use. This challenge will be greatly magnified if agreements to share water do not include flexibility to react to unexpected changes in both demand and availability.

> *The critical challenge in 2050 will be the same as we face today: to minimize water sharing conflicts through cooperative actions.*

Evidence of climate change exists today in documented melting of glaciers, thawing of permafrost and thinning of sea ice in Arctic regions. Collapse of ice shelves in Antarctic regions as well as melting of continental glaciers throughout the world are significant proof of climate change (Karl et al. 2009; Monaghan and Bromwich 2008). Whether this climate change is man-made or a natural fluctuation in the long-term climate time frame is irrelevant to water management. The impacts on water resources will be substantial.

As noted by the Intergovernmental Panel on Climate Change (IPCC), among others, climate change will disrupt normal historic patterns of rainfall in terms of amount, distribution and/or timing. River flows and aquifer recharge will be affected (Draper and Kundell 2007; IPCC 2001, 2007; Karl et al. 2009; National Science and Technology Council 2008). Water users such as municipal water utilities that are dependent on a consistent, reliable water supply source may have to contend with less reliability than experienced in the past. Governments and water management strategists may have to struggle to manage an increasingly erratic supply of water to meet higher demands for dependable water supplies. The critical challenge in 2050 will be the same as we face today: to minimize water sharing conflicts through cooperative actions. However, these 2050 challenges will be far greater in both size and scope.

MEETING THE WATER SHARING CHALLENGE

Meeting the challenges of water sharing in a time of water scarcity will be a major task. States and nations will have to reorder their thoughts and ideas about sovereignty and individuality. Cooperation will be essential. While states and nations can work towards maximizing their own economic and social well-being from the use of the shared water resource, they must also be willing to acknowledge and accommodate the goals and objectives of their riparian neighbors.

The struggle to share source water between and among distinct, sovereign political authorities has existed at least as long as man has been civilized. One of the astonishing lessons of history is that water scarcity conflict has been most often resolved by formal agreement to share the water in some fashion rather than through the use of military force (Barnaby 2009; Draper 2006; Gleick 2006).

The task of managing transboundary water is immense. While some form of interstate compact covers a number of the shared river basins in the United States, many were drafted in the first half of the 20th century. These agreements were often limited in scope and oriented to specific problems rather than towards comprehensive management of the shared surface and underground water. These compacts will require significant changes, if not replacement. In other areas, new compacts must be formed as the geographic scope of water scarcity enlarges.

Internationally, water sharing problems are more acute. Over a third of the 200 international river basins are not covered by international agreements, and only 30 of the agreements in force have truly cooperative institutional arrangements (Draper 2002, 2006; Oregon State University 2005).

RESOLUTION BY WATER SHARING AGREEMENTS

Effective and efficient water sharing is predicated on appropriate water sharing agreements. In the development and implementation of a viable water sharing agreement, certain principles of negotiations are essential. These principles are equally necessary for the agreement's ongoing effectiveness. They include an obligation to cooperate and negotiate in good faith and an obligation to prevent unreasonable harm to other parties. Other principles of negotiation include a commitment to the equitable use of the shared water, an obligation to exchange adequate data with the other parties and a commitment to the values of water resource sustainability (Albert 2000; Caponera 1995; Dellapenna 2001; Draper 1997; Hey 1995).

Water sharing agreements must reconcile an array of issues: political, geographical, hydrological, environmental, and functional. Political issues are an especially important concern. National and local government water management agencies may disagree among themselves on specific provisions since the different agencies respond to divergent constituencies and interest groups. Not only may political issues divide agencies, constituencies and interest groups horizontally (e.g., national agencies for agriculture, environmental protection, and industry and trade may disagree), but vertical deviations exist as well (i.e., national, state, and local agencies may disagree).

Although the variation among water allocation strategies is infinite, the history of water sharing agreements in the United States has shown that the number of successful water sharing strategies is limited (McCormick 1994). The specific manner of allocating water can vary according to a variety of influences, but successful strategies for allocating surface water and groundwater can be based on either flows or storage volumes. With respect to sharing underground water, choices are limited to flow allocations based on either restrictions on the rate of extraction or total volume of withdrawal over a specific period of time. Choice of method depends on what the parties want to accomplish and how they want to divide the risk of shortage (McCormick 1994).

Active, comprehensive management is the alternative to strategies that define a specific method of restricting flow or storage allocations. These comprehensive management strategies usually allocate water according to some designated priority of type of use. Such a management style is arguably the most appropriate for the acute water scarcity expected. Whatever the choice, however, the struggle between politics, economic needs and sound water science and engineering will continue.

> *The struggle between politics, economic needs and sound water science and engineering will continue.*

Equally important to the success of the water sharing agreement is the administrative and institutional provisions of the agreement. Without effective administration, implementation of the agreement will falter and enforcement of its provisions will be limited. Without an effective institutional framework, the parties will spend much of their time and resources in dispute resolution rather than effective water management.

The administrative and institutional provisions must address geographical issues that refer to scale of the agreement: river basin drainage area, region, nation subdivisions or global. There is little disagreement among experts that water should be allocated and managed according to watershed and river basin boundaries (Gooch et al. 2002). Unfortunately, political boundaries rarely coincide with river basin boundaries. Economic and environmental issues must merge water quantity and quality issues, as well as related biological and wildlife issues. Functional issues focus on consideration of diverse water use applications, such as urban water supply, wastewater management, navigation, and irrigation, among others (Kliot et al. 1998).

The management institution should be structured to ensure that implementation of the agreement is feasible, efficient, and effective. The agreement should provide the means for resolving intra- and interagency, intra- and interstate conflict, and international conflicts if and as appropriate. At the political level, the agreement must include policy decision-making mechanisms that satisfy, or at least acknowledge, all political viewpoints associated with potential problems. Stakeholder involvement is essential.

A mechanism for resolving conflicting interpretations of the terms of the agreement is a critical component. A law, contract or agreement is only as good as its ongoing oversight and enforcement. The effectiveness of any water sharing agreement or law depends on how effectively it is administered and how rigorously its provisions are enforced.

A review of water sharing agreements in the United States and around the world illustrates several essential features to the administrative provisions (Draper 2006). The management institution should possess adequate legal authority (Eheart 2002). The agreement should be validated by a political consensus among the governmental entities involved as well as, whenever possible, the non-governmental organizations representing the various private stakeholders (Kakebeeke et al. 2000). A financial capability to perform the responsibilities outlined in the agreement must be included (Arcadus Euroconsult 2001; Lintner 1998).

THE COOPERATIVE APPROACH TO EFFECTIVE TRANSBOUNDARY WATER SHARING

Traditionally, the creation and implementation of transboundary water sharing agreements have been carried out by governmental institutions. Typically the issue of sovereign control of water allocation and management is paramount. Recently a number of water policy analysts have concluded that basing water management solely on the notion of sovereignty, and all the encumbrances therefrom, is not effective (Conca 2009; Finger et al. 2009; Warner 2007).

While some agreements developed within the international public institutions have been effective for certain environmental issues such as ozone-depleting chlorofluorocarbons (CFCs), a mixture of public and private concordance provides a better model for transboundary water sharing (Conca 2006). The basic tenant is that cooperative management that engages government, quasi-government and private, non-state actors provides a better path to effective water sharing. Several alternative non-state forms of water sharing governance have been proposed to supplement formal international water sharing agreements: international networking among water experts and professionals, socio-ecological movements, and source water privatization and marketing (Conca 2006).

The role of non-state actors in formulating source water management law and policy has become increasingly relevant. Formal commissions, informal advisory groups and stakeholder forums established by government provide significant contribution to both internal water management and transboundary water sharing. These institutional forms may be directly created and state-sponsored through legislation. For instance, the Georgia Joint Study Committee for Statewide Water Management Planning is composed of both legislators and stakeholders and was formed by the Georgia Legislature to negotiate the text of the statewide water planning law through a consensus process (Georgia Joint Comprehensive Water Plan Study Committee 2002). Alternatively, these institutional forms may be informally constituted by the executive branch as was the Georgia Governor's stakeholder advisory committee for negotiations between Alabama, Florida and Georgia for interstate sharing of the water in the Apalachicola-Chattahoochee-Flint River Basins. A private law firm, rather than the State's Department of Law, reportedly guided the State in negotiations and litigation for Georgia. In both of these cases, non-state actors in the form of stakeholders and lobbyists for interest groups developed a consensus for the text of laws and/or agreements (Georgia Joint Comprehensive Water Plan Study Committee 2002).

Two important "lessons-learned" should be considered with respect to the advantages of these "non-state forms of water governance." First, active participation by the states involved was essential and formal, legal documentation was needed. Second, the most influential "non-state actors" were business, commerce and agricultural interests within Georgia. Since political response is generally much more responsive to business and commercial interests, recommendations from "non-state actors" not associated with internal economic interests (including water policy experts) were accommodated only when no clear conflict with economic interests arose.

A final "lesson-learned" is especially important because of the anticipated increased need for transboundary water sharing agreements. For political entities with little or no historical experience with water sharing, the inherent degree of cooperation between and among the parties is likely to be minimal. Such parties tend to establish relatively inflexible positions without consideration for the needs and objectives of other entities. This inflexibility is extremely damaging to achieving effective use of the shared resource.

Although the two Georgia examples involve water management and water sharing of a sovereign state within a federal system of government, these three "lessons learned" apply to international water sharing as well. In addition, the need for a formal water sharing agreement remains essential despite the heavy involvement of non-state actors.

IMPLICATIONS FOR TRANSBOUNDARY WATER SHARING IN 2050

Water scarcity arguably poses the most important natural resources challenge of the 21st century. Water scarcity exists today and may dramatically increase by 2050.

Water scarcity can inhibit economic growth and undermine quality of life. Conflict between and among users of the shared water often emerges. Since shared surface and underground water comprise a significant part of the world's fresh water, it can be expected that conflict between and among governments and political jurisdictions will intensify.

> *Water scarcity arguably poses the most important natural resources challenge of the 21st century.*

Transboundary water sharing will continue to increase in importance. Likewise, water scarcity challenges will increase in importance due to continued increase in demand for water by a growing population and decrease in water supply exacerbated by climate change. In 2009, the burdens of increasing water scarcity are caused primarily by an increasing demand for reliable and consistent supplies of clean water. By 2050, the challenge will be significantly aggravated, not only because of steadily increasing demand but also because the supply of accessible water will shrink as predicted effects of climate change disrupt the pattern and distribution of water available for use.

Meeting these challenges will be a major task, one that will require states and nations to reorder their thoughts and ideas about sovereignty and individuality. Cooperation will be essential. Only cooperative management that engages government, quasi-government and private, non-state actors can achieve equitable and effective management of water in 2050.

Central to meeting the challenge is the need to create, implement and enforce effective water sharing agreements between and among riparian governments. Certain principles of negotiation are essential to the creation of these agreements and certain sharing strategies have historically demonstrated their effectiveness. These must be integrated into an administrative and institutional framework that assures implementation of the agreement is feasible, efficient, and effective.

REFERENCES

Albert, J. (2000). "Rethinking the management of transboundary freshwater resources: a critical examination of modern international law and practice." *Nat. Resour. Forum,* 24 (1), 21-30.

Arcadis Euroconsult. (2001). *Transboundary water management as an international public good.* Prepared for the Swedish Ministry for Foreign Affairs. Arcadis Euroconsult, Stockholm, Sweden, <http://www.odi.org.uk/resources/download/2972.pdf> (August 2010)

Barnaby, W. (2009). "Do nations go to war?" *Nature,* 458, 282-283.

Caponera, D. A. (1995). "Shared waters and international law." *The peaceful management of transboundary resources,* G. H. Blake, ed., 121-126.

Conca, K. (2006). *Governing water: contentious transnational politics and global institution building.* MIT, Cambridge, MA.

Dellapenna, J. W. (2001). "The customary international law of transboundary fresh waters." *Int. J. Global Environ.,* 1 (3/4), 264-395.

Draper, S. E. (1997). "International duties and obligations for transboundary water sharing." *J. Water Res. Pl.-ASCE,* 123(6), 344-349.

Draper, S. E., ed. (2002). *Model water sharing agreements for the 21st century,* American Society of Civil Engineers.

Draper, S. E., ed. (2006). *Sharing water in times of scarcity,* American Society of Civil Engineers, Environmental and Water Resources Institute, Reston, VA.

Draper, S. E., and Kundell, J. E. (2007). "Impact of climate change on transboundary water sharing." *J. Water Res. Pl.-ASCE.,* 133(5), 405-415.

Eheart, J. W. (2002). *Riparian water regulations: guidelines for withdrawal limitations and permit trading.* American Society of Civil Engineers, Environmental and Water Resources Institute, Reston, VA.

Finger, M., Tamiotti, L., and Allouche, J., eds. (2009). *The multi-governance of water*, State University of New York, Albany, NY.

Georgia Joint Comprehensive Water Plan Study Committee. (2002). *Final report of the Joint Comprehensive Water Plan Study Committee*, Athens, GA, <http://www.cviog.uga.edu/water/finalreport.pdf> (Oct, 2009).

Gleick, P. H. (2006). *Water conflict chronology*. Pacific Institute for Studies in Development, Environment, and Security. <www.worldwater.org/conflictchronology.pdf> (Oct, 2009).

Gooch, G., Höglund, P., Roll, G., Lopman, E., and Aliakseyeva, N. (2002). "Review of existing structures, models and practices for transboundary water management in Europe - the implementation of transboundary water management - identification of present problems and a design for future research." *Proceedings of the international, conference on sustainable management of transboundary waters in Europe*, F. Bernardini, M. Landsberg-Uczciwek, S. Haunia, M. Adriaanse, and R. Enderlein, eds., UN ECE, Geneva, Switzerland, 285 - 293.

Hey, E. (1995). "Sustainable use of shared water resources: the need for a paradigmatic shift in international watercourses law." *The peaceful management of transboundary resources,* G. H. Blake, ed., 121-126.

Intergovernmental Panel on Climate Change (IPCC). (2001). *Climate change 2001: the scientific basis. Contribution of Working Group I to the third assessment report of the Intergovernmental Panel on Climate Change* (J. T. Houghton, Y. Ding, D. J. Griggs, M. Noguer, P. J. van der Linden, X. Dai, K. Maskell, and C. A. Johnson, eds.), Cambridge University Press, Cambridge, UK, <http://www.grida.no/publications/other/ipcc_tar/> (Oct, 2009).

Intergovernmental Panel on Climate Change (IPCC). (2007). "IPCC-Intergovernmental Panel on Climate Change." <www.ipcc.ch> (Oct, 2009).

Kakebeeke, W., Wouters, P., and Bouman, N. (2000). *Water management: guidance on public participation and compliance with agreements*, ECE/UNEP Network of Expert on Public Participation and Compliance, Geneva, Switzerland.

Karl, T. R., Melillo, J. M., and Peterson, T. C., eds. (2009). *Global climate change impacts in the United States*, Cambridge University Press.

Kliot, N., Shmueli, D., and Shamir, U. (1998). *Institutional frameworks for the management of transboundary water resources.* Water Research Institute, Technion University, Haifa, Israel.

Lintner, S. F. (1998). *International round table : transboundary water management : experiences of international river and lake commissions*, German Foundation for International Development (DSE), Berlin, Germany. <http://www.umweltdaten.de/wasser-e/twmb98.pdf> (May, 2010).

McCormick, Z. L. (1994). "The use of interstate compacts to resolve transboundary allocation issues." Ph.D. dissertation, Oklahoma State University, Stillwater, OK.

Monaghan, A. J., and Bromwich, D. H. (2008). "Advances in describing recent Antarctic climate variability." *B. Am. Meteorol. Soc.*, 89, 1295-1306.

Oregon State University. (2005). "The transboundary freshwater dispute database." *Oregon State University*, <www.transboundarywaters.orst.edu> (Feb, 2010).

National Science and Technology Council. (2008). *Scientific assessment of the effects of global change on the United States*, Report of Committee on Environment and Natural Resources, National Science and Technology Council, · <www.climatescience.gov/Library/scientific-assessment/Scientific-AssessmentFINAL.pdf > (Oct, 2009).

Warner, J. (2007). *Multi-stakeholder platforms for integrated water management*, Ashgate Publishing, Limited, Hampshire, UK.

AUTHOR INFORMATION

Stephen E. Draper, PhD, PE, JD is a graduate of the US Military Academy, Georgia Tech, Long Island University, and the Georgia State University School of Law. His professional qualifications include awards of four post-graduate degrees and registration as a PE in Georgia and Florida. His forty-year career in water science, engineering, law and policy includes service in the public and private sectors within the United States and overseas. Draper currently serves as the Chair of the ASCE Task Committee developing the ASCE National Standard for Transboundary Water Sharing Agreements. He is the editor and principal author of *Model water sharing agreements for the twenty-first century* published by ASCE in 2002 and *Sharing water in times of scarcity* published by ASCE in 2006. Email: sedrap@aol.com

Chapter 6

Sanitation and Hygiene for All by 2050

Roberto Lenton and Jon Lane

ABSTRACT

This article outlines a vision of what the state of access to sanitation and hygiene worldwide, and particularly in the poorest countries, could and should look like in 2050, and identifies the actions needed now and into the future to make that state a reality. Achieving a vision of sanitation and hygiene for all by 2050 is well within our reach, but it will not be achieved without significant effort. Realizing this vision will require both a substantial ratcheting up of political commitment and an unleashing of energy and innovation – institutional, financial and technical – at all levels. We must dovetail our vision of sanitation access for all with the larger societal concerns for environmental sustainability. Our vision for 2050 must be one of sustainable sanitation, and involve not only access to basic sanitation and hygiene but also the safe disposal of human waste, proper attention to pollution and environmental degradation, and a commitment to sustainability more generally.

"It's not fair that I have to share a bathroom with my sister!"

"It's so wonderful that our village now has a clean sanitation facility."

THE CURRENT SITUATION

Sanitation was chosen by readers of the British Medical Journal as "the most important medical advance since 1840," beating out the development of antibiotics, anesthesia and vaccines as well as the discovery of the structure of DNA (Ferriman 2007). Indeed, in industrialized countries virtually everybody has access to good sanitation and personal hygiene facilities. As a result, in the industrialized world sanitation access is taken for granted, and much more attention and investment quite properly goes into the "second generation" challenges of waste disposal and pollution control.

However, the situation in much of the developing world is vastly different. Here, the magnitude of the sanitation and hygiene challenge defies belief. According to the most recent report of the Joint Monitoring Programme of the WHO and UNICEF (WHO/UNICEF 2008), at present some 2.5 billion people do not have access to a private sanitation facility that meets basic hygienic standards – i.e., that ensures the hygienic separation of human excreta from human contact. These 2.5 billion people are instead forced to share a facility that meets these standards with one or more households, use a sanitation facility that does not ensure hygienic separation of excreta from human contact, or practice indiscriminate or "open" defecation. If collected, the quantity of openly defecated excreta produced by the 1.2 billion people forced to do so would fill an 80,000 seat stadium *every day*.

The health consequences of this state of affairs are severe. More than two million children die each year from sanitation-related diseases. Diseases associated with poor sanitation are particularly correlated with poverty and infancy – they account for about 10% of the global burden of disease, most of which is diarrheal disease in children under 5 years of age. But it is not only the health of children and their parents that are at stake here. Lack of ready access to sanitation is a daily affront to the human dignity of billions of people around the world. Women are especially vulnerable to the dangers that come with defecating in the open: sexual harassment and rape occur in rural areas where women often seek privacy to defecate only at night, and in refugee camps which usually fail to provide safely located, women-only toilets. The lack of adequate sanitation facilities in schools prevents girls from attending school, especially when they are menstruating.

And poor sanitation constitutes a severe hindrance to the economic development of the poorest countries. Studies show that the broad benefits associated with averting mortality and morbidity from poor sanitation far outweigh the costs of implementing and maintaining low cost sanitation systems (Hutton et al. 2006). Research related to Sub-Saharan Africa and Asia (home to nearly 2.35 billion of the 2.5 billion lacking access) suggests that one dollar invested in sanitation generates nine dollars in economic benefit; healthy people are more productive than sick ones.

Despite the gravity of the situation, the sanitation crisis in the world's poorest countries remains largely a forgotten subject, in part because of the strong social taboos associated with human waste. Few political leaders are keen to make sanitation access a major part of their political platform. The international media and many celebrities, while increasing attention to drinking water issues, seem reluctant to focus on the far more widespread, but less attractive subject of sanitation. This has, nonetheless, helped sustain progress on access to safe drinking water. Absolute numbers of people without access to safe drinking water shrank from 1.2 billion in 2000 to 894 million in 2006. In many countries, open discussions of sanitation and hygiene practices at all levels remain rare. Often ignored is that "water-related diseases" such as diarrhea are, in fact, sanitation-related diseases. Similarly, it is not well known that hygiene promotion to prevent diarrhea is the most cost-effective health intervention in the world (Jamison et al. 2006).

> *One dollar invested in sanitation generates nine dollars in economic benefit; healthy people are more productive than sick ones.*

VISION FOR 2050

The current state of sanitation and hygiene in the developing world need not continue this way. Partners in the Water Supply and Sanitation Collaborative Council (WSSCC) described a vastly different future scenario in a visioning exercise at the turn of the new Millennium (WSSCC 2001):

> *"Virtually every man, woman and child on the planet knows the importance of hygiene and enjoys safe and adequate water and sanitation. People work closely with local governments and non-governmental organizations to manage water and sanitation systems so as to meet basic needs while protecting the environment. People contribute to these services according to the level of service they want and are willing to pay for. Everywhere in the world, people live in clean and healthy environments. Communities and governments benefit from the resulting improved health and the related economic development."*

Simply put, this vision of the future entails ensuring sanitation and hygiene for all by 2050. It contrasts sharply with the current situation. The change is not simply one of increased access to sanitation facilities. It also means a change in mindsets and attitudes – the transformation of sanitation and hygiene in the developing world from a taboo subject and minor sub-sector of international development into something that is taken for granted as a necessary but uncomplicated, safe and natural part of everyday life. "Sanitation and hygiene for all by 2050" should be considered as relevant a part of a future scenario as "a cell phone for all by 2050." To wit, half the global population was without a cell phone in 2007, but by 2009 this figure shrank to around 34%, or about 2.3 billion people out of a total global population of 6.7 billion.

Achieving this vision of sanitation and hygiene for all is not a pipe dream, but a goal that is well within the realm of possibility. It does not require rocket science, but rather dedication and commitment manifested through hard work, plain talk, political will and creation of demand for improved sanitation. As highlighted in WSSCC (2001), achieving sanitation and hygiene for all requires collaborative action by empowered people in households, communities and authorities. It demands fresh attitudes and commitment and new sanitation policies and activities where they do not exist at every level of society and governance. And while resources are important, the amount required – an estimated $10 billion each year for both basic sanitation and drinking water (UNDP 2006) — is affordable, available and more often than not, financed by poor people themselves. Whoever pays, the figure is less than one percent of world military spending in 2006 (SIPRI 2007).

PROGRESS IN THE LAST FORTY YEARS

By 1970 we had placed a man on the moon, but large parts of the developing world were locked in poverty. Despite the huge technological revolution since then, much of the world is still living in poverty. Technological progress has failed to make much difference in eradicating poverty in all its manifold dimensions in the world's poorest countries.

On the sanitation front, progress has been uneven at best. Some countries, such as Singapore, South Africa and South Korea – extremely poor places until the 1960s – have made truly impressive gains in access to sanitation and hygiene. National and individual economic well-being and quality of life there took quantum leaps. However, global data on access to basic sanitation suggest that the proportion of both rural and urban populations with access to an improved sanitation facility has increased only marginally in the last two decades in virtually all the developing regions of the world (WWAP 2009).

Indeed, progress has been much less than is needed to make a real difference on the levels of sanitation and hygiene access. At current rates of progress, simply achieving the Millennium Development Goal target of halving the proportion of people without sustainable access to basic sanitation would not be achieved until well into the second half of the this century – 2077, to be exact – a far cry from our 2050 vision.

Nevertheless, while the improvement in access levels has been extremely disappointing, there has been important progress over the last forty years. First, while sanitation remains a taboo subject in many countries and is still largely regarded as a less significant element of the "water and sanitation" duo, the pace of specific attention to sanitation and hygiene issues, as distinct from drinking water issues more generally, has picked up in recent years. The declaration by the United Nations (UN) General Assembly that 2008 was to be the International Year of Sanitation helped mobilize governments and other stakeholders to move sanitation to the top of the development agenda, and helped induce other development partners such as the Bill and Melinda Gates Foundation to accord priority to sanitation and hygiene issues. The recent establishment of the Global Framework for Action, an international partnership of national governments and a range of development partners, is helping to galvanize political commitment to increase global access to sanitation and water and serve as a platform to put sanitation on the global agenda, improve targeting and effectiveness of overseas development assistance and advocate for increased budgets. Media also seem to understand the importance of the issue. From the biggest global mass broadcasters to the tiniest local newspapers, reporting on sanitation improved beginning in 2008; sanitation-related specials and opinion-editorial articles appeared in general publications such as the *New York Times* (Friedman 2009) and more specialised ones like the respected medical journal *The Lancet* (The Lancet 2008). Best-selling sanitation-related books were even reviewed by *The Economist*.

Second, there is much greater international consensus on the importance of sanitation and the critical need for action to improve access to basic sanitation than there was 40 years ago. Several international conferences in the last 40 years have helped place water and sanitation on the international agenda, beginning with the UN Water Conference at Mar del Plata in 1977, followed by the UN Conference on Environment and Development (also known as the Earth Summit in Rio de Janeiro) in 1992, and perhaps most importantly, the World Summit for Sustainable Development in Johannesburg in 2002. This Summit agreed to amend the "Millennium Development Goals" endorsed by the world's governments in 2000 by adding the conspicuously missing target to halve, by 2015 the proportion of people without sustainable access to basic sanitation, which really helped increase recognition of sanitation as an issue of fundamental development significance.

Third, while much remains to be done, there is now a better institutional architecture for progress on sanitation than there was 40 years ago. The International Drinking Water Supply and Sanitation Decade from 1981 to 1990 led to some important institutional innovations, including in particular the creation of the Water Supply and Sanitation Collaborative Council, the establishment of the Joint Monitoring Programme (JMP) by the World Health Organization (WHO) and UNICEF and the formation of the World Bank/UN Development Programme Water and Sanitation Program (WSP). Forty years ago, the international community had no mechanisms to monitor progress in access to sanitation or to conduct research and development on sanitation issues in the poorest countries, but now such monitoring is possible through these organizations. More and more, governments in developing countries are realizing the importance of having a separate budget line for sanitation work as well as distinct institutional ownership and policies for sanitation in the country.

Fourth and perhaps most importantly, there is now a much better understanding of what it would really take to achieve a world with sanitation and hygiene for all. Experience over the last 40 years, including that of the Water Supply and Sanitation Decade, together with extensive research by such organizations as WSP and the International Reference Center for Water and Sanitation, has provided real evidence of what works and what does not in efforts to advance sanitation and hygiene in the developing world. For example, while 40 years ago it was thought that technological innovation would be the key to progress, it is now recognized that technology, while important, is not the only answer and that institutional as well as technical innovation are required. It is also now recognized that as much or more effort is needed on the demand side as on the supply side -- to unlock latent demand for sanitation by households and communities in the poorest countries, and to understand the cultural and social dimensions of sanitation. Top-down, supply-side, government-led construction programs have proven ineffective on their own (WSSCC 2009).

> *There is now a much better understanding of what it would really take to achieve a world with sanitation and hygiene for all.*

Further, the importance of political will and leadership, often overlooked in the past, is now increasingly viewed as critical – especially for political leadership that really understands economic benefits and internalizes them, and of a professional sector that recognizes the importance of making the argument for sanitation in economic terms and not only in terms of health and human rights. Several landmark reports such as those from the UN Millennium Project (Lenton et al. 2005) and the UNDP (UNDP 2006) have laid out what needs to be done to achieve a world of sanitation and hygiene for all (see Box 1).

With these basic building blocks in place, progress over the next 40 years could potentially be much more rapid than in the last 40 years, as long as proper and concerted action – guided by the results of experience and research -- is taken.

ACTIONS NEEDED NOW AND INTO THE FUTURE

While achieving the vision of sanitation and hygiene for all by 2050 is well within our reach, this vision will not be achieved without a significant effort. Realizing this vision will require both a significant ratcheting up of political commitment and an unleashing of energy and innovation – institutional, financial and technical – at all levels. Some of the actions needed, adapted from Lenton et al. (2005), are summarized in Box 1. For each of these actions there are numerous examples of initiatives currently underway that provide a model for the future.

Action 8, for example, calls for institutional, financial and technological innovation to be promoted in strategic areas. Some recent examples of innovative efforts illustrate what can be done on this front:

- The Community Led Total Sanitation (CLTS) approach, pioneered by Kamal Kar of India together with the Village Education Resource Centre, a partner of WaterAid, in Bangladesh (Kar and Bongartz 2006; Kar and Chambers 2008), has attracted significant attention in recent years as an innovative methodology for mobilizing communities to completely eliminate open defecation. Under the CLTS approach, communities are helped to conduct their own appraisal and analysis of open defecation and take action to become free of such defecation practices. CLTS focuses on behavioral change, investing in community mobilization instead of hardware and shifting the focus from toilet construction towards triggering a community's desire for change. CLTS has spread fast in Bangladesh and elsewhere and is now practiced in more than 20 countries in Asia, Africa, Latin America and the Middle East. (http://www.communityledtotalsanitation.org/)

- The need for innovative funding approaches is exemplified by the work of the Global Sanitation Fund, an important initiative established by the WSSCC in 2008 to help large numbers of poor people attain safe and sustainable sanitation services and adopt good hygiene practices through a single pooled fund open to contribution from any source including governments, foundations, private sector and individuals, and which focuses on demand- and sanitation-market creation.

- Combining institutional and technological innovation is well exemplified by the work of Sulabh International, a pioneering non-governmental organization in India headed by Dr. B. Pathak, who received the Stockholm Water Prize in 2009. Sulabh's approach involves innovative modifications of the pour flush system – an existing low cost technology – and equally innovative institutional and social programs. Sulabh popularised the use of the pour flush system in India as a domestic latrine, with some 1 million household units already in place. Sulabh has also developed over 5,000 public "pay-for-use" facilities, which now serve over 10 million people a day. Sulabh's approach also liberated approximately 270,000 women from the demeaning and undignified profession of "manual scavenging."

However, achieving the vision of sanitation and hygiene for all by 2050 cannot be conceived of in isolation of other global challenges. As a recent column by Friedman (2009) noted, the world is facing a whole array of integrated problems such as climate change and poverty alleviation. We must stop thinking about these issues in isolation and deal with them in an integrated way. This means we must dovetail our vision of sanitation access for all with the larger societal concerns for environmental sustainability. This will in turn require aligning sanitation efforts with current efforts to mitigate and adapt to climate change and ensure sustainability more generally -- ensuring that sanitation systems, processes and facilities can themselves be sustained on a long-term basis and that they do not pollute the local living environment and/or downstream water resources, or lead to other environmental damages. All this suggests the need for our vision for 2050 to be one of sustainable sanitation, as articulated by the Sustainable Sanitation Alliance (www.susana.org), and involve not only access to basic sanitation and hygiene, but also the safe disposal of human waste, proper attention to pollution and environmental degradation, and a commitment to sustainability more generally.

Box 1: Nine critical actions for achieving sanitation (adapted from Lenton et al. 2005)

1. Governments and other stakeholders must move the sanitation crisis to the top of the agenda. In February 2008 some thirty-two African ministers showed such initiative by signing the eThekwini Declaration, which recognised the importance of spending at least 0.5% of GDP on sanitation and hygiene in order to avoid the 2.0% of GDP lost annually through poor sanitation.

2. Countries must ensure that policies and institutions for sanitation service delivery respond equally to the different roles, needs, and priorities of women and men.

3. Governments and donor agencies must simultaneously pursue investment and reforms for improved sanitation. A good start is the Global Annual Assessment of Sanitation and Drinking-Water (GLAAS), a UN-Water pilot initiative led by the World Health Organization (WHO) which will disaggregate water supply and sanitation investments by governments so as to make them more effective.

4. Efforts to expand sanitation access must focus on sustainable service delivery, rather than construction of facilities alone. Privacy, dignity, convenience and safety are motivating factors which get people to change their behaviors, i.e. to build, use and maintain toilets, to wash their hands after using the toilet, and so on. But when the latrine pit is full, it needs to be emptied.

5. Governments and donor agencies must empower local authorities and communities with the authority, resources, and professional capacity required to manage sanitation service delivery. Sanitation coverage is typically increased through a combination of community-based promotion and enforcement of national or local legislation that every house must have a toilet.

6. Governments and utilities must ensure that users who can pay do pay in order to fund the operation, maintenance, and expansion of services – but they must also ensure that the needs of poor households are met.

7. Governments and their civil society and private sector partners must support a wide range of sanitation technologies and service levels that are technically, socially, environmentally, and financially appropriate. Examples of these are readily available in the Compendium of Sanitation Systems and Technologies produced by WSSCC and the Swiss agency EAWAG/SANDEC in 2008.

8. Institutional, financial and technological innovation must be promoted in strategic areas. The raising of awareness about sanitation must also be about the raising of new resources -- people, ideas and money -- for the subject.

9. The United Nations system organizations and their Member States must ensure that the UN system and its international partners provide strong and effective support for the achievement of the sanitation target.

ACKNOWLEDGEMENTS

The authors would like to acknowledge, with thanks, the very helpful assistance received from David Trouba in the preparation of this paper.

REFERENCES

Ferriman, A. (2007). "BMJ readers choose the 'sanitary revolution' as greatest medical advance since 1840." *Brit. Med. J.*, 334, 111.

Friedman, T. L. (2009). "Connecting nature's dots." *New York Times*, Aug 22, 2009.

Hutton, G., Haller L., and Bartram, J. (2006). *Economic and health effects of increasing coverage of low cost water and sanitation interventions to countries off-track to meet MDG target 10.* Report prepared for the United Nations Development Programme, World Health Organization, Geneva, Switzerland, <http://www.who.int/water_sanitation_health/economic/mdg10_offtrack.pdf> (Aug, 2010)

Jamison, D. T., Breman, J. G., Measham, A. R., Alleyne, G., Claeson, M., Evans, D., Jha, P., Mills, A. and Musgrove, P., eds. (2006). *Disease control priorities in developing countries*, The World Bank and Oxford University Press, New York, NY.

Kar, K., and Bongartz, P. (2006). *Update of some recent developments in community-led total sanitation.* Update to IDS Working Paper 257, Institute of Development Studies, Brighton, UK, <http://www.communityledtotalsanitation.org/resource/latest-update-subsidy-or-self-respect-update-ids-working-paper-257> (Aug, 2010).

Kar, K., and Chambers, R. (2008). *Handbook on community-led total sanitation*, Institute of Development Studies and Plan International, Brighton, UK, <http://www.communityledtotalsanitation.org/resource/handbook-community-led-total-sanitation> (Aug, 2010).

Lenton, R., Wright, A. M., and Lewis, K. (2005). *Health, dignity and development: what will it take?*, UN Millennium Project, Task Force on Water and Sanitation, Earthscan, London, UK, <http://www.unmillenniumproject.org/reports/tf_watersanitation.htm> (Aug, 2010).

Stockholm International Peace Research Institute (SIPRI). (2007). *Armaments, disarmament and international security,* SIPRI, Stockholm, Sweden.

The Lancet. (2008). "Keeping sanitation in the international spotlight (editorial)." *The Lancet,* 371(9618), 1045.

United Nations Development Programme (UNDP). (2006). *Human development report 2006. Beyond scarcity: power, poverty and the global water crisis*, United Nations Development Programme, New York, NY, <http://hdr.undp.org/en/reports/global/hdr2006/> (Aug, 2010).

Water Supply and Sanitation Collaborative Council (WSSCC). (2001). *Vision 21: a shared vision for hygiene, sanitation and water supply, and a framework for action*, Geneva, Switzerland.

Water Supply and Sanitation Collaborative Council (WSSCC). (2009). *Public funding for sanitation: the many faces of sanitation subsidies*, Geneva, Switzerland, <http://www.wsscc.org/fileadmin/files/pdf/publication/Public_Funding_for_S anitation_the_many_faces_of_sanitation_subsidies.pdf> (Oct, 2009).

World Health Organization (WHO)/ United Nations International Children's Emergency Fund (UNICEF). (2008). *Progress on drinking water and sanitation - special focus on sanitation*, Joint Monitoring Programme for Water Supply and Sanitation, UNICEF, New York, NY, <http://www.who.int/water_sanitation_health/monitoring/jmp2008/en/index.h tml> (Aug, 2010).

World Water Assessment Programme (WWAP). 2009. *The United Nations world water development report 3: water in a changing world*, United Nations Educational, Scientific, and Cultural Organization, Paris, France, <http://www.unesco.org/water/wwap/wwdr/wwdr3/> (Aug, 2010).

AUTHOR INFORMATION

Roberto Lenton is Chairman of the Inspection Panel of the World Bank. A specialist in water resources and sustainable development with over 30 years of international experience in the field, he currently serves as Chair of the Water Supply and Sanitation Collaborative Council. He holds a PhD from the Massachusetts Institute of Technology. Email: rlenton@worldbank.org

Jon Lane is Executive Director of the Water Supply and Sanitation Collaborative Council. Previously he served as a consultant in water and sanitation for developing countries, concerned mainly with global and regional policy and strategy issues. He is a former Director of WaterAid for which he was awarded the OBE. By training he is a civil engineer. Email: Jon.Lane@wsscc.org

Chapter 7

Integrated Water Management in 2050: Institutional and Governance Challenges

Neil S. Grigg

ABSTRACT

The tools of integrated water management include multi-objective analyses, involvement of stakeholders, and a search for balanced solutions. These were used in their early versions forty years ago, but the high level of conflict in water management has blocked the implementation of balanced solutions through planning and cooperation and has pushed many decision processes into the legal and political camps. Examination of the historical record and some case studies show that, while the concepts of integration are visionary and desirable, new approaches are needed to use them more effectively. Foremost among these are use of incentives, accountability, and transparency. Integrated water management is a core practice needed in today's complex world, and water managers, engineers, and scientists have a lead role in promoting it.

"Integrated Water Resources Management"

WHY INTEGRATED WATER MANAGEMENT IS NEEDED

Society's total dependence on water to sustain economic, social, and environmental, systems is unquestioned, and this dependence explains the popularity of "triple bottom line" accounting, which tracks the positive and negative impacts of water actions on the three systems. In addition to the economic, social, and environmental accounts, water managers must address the competing goals of stakeholders and whether they are driven by beliefs and value systems, goals for regional development, or simply different ways to use water. As a result of these complexities, the water management community has learned that single-purpose approaches to managing water do not work and that multi-purpose and integrated approaches are required.

As a result of these lessons, water managers have learned to balance aspects of water management such as its purposes and stakeholder views when making decisions and taking management actions. The paradigms and approaches they use are lumped in this chapter under the term "integrated water management," but this lumping recognizes that there are many opinions about what it means and what it includes.

The questions addressed in this chapter are: 1) what is meant by integrated water management; 2) how well are we using it to manage water resources; 3) how successful will we be in 2050 given current trajectories; and 4) what should we do to improve the prospects of integration?

WHAT IS MEANT BY "INTEGRATED WATER MANAGEMENT?"

Given the many opinions about integrated water management, it would be naïve to think that broad-based agreement can be reached on its definition. The words "integrated" and "management" are too abstract, so when you combine them the resulting phrase can take on even more meanings. When applied to water, the phrase addresses how decisions are made in the complex arena of water management where many diverse stakeholders are involved in the arena, and where their interests converge and decisions are made. Therefore, the integration concept has been developed to provide a framework to balance conflicting views about how to manage water in complex situations. There is no "right answer" as to what integrated water management is; to some it is a clear concept, but to others it amounts to a mixed bag of best practices, such as data collection and use of conservation.

> *Integrated water resources management is a framework for planning, organizing and operating water systems to unify and balance the relevant views and goals of stakeholders.*

My recommendation for a definition is (Grigg 2008a): "Integrated water resources management is a framework for planning, organizing and operating water systems to unify and balance the relevant views and goals of stakeholders." Put into practice, this framework provides a way to achieve a balance among the demands for drinking water, for controlling wastewater, stormwater and floods, and for all other uses of water including for environmental and instream purposes. It provides a focus on what integration adds to the water management mix.

This is, of course, a simple definition. More complex ones incorporate many attributes of systems analysis and systems thinking. For example, integrated water management links closely to systems thinking, which is a framework to view problems holistically and deal with complexity. It has been promoted by Senge (1990) with a focus on systems thinking, models, shared values, and team learning, which are attributes of the integrated approach.

Unless a discussion of integrated water management is illustrated with examples, it will be too abstract and easily misunderstood. Therefore, I offer four examples of different water decision processes, places, and issues. The examples illustrate that the higher you go toward policy and the more complex the issues, the more you need integrated water management. Operational decisions involving only one or a few players need less integration. This phenomenon is illustrated in Figure 7-1, which shows two variables. On the vertical axis is the variable of problem scale, as measured by the political and geographic scopes of the problem space. At the top, a scale level of national politics and broad playing field size is shown, and at the bottom, a scale of local politics and small playing field size is represented.

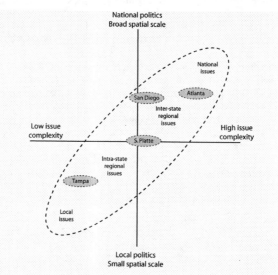

Figure 7-1. Integration as a function of scale and complexity

The horizontal axis represents issue complexity, which is a function of the number of water management purposes, diversity of stakeholders, inter-sectoral impacts of water decisions, and other factors that make decisions more complex. The two variables—

problem scale and issue complexity—are not independent of each other, so the range of problems is shown by a problem space in a 45-degree ellipse. The four case examples, to be explained next, are shown on the diagram. Their positions on the map can be debated, of course.

Regional Examples

The four regional case examples illustrate water supplies for two large and growing cities on opposite sides of the country (Atlanta and San Diego), a conjunctive use problem in Colorado involving cities and agriculture, and an integrated operations plan for Tampa Bay Water (Florida), which manages ground and surface supplies jointly and subject to unique environmental constraints. The cases are summarized very briefly with only enough detail to identify the nature of integration in the solutions.

- *Atlanta water supply*: The key feature of this case is the need for additional water for Atlanta, a rapidly-growing metropolitan area with a population of over five million. The case involves operation of a federal reservoir, court cases over interbasin transfers, upstream-downstream conflicts, and environmental conflicts with Florida, among other issues. The decision is at the interstate and regional level and involves numerous issues and stakeholders. This case illustrates the need to involve stakeholders in multiple states and regions within Georgia. It pits water supply, energy, and environmental water purposes against each other.

- *San Diego water supply*: The focus of this case is a decision to transfer water from the Imperial Valley by lining a large canal of the Imperial Irrigation District to salvage water for transfer. The raw water authority is the San Diego County Water Authority, which is a member of the larger Metropolitan Water District of Southern California. Groundwater seepage that is changed may affect the Salton Sea and agricultural zones in Mexico. The decision involves the United States Bureau of Reclamation, which operates Colorado River facilities, and a number of management entities in Southern California. The integration needed is among cities and farms, ground and surface water, two nations, and local, state, and federal water interests.

- *South Platte conjunctive use*: The case is focused on the need to improve use of a large regional aquifer with some 1.23×10^{10} m^3 (10 million acre-feet) of storage space. Colorado's water law, based on a strict version of the appropriation doctrine, has been interpreted through recent state court decisions to prohibit aquifer pumping for water users who lack appropriate surface water augmentation rights. Opposition to relaxation of strict augmentation requirements resulted in the cutoff of well supplies to many farmers who are in economic distress. The situation was exacerbated by a severe drought in 2002. The decision is at the intra-state and regional level and integration should be among regional surface water right owners, well-pumpers, state water courts, and legislators.

- *Tampa Bay operational plan*: Tampa Bay Water operates a series of wells and some surface supplies, including a new desalting plant. The water is provided to local water supply agencies, who distribute it to their customers in the region. Groundwater pumping has environmental effects that include lowered water tables that deprive trees and other plants of vital water supplies, as well as land subsidence. Therefore, it is important that a mixture of water sources be used to optimize both economic costs and environmental sustainability. The decision is at the local level, but is a regional issue that extends throughout the Tampa Bay area. Integration is required among regional agencies, a state regulatory agency, ground and surface water, and urban versus environmental interests.

If we turn first to the cases in Atlanta, San Diego, and the South Platte Basin, the attributes of integration were not applied successfully. In all three cases, decisions were or are being made through court processes or forced negotiations. The legal and political cards have trumped the technical and management cards. In the case of Tampa, the collaborative management approach has been more successful, but it deals with a more controlled situation.

National Issues
If we view the status of water systems, we would not be encouraged by the American Society of Civil Engineers (ASCE) Infrastructure Report Card, which most recently rated drinking water, wastewater, levees, and inland waterways at D⁻ (ASCE 2009). The only water-related score that was higher was dams, rated as D. We might also turn to United States Environmental Protection Agency (USEPA) reports on the status of clean streams and drinking water for further information, but we might be confused by the detail and lack of conclusions in them. For example, USEPA's (2008) Report on the Environment contains many indicators, but it does not provide yes or no answers as to whether things are improving or not. These statistics are difficult to interpret, both because of data quality and because of annual fluctuations and the difficulty in identifying trends. In fact, assessment programs such as the Water Resource Council's National Water Assessment and US Geological Survey's National Water Summary have been shelved. We simply lack any kind of national water assessment program that reaches integrated conclusions.

Discussion
Given the difficulty in reaching conclusions supported by rigorous analysis, we might conclude some general statements, such as that streams are much cleaner than in 1970, drinking water quality is, on the whole, better, flood damages are lower (with the exception of Katrina damages), and some environmental concerns, such as the need for instream flows, are being addressed better now than in 1970.

While we cannot really assess outcomes of integrated water management, we can look at how its three parts (recognition of the multi-objective nature of water, involvement of stakeholders, and reaching decisions that balance the views) have been implemented. Clearly, the multi-objective nature of water is widely-recognized. Prior to the Flood Control Act of 1917, there was little recognition of multi-objective approaches, and the concepts are now widely-embraced, not only in the water sector but in other public sectors, especially the closely-related field of land use planning. The involvement of stakeholders is also much better now than in 1970, but this development has also occurred across-the-board in public sector planning. Stakeholders are involved in any public sector decision that affects varied interest groups, such as, for example, capital budgeting for community investments such as libraries, arts centers, and other shared facilities. Reaching decisions that balance the views has been the hard part of integrated water management, but again it seems that society has become more contentious and it is difficult to reach decisions on many fronts.

In summary, big advances have occurred in the multi-objective purpose approach involving stakeholders. These were not so much the results of integrated water management as they were drivers of it. The difficult goal of integration—reaching balanced decisions—is hard to measure but it seems that conflict and the cost of planning have increased. Perhaps the best indicator of whether greater equity has been achieved would be some sort of political variable of public satisfaction with water management. This indicator would be difficult to develop and to measure.

> *The difficult goal of integration—reaching balanced decisions—is hard to measure but it seems that conflict and the cost of planning have increased.*

The indicator is not only difficult in a scientific way, but it is also difficult to develop for levels of water management scenarios. Should we try to assess the aggregated national status, regional issues, or local projects, for example? Intra-state regional issues lend themselves to this kind of analysis because one is at least within one state-level political unit. Once two or more states are involved, the basis for interstate conflicts exists. Local projects are easier to describe and analyze because the numbers of issues and stakeholders are smaller.

PROSPECTS FOR 2050—WHAT THE CASES SHOW US

The premises and conclusions so far are these: 1) the main features of integrated water management are recognizing the multiple objectives of water, involving stakeholders, and balancing the solutions, and 2) the multiple purpose approach and involvement of stakeholders have improved, but finding balanced solutions involves much more conflict than in the past.

In my view, the cases bolster the conclusions. In the Atlanta case, what began in the 1990s as a limited dispute over the rights of Atlanta to take additional supplies from the Chattahoochee River and some interbasin transfers has mushroomed into a two-decade long case involving Congress, District Courts, gubernatorial negotiations, and costs involving hundreds of engineers, lawyers, and public officials. No one has counted the mounting costs, but legal and other fees and costs seem sure to have exceeded the level of $1 billion and may be much, much higher. While the tools of water management—models, expert opinion, and planning councils—have been applied extensively, they have not brought the parties to a balanced solution.

> *While the tools of water management—models, expert opinion, and planning councils—have been applied extensively, they have not brought the parties to a balanced solution.*

The San Diego water transfer project that focused on the All-American Canal Lining Project seems to offer more hope, as it did involve a negotiated multi-stakeholder approach to problem-solving. However, the extent to which some stakeholders—particularly those relying on past groundwater seepage—participated in the negotiations is not as clear. By restricting the scope of the negotiations to the stakeholders that were directly concerned and affected, the project was allowed to proceed. Time will tell us more about the success of the integrated approach on this project.

The South Platte conjunctive use program is in gridlock. Given the high-level of conflict that inhibits flexible and shared approaches to water management in a system, balanced solutions through negotiation appear unrealistic. Consequently, use of integrated water management in this venue appears much more difficult than in venues with more built-in flexibility.

The Tampa Bay program involving development of an integrated operations plan appears to be successful, due to development of a technically-sound management tool, involvement of stakeholders, and a decision that is within the control of a single management agency. Success is based on finding scenarios that will meet regional demands at minimum economic and environmental cost.

Now, to the question, "what will be the score of using integrated water management in 2050 given current trajectories?" To answer the question, we focus on the arena of conflict where balance is to be achieved. Four general solution methods are used, representing escalating levels of conflict: voluntary cooperation, facilitated or negotiated consensus-building, legislative mandates, and court decisions. Executive decision-making is not included because most problems lie outside the authority of single agencies.

Of the four regional cases, Tampa and San Diego have proceeded based on facilitated or negotiated consensus-building. In the case of San Diego, the powers of executive agencies at all three levels of government were used to seal agreements. In the South Platte case, the gridlock has already been addressed by court decisions, but the court cases were not comprehensive enough to solve the integrated problem. Consequently, this issue remains unresolved. In the case of Atlanta, we have nearly two decades of conflict, in spite of studies and environmental assessment processes costing millions of dollars, and it seems certain to continue toward some form of a legal settlement within, say, five years. The most likely form of the solution seems to be a comprehensive court decree, which may be administered in the future like an interstate compact.

So, the answer to the question seems to point toward more of the same. The institutions involved—water agencies at three levels of government and the court systems—will continue to act according to their legal mandates and powers. The drivers of the system continue to be politicians, lawyers, engineers, and others acting according to their perceptions of the public interest and in their own interests. It appears that the defining statement might be a quote that is ascribed to Winston Churchill, "It has been said that democracy is the worst form of government except all the others that have been tried."

HOW TO IMPROVE THE PROSPECTS FOR INTEGRATION

For someone in my age category, the year 2050 seems just down the road. Will the next 40 years make much difference? What big drivers will change things? Comparing 2010 to 1970, many things do not seem much different, but others do, such as technologies, the legal environment, and globalization. It seems certain that new technologies will create wonderful possibilities to improve life, but the biggest difficulties will continue to be in the political, legal, and financial arenas, where the fruits of integrated water management have mostly eluded us.

> *The biggest difficulties in water resources management will continue to be in the political, legal, and financial arenas.*

So we see that integrated water management as a framework to balance the views and goals of stakeholders is a political tool that relies on technology and management methods as necessary but not sufficient conditions for advancement. This tool works fairly well for local issues, but the difficulty rises with the scales and complexities of problems.

The incentive system to improve the use of integration tools is often perverse because lawyers, engineers, and even public officials may actually gain from conflict. There are many situations of moral hazard where officials have authority but do not feel the consequences of their actions. In fact, they may benefit personally from those actions, with the public being the loser. Various avenues such as shared vision planning are available to mitigate conflicts, but unless the stakeholders who participate in these negotiations have the incentives to agree and to find solutions, the processes will fall apart.

The arena for conflict seems to have gotten worse, but that may be a symptom of larger issues in society. After all, it has been hard to reach consensus on big issues of war and peace, health care, social security, and government bailouts for large companies, among others. Looking at integrated water management this way, we see that it is one of many attempts to find solutions to complex problems, in spite of the many divisive forces at play. Water is a unique resource, of course, because its use draws in so many interdependences among society and the environment.

Many writers point to the need for integration, but we should not underestimate the difficulty in implementing the integrated approach. As an example, Peter Gleick (2009) wrote that a judge in the Atlanta water wars described water problems with "stunning clarity." The judge wrote that "only by cooperating, planning, and conserving can we avoid the situations that gave rise to this litigation." To anyone working on integrated water management, the statement is a declaration of what we have said all along. However, the real issue is, how do we bring this about?

Here are a few thoughts for how to improve things. We start with the generalities, such as in the judge's statement, which emphasize cooperation, planning, conservation, and the like. In my book on *Total Water Management*, 15 principles for the process are identified and divided into two groups (Grigg, 2008b). The first group includes the "ought to" suggestions that are so common among writers about integrated approaches. They include powerful ideas such as:

- Effective policy-setting and processes
- Planning for sustainability on watershed basis
- Adaptive management
- Shared governance
- Focus on roles and relationships
- Coordination mechanisms
- Equitable allocation
- Shared goals
- Assessment and "triple bottom line" reporting of environmental, social and economic outcomes against established benchmarks.
- Corporate social responsibility
- Engagement of workforce, public and customers
- Effective regulation

The other group focuses on incentives and accountability and is more difficult. The first principle is to have rules for consensus and conflict resolution so that stakeholders cannot disrupt the process by pushing divisive agendas that work against the public interest, broadly defined. The second is to use effective incentives to bring about the desired outcomes in conservation, management practices, and other behaviors. Finally, transparency and accountability should be the rule so that the public can know what is happening and take appropriate actions through democratic and governance processes to correct situations and change course toward the water management actions needed.

At the end of the day, integrated water management is a hard thing to define, measure, and implement. Single-issue advocates are able to bring passion and force to the table. It is more difficult to generate equal levels of passion about improved understanding, balanced solutions, and equity for stakeholders. Integrated water management is one of the core practices required to make democracy work in a complex world. Water managers, engineers, and scientists should promote it wherever it is possible, especially taking multi-objective approaches, involving stakeholders honestly, and seeking balanced win-win solutions.

REFERENCES

American Society of Civil Engineers (ASCE). (2009). *Report card for America's infrastructure*, ASCE, Reston, VA, <http://www.asce.org/reportcard/2009/> (Mar 20, 2009).

Gleick, P. (2009). "An Eastern judge points the way to solving Western water problems." *SFGate*, <http://www.sfgate.com/cgi-bin/blogs/gleick/detail?entry_id=43844> (Jul 17, 2009)

Grigg, N. S. (2008a). "Integrated water resources management: balancing views and improving practice." *Water Int.*, 33(3), 279-292.

Grigg, N. S. (2008b). "Total water management: leadership practices for a sustainable future." *Water Int.*, 34(2), 290-293.

Senge, P.M. (1990). *The fifth discipline: the art and practice of the learning organization*, Doubleday Currency, New York, NY.

United States Environmental Protection Agency (USEPA). (2008). *Report on the environment: water*, USEPA, <http://www.epa.gov/roe/> (Jul 19, 2009).

AUTHOR INFORMATION

Neil Grigg is a Professor of Civil and Environmental Engineering at Colorado State University. He holds a PhD in civil engineering from Colorado State, a MS in civil engineering from Auburn, and a BS from the US Military Academy. He has been involved in water resources management for over forty years, and has received awards from ASCE, AWWA, UCOWR, AAAS, and APWA for his work. Email: neil.grigg@colostate.edu

Chapter 8

River Basin Planning and Management in 2050

Alan H. Vicory and Peter A. Tennant

ABSTRACT

Best practice in river basin planning and management is characterized by use of a framework whereby all issues are addressed in an integrated fashion. Current barriers to achieving this ideal practice include, principally, the "silo" nature of the many legislative statutes to address environmental stewardship goals, the absence of facilitating provisions in legislation, and the lack of institutional mechanisms in place in most river basins and watersheds. The basic components of river basin-based planning and management are: defining the planning (i.e. the watershed) unit; investigating/understanding water quantity and quality, water uses and users and pollutant sources; setting goals and necessary regulatory regimes that represent sustainable management; establishing an institutional mechanism under whose aegis the planning and integrative management authoritatively occurs; and insuring adequate funding is available in support of the process. Advances have been made in technologies and tools to facilitate integrated approaches, but constraints remain in financial resources for appropriate levels of monitoring. A "vision" for river basin planning and management in 2050 is one where plans are in place for local watersheds and they are facilitated by well-coordinated legislative mandates and policies and take advantage of available data. Appropriate institutions are in place to guide planning and programs across political jurisdictions. The planning process insures that impacted stakeholders and citizens are equal partners.

IMPORTANCE AND NEED FOR RIVER BASIN PLANNING

Best practice in river basin planning and management is characterized by use of a framework whereby all issues are addressed in an integrated fashion. While this concept is well accepted, it is difficult to implement principally because conducting integrated management is, in essence, about relationships: relationships among the political jurisdictions sharing the watershed; relationships among the programs for the collection and assessment of data; relationships among the on-the-ground programs for remediation and protection; relationships among the supporting legislations and interpretive policies; and relationships between the local citizens and stakeholders and those ultimately implementing the planning process.

All relationships inherently require significant resources to build and maintain. Thus, current barriers to achieving this ideal practice include the "silo" nature of the many legislative statutes that address environmental stewardship goals, the absence of facilitating provisions in legislation, the lack of institutional mechanisms in most river basins and watersheds, and a history of top-down planning and management in which the local citizens and impacted stakeholders are frequently marginalized or even ignored (Collier 2008).

The importance of integrated approaches is illustrated by the top three pollutants responsible for water quality impairments of water quality in the US: sediment, nutrients and pathogens. The nature of the sources of these contaminants in most waters can only be addressed by a suite of activities which are implemented in a coordinated, or integrated, fashion on a watershed basis and that typically involve the direct participation of local stakeholders.

Within the US and globally, the availability of water is at a critical juncture, with many areas in a state of deficit or on an unsustainable path. Given the projected increase in global population as of 2050, it is clear that better, more effective, planning and management is required to avoid impacts of catastrophic proportions. It is critically important that efforts be aggressively pursued, now and into the coming several decades, that serve to free the deployment of integrated river basin-based planning and management in the US and around the world.

> *The availability of water, in the US and globally, is at a critical juncture, with many areas in a state of deficit or on an unsustainable path.*

THE BUILDING BLOCKS

The basic components of river basin-based planning and management are: defining the planning (i.e. the watershed) unit; investigating/understanding water quantity and quality, water uses and users and pollutant sources; setting goals and necessary regulatory regimes that represent sustainable management; establishing an institutional mechanism under whose aegis the planning and integrative management authoritatively occurs; providing a sufficient and sustainable funding stream; and having a strategy for meaningful involvement of the public in the planning process.

Planning Unit

There are no clear guidelines regarding the scale at which river basin planning and management is most effective. Each basin is unique. Organizations currently exist that focus on very small local watersheds while others focus at the scale of the Ohio River Basin in the US, the Danube River Basin in Europe and the Mekong River Basin in Asia (Vicory and Tennant 1998). Certainly, river basins comprise the aggregate of sub-basins within, and moreover, there are watersheds within the sub-basins. Thus, planning and management needs to be applied, directly or indirectly, at all scales within a basin, with inter-scale relationships designed such that the information and actions at the lowest scale simultaneously address the needs of the locale but also serve as a component of, and integrate into, the larger scale planning units (e.g., watershed → sub-basin→ basin).

> *There are no clear guidelines regarding the scale at which river basin planning and management is most effective.*

Investigating and Understanding Water Quality and Quantity

River basin planning and management requires adequate diagnostic data that provide an understanding of basin hydrology and quality. However, the scope of current monitoring and assessment in most river basins is insufficient to optimize planning and management activities. This is due in part to declining resources, and in part to the different entities with different missions that collect water quality and quantity data.

In the US, water quality monitoring is primarily conducted by state environmental protection agencies, many of which are moving to deployment of basin-based designs integrating water quality and biological measurements. However, where watersheds cross state boundaries or waters form state boundaries, these programs are poorly coordinated. Moreover, data assessment protocols vary from state to state and, as a result, it is difficult to combine databases for unified assessment. On a positive note, there have been attempts to provide at least partial coordination of water management activities over entire river basins via commissions or authorities such as the Ohio River Valley Water Sanitation Commission (ORSANCO), the Delaware River Basin Commission and the Interstate Commission on the Potomac River Basin (ICPRB) (see Reference section for web addresses for these and other river basin commissions).

In the past 30 years, major advancements have been made in technologies for water quality and quantity measurement, data storage and transmission and analytical tools. Models such as BASINS (USEPA 2007) and WARMF (Goldstein 2001) permit a holistic assessment of impacts from different land uses. Other contemporary challenges include, but are not limited to, hydrological impacts from climate change and continuing discovery of contaminants, such as endocrine disrupting compounds and personal care products. These emerging concerns are adding additional complexities to the challenge of river basin management. Use of current and emerging technologies is critical to make best use of available data, and new protocols are needed to align advances in measurement science and discovery with understanding of ecological and human risk, both from floods and droughts as well as from the presence of contaminants.

Demands and Uses

Demands and uses can be generally categorized into anthropogenic and ecological. Anthropogenic uses are subject to changes over time as influenced by population shifts and economic, industrial, agricultural and silvicultural activities. Ecological demands, which comprise the water needs to sustain aquatic and terrestrial life and to maintain riparian vegetation, can also vary over time partially due to anthropogenic impacts.

Ecological uses and demands can only be understood through scientific study and observation and cannot be changed per governmental mandates. On the other hand, anthropogenic demands and uses can, and are, highly influenced by social policy and economic conditions. Thus, the challenge for river basin management is one of determining the basin's water dynamics as necessary to serve the needs of nature and protecting that need by anthropogenic demand management and/or infrastructure. The current state of science regarding determination of ecological flow needs is rapidly evolving and has yet to be commonly applied.

Sources of Pollution

A full understanding of sources of pollution is necessary to construct appropriate controls to achieve water quality and ecological objectives. Programs for source controls can include development of emission regulations (the approach for point sources) and economic incentives as an encouragement for action (commonly used to abate non-point sources). In the context of integrated water resources management, conflicts can and do arise when pollutant levels create water quality conditions unsuitable for recreational use or for withdrawal for irrigation, industrial processes or for treatment to potable drinking water standards.

Today in the US, the most widespread water quality problems are caused by nonpoint sources. While some success has been achieved in addressing the nonpoint source categories of urban runoff, construction site runoff, and animal feeding operations, much less has been realized in addressing row crop agriculture. Agricultural cropland represents the largest nonpoint source in terms of areal extent; however efforts to control its impacts on the environment have been through voluntary incentive-based programs. The concept of controlling farm runoff through regulation is frequently discussed, but to date has not been pursued.

Goals and Regulatory Regimes in Support of Sustainability

Goals and regulatory regimes provide directions and methods to help achieve a desired state of the system. Goals are often embodied in basin management plans.

However, because plans are "plans," they do not impose mandates for action. As most basin settings span multiple political jurisdictions, parochial interests often override adherence to a plan's goals. While regulatory mandates can serve to move water resources management to a desired operational state, they are very difficult to put in place.

Institutional Mechanisms

River basin planning and management involves integrating management of water quantity and water quality which, in turn, requires monitoring, assessment, land management, and grey and green infrastructure. Because commonly, multiple political jurisdictions are within the watershed land area as well as different levels of government (local, state, provincial, and national), appropriate institutional mechanisms are required to provide necessary coordination, oversight, focus and advocacy. In many basins, such central authorities exist both formally and informally.

Of particular note, the European Water Framework Directive requires the establishment of River Basin authorities to carry out management and planning, and in the United States, commissions have been established under formal compacts in several basins. International Commissions exist for the Mekong River and the Rhine River. Still, in most basins, mechanisms that exist are less formal in law and charter.

OUTLOOK

Experience in the US indicates that planning and management of water resources increases in response to increased demand. In order to speculate on how water resource management might change over time, it is useful to consider possible changes in demand and other factors.

Water Supply Demand

Population growth requires an increase in demand for public water supply. Large municipal utilities are experiencing greater increases in demand as smaller outlying communities are added to their systems. Smaller communities are getting out of the water supply business due to increased costs which are partially offset by economies of scale in larger systems. In some instances, contamination of ground water supplies has forced small communities to turn to nearby larger systems. The larger systems generally use surface waters for their supplies. Increases in both population and climate extremes will make drought management even more challenging than it is now. The combined impact of these developments is an overall increase in demand for water supply.

Energy

Direct use of surface water for hydroelectric power generation is likely to increase as the cost of energy from other sources increases. Hydropower facilities require reliable quantities of water in order to operate. These facilities can impact aquatic life, either directly though hydrologic modification, or indirectly by diverting flow around dams, thereby reducing reaeration.

Traditional combustion of coal for electric power generation requires huge quantities of water for cooling. Current regulations mandate the use of cooling towers at new power plants. While this minimizes the environmental effects of heated discharges, it also increases consumptive use of water. Coal conversion processes may offer reduced emissions to the environment, but will also mean increases in consumptive water use.

New extraction techniques make it feasible to drill for natural gas in places that heretofore have been considered unavailable. These techniques require large volumes of water. Meanwhile, use of corn to produce biofuels has increased demand for that crop. Cultivation of corn requires considerable use of agricultural chemicals, and its conversion to biofuel requires large quantities of water.

Flood Control
It is unlikely that any more large structural projects for flood control will be undertaken in the US; more likely, the roles of wetlands and preserved open space will be emphasized. Diversion of excess flows for storage and later use ("flood skimming") might be a promising option.

Climate Change
Projections of changes anticipated due to climate change include increases in extreme river flows –i.e., higher maximums and lower minimums. Under this scenario, it will be necessary to deal with greater volumes of water on a short term basis. Projected changes due to climate change will also add impetus to planning for drought management.

Water Quality
While considerable progress has been made in controlling pollution from sewage and industrial wastes, the pressures of aging infrastructure and increasing population assure that these sources will continue to pose challenges to meeting water quality goals. The debate over nonpoint source control – whether to continue reliance on voluntary solutions or to adopt regulatory approaches – is likely to continue. It is likely that a mixture of the two approaches will prevail.

THE VISION FOR RIVER BASIN PLANNING AND MANAGEMENT IN 2050

The river basin approach is virtually universally accepted as the most effective approach for water resources planning and management (Loucks 2004). Even as pressures mount to divert water from one river basin to another in order to meet demand, the river basin remains the most logical unit from which to operate. However, the basin management approach is also the most difficult to successfully implement due to the demands on relationships and technical support systems. Attention is needed to the water resources management aspect of basins.

By 2050, there will be a national baseline framework for water resources management in the US. Some of the steps needed to achieve this vision include building support for basin-based planning and management, improving technologies for efficient delivery of programs, and modifying legal and programmatic underpinnings. A "vision" for river basin planning and management in 2050 is one where plans are in place that comprise sub-plans for local watersheds. They are facilitated by well-coordinated legislative mandates and policies and take advantage of available data. Appropriate institutions are in place to guide planning and programs across political jurisdictions.

Building Support

The first and foremost challenge and need is for higher levels of appreciation and support for basin-based planning and management; to the extent that will prompt action politically to establish, strengthen and fund institutions and basin level management activities. One needed activity is comparative assessments of a basin's future with and without a basin management approach and managing institution, and with costs assessed in not only financial terms but in terms of conflict among sovereigns and resource users.

Technologies for Harnessing Existing and Developmental Needs

Levels of management activities will commonly be dictated by financial constraints. Therefore, it is imperative that maximum use be made of available technologies that serve to achieve efficient delivery of programs. There have been recently, and will continue to be, rapid developments in technologies as regards measurements, data logging and telemetry, data analysis and modeling and general business communications.

> *We need legislation requiring the creation of a management plan for each basin and a proper authority to implement it.*

Legal and Programmatic Underpinnings

River basin management must be unconstrained by conflicting and uncoordinated legislative mandates. Legislative flexibility is a necessity to the development of structures and programs customized to the resource, political, institutional and economic "lay of the land" unique to each basin. Most desirably, supporting legislation requiring a management plan for each basin and the identification, strengthening, or creation of a proper authority under whose aegis the planning and management function of each basin rests, is needed.

Other changes that are needed include support for emerging programs in water quality trading that are used to inform the development of model approaches and enabling legislation. Reviews of cross-impacting legislation (e.g., the Clean Air, Clean Water and Safe Drinking Water Acts and other peripheral legislation such as the Federal Insecticide, Fungicide, and Rodenticide Act and the Endangered Species Act in the US) must be undertaken and changes incorporated therein to allow their synergistic application within the context of adopted basin plans.

REFERENCES

Collier, C. R. (2008). *Comprehensive watershed management and planning*,
    Statement before Subcommittee on Water Resources and Environment,
    Committee on Transportation and Infrastructure, United States House of
    Representatives, Jun 24, 2008.
Goldstein, R. A. (2001) *Watershed analysis risk management framework (WARMF):
    update one.* Topical Report. EPRI, Palo Alto, CA.
Loucks, D. P. (2004). "Federal leadership in managing America's rivers." *Water
    Resources Update*, 127, 198-111.
River Basin Commissions:
    Danube River. http://www.icpdr.org/
    Mekong River. http://www.mrcmekong.org/
    Ohio River. http://www.orsanco.org/
    Delaware River. http://www.state.nj.us/drbc/
    Potomac River. http://www.potomacriver.org/cms/
United States Environmental Protection Agency (USEPA). (2007). *BASINS 4.0 fact
    sheet: better assessment science integrating point and non-point sources*,
    <http://www.epa.gov/waterscience/basins/fs-basins4.html> (Dec, 2009).
Vicory, A., and Tennant, P. (1998). "The case for river basin management."
    Watershed management: practices, policies, and coordination, R. J. Reimold,
    ed., McGraw-Hill, New York, NY, 221-234.

AUTHOR INFORMATION

Alan H. Vicory is the Executive Director and Chief Engineer for the Ohio River
Valley Water Sanitation Commission (ORSANCO), as position he has held for over
20 years. ORSANCO is known worldwide for its accomplishments and programs in
river basin management. He holds a BS in Civil Engineering from Virginia Military
Institute and is a member of the American Academy of Environmental Engineers
(AAEE). He is past Chairman of the International Water Association's Watershed
and River Basin Management Specialist Group and Past President of AAEE and the
Association of State and Interstate Water Pollution Control Administrators. Email:
avicory@orsanco.org

Peter A. Tennant is Deputy Executive Director with ORSANCO. He has over 35
years of experience in river basin planning and management and in delivery of state
agency water programs. He holds a BS in Civil Engineering from Northeastern
University and is a member of the American Academy of Environmental Engineers.
Email: ptennant@orsanco.org

Chapter 9

The Law Applicable to Surface Waters in 2050

Joseph W. Dellapenna

ABSTRACT

Technological change and population growth already stress legal regimes for managing surface waters. Significant climate change complicates the picture. These stresses require major reforms to water law at the local, national, and even the international levels. While security of investment and incentives to promote the highest and best use of water are necessary, it is also necessary to protect and enhance the public and ecological dimensions of water management. Water law must become a tool for accomplishing these objectives rather than merely serving to perpetuate an increasingly dysfunctional status quo. The public nature of water largely precludes markets as a management tool.

"It looks like you need a law degree
to be a protester these days."

INTRODUCTION

While water is found nearly everywhere, because of its variability in quantity and quality, the desired amount and quality of water is not always found where and when it is needed for human needs. Usable water is a scarce and valuable commodity. This reality gives rise to the need for appropriate and effective legal regimes to define and limit water rights. Judges, lawyers, and others working within existing legal regimes governing water management in the United States, however, are struggling to respond to the growing stresses on those regimes that have arisen from increasing and changing demands for water, without unduly destabilizing existing expectations expressed in investments in water use facilities. Stresses on water law regimes grew throughout the twentieth century, in part because of the quadrupling of the national population to nearly 300,000,000 during the century, and perhaps even more from the dramatic, six-fold growth of *per capita* demand for water resulting from the unprecedented affluence of the second half of the century (Dellapenna 1997). Because of increasing human populations, the great increases in *per capita* demand, and the belated recognition of the necessity of reserving water for ecological and other in-place water uses, legally protected water uses continued to grow exponentially.

Global climate disruption adds further complexities to the stresses facing water law regimes in the United States (Dellapenna 1999). Adaptation to climate change will necessarily center on water—one of the most essential resources for human survival and welfare. Global climate change adds stress to existing water law regimes as water management systems struggle to adapt. Our responses, whatever they are, will have to be carefully planned in order to be sustainable, rather than ultimately self-destructive.

> *Can existing legal regimes accommodate change without provoking extensive, perhaps violent, resistance among water users?*

In attempting to predict what law regimes in the United States will look like in 2050, one cannot simply project forward existing legal regimes. Those regimes will have to adapt, and if they don't they will be swept aside (Dellapenna 2008). The only questions are when that will happen and whether the existing legal regimes can be modified to accommodate change better without unsettling water users and provoking extensive, perhaps violent, resistance. Too much legal response can produce as much social turmoil as inadequate legal response. To consider how existing legal regimes should change, we must begin by understanding the three water law regimes now existing at the state level as well as the role of federal law in water management.

EXISTING STATE WATER LAW IN THE UNITED STATES

The basic allocation rules for surface waters in the United States are matters of state law, derived through the common law tradition from principles brought to the United

States in the English colonization of North America. While parts of the United States were first settled from France or Spain, the water laws those settlers brought to the country were largely swept aside with the spread of "Anglo" culture across the continent, with only vestigial remains found in a few states (Dellapenna 2009a). Aboriginal law, which might have proven better adapted to local conditions than the European imports, was ignored almost entirely, apart from Hawaii. In Hawaii, vestiges of indigenous law survive in an uneasy amalgam of aboriginal law, riparian rights, notions drawn from appropriative rights but expressed as prescriptive rights, and public management (Dellapenna 2009e).

When the English colonists settled along the east coast, they found a land that in many respects was similar to England—short streams that were seldom navigable above the ebb and flow of the tide, but which were easily adaptable to the generation of power through water mills. The climate was humid, allowing rain-fed agriculture. Thus, the early disputes over access to water dealt with disputes over access to water to drive mills, disputes that were relatively easy to resolve by a few simple rules (Dellapenna 2009c). The rules came to be known as "riparian rights," taking their name from the Latin term *ripa,* meaning the bank of a stream. Riparian rights limited the right to use water to those who owned or leased land contiguous to the water source. For the most part, a riparian landowner was free to make any use she wanted so long as no one else complained, and no one complained unless there was direct interference with the complainant's water use—if only because the mechanism for resolving the complaints was the slow and expensive process of litigation.

Legal complaints remained rare so long as rain and river flows were adequate to meet all needs, as they were most of the time. Yet industrial development and occasional droughts did give rise to litigation, as a result of which courts developed the rule that in a conflict between uses, the riparian user making a "reasonable use" would prevail (Red River Roller Mill v. Wright 1883). Apart from disputes involving the use of water on non-riparian land (which were always deemed unreasonable), this test required the court to exercise judgment as to which of the competing uses, on balance, best served society's needs. Results were highly unpredictable and no water user could be certain, if his use were challenged in court, whether he would prevail. Even long-established uses could be wiped out in favor of recently begun competing uses. This system, a common property approach to water, was carried by the Anglo settlers as they spread across the country. The results were a highly unpredictable and unstable system that survived in large part only so long as there was generally more than enough water to go around. As recently as 1950, riparian rights applied in 32 states and today it still survives in 14 or so states (the exact status of the state law in some states within the riparian rights tradition is in dispute).

When large-scale Anglo settlement reached California, the settlers were compelled to confront the problems of allocating consumptive uses without any organized government in the state (Hundley 2001; Pisani 1992). The discovery of gold at Sutter's Mill in 1848 resulted in an increase in population of several hundred thousand within five years. The sudden peopling of California occurred without any organized government in place. Whatever law might have been established among the Spanish-founded missions, presidios, and pueblos was virtually swept away, ignored by the mass of would-be miners (Bakken 1983). These Yankee intruders brought with them the only law with which they were familiar—the common law of the eastern United States (Reid 1980). However, regarding the two most central material factors in their lives—land and water—they were unable to do so. Under that law, the land belonged to the government and the waters went with the land. The "forty-niners" were unable to acquire title to the land without the establishment of regular government and comprehensive surveys, yet they were unwilling to wait for that to occur. The newcomers simply sought out the gold as trespassers, and took what water they needed. They often needed a great deal of water, sometimes at a considerable distance from where the water was naturally located.

The results helped to give Americans a national mythology based on stories of violent disputes, blood feuds, and sudden death. The miners sought to bring order through vigilante law which adopted the most elementary notion of justice to their situation: the first to grab it owns it, or, as it would be put more eloquently by lawyers and judges, "first in time is first in right" (Beck and Anderson 2009). This became known as the doctrine of prior appropriation or appropriative rights. This process was well established on the ground before effective formal governments could be created. When governments were created, they could do little but ratify the "customs of the miners" (Jennison v. Kirk 1879). This system of appropriative rights (based upon the prior appropriation of water) became the dominant form of water law in the 18 states west of Kansas City. Today this essentially private property system is applied through elaborate state administrative arrangements (Goplerud 2009), while vestiges of riparian rights survive in some appropriative rights states, creating "dual systems" that suffer from needlessly complex water law regimes (Dellapenna 2009a). There is a certain irony in the result: "A legal system that arose from the relatively lawless mining camps of the Wild West would come to be viewed as though it had been handed down directly from God" (Benson 2006).

The explosion in water demand after World War II coupled with changing precipitation patterns in the last decades of the twentieth century, combined to undermine the continued vitality of riparian rights in the eastern states. Those states, however, did not simply adopt appropriative rights, for the experience of dual systems in the western states demonstrated that it was necessary to address the growing water management problems in the east within the riparian tradition (Dellapenna 2009a). Instead, about 17 eastern states and Hawaii developed a system of regulated riparianism based upon treating water as public property (Dellapenna 2009d). Under regulated riparianism, the right to use water is obtained not through the ownership of riparian land, but through the granting of a time-limited state permit. Permits are determined by the criterion of reasonableness, as in traditional riparian rights, applied by an administrative agency before the use begins (Dellapenna 2003). Special provisions apply to uses begun before the permit system was put in place. The permits provide greater security for investors in water-use facilities, while the periodic expiration of the permits allows for orderly re-examination of the continuing social utility of particular waters uses. Additional provisions in regulated riparian laws provide protections for the public interest in waters, including the power to override permits during water emergencies.

THE FEDERAL ROLE IN WATER LAW

The federal government has been involved from its beginning in water management, although for the first century that role was largely limited to regulating, protecting, or improving the navigability of watercourses. At the beginning of the twentieth century, the federal government began to finance, build, and operate facilities to provide water for irrigation, to prevent flood control, and (eventually) to regulate pollution and other environmental aspects of water usage (Huffman 2008). The federal government also became active in resolving interstate disputes (Dellapenna 2005) and in protecting the water rights of Indian reservations (Thorson et al. 2006). After 1970, the enactment of the Clean Water Act, the Endangered Species Act, and numerous other federal environmental laws, coupled with the inability of states applying appropriative rights to enforce these laws given the built in rigidities of that system, led to federal intervention to override state water rights to achieve the federal goals, perhaps most notably in the Klamath River valley (Fimrite 2009; McKinley 2009; Symposium 2007).

THE NEXT 40 YEARS

The combination of increasing population, increasing demand (including the recent recognition of ecological demand), and climate disruption has rendered obsolete both traditional riparian rights and traditional appropriative rights. Growing climate disruption will create demands for a more equitable distribution of what water there is and therefore for water law reform. For both the riparian tradition and appropriative rights, the difficulty arises from the fact, virtually unique to water, that it is consumed over and over again by different users as it progresses through the hydrological cycle. Thus the water I use today is the water you use tomorrow, or *vice versa*. Contrast this aspect of water to oil, another liquid resource. Because of this pattern of use and re-use, private property systems simply don't work for water in nature, and water markets are more of a myth than a reality (Dellapenna 2000). Instead, the practical effect of reaching a point where most or all available waters have been appropriated, given the need to protect third parties who have perfected water rights, was to freeze uses in place rather than giving rise to markets among property owners (Dellapenna 2008). On the other hand, the common property approach of traditional riparian rights has become a paradigm of the tragedy of the commons (Hardin 1968). Lack of effective restraint on water use under riparian rights allows, and almost requires, users to exhaust the resource either by withdrawing and consuming the water or by polluting the water.

Because of their very different legal traditions, governments in the 32 riparian rights states and the 18 appropriative rights states faced (and face) very different challenges. In riparian rights states, the problem is to provide security of investment for water users while tightening protections for the public interest in the waters. In appropriative rights states, the problem is to introduce needed flexibility into an increasingly sclerotic system of water rights while also beginning to provide adequate protection to the public interest in waters. Devising proper responses in riparian rights states is easier than in appropriative rights states because the water rights in riparian rights states are less firmly established than in appropriative rights states, and thus governments face fewer strictures arising from the constitutional prohibition of the taking of property without compensation.

> *The combination of increasing population, increasing demand (including ecological demand), and climate disruption has rendered obsolete traditional riparian and appropriative rights.*

State governments have already begun to transform the established systems of water rights. Table 9-1 lists the current (2009) surface water law regime in place by state. More than half of the states within the riparian tradition have abandoned traditional riparian rights in favor of publicly managed regulated riparianism. That transition is likely to spread until traditional riparian rights have been entirely supplanted by regulated riparianism in the 32 states within the riparian tradition, although in some states it might only be applied in more developed parts of the state. In the 18 appropriative rights states, many claims are being made that markets will solve water management problems (Anderson and Snyder 1997). Close examination, however, demonstrates that true markets for water have only operated at small scales and over short distances. Instead, such changes as there have been in the west have resulted not from market transactions but from state intervention to re-allocate the water (Dellapenna 2009b). Such state-managed reallocation is likely to increase over the next 40 years, using legal fictions like pseudo-markets to accomplish what cannot be done directly because of constraints on the taking of property. At the same time, federal government interventions to ensure the protection of the public interest in western waters might continue and grow, unless the states are willing and able to take advantage of re-allocation of water rights and the de-stabilizing effects of federal intervention to begin to do this on their own.

Transitions such as those predicted here will not be easy to accomplish. There will be resistance from water users who believe that they have vested rights in the water they have been using, particularly in the western (appropriative rights) states where the rhetoric of private property in water rights is well entrenched. In such a setting, appeals to public concerns about how water is used will be met with demands for compensation for the taking of property. The politically expedient response will be to pay compensation, but in a world of tight budgets the need to compensate might prevent timely responses to the growing need for water law reform. Those same tight budgets, not to mention concerns about protecting ecosystems and impacts of "vested" property rights, might also impede the construction of new reservoirs or other infrastructure that might be necessary to cope with changes in precipitation patterns and natural water storage. Careful attention to the true dimensions of legal rights might help alleviate these problems, but they remain at bottom political rather than legal.

Table 9-1. States by Surface Water Law Regime in 2009

Appropriative Rights	Dual Systems (appropriative & riparian rights)	Regulated Riparianism	Riparian Rights
Arizona[1]	Alaska	Connecticut	Alabama[2]
Colorado	California	Delaware	Arkansas[2]
Idaho	Kansas	Florida	Illinois[1]
Montana	Nebraska	Georgia	Indiana
Nevada	North Dakota	Hawaii[3]	Louisiana[4]
New Mexico	Oklahoma	Iowa	Maine
Utah	Oregon	Kentucky	Missouri
Wyoming	South Dakota	Maryland	New Hampshire
	Texas	Massachusetts	Ohio
	Washington	Michigan[5]	Pennsylvania
		Minnesota	Rhode Island
		Mississippi	South Carolina[1]
		New Jersey	Tennessee
		New York[5]	Vermont
		North Carolina[2]	Virginia[2]
		Wisconsin	West Virginia

---

[1] The state has a regulated riparian system for groundwater, but not for surface water.
[2] The state has enacted a regulated riparian system but has largely not implemented it.
[3] Hawaii has a compound of ancient customary and prescriptive rights and regulated riparian rights.
[4] Louisiana follows riparian principles, but as derived from French law and expressed in its civil code rather than as part of the common law tradition.
[5] The state has enacted a regulated riparian statute that applies only to very large users on certain limited water sources.

REFERENCES

Anderson, T. L., and Snyder, P. (1997). *Water markets: priming the invisible pump*, Cato Institute, Washington, DC.

Bakken, G. M. (1983). *The development of law on the Rocky Mountain frontier: civil law and society, 1850-1912*, Greenwood Press, Westport, CT.

Beck, R. E., and Anderson, O. L. (2009). "Elements of prior appropriation." *Waters and Water Rights*, 3rd Ed., Vol. 1, R. E. Beck and A. K. Kelley, eds., LexisNexis, Newark, NJ, 12-1 to 12-73.

Benson, R. D. (2006). "A few ironies of western water law." *Wyoming Law Rev.*, 6, 331-37.

Dellapenna, J. W. (1997). "Population and water in the Middle East: the challenge and opportunity for law." *Int. J. Environ. Pollut.*, 7, 72–111.

Dellapenna, J. W. (1999). "Adapting the law of water management to global climate change and other hydropolitical stresses." *J. Am. Water Resour. As.*, 35, 1301-26.

Dellapenna, J. W. (2000). "The importance of getting names right: the myth of markets for water." *William and Mary Environ. Law and Policy Review*, 25, 317-77.

Dellapenna, J. W., ed. (2003). *Regulated riparian model water code*, ASCE Std. 40-03, American Society of Civil Engineers, Reston, VA.

Dellapenna, J. W. (2005). "Interstate struggles over rivers: the southeastern states and the struggle over the 'Hooch." *New York Univ. Environ. Law J.*, 12, 828-900.

Dellapenna, J. W. (2008). "Climate disruption, the Washington consensus, and water law reform." *Temple Law Rev.*, 81, 383-432.

Dellapenna, J. W. (2009a). "Dual systems." *Waters and water rights*, 3rd Ed., Vol. 1, R. E. Beck and A. K. Kelley, eds., LexisNexis, Newark, NJ, 8-1 to 8-72.

Dellapena, J. W. (2009b). "Introduction to riparian rights." *Waters and water rights*, 3rd Ed., Vol. 1, R. E. Beck and A. K. Kelley, eds., LexisNexis, Newark, NJ, 6-3 to 6-213.

Dellapenna, J. W. (2009c). "The right to consume water under 'pure' riparian rights." *Waters and water rights*, 3rd Ed., Vol. 1, R. E. Beck and A. K. Kelley, eds., LexisNexis, Newark, NJ, 7-1 to 7-178.

Dellapenna, J. W. (2009d). "Regulated riparianism." *Waters and water rights*, 3rd Ed., Vol. 1, R. E. Beck and A. K. Kelley, eds., LexisNexis, Newark, NJ, 9-1 to 9-261.

Dellapenna, J. W. (2009e). "Related systems of water." *Waters and water rights*, 3rd Ed., Vol. 1, R. E. Beck and A. K. Kelley, eds., LexisNexis, Newark, NJ, 10-1 to 10-96.

Fimrite, P. (2009). "Deal to raze four Klamath dams." *San Francisco Chronicle*, September 30, 2009, p A1.

Goplerud, III, C. P. (2009). "The permit process and Colorado's exception." *Waters and water rights*, 3rd Ed., Vol. 1, R. E. Beck and A. K. Kelley, eds., LexisNexis, Newark, NJ, 15-1 to 15-49.

Hardin, G. (1968). "The tragedy of the commons." *Science*, 162 (3859), 1243-50.

Huffman, J. L. (2008). "The federal role in water resource management." *New York*

Univ. Environ. Law J., 17, 669-702.

Hundley, Jr., N. (2001). *The great thirst: Californians and their water, 1770-1990*, 2nd ed., University of California Press, Berkeley, CA.

Jennison v. Kirk (1879). *United States Reports*, 98, 453-62.

McKinley, J. (2009). "Plan outlines removal of four dams on Klamath River." *NY Times*, October 1, 2009, p. A22.

Pisani, D. J. (1992). *To reclaim a divided West: water, law, and policy, 1848-1902*, University of New Mexico Press, Albuquerque, NM.

Red River Roller Mill v. Wright (1883). *Minnesota Law Reports*, 30, 249-56; *Northwestern Reporter*, 14, 167-70.

Reid, J. P. (1980). *Law for the elephant: property and social behavior on the Overland Trail*, Huntington Library, San Marino, CA.

Symposium. (2007). "At the crossroads: the search for sustainable solutions in the Klamath basin." *J. Environ. Law and Litigation*, 22, 1-129.

Thorson, J. E., Britton, S., and Colby, B. G., eds. (2006). *Tribal water rights: essays in contemporary law, policy, and economics*, University of Arizona Press, Tucson, AZ.

AUTHOR INFORMATION

Joseph W. Dellapenna is a professor of law at Villanova University, where he teaches water law, among other subjects. He holds a BBA with distinction from the University of Michigan, a JD *cum laude* from the Detroit College of Law, an LL.M. in International and Comparative Law from the George Washington University, and an LL.M. in Environmental Law from Columbia University. He serves as Director of the Model Water Code Project of ASCE and served as rapporteur for the *Berlin Rules on Water Resources* for the International Law Association. He has received several awards from ASCE for his work on water law reform. Email: dellapen@law.villanova.edu

Chapter 10

A Vision of Unified River Basin Planning and Management

Charles W. Howe

ABSTRACT

This chapter looks at the history and importance of the river basin as the natural unit for river administration and, as we move towards 2050, why it is increasingly important for water administration to get back to the river basin framework. Since there is a long history of dividing the river basin into jurisdictions that often have little to do with water, recommendations are made for moving back to the unified basin in ways that recognize the legitimate objectives of these jurisdictions. Under increasing demands and possible climate change, there will be a greater need for more flexibility in water re-allocation. Water markets promise to provide this flexibility and, on broader geographical scales, to take planning and management back to the river basin level.

THE RIVER BASIN AS A PLANNING AND MANAGEMENT UNIT[1]

There is a long history of recognition of the river basin as the natural unit for river development, planning and management. However, globally there has been a long history of breaking up river basins into multiple jurisdictions, many having nothing to do with water. At present, because of the failure to focus development, planning, and management on the entire river basin, unplanned detrimental impacts (negative externalities) increasingly appear. The question is "What politically feasible steps can be taken to move planning and management back to the river basin?"

Over past millennia, the river basin has been used as the entity for river planning and management. The origins of irrigation development in the Tigris and Euphrates Valleys go back to 6000 BC and involved interdependent diversions from both rivers (Christensen 1993; Postel 1999). China's attempts to control the Yellow River go back to 4000 BC. The Indus Basin was settled and managed by 2300 BC (Postel 1999), while the ingenious Dujianyang irrigation and flood control project on the Min River in Szechwan Province of China was designed and built around 1600 BC by the still revered engineer, Li Bao (Van Slyke 1988).

In the mid-nineteenth century, the faculty of the École nationale des ponts et chaussées (ENPC) in Paris was one of the most prominent promoters of the river basin approach. The "Agences de Bassin" proposed by ENPC still constitute the river

---

[1] This section draws on Howe's work as partially reported in Howe (2005).

planning and management agencies of France (Ekelund and Hebert 1973). In the US, the Inland Waterway Commission appointed by President Theodore Roosevelt in 1907 during the early era of "scientific management and the gospel of efficiency" of natural resources (Hays 1958) strongly promoted centralized control of the major rivers and multi-purpose river development.

During the depression of the 1930s, the federal government of the US developed the Tennessee Valley Project, the only attempt in the US at basin-wide comprehensive development (Trelease 1971). The 1965 federal Water Resources Planning Act created the Water Resources Council to coordinate federal water development and management activities (Rogers 1993) and also authorized the establishment of new river basin commissions to coordinate federal and state efforts of basin-wide planning.

During 1968–1973, the US National Water Commission carried out an extensive set of studies leading to a landmark report, *Water Policies for the Future* (US National Water Commission, 1973). The report strongly emphasized the importance of the basin approach. Under Commission sponsorship, a group chaired by Gary Hart produced a major study, *Institutions for Water Planning-Institutional Arrangements: River Basin Commissions, Inter-Agency Committees and Ad Hoc Coordinating Committees* (Hart 1971) that emphasized the need for a whole basin approach. More recently in 1998, the US Western Water Policy Review Advisory Commission issued an incisive report, *Water in the West: Challenge for the Next Century* that emphasized the need to coordinate watershed initiatives with river basin goals (US Western Water Policy Review Advisory Commission 1998)[2].

In contrast to this long history of focusing on the river basin, many federal policies in the US since the mid-19th century have had the effect of reducing federal control over water resources and reducing possibilities for basin-wide management (Trelease 1971). The 1877 Desert Land Act required that settlers make water claims under state law. The 1897 National Forest Act required those using forest lands to claim water under state laws. The 1902 Reclamation Act required authorized projects to proceed in conformity with state laws for claiming water, as did the Federal Power Act of 1920. The McCarran Amendment (US Code 43 1988) requires all federal agencies to pursue claims for water under state laws.

Many of the institutional arrangements that stand as impediments to comprehensive river basin planning were intended to achieve valid water- and non-water-related objectives including the recognition of national sovereignty in the case of international rivers, the goal of stronger roles for the states in water and natural

---

[2] In 1982, the Reagan administration down-graded the Water Resources Council to a non-policy status and abolished the river basin commissions that had been established under the 1965 Act. This has left an uncertain, mixed picture of state versus federal water administration, especially across the western states.

resources management, safeguarding basins of origin and states' water supplies through prohibitions of inter-basin and/or interstate transfers, and reluctance to recognize the newer, emerging uses of water. Examples are found on the Colorado River under the Compact of 1922 (Meyers 1966; Water Education Foundation 1997, 1999) and in the repeated attempts at joint river management of the Apalachicola, Chattahoochee and Flint Rivers shared among Georgia, Alabama and Florida (Lipford 2004). Thus there are trade-offs between the water-based benefits that might be achieved through basin-wide management and other public policy objectives.

> *There are trade-offs between the water-based benefits that might be achieved through basin-wide management and other public policy objectives.*

RETURNING TO "VIRTUAL RIVER BASINS"

It seems unlikely that nations, states, and all the special districts that currently have a say in water planning and management will simply surrender their prerogatives to unified river basin initiatives. Steps towards basin-wide integration will have to involve rewards to all parties involved. Since institutional change always involves losers as well as winners, progress depends in part on devising ways of creating "win-win" opportunities and/or efficiently compensating the losers.

Several steps could take us toward what we might call "virtual river basins," i.e., not politically nor jurisdictionally unified regions but agreed upon basin-wide water allocation principles and mechanisms that can result in "win-win" improvements. A first step would be the adoption of the principle of "benefit sharing" or parallel negotiations in place of just water sharing. In his analysis of the negotiations between the United States and Canada over Columbia River development, Krutilla (1967) described the "benefit-sharing" incorporated in the treaty. Since the Columbia originates in the US, sweeps into the canyons of British Columbia, and then returns to the US, efficient development required reservoir storage in the canyons of British Columbia to support power generation, navigation and fisheries downstream in the US. The solution was to arrange monetary payments and the sharing of electric power from the lower river with British Columbia.

Similar arrangements can be envisioned on other rivers. The treaties between Mexico and the US on the Colorado and Rio Grande Rivers in 1944 involved simultaneous negotiation over the two rivers, since Mexico provided a major portion of the water to the lower Rio Grande while the US commanded all the water of the Colorado. This type of bargaining is referred to as an "interconnected game" (Folmer v. Mouche and Ragland 1993) and promises to play a role in some situations in getting back to the river basin. The potential gains may be sufficient to overcome the reluctance of nations and states to enter into more comprehensive river management arrangements.

Benefit sharing is most often accomplished through extra-market compensation. This is seen in payments to the basin of origin accompanying out-of-basin water transfers in the western US. For example, the State of Colorado requires "compensatory storage" for any project exporting water from the Colorado River Basin to other basins in the State (Grigg 2003) to provide insurance against diversion-induced shortages in the state's Colorado River Basin. The US Bureau of Reclamation built Green Mountain Reservoir on the Blue River (a tributary to the Colorado) as compensatory storage for the Colorado-Big Thompson Project that diverts water from the Upper Colorado to the eastern side of the Rocky Mountains. Naturally, compensatory storage may not always be the most efficient form of compensation.

A second step would be to take advantage of newly developed optimization and surveillance technologies that can facilitate basin-wide real time management. Technological developments have made basin-wide, real-time modes of river management practical. Tele-monitoring of streamflows is highly developed while satellite imagery of weather and flood events now makes it possible to allocate water on a basin-wide, real-time basis rather than basing allocation on monthly or annual average flows. Kilgour and Dinar (2001) have shown that real time basin-wide river allocation rules are economically more efficient than administration based on periodic accounting with fixed or proportional allocations.

> *Satellite imagery of weather and flood events now makes it possible to allocate water on a basin-wide, real-time basis rather than based on monthly or annual average flows.*

A third step would be to expand the geographical scope of water markets to an interstate (or even international) basis. Selling or even leasing water out-of-state has not been permitted by the states because of fear of losing the water forever. These fears can be overcome by the establishment of continuous, low transaction cost water markets extending across state lines. Recently, the States of Arizona and Nevada entered into an interstate agreement under which Arizona will "bank" 4.93×10^7 m^3 (40,000 acre-feet) of water per year from its currently unused portion of the Colorado River. This water will be provided to Nevada as needed in the future, with Nevada paying $23 million per year to cover Arizona's costs of groundwater recharge, plus $100 million "up front" (Fischer 2004).

Because of pervasive externalities, water markets must be supervised to avoid third party injury, in keeping with appropriations doctrine (Howe 2002)[3]. Water markets are often limited in their ability to protect non-consumptive instream benefits such as recreation, ecosystem maintenance, and hydropower if they are not represented by water rights. Booker (1995) and Young (1995) found that the greatest losses from

---

[3] From an economic efficiency point-of-view, it may not pay to enforce "no injury" in all situations. Rather, some degree of injury would be allowed to a point where marginal injury damages to other water users are offset by the benefits of a more flexible transfer.

extended drought on the Colorado River would be to recreation, power and environmental values.

The magnitude of transaction costs associated with transfers is crucial to the working of water markets. Transaction costs arise from the search for information about potential buyers and sellers and from the legal requirements imposed on transfers. The water court process used in Colorado guarantees orderly oversight of transfers, but can be costly to buyers and sellers. Greater reliance on oversight by administrative agencies like the state engineer's office can reduce these costs and expedite market transfers.

Conflict between the enforcement of priorities and the efficient allocation of water can arise when priority dates of water rights are not correlated with marginal values in use. In the South Platte Basin of Colorado and on the Snake River in Idaho, serious economic and social losses have resulted from administering the priority system (Howe 2008). While these cases suggest that river calls are likely to be economically inefficient, water markets with low transaction costs can eliminate these inconsistencies over time.

The appropriations doctrine has proven to be flexible in accommodating to changing economic conditions. Water markets, too, have evolved through experience with water banks, drought relief schemes, and rotating fallow schemes proving to be effective in allocating water flexibly and efficiently. These water institutions will continue to evolve in response to the pressures of demand, environment and likely climate change.

REFERENCES

Booker, J. F. (1995). "Hydrologic and economic impacts of drought under alternative policy responses." *Water Resour. Bull.*, 31(5), 889-906.

Christensen, P. (1993). *The decline of Iranshahr*, Museum Tusculanum Press, Copenhagen, Denmark.

Ekelund, Jr., R. B., and Hebert, R. F. (1973). "Public economics at the Ecole des Ponts et Chausees: 1830-1850." *J. Public Econ.*, 2, 241-256.

Fischer, H. (2004). "Arizona OKs Nevada deal to bank CAP water." *Arizona Daily Star*, Dec. 9, 2004.

Folmer, H. v. Mouche, P., and Ragland, S. (1993). "Interconnected games and international environmental problems." *Environ. Resour. Econ.*, 3(4), 313-335.

Grigg, N. S. (2003). *Colorado's water: science and management, history and politics*, Aquamedia Publishing, Fort Collins, CO.

Hart, G. W. (1971). *Institutions for water planning-institutional arrangements: river basin commissions*, Inter-Agency Committees and Ad Hoc Coordinating Committees Report PB 204 244 to the National Water Commission, National Technical Information Service, Springfield, VA.

Hays, S. P. (1958). *Conservation and the gospel of efficiency: the progressive conservation movement, 1890-1920*, Harvard University Press, Cambridge, MA.

Howe, C. W. (2002). "Protecting public values in a water market setting: improving water markets to increase economic efficiency and equity." *Univ. of Denver Water Law Review*, 31(2), 357-372.

Howe, C. W. (2005). "The return to the river basin: the increasing costs of 'Jurisdictional Externalities.'" *J. Contemp. Water Res. and Educ.*, 131, 26-32.

Howe, C. W. (2008). "Water law and economics: an assessment of river calls and the South Platte well shut-down." *Univ. of Denver Water Law Review*, 12(1), 181.

Kilgour, D. M., and Dinar, A. (2001). "Flexible water sharing within an international river basin." *Environ. Resour. Econ.*, 18, 43-60.

Krutilla, J. V. (1967). *The Columbia River treaty: the economics of an international river basin development*, Johns Hopkins Press, Baltimore, MD.

Lipford, J. W. (2004), "Averting water disputes: a southeastern case study." *PERC Policy Series*, PS-30, Property and Environment Research Center, Bozeman, MT.

Meyers, C. J. (1966). "The Colorado River." *Stanford Law Review*, 19(1), 1-75.

Postel, S. (1999). *Pillar of sand: can the irrigation miracle last?,* W.W. Norton & Company for the Worldwatch Institute, New York, NY.

Rogers, P. (1993). *America's water: federal roles and responsibilities*, MIT Press, Cambridge, MA.

Trelease, F. J. (1971). *Federal-state relations in water law*, Report PB 203 600 to the National Water Commission, National Technical Information Service, Springfield, VA.

US Code: 43 USC §666. (1988). *McCarran amendment.*

US National Water Commission. (1973). *Water policies for the future: final report to the president and to the Congress of the United States by the National Water Commission,* US Government Printing Office, Washington, DC.

US Western Water Policy Review Advisory Commission. (1998). *Water in the west: challenge for the next century,* University of New Mexico, Albuquerque, NM.

Van Slyke, L. P. (1988). *Yangtze: nature, history and the river*, Addisson-Wesley Publishing Company, Menlo Park, CA.

Water Education Foundation. (1997). *Proc., 75th anniversary Colorado River Compact symposium*, Sacramento, CA.

Water Education Foundation. (1999). *Proc., Colorado River project symposium*, Sacramento, CA.

Young, R. A. (1995). "Coping with a severe sustained drought on the Colorado River: introduction and overview." *Water Resour. Bull.*, 31(5), 779-788.

AUTHOR INFORMATION

Charles W. Howe, professor emeritus of economics at the University of Colorado-Boulder and director emeritus and currently faculty research associate at the Environment and Behavior Program, Institute of Behavioral Science, University of Colorado-Boulder, has focused his research on environmental and natural resource economics with an emphasis on water resources, including water resources development, water rights, and river basin and watershed management. He frequently contributed his expertise in water issues as a consultant in the United States and overseas. Email: Charles.Howe@Colorado.edu

Chapter 11

Water Resources Policy: Foundation, Evolution, and Future

Warren Viessman and Elizabeth M. Perez

ABSTRACT

This chapter summarizes the development and evolution of four decades of water resources policy in the United States, offers a view of what would be desirable in the future, and suggests actions that we can take to get to that future. The foundation of US water resources policy is based on the need for humans to develop safe water sources and, over the past 40 years, has been implemented through the use of environmental regulations. Water resources policy planning and analyses now regularly include the integration of water, land, and air considerations. Current water resources policy substantially impacts our ecological, economical, financial, and social systems as well as our public health. These impacts will only become more pronounced in the future. It is thus critical that future policy continue to become more efficient, integrated, sustainable, and transparent.

"It must be a mirage! Agencies agreeing with each other?"

FOUNDATION

Policies for water, land, air, or other resources are courses of action flowing from legislative or other decision-making bodies. These policies are the foundation for all water resources planning and management actions and often affect large numbers of individuals. Usually, these decisions favor some and disfavor others.

Policy-making is a sequential process of identifying problems, searching for options, negotiating among contending stakeholders, and establishing a democratic forum to support resolution of the issue of concern. Basic negotiation requires knowing what outcome is desired and what outcomes will result from each option under consideration.

Water policy in spoken or written form most likely existed since prehistoric times. It may have resulted from the observation of cave dwellers who noted that lightening caused a tree to fall and dam a small stream. An incident like this would have created a reservoir of useful water and the subsequent allocation of this important resource.

Moving forward in time to the 19th century, reservoir construction took hold in the US as a major option for supplying water to thirsty citizens and for other traditional (beneficial) purposes. This continued until the late 1960s when the environmental era changed everything. New federal, state, and local governmental mandates were needed to address an array of emerging water-environment issues and to deal with widespread national support for environmental protection and restoration. As a result, water resources planners had to develop new scenarios embracing attributes of physical, biological, social, and monetary systems (Loucks and van Beek 2005).

> *Water resources planners have had to develop new scenarios embracing attributes of physical, biological, social, and monetary systems.*

Thus, from early in the 19th century through present, a host of water-related statutes and regulations have emerged to form the current patchwork of water policy. For a detailed history of federal water resources programs see Holmes (1972, 1979) and Viessman (2009). Since the 1800s, water resources planning and management have evolved from single purpose to multiple purpose to multiple objective, and finally to integrated water management (IWM). This is conceptually a preferred approach but can be difficult to implement. And while a number of agencies report that they are using it, their definitions of IWM vary considerably (Viessman and Feather 2006).

IWM is a holistic approach to water management that considers water, land and air. It features:

- Analyzing the right spatial and temporal dimensions of the problem (the "problemshed");
- Getting agreement from stakeholders on what should be achieved;

- Initiating and institutionalizing a broad water resources assessment and appraisal process;
- Forming collaborative coalitions of stakeholders—see Potomac River case study in Perez and Viessman (2009);
- Developing plausible forecasts for the future;
- Incorporating adaptive management;
- Monitoring option impacts (i.e., if you don't know what is happening, how can you determine if your policy is working?);
- Providing for stakeholder involvement (including non-governmental organizations (NGOs) in planning processes;
- Addressing the national infrastructure problem; and
- Providing for plan implementation.

Today, traditional water uses remain important, but environmental protection and restoration, ensuring safe drinking water, and providing aesthetic and recreational experiences compete equally for attention and funds.   Furthermore, the environmentally-conscious public is placing an increasing emphasis on water management practices with fewer structural components. The notion of continually striving to provide more water has been replaced with addressing an entire spectrum of environmental, social, and financial concerns.

"It must be a mirage! Stakeholders
agreeing with each other?"

FUTURE

Similar to so many issues the US is currently tackling, water resources policy is now at a critical tipping point. A number of regulations and techniques have been tested for over 40 years. Planners now know that they need to address the entire spectrum of environmental and water resources challenges. However, financing these efforts has become challenging and in many cases, stakeholders expect sophisticated solutions with minimal impacts to their quality of life. All of these constraints and expectations are now coupled with what is now a general acceptance of climate change and a need to adopt more sustainable approaches. There is also greater movement towards increased transparency and making water resources planning considerably more efficient. Perhaps all of our processes can now be described as being embedded in greater simplification and an urgent need to move beyond jargon and getting effective programs underway. Planners and policy-makers now need to bring these years of research and planning to fruition and effectively address and prepare for the future.

> *There is an urgent need to move beyond jargon and get effective water resources policies underway.*

Changes and issues in water resources policy over the next ten years, and perhaps beyond, will likely include:

- *Changes in forecasting*: Planning is about the future. It requires that we guess at what the future will be like. Current forecasting processes may be classified as extrapolation of trends in population and per capita water use, and integrated forecasting using unit use coefficients and disaggregation. Both methods imbed levels of uncertainty and are influenced by the past. It is perhaps time to consider the use of scenarios for developing alternatives. Scenarios are defined as plausible descriptions of the state of the future. They incorporate many features that traditional forecasts do not (new practices in urbanization and work-at-home practices, for example). They can offer a range of plausible futures that provide a different basis for determining water and other requirements (Langsdale 2008), but scenario development will require planning staffs that include futurists, those with the ability to imagine a series of plausible options for the future. A well-known futurist was Jules Verne, who wrote many scenarios that have since come to pass.

- *More efficient application of technology*: With the emergence of high-speed computers, we have at our command an extraordinary analytic capability. Unfortunately, institutionalized compartmentalization constrains our ability to explore alternatives that do not fit traditional political or institutional boundaries. This is a critical issue that will be addressed in the near future.

- *Climate change*: Most agree that now is the time to address climate change. We should consider what needs to be done to provide adequate water supplies at reasonable costs and to keep new land use developments out of harm's way, in addition to reducing the level of risk associated with those developments that already exist. We must encourage state and federal actions and support appropriation of funds for taking action now.

- *Sustainability*:   Sustainability criteria will be further imbedded in water resource plans. This will require changes in how we think about the future and how we develop and use water.   The crux of sustainable development is forecasting impacts on future generations of actions taken today. It is difficult enough to forecast what the future population will be, but that pales in comparison to the need to forecast what future residents will want their environment to be like. For example, would planners in the early 20th century have been able to forecast the wishes of residents of the 1980s regarding restoring the Everglades ecosystem to something more like the original system (Loucks and van Beek 2005)?

- *Clash of values*: A process for dealing effectively with the clash of values between those interested in economic development and those concerned with environmental protection and restoration must be designed. The result of such conflict is often stagnation and failure to arrive at an acceptable course of action. The problem is partially created by the inability to quantify many environmental benefits monetarily. Perhaps it is time to put aside what seems to be an impossible task and instead focus on what it is that the parties involved want to happen. If that can be agreed upon, then both sides could spend their energies trying to identify alternatives that offer something for each of them. Such an approach could increase the likelihood of a successful outcome. It eliminates the argument of economic values and puts the effort on finding common ground.

- *Institutional reform*: Compartmentalized approaches used by institutions today will be modified to support analyses and actions that recognize the true temporal and spatial dimensions of identified problems. Water resource planners will likely catalog existing institutional constraints up-front and identify those that could likely be changed and those that could not. Experimentation with scenarios with and without these constraints could be considered in developing alternatives. If the outcomes without some of the identified constraints are found to be attractive, such information could be used in efforts to relax some binding conditions. Non-conventional analyses may also divulge solutions worth considering.

- *Assessments*:   A new federal institution for assessing and coordinating national interests in water resources planning and management might be considered. The institution should have the authority to: (1) analyze and propose federal water policy, (2) assist in coordinating the activities of federal, state, and regional water planning agencies, (3) assess the status of national and global water resources, (4) provide foresight capability, and (5) identify needed water research. The institution should also have authority to stimulate and facilitate regional water resources initiatives. There is a rationale for having the new institution attached to the White House in a manner similar to that of the Council on Environmental Policy that was formed by the National Environmental Policy Act of 1969. There should be representation from federal agencies, states and NGOs.

- *Experimentation*: Water resources planning institutions (or some other institution) might be given the authority to experiment with the development of alternatives external to their usual planning demarcation. We are not going to uncover the advantages of problemshed analyses if we do not explore them. The potential for payoff in doing this has been demonstrated by the solution to the water supply problem of the Washington DC metropolitan area. The Washington DC metropolitan area project used an emerging type of planning that facilitated collaboration and an expedient resolution to D.C.'s urgent water supply needs. This analysis illustrated that multi-objective regional-scale water supply planning is possible and can be successful if executed properly (Viessman and Welty 1985).

- *Outcome assessment*: Impact analysis will be further imbedded in planning and management practices. We need to know what we get when we choose a particular option. Armed with that information, we can adapt our designs and practices accordingly.

- *Choice of "problemsheds:"* Water resources planning will further focus on river basins, watersheds, or "problemsheds." Planning institutions might be designed "bottom-up" to reflect the needs and features of the area to be served. Concerned citizens, local governments, representatives of federal and state agencies and NGOs could be directly involved. Planners would have authority to conduct assessments, suggest relevant policies and identify alternative strategies for meeting plausible future scenarios.

- *Education*: Universities could revise their water-related research and education programs so that they meet the needs of those engaged professionally in water resources planning and management. They have an obligation to graduate students who are qualified to fill the voids in state and federal water planning agencies created by retirement and other staff losses. Education is important. Scientists and engineers of tomorrow must be society-wise as well as technology-wise. For example, engineers and scientists should receive more academic training in social perspectives, emotional intelligence, and the history of environmental justice.

- *Collaborative research*: University-agency research will be more collaborative. Academicians must become full partners in applied research if their efforts are to be effective. Research projects could be designed to contribute to the body of knowledge needed by water resources practitioners.

Relevant research topics include: the functioning of natural systems, the nature of social processes, forecasting goals of future generations, analytical tool development, design and management of information systems, and the development of new technologies.

CONCLUSIONS

The structured and compartmentalized approach to water resources policy has evolved over the past 40 years. Both the general public and water resources policy-makers now recognize that our thoughts on the environment, water, and sustainability have brought us to a place where transparency and urgent action are needed. Based on these lessons, it is believed that 21st century water resources professionals will:

- Drive policy making, not be driven by it.
- More accurately assess prevailing views of stakeholders and decision–makers, but still remain grounded in sound science and technology.
- Identify options that society will accept and that are better than the status quo even if they are inferior to a so-called "optimal" plan. Positive incremental gains may be the way to go. Better forecasting methodologies will likely accompany this shift.
- Recognize the importance of the time line. At a meeting of the Universities Council on Water Resources in 2000, Daniel Bromley of the University of Wisconsin commented that "truth is at the moment." What will be the desires of future generations regarding water management? We don't have the answer, but we can and must take a guess. If we are to achieve the goal of sustainable water development, the impact on future generations of actions taken today must be based on forecasts of what society will want at some future time.
- Recognize that water resources planning for long-term projects (such as the Everglades restoration) should include a time-line analysis incorporating the potential occurrence of events similar to those that affected the integrity of the Lake Pontchartrain and Vicinity Hurricane Protection Project as a result of Hurricane Katrina. It is likely that other projects scheduled for development over long time frames may be subjected to many of these modifying influences. Taking this into consideration will add a new dimension to the planning process and it could raise important flags that may not be considered otherwise.
- Consider the true temporal and spatial dimensions of the entire "problemshed." Attention should be placed on shifts in actors and events over time, funding shifts, policy maker changes, and changes in the attitudes of society.
- Develop more consistency in state, regional, and local planning objectives and processes.
- Develop strong, effective leadership through the development of objective, imaginative, and interdisciplinary planning teams. Diversity of thought and non-structural solutions will be more heavily valued.

- Further institutionalize IWM or a similar approach that involves holistic, adaptive policy in the future.
- Develop educational programs that are a means to the desired end—more collaborative research will likely result.

It is now clear that many aspects of water resources policy were and are effective. However, significant work remains. Policy-makers and planners now need to combine the many lessons learned over the past 40 years with the best emerging methodologies and technologies to address the important challenges that lay ahead. This task is not an easy one but the foundation of water resources policy has provided significant insight into the strengths of integration, adaptation, transparency, and perhaps most importantly, simple action.

REFERENCES

Holmes, B. H. (1972). *A history of federal water resources programs 1800-1960.* Miscellaneous Publication No. 1233, US Department of Agriculture, Washington, DC.

Holmes, B. H. (1979). *A history of federal water resources programs 1961-1970,* Miscellaneous Publication No. 1379, US Department of Agriculture, Washington, DC.

Langsdale, S. (2008). "Communication of climate change uncertainty in stakeholders using the scenario approach." *J. Contemp. Water Res. Educ.,* 140, 24-29.

Loucks, D. P., and van Beek, E. (2005). *Water resources systems planning and management: an introduction to methods, models and applications,* UNESCO Publishing, ISBN 92-3-13998-9, Paris, France.

Perez, E. M., and Viessman, Jr., W., eds. (2009). *The role of technology in water resources planning and management,* American Society of Civil Engineers, Reston, VA.

Viessman, Jr., W. (2009). "A history of the United States water resources planning and development." *The evolution of water resources planning and decision making,* C. S. Russell and D. D. Baumann, eds., Edward Elgar Publishers, Cheltenham, UK, 14-61.

Viessman, Jr., W., and Feather, T. D., eds. (2006). *State water resources planning in the United States,* American Society of Civil Engineers, Reston, VA.

Viessman, Jr., W., and Welty, C. (1985). *Water management: technology and institutions,* Harper & Row Publishers. New York, NY.

AUTHOR INFORMATION

Dr. Warren Viessman (deceased 2010) was a Professor Emeritus at the University of Florida. He received his Doctorate in Engineering from Johns Hopkins University. For over 50 years, Dr. Viessman published papers and books on a wide variety of water resources and environmental topics and won numerous awards for his involvement and dedication to the water resources community. He was a distinguished member of ASCE, an honorary member of the American Academy of

Water Resources Engineers, and a former president of the American Water Resources Association.

Ms. Elizabeth Perez received her MS in Civil Engineering from the Georgia Institute of Technology and her BS in Environmental Engineering from the University of Florida. She is a member of the American Academy of Water Resources Engineers, a Director-at-Large for the Florida Water Environment Association, and a co-author on the 8th Edition of the well-known textbook *Water Supply and Pollution Control.* Email: lizperez516-ec@yahoo.com

Chapter 12

Water Utilities Recognizing and Adapting to a 2050 Climate

Patricia Mulroy

ABSTRACT

As though challenges such as aging infrastructure, emerging contaminants and increasing water demand did not exert enough pressure on water managers, the implications of climate change have added an entirely new dimension to water utilities' planning calculus. This chapter examines the implications of climate change on water resource availability and water quality, as well as exploring strategies to help water agencies adapt to this new reality. The 2050 vision presented foresees an unprecedented integration of water resource and demand management policies that accounts for increased variability in climatic conditions, as well as a level of interagency collaboration presently considered by some to be unattainable. While the author's experience focuses on the American Southwest, the ramifications of climate change--and the application of mitigation strategies--are not confined to arid regions.

"Cooperation on the Lower Colorado River"

BACKGROUND

For nearly a decade, the American Southwest—including southern Nevada—has been mired in a severe drought. However, other parts of the country, including areas unaccustomed to prolonged water shortages, are enduring similar if not worse drought conditions. Texas went through one of its worst droughts on record in 2005 and 2006; the Southeast—including metropolitan Atlanta and much of Florida—also in recent years has experienced a drought so severe that many areas had but a few months of water supply on hand. Population growth in these Sunbelt regions, which until recently was robust, is no doubt contributing to water resource challenges. However, many leading climatologists believe global climate change is already affecting precipitation patterns.

While we do not completely know how climate change is affecting water resources, it is understood that water resources are already stressed due to a variety of factors, including population growth, point and non-point sources of waterborne pollutants, groundwater overdrafting and high system water losses due to aging infrastructure. While natural climate variability may be concealing the true effects of climate change on water resources, a warmer climate is expected to increase the frequency of severe and longer-lasting droughts and floods. As these variables increase, so too do their adverse impacts on existing water resources.

A VISION FOR 2050

By 2050 we will have a much better understanding of just how much climate is changing and the impacts of climate change on our water resources, how it is managed, and on aquatic ecosystems. Climate models will be providing relevant inputs to hydrologic models at relevant scales, and hydrologic models will be providing inputs to models used for planning and operating water resources infrastructure.

By 2050 water utilities will be managing complete watersheds. The management of groundwater aquifers, rivers and lakes will be done in an integrated manner, not separately and independently. Parochial attitudes prevalent in the water industry for decades will be replaced by an atmosphere of flexibility and cooperation. There will still be multiple agencies of government at all levels, and each will have its own authorities and responsibilities, but there will be a high degree of collaboration among them.

> *By 2050 water utilities will be managing complete watersheds in an integrated manner.*

By 2050 water utilities serving communities, both small and large, will have recognized just how vulnerable they may be in the face of extreme hydrological events. They will recognize that they can no longer consider themselves self-sufficient. Hence the need for cooperation among groups of utilities, sometimes involving transport of water from one region to another, will be fully understood, and agreements will be in place to allow this cooperation and collaboration when conditions warrant. In some sense this replaces the concept of large regional authorities, such as river basin commissions. Political boundaries still do not coincide with watershed or basin boundaries, but by 2050 this is not a problem because of the increased cooperation.

Water conservation measures and water reuse will be commonplace. For example, the use of sewers to carry wastes to regional wastewater treatment plants with drinking water quality water will be rare. Large city apartment buildings will have their own internal wastewater treatment systems. Most stormwater runoff basins will serve as recreation areas and road and parking lot pavements will allow water to enter the ground before running off to storm sewers. By 2050 we all will have recognized the major impact changes in land use and land cover have on our water resource demands and supplies, and utilities will be working closely with city and regional planners in the management of land use change.

GETTING TO THAT VISION OF 2050

Commensurate with the expanding threat of climate change are numerous challenges for water agencies across the United States, not the least of which is understanding what climate change is and developing a consensus about its impacts on domestic water supplies and water quality. Key to recognizing and quantifying the effects of climate change is assessing available scientific data and studies into the phenomenon. Despite all of the work that has been done in this realm in recent years, there still is a lack of reliable data that water managers can use to develop long-range climate models. Consolidation of existing data is needed to help build public support for infrastructure investment by water agencies to prepare for and insulate themselves against the long-term ramifications of climate change. Defining what exactly constitutes "climate change" and acknowledging its existence are critical for water utilities to take necessary subsequent action. For that to happen, coordinating the work of the disparate groups studying climate change is crucial.

Despite the scientific research and studies that have been done to date, more analysis is needed that will directly support water utilities' ability to grapple with climate change. Most notably, research into the geophysics of climate change—such as the causes and effects of glaciation and deglaciation, past and present sea-level change and evidence of past and future weather patterns—is, by and large, improving, but still relatively crude. Developing a streamlined approach to understanding climate change in turn could spur creation of a customized climate change predictor, which water utilities across the country could share to help them better assess their unique situations and develop responses to the threat posed by climate change.

Ultimately, interpretation of this information by water utilities will be critical for their combined successes and for engendering an understanding of the consequences and solutions. To address these questions, water utilities should begin thinking on a watershed basis - i.e., management of rivers and lakes should be done conjunctively and holistically rather than in a piecemeal fashion. Parochial attitudes prevalent in the water industry for decades must give way to an atmosphere of flexibility and cooperation. The era of "win-lose" management is over. The ability of water utilities to adapt to a global problem like climate change calls for a greater degree of collaboration among regional entities. Such partnerships strive for the common good and serve to end adversarial relationships and territorialism.

> **More analysis is needed that will directly support water utilities' ability to grapple with climate change.**

Some measures, such as regional or interstate agreements that are inherently time-intensive, can and should be taken early. An example is the cooperation and collaboration among entities in the Colorado River basin (SNWA 2009). Through a series of water-banking agreements and other exchanges, the three Lower Basin states—California, Arizona and Nevada—are addressing the ramifications of climate change and its role in prolonging the decade-long drought along the Colorado River. On a larger scale, relations between the Upper and Lower Basin states have improved as all of the entities involved recognized their mutual vulnerability and reached an accord to conjunctively manage the river's two primary reservoirs.

Another example of two municipalities working together in such collaboration is an agreement between the Metropolitan Water District of Southern California (MWD) and the Southern Nevada Water Authority (SNWA) on a water banking agreement. Under terms of the pact, the SNWA had available water it wanted to store as a drought reserve, while MWD needed additional Colorado River water to address a water supply shortfall resulting from cutbacks in in-state supplies. The two agencies approached each other in a spirit of cooperation, rather than as resource competitors, and worked together to meet their mutual needs in a creative manner.

A more recent agreement among Nevada, California and Arizona led to the creation of the Drop 2 Reservoir by the US Bureau of Reclamation. The Drop 2 project, approved as one of a series of pacts related to Colorado River drought management, calls for all three states to receive a specified quantity of water in exchange for financing construction of the federal reservoir, which was developed to improve Colorado River storage below Parker Dam and to capture non-storable flows for use in the United States. An important regulatory aspect of this agreement is that a portion of the water conserved through this project is reserved for the Colorado River system, rather than a specific water user, which helps to maintain water levels in the system's two primary reservoirs, Lake Powell and Lake Mead, for everyone's benefit.

Cities in the Southwest have a more established record of accomplishment of water resource management than those in other regions, in part due to their acclimation to dry conditions. Still, climate change-induced variations in weather patterns continue to render old assumptions obsolete. Consequently, water managers throughout the region are rethinking the methods they currently use to address the stresses on water supplies while building flexibility into their systems to provide a quick response to changing conditions. This approach to planning should enable water managers to better adapt to the uncertain effects of climate change, while better equipping them to address existing climate variables.

Collaborative efforts such as these should be of particular interest to coastal zones and other areas long insulated from the effects of climate change on their water supplies. In these locations, water utilities must adapt their response strategies to climate change based on their unique circumstances. For example, forecasts for more precipitation in higher latitudes and the tropics call for responses predicated on the need for reservoir management and flood control. And in coastal areas—particularly in Florida—these issues are compounded by salt water intrusion into groundwater aquifers caused by rising sea levels resulting from glacial melting and expansion of water from higher temperatures, a potentially devastating prospect from a water resource perspective.

In short, water managers in areas that typically are subject to frequent and prolonged drought should move forward with measures to address climate change as a matter of course. Meanwhile, water managers in areas that typically are subject to higher levels of precipitation and flooding—those in the Mississippi River watershed, for example—should move ahead with similar "no regrets" strategies. Utilities should consider building projects based on the near-term effects of climate change and almost certain increases in population, as these predictions are more precise than long-range forecasts (which require such responses as footprint reduction, diversification, etc.).

Vulnerability Assessments
Water utilities should pursue the same course of action in evaluating the vulnerability of their water resource options to climate change. Over-reliance upon a single water resource for a municipal supply poses great risks to utilities and their customers. An example is Lake Mead, the country's largest manmade reservoir, which for many years was considered drought-proof. However, after nearly a decade of drought, the lake has lost millions of cubic meters (trillions of gallons) of water; meanwhile, Las Vegas and its nearly 2 million residents rely on this resource for 90 percent of its municipal supply. Consequently, the SNWA is accelerating work on developing hydrologically independent, non-Colorado River water supplies.

The problem is not limited to the historically dry Southwest. Atlanta has seen its reliance on Lake Lanier tested as that reservoir's levels continue to drop. States surrounding the Great Lakes are witnessing unforeseen declines in water levels in the lakes that hold 84 percent of the country's fresh water reserves. In light of these unanticipated occurrences, utilities with water resource planning responsibilities should analyze their water sources' vulnerabilities to shortage given changing climate conditions. By initiating the process immediately, water utilities should have sufficient time to take the steps necessary to ensure a reliable water supply since these changing climate conditions are mid- to long-term in nature.

Water utilities can and must begin planning their adaptation measures based on best-available information, which drives operating assumptions and prioritization of climate-change responses that could dramatically hinder their ability to provide critical services. Simultaneously, water providers should resist limiting their analyses to development of additional infrastructure needed to counter the effects of climate change, and should also consider what impacts rising temperatures have on their existing facilities.

> *Utilities with water resource planning responsibilities should analyze their system's vulnerability to changing climate and demand conditions.*

Adaptation Strategies

In the growing Southwest, an expanding population base absorbs a significant amount of capital expenditures, meaning that infrastructure investment might be more economically viable and pose less of an encumbrance to ratepayers. However, in areas of the country experiencing minimal or even negative growth—and in those served by small- and mid-sized providers—a shrinking revenue stream means that water utilities are struggling to replace or upgrade their infrastructure. As a result, the challenge of climate change could lead to increased financial strains that some communities may be unable to endure.

Meanwhile, the federal government is beginning to incorporate climate change into National Environmental Policy Act (NEPA) documents. NEPA regulations now accommodate scientific uncertainty, address cumulative impacts and require consideration of "reasonably foreseeable" effects, including changes to the environment caused by climate change, and contributions to climate change by the proposed action and its alternatives. While recognition of this issue is not a recent occurrence—the 1997 Council on Environmental Quality draft guidelines called for consideration of climate change in NEPA documents, notably the agencies' "programmatic" environmental impact statements—the issue's recent prominence could have significant legal and permitting ramifications for water managers well into the future.

At the same time, water managers should not dismiss or ignore environmental issues when determining a course of action. Instead, they should investigate what opportunities are available to them when developing strategies to confront climate change. In addition, water managers—indeed, the public as well—should avoid the myopic focus on attribution of the root cause of climate change. Ultimately, debates about who is responsible for climate change do little more than create an excuse for inaction. Irrespective of cause, climate change has the unprecedented potential to have a profound effect on the regional water supplies of the world, including their spatial and temporal distributions.

While some actions, such as infrastructure investment, may be deemed premature by some managers, other steps—such as investment in renewable energy and conservation—are not. For instance, water efficiency measures are critical based upon the nexus to electrical energy; because water and wastewater utilities are leading consumers of electricity, they have a significant opportunity to impact energy use. Additionally, these same utilities can influence energy providers by supporting the development and deployment of renewable energy resources. By working closely with state and federal agencies on efforts to increase investments in this area, water utilities have an opportunity to send a clear message to producers of electricity that renewable sources are desirable. Certainly cost considerations must be factored into the equation; however, only greater adoption and implementation of renewable energy will serve as a catalyst to spark investment that will lay the foundation for the long-term economic feasibility of those sources.

If water agencies choose to take such a course of action, they should begin by completing a comprehensive appraisal of their total energy use and emissions, in order to quantify the environmental loading that can be attributed to the organization. For instance, the SNWA's primary source of emissions is the massive amounts of electrical energy needed to treat and pump water throughout the region's infrastructure. Emissions from fleet vehicles and those associated with day-to-day energy use at various facilities also should be included in the audit. After identifying these and other factors, and subtracting energy derived from renewable resources, analysts can calculate the SNWA's total net annual greenhouse gas (GHG) contributions. This resulting figure would then be used as a baseline from which emission reductions can be measured.

Utilities also can bring to bear great influence over water demand as a way to decrease electrical consumption. By reducing customer demand through a variety of innovative water-efficiency programs, water utilities can effectively reduce their carbon footprints, since the bulk of their energy demand goes toward treating and delivering water.

In 2003, the SNWA responded to the continued and worsening drought on the Colorado River by leading a comprehensive community-wide conservation initiative. As a result of these efforts, Colorado River consumption by Southern Nevada was about 75 million cubic meters (26 billion gallons) less in 2009 than in 2002, despite a population increase of 400,000 during that span.

In addition, even as many in the community celebrated the initiative's success in reducing water consumption, few noticed how the program helped to reduce the amount of energy the SNWA needed to draw, treat and deliver water to customers— and which, in turn, reduced the utility's GHG emissions. Using the 2001 per capita consumption rate as a benchmark, avoided water deliveries cumulatively totaled almost one billion cubic meters (more than 800,000 acre-feet) during that decade, reducing the amount of energy that would have otherwise been required for water treatment and conveyance by nearly 17 million megawatt hours. This equates to a carbon equivalent of almost 715,000 metric tons that were not contributed to the environment as a result of water conservation activities. Based on those results, it is easy to see how the SNWA initiative serves as an example of methods water utilities around the country can implement to achieve cumulative energy-use and GHG reductions through comprehensive water-efficiency programs.

CONCLUSION

Taken individually, none of the effects associated with climate change poses an insurmountable challenge to well-prepared water managers and agencies. However, taken as a whole, they become significantly more daunting. As aging infrastructure brings asset management and reinvestment to the center stage nationally, the idea of being compelled to devote resources to several climate change-induced problems simultaneously is less than appealing. Similarly, in water-rich areas, aggressive pursuit of revenue-reducing conservation programs highlights the inherent conflict between water efficiency and financial pressures.

There is little doubt that climate change will have a dramatic effect on the affected organizations and communities for years to come. Acknowledging this reality and enacting the appropriate adaptation and mitigation measures will be critical to weathering the unprecedented storm that looms on the horizon.

REFERENCES

Southern Nevada Water Authority (SNWA). (2009). *Water resource plan 09*, SNWA, Las Vegas, NV, <http://www.snwa.com/assets/pdf/wr_plan.pdf> (Feb, 2010).

AUTHOR INFORMATION

Patricia Mulroy oversees the operations of the Southern Nevada Water Authority and the Las Vegas Valley Water District. She joined the Water District more than 20 years ago and began serving as its general manager in 1989. She was a principal architect of the Water Authority, which has served as a model for other Western water agencies since its creation in 1991. Mulroy serves on the boards of the Association of Metropolitan Water Agencies, the National Water Resources Association and the Water Research Foundation. Email: pat.mulroy@lvvwd.com

Chapter 13

Water 2050: Attributes of Sustainable Water Supply Development

Edward G. Means III

ABSTRACT

There are fundamental trends at work today that will significantly impact mid-century provision of adequate supplies of safe drinking water in the developed world. This chapter describes some of the trends that will drive a water supply and governance paradigm shift. Five key drivers will shape the 2050 world of water: demographics, water supply constraints, rising water costs, growing energy/water nexus, and regional collaboration. These water utility drivers will require changes in infrastructure, finance, environment, community and workforce. Because each water utility has its own unique attributes (related to geography, financial base and social setting) the pace of transition to this new world will vary accordingly.

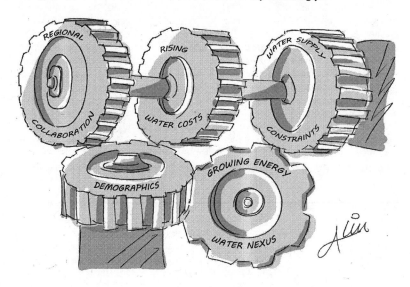

KEY DRIVERS

Five key drivers (supported by multiple secondary drivers) will shape the 2050 world of water. These are demographics, water supply constraints, rising water costs, growing energy/water nexus, and regional collaboration. These water utility drivers will require changes in infrastructure, finance, environment, community and workforce.

> *Demographics, water supply constraints, rising water costs,*
> *growing energy/water nexus, and regional collaboration will*
> *shape the 2050 world of water.*

Demographics

Population growth will exacerbate water supply conflicts. World population growth is projected to increase from 6.9 billion in 2010 to 9.1 billion in 2050 according to the Population Division of the Department of Economic and Social Affairs of the United Nations Secretariat (2009). The majority of that growth will be in less developed countries. In the absence of greater conservation, the planet will require an approximate 30% increase in water supply (or reduction in per capita water use) to accommodate that growth. In many areas this increase must come from already water-stressed environments and will come at great economic and environmental cost. Countries or regions where population contraction is occurring will face shrinking rate bases and escalating costs for repair and rehabilitation of existing water infrastructure.

In the US, population will rise from 318 million (projected for 2010) to 404 million in 2050. Much of this growth continues to be forecast to occur in the southern and western US, areas that are already facing water supply shortages. Ironically, water supplies in some of the same areas are expected to be disproportionately impacted by climate change. Continued development of watersheds will contribute contaminant loading to water sources. Shifts from agricultural to urban land uses will also change the nature of the contaminant loading.

Supply Constraints

Conflicts over water supply have been a fixture in world politics for centuries. Gleick (2009) placed these conflicts in various categories: Control of Water Resources, Military Tool, Political Tool, Terrorism, Military Target and Development Disputes. These "traditional" conflicts will be exacerbated by climate change.

The Colorado River basin continues to be in a decade-long drought (USBR 2009), population growth in the west will continue (Campbell 1996) and climate change will increase temperatures and, in many areas, increase water demands (Field et al. 2007). Through 2025 the West is projected to grow at nearly twice the national average. From 1995 to 2025 California alone is projected to add 17.7 million people (56 percent growth). The first eight of the fastest growing U.S. states are western states.

According to the International Panel on Climate Change (IPCC) (Field et al. 2007), by late in the 21st century, projected annual warming is likely to be 2-3°C across the western, southern, and eastern continental edges of North America, but more than 5°C at high latitudes. The projected warming is greatest in the winter at high latitudes and greatest in the summer in the Southwest US. Warm extremes across North America are projected to become both more frequent and longer.

Forty-one percent of the water supply to southern California is likely to be vulnerable to warming from loss of Sierra Nevada and Colorado River basin snowpack. Additionally, April 1 snow water equivalent (SWE) has declined 15-30% since 1950 in the western mountains of North America, particularly at lower elevations and primarily due to warming rather than changes in precipitation. Streamflow peaks in the snowmelt-dominated western mountains of the US occurred one to four weeks earlier in 2002 than in 1948 (Field et al. 2007).

In other parts of the US and in the world, this pattern will be repeated. While not discussed here, there will be "climate change winners" from the water supply standpoint. Areas where precipitation increases will be awash in water, creating other problems (like flood management and combined sewer overflow challenges).

Impacts to surface water resources will also affect aquatic ecosystems and the regulatory systems that have been developed to protect them. Streams and rivers deemed impaired under the Clean Water Act will be further challenged under climate change stress. Seasonal flow reductions and their impacts on species will further complicate the development of traditional surface water supplies in many areas. At some point, these systems will be effectively "off-limits" to development as we struggle to recover species.

In water supply and climate stressed areas, 2050 water supply will have to evolve from heavy reliance on traditional surface supplies to increasing reliance on:

1. Managing water demand through water demand and water loss management: We will either store more water in the ground and behind off-stream dams or we will desalinate seawater.
2. Effectively managing groundwater supplies: Where surface supplies are inadequate, groundwater replenishment strategies (conjunctive use of surface and ground supplies) may be seriously affected. Increased salinity of surface water supplies may further complicate groundwater conjunctive use,
3. Managing what crops are grown where and transferring water from low value uses to high value uses (these policies will be hotly debated): The water intensity of crops will be carefully scrutinized,
4. Recycling water (and aggressive salt management),
5. Recovering impaired water supplies (e.g. brackish groundwater, contaminated groundwater, etc.), and
6. Desalinating seawater.

Rising Costs

The heavy water use that characterized the late 20th century will be a costly lifestyle in 2050 in many parts of the US. The public in 2050 will "value water" (ironically answering the lamentations of the 20th century water managers that the public doesn't value water). This new-found appreciation will develop as the price of water rises dramatically through the early part of the 21st century. It will also develop as the public begins to understand the linkages between water use, energy and environmental (aquatic ecosystem) health. These rising costs will be driven by:

- Drought
- Rising energy costs (in part driven by reductions in relatively inexpensive hydro electricity generation due to climate induced hydrologic changes)
- Rising utility labor costs
- Repair and replacement of existing infrastructure, much of which was built in decades past
- Development of costly new incremental supplies including water recycling, contaminated water recovery, and brackish and ocean desalination
- Lower water sales through conservation in a high fixed-cost utility environment.

It is easy to imagine coastal areas becoming home to large desalination plants that exchange water with upstream mega-cities (e.g., Phoenix, Denver, Atlanta, etc.). Agricultural water use will continue as national food security will remain important, but there will likely be a shift to high value/less water intensive crops that can still be grown profitably with more expensive water.

In 2009, the average US household spends less on both monthly water and wastewater bills than on bills for phone, television, high speed internet and electricity (AWWA and Raftelis Financial 2006; The WhiteFence Index 2009). Water is a comparative bargain today, but that will change by 2050.

> *Water is a comparative bargain today, but that will change by 2050.*

Fisher et al. (2006) examined water and sewer rates obtained from several national surveys and concluded that water and wastewater rates are rising faster than the rate of inflation. From 1996 to 2004 the average water rate increased 39.5 percent, average wastewater rate increased 37.8 percent, and the Consumer Price Index (CPI) for all urban areas increased 20.1 percent (Fisher et al. 2006); collectively water and wastewater rates are rising at about double the CPI.

With upward pressure on water system supply and operations and maintenance costs, it is easy to imagine average water rates doubling within the next 10 years. Beyond, water and wastewater costs will likely outstrip our other utility costs with the possible exception of electricity costs (both will be driven by the increase in the cost of supply development, infrastructure development and environmental mitigation). The conservation message that rising rates will send will be significant. Landscaping will inexorably evolve to drought tolerant/native landscaping except for consumers that are willing to pay a large premium to water non-native water intensive landscaping. To this end, water budget-based rates will become the norm in 2050 to reward low water use and discourage heavy water use. Cost sensitive and water intensive industry may well move to areas of the country where water costs are low.

Energy/Water Nexus
Water conservation will be driven from several perspectives including:
- Pressure to reduce water use for aquatic environmental reasons,
- Pressure to reduce water use to reduce energy use, cost, and greenhouse gas emissions, and
- Price elasticity effects –as costs rise, demand will be pressured downward.

Since energy is a substantial portion of the operating budgets of water utilities, cost pressure due to rising rates will continue to drive utilities to be more energy efficient. The US Environmental Protection Agency (USEPA) estimates that 3% of national energy consumption, equivalent to approximately 56 billion kilowatt hours (kWh), is used for drinking water and wastewater services. Assuming the average mix of energy sources in the country, this equates to adding approximately 41 million metric tons of greenhouse gas to the atmosphere. While water and wastewater utilities are minor direct contributors to national greenhouse gas emissions (USEPA 2010), the water and wastewater facilities account for up to 35 percent of municipal energy usage (Consortium for Energy Efficiency 2009). Studies have estimated the energy savings potential at 15-30 percent, which translates into as much as 31 billion kWh. Since facilities operate 24 hours a day, the potential to reduce peak demand is also a significant factor.

By 2050, cost pressures will have driven utilities to optimizing energy efficiency. Energy recovery from the distribution system will be standard practice and utilities will use their alternative energy assets (land for wind and solar installations) to maximum advantage. They will either do so themselves or contract to private energy developers to help them develop alternative energy.

Regional Collaboration
The luxury of independence will fade as consumers demand more from public institutions. Economies of scale will become increasingly apparent and harder to ignore. For example, there are approximately 155 thousand public water systems in the US. Each has its own billing system, governance structure, operating and maintenance standards, water quality objectives, energy efficiencies, human resources management, administration, etc. These systems necessarily developed as the country developed, often around the availability of a substantial and high quality local water supply. Now, many of these population centers have essentially grown together creating contiguous systems and using regional resources (power, materials, labor, water, etc.). The power of the historical arguments for maintaining "sovereignty" may well diminish as the benefit of working together and leveraging resources grows.

The cost of repair and replacement of infrastructure (especially for smaller systems) and the rate increases necessary to support such costs will encourage utilities to seek cost reducing collaborations (including regionalization of utilities). Thirty years ago it was difficult to imagine the megalopolises that have developed in southern California, southern Arizona, the front range of the Rocky Mountains and in numerous other urban/suburban corridors today. Fast-forward to 2050 under current population projections and the rationale for separate water systems will be weaker yet. We will witness the battle between "local control" versus efficient use of public capital unfold in a context of high water rates.

Collaboration among utilities is already quite common. It includes such activities as financial contribution to research foundations, establishment of emergency response networks, sharing of best practices, development of cooperative procurement systems, sharing of workforce training, cooperating on water sampling networks, and others. This trend will accelerate as financial pressures and population growth underscore the value of collaboration.

WATER SUSTAINABILITY IN 2050

From the water utility perspective, 2050 sustainability can be viewed through five broad "lenses:"

- Infrastructure – Planning, constructing, operating and maintaining infrastructure to optimize the useful life of water facilities,
- Finance – Having sufficient financial capacity to sustain capital investment and operations of the utility while providing affordable water to the community,
- Community – Managing the utility to reflect the needs and values of the stakeholders that depend on the utility for their quality of life,
- Environment – Minimizing or mitigating the direct and indirect impact of the water utility on the natural environment, and
- Workforce – Establishing workplace systems, practices and policies that create a workplace environment that motivates and retains talented people.

Table 13-1 summarizes some of the sustainability implications of these drivers.

Table 13-1: Utility Drivers for Sustainability

2050 Utility Drivers	Implications for Key Sustainability Drivers				
	Infrastructure	Finance	Environment	Community	Workplace
Demographics	Population growth will drive expansion, repair and replacement in some geographies and population contraction will accelerate higher rate increases in shrinking areas.	Growing areas will expand rate bases, contracting areas will see upward pressure on rates.	Source water quality degradation will require greater controls on development and fertilizer/pesticide use.	Densification and urbanization will create challenges and opportunities for community engagement.	Development of scientists and engineers will be a priority for water utilities as will retention and recruitment.
Water supply constraints	Shifts in resource mix will generate different infrastructure needs. Brine lines and salt removal technologies will be increasingly needed. Water conservation will minimize infrastructure expansion.	Water budget based rate structures will prevail (even in "water rich" areas). Water will be more expensive than other household utilities.	Pressure on natural ecosystems will drive efforts to minimize our water footprint. Mitigation for environmental effects of current water projects will be required.	The public will be sensitive to water as a resource. Native landscaping will prevail. Per capita water use will drop dramatically.	Skill sets related to advanced treatment technology, community outreach and automation will be prized.
Rising water costs	Utilities will be expert at linking infrastructure benefits to the required costs/rates.	Rate structures will be based on full cost of service with powerful incentives for sutainable water use.	Ensuring that water use minimizes impacts on the environment will be a key cost driver.	Political "push back" on rising water rates will require deft communication skills of utility managers.	Pressure for cost containment in utility operations will grow. Automation to reduce labor costs will be optimized and leverage new technologies.
Growing energy/water nexus	Energy and chemical intensive infrastructure (e.g. treatment) will be carefully scrutinized. Life cycle costing will be standard practice.	Energy costs will rise. Water utilities will maximize assets for alternative energy generation.	Alternative energy projects will be standard aspects of new water infrastructure development. Greenhouse gas offsets will be required for new water infrastructure and operations.	The public will understand the relationship between energy and water costs and the value of water.	Energy efficiency in utility design and operations will be a priority.
Regionalization	Consolidation and increasing levels of cooperation in development of regional infrastructure will be required.	Collaboration on financing of regional infrastructure will be necessary.	Regional water planning will become the norm.	The public will question the efficiency of fragmented service provision. Rising costs will force examination of mergers/consolidations among adjacent water utilities.	Pressures to operate efficiently will lead to regional billing systems, administration and sharing of call center functions, maintenance centers, etc.

CONCLUSIONS

The water utility societal charge to provide high quality and adequate supplies to sustain community-defined quality of life will remain unchanged in 2050. Water utilities will become sustainable because, almost by definition, they have to – they are too important to our communities. However, they may look quite different in 2050 as economic and environmental pressures shift and optimize their business models (forcing consolidation and greater regional collaboration) and operations, and new sources of supply (and the technology to deliver it) command their attention. Conservation will be a core water supply strategy for all utilities regardless of location. Leaving as much water in our natural systems as possible will be a societal goal.

REFERENCES

American Water Works Association (AWWA) and Raftelis Financial. (2006). *2006 water and wastewater rate survey*, AWWA, Denver, CO.

Campbell, P. R. (1996). *Population projections for states by age, sex, race, and Hispanic origin: 1995 to 2025*, US Bureau of the Census, <http://www.census.gov/population/www/projections/ppl47.html> (Jul, 2009).

Consortium for Energy Efficiency. (2009). *Industrial programs: national municipal water and wastewater facility initiative*, <http://www.cee1.org/ind/mot-sys/ww/ww.php3> (Jul, 2009).

Field, C. B., Mortsch, L. D., Brklacich, M., Forbes, D. L., Kovacs, P., Patz, J. A., Running, S. W., and Scott, M., J. (2007). "North America." *Climate change 2007: impacts, adaptation and vulnerability. Contribution of working group II to the fourth assessment report of the Intergovernmental Panel on Climate Change*, M. L. Parry, O. F. Canziani, J. P. Palutikof, P. J. van der Linden, and C. E. Hanson, eds., Cambridge University Press, Cambridge, UK, 617-652, <http://www.ipcc.ch/pdf/assessment-report/ar4/wg2/ar4-wg2-chapter14.pdf> (Aug, 2010).

Fisher, D. C.,Whitehead, C. D., and Melody, M. (2006). *National and regional water and wastewater rates for use in cost-benefit models and evaluations of water efficiency programs*, Lawrence Berkeley National Laboratory, University of California, Berkeley, CA.

Gleick, P. R. (2009). *Water conflict chronology*, Pacific Institute for Studies in Development, Environment, and Security, <http://www.worldwater.org/conflict/> (Nov, 2009).

Population Division of the Department of Economic and Social Affairs of the United Nations Secretariat. (2009). *World population prospects: the 2008 revision*, United Nations, New York, NY, <www.un.org/esa/population/publications/wpp2008/wpp2008_highlights.pdf > (Jul, 2009).

The WhiteFence Index. (2009). *Compare utility & essential home services prices among top U.S. cities*, < http://www.whitefenceindex.com/> (Jul, 2009)

US Bureau of Reclamation (USBR). (2009). *Drought monitor*, <http://www.drought.unl.edu/dm/monitor.html> (Jul, 2009).
USEPA (2010). Inventory of U.S. greenhouse gas emissions and sinks: 1990 – 2008. EPA 430-R-10-006. Washington, DC. http://epa.gov/climatechange/emissions/downloads10/US-GHG-Inventory-2010_Report.pdf (Aug, 2010).

AUTHOR INFORMATION

Edward G. Means III is a Vice President with Malcolm Pirnie, Inc., a subsidiary of ARCADIS, NV. He holds a Bachelors and Masters degree from University of California Irvine in Social Ecology with an emphasis in environmental analysis. He is author of over 100 articles and two books on water resources, water quality and utility management. He was the principal investigator for two Water Research Foundation projects related to a Strategic Assessment of the Future of Water Utilities. Mr. Means has received awards from AWWA, AMWA, and NWRA for his work. Email: emeans@pirnie.com

Chapter 14

Flood Risk Management in 2050

Gerald Galloway

ABSTRACT

Today the United States faces increasing annual flood damages. Climate change and sea level rise will only exacerbate this problem. In spite of over 74 years of flood control and 42 years of floodplain management, the challenge continues. We cannot control floods or even focus on simply reducing damages, but rather must identify and manage our growing flood risks. Over the next 40 years, if action is not taken to deal with the problem, it will grow substantially worse. Climate change, population growth, unbridled development in hazardous areas, and a lack of personal responsibility on the part of individuals subject to flooding will lead to an untenable situation by the middle of the 21st century. With attention to these opportunities, the American floodplain of the future can be far different than it is today. Civil engineers are at the nexus of this challenge and must take on the task of ensuring that the floodplain of 2050 is sustainably developed and managed. This chapter provides a positive vision of how the floodplains of 2050 might appear if appropriate measures are taken by governments and the public at large in the years ahead. It is based on the results of the 2007 Association of State Floodplain Managers Foundation Gilbert F. White National Flood Policy Forum that examined this topic.

"Sustainable Floodplain Development"

YEARS OF FLOODS

Floods have been a constant part of American history. Early eastern colonists battled overflows from the Delaware River into nearby agricultural lands. At the start of the 18th century, the founders of New Orleans initiated levee building to protect their growing city. Over time, as the nation moved to the west, it established its towns and cities alongside rivers, the principal highways for movement of goods and people. As these new communities grew, they had to address the problems of periodic flooding. By the middle of the 19th century, the federal government began to take limited actions to reduce flood losses, and, as the 20th century began, it actively assisted states and municipalities in dealing with the flood challenge. Major floods in 1927 and 1936 caused Congress to reevaluate the federal role and legislate a national approach to flooding that would drive federal and state efforts for the rest of the 20th century. The Flood Control Act of 1936 defined the method by which engineers would address flooding - *control* the waters by keeping them off the land, storing them behind dams, and speeding them to the oceans through channel works and floodways. Acts of 1928 and 1936 targeted at the lower Mississippi Valley were focused on preventing disasters - no more destructive flooding. These acts led to the construction of large systems such as the Mississippi River and Tributaries project that still protects the lower Mississippi Valley from Cairo, Illinois to the Gulf of Mexico against inundation, as well as countless smaller projects designed to protect individual communities, agricultural areas, and critical infrastructure.

The environmental movement of the 1960s, coupled with the growing knowledge of the work of the University of Chicago geographer Gilbert F. White, who focused on adjusting human use of the floodplain to avoid flood losses as opposed to protecting humans in the floodplain from flooding, began to slow down the construction of large flood control structures and to seek alternative approaches - nonstructural methods - to deal with flooding. These methods included land-use controls to prevent unwise development in the floodplain, floodproofing and elevation of structures, acquisition of most frequently flooded lands, use of natural storage of flood waters in upstream wetlands and the development of early warning systems to permit timely evacuation of flood hazard areas. In 1968, Congress established the National Flood Insurance Program (NFIP) to sell previously unavailable insurance to those at risk in the floodplain. Today over 20,000 communities and more than 5.7 million policyholders participate in the program.

In 1993, the Midwest was devastated by massive flooding that took 38 lives and caused over $16 billion in damages in eight Midwestern states. Because the flooding was extensive (water remained in homes and on the land in some places for over six months) the nation was exposed through media coverage to the devastation and human trauma that resulted from this flood. Calls for action in Congress and by the Administration led to a White House study of the flood's causes and the development of recommendations to deal with future such events. The Interagency Floodplain Management Review Committee (IFMRC) report, which was issued in 1994, indicated that although the flood was a significant event, floods of that magnitude were natural events and would continue to occur. It pointed out that national flood damages were growing and that people and property across the country were at risk. It noted that occupation of the floodplain and attempts to protect those in the floodplain had caused significant environmental damage and threatened ecosystems that provided substantial goods and services to both the natural and human environment. The report acknowledged that flood control structures had prevented $18 billion in damages during the 1993 flood, and it recommended that, in moving forward with efforts to reduce flood damages, the nation should not only strive to reduce flood losses, but also concurrently protect and enhance the floodplain's natural environment. The report offered a vision for the future of the floodplain that would carefully balance the use of both structural and nonstructural methods to bring about both sustainable occupation of lands that were already the home for many long settled communities and important for the conduct of commerce, as well as ensuring that the degradation of riverine and coastal ecosystems was reversed (IFMRC 1994). Although there was some support for action on the recommendations, other national priorities moved onto the scene and the report was soon forgotten.

> *The 1993 Mississippi River Flood was another wake up call for improved floodplain management, but once again the nation went back to sleep.*

INTO THE 21ST CENTURY

While non-governmental organizations, such as the Association of State Floodplain Managers (ASFPM), pointed out the escalation of flood losses in the latter half of the 20th century, entreaties for a retrospective look at the national approach generally fell on deaf ears. Although these organizations were unable to promote any detailed examination by Congress of the flood problem, they were at least able to convince Congress to support a $1 billion modernization of flood mapping by the National Flood Insurance Program (NFIP) in order to more accurately depict the threat faced by those who live in and near floodplains and coastal hazard areas.

On August 29, 2005, Hurricane Katrina smashed into the Louisiana-Mississippi Gulf Coast and inflicted massive damages on the people and the built and natural environment of the region. Over 1800 people lost their lives. The costs of property losses, response and recovery operations, and insurance claims payouts have not been completely identified but likely will exceed $100 billion. Over 300 km^2 (120 mi.^{2}) of the wetland buffer that existed between New Orleans and the Gulf were also destroyed by the hurricane. Four years after the hurricane, only 70% of the pre-Katrina population had returned to the region and many parts of the city of New Orleans and the Gulf Coast had yet to be restored or have plans made for their eventual resettlement or reuse (Galloway et al. 2009). Once again, just as it occurred after the 1993 Flood, the outcries about the need to deal with flooding were loud and the promises great. Some initial debate about alternative approaches to the restoration of below-sea level areas of New Orleans (move people out) were quickly seen to be impolitic and President George W. Bush appeared in that city on September 15, 2005 with a promise to make " the flood protection system stronger than it has ever been." Since 2005, the focus of federal effort in New Orleans has been on restoration of the hurricane protection system (levees, pumps and other structures) to a level that would protect the city against the 100-year (1% annual chance of occurrence) flood event, a level that is far less than the return interval of the approximately 400-year Katrina storm surge event.

> *The property losses, response and recovery operations, and insurance claims payouts resulting from the 2005 Katrina storm surge event likely will exceed $100 billion.*

Questions about why levees failed in New Orleans during the hurricane and why the destruction along the Mississippi coastline was so complete did bring calls for investigations, reviews, studies and Congressional hearings. Two reports by the US Army Corps of Engineers (USACE) dealt with the technical issues surrounding the levee failures as well as the flaws in the decision-making from Washington to New Orleans over the 40-year history of the New Orleans hurricane protection project (IPET 2009a, 2009b; Woolley and Shabman 2007). The Interagency Performance Evaluation Task Force (IPET) report was supplemented by reports from the American Society of Civil Engineers (ASCE 2008) and a blue ribbon panel of the National Research Council (NAE/NRC 2009). The Federal Emergency Management Agency (FEMA) commissioned an Interagency Levee Policy Review Committee (ILPRC) to examine how levees were treated in the NFIP (ILPRC 2006). The net result of the conduct of these studies, together with the attention of the Association of State Floodplain Managers (ASFPM) and the National Association of Flood and Storm Water Management Agencies (NAFSMA), was the identification of the fragile nature of tens of thousands of kilometers of levees across the entire nation and the need for evaluation of the condition of these levees (a conclusion also reached in IFMRC (1994)). This attention eventually led to the passage, in the Water Resources Development Act of 2007, of provisions to establish a national levee safety program (NCLS 2009).

FLOOD RISK MANAGEMENT

In recognition of the gradual shift away from a structural-only approach, during the last decades of the 20th century organizations such as FEMA and the USACE began to drop use of "flood control" in favor of "flood damage reduction" in describing activities related to floodplain management. However, in Europe, the approach was to move even farther away from flood control.

Under flood control, those responsible for reducing damages chose a level of protection for areas in danger based on either an economic analysis that determined that benefits of providing the protection (i.e., flood damages avoided) exceeded the cost of constructing the protection, or a national policy such as "no more floods." Following the disastrous floods in 1953, the government of the Netherlands took action to prevent recurrence of such catastrophic events and eventually established a

10,000-year level of protection for coastal areas (in 2008 a Netherlands Delta Committee recommended that, to accommodate potential climate change, the level be increased to 100,000-year protection (Royal Netherlands Embassy 2008)). In the late 1990s, the European Community began to consider a different approach, flood risk management. Under this approach, the risk to a given area would be defined by examining the probability that the flood might occur, the probability that whatever protection system existed would function as designed, and the consequences that would result should the area actually flood. Establishing a risk-based approach not only identified the level of risk faced by each community, but also offered a method of prioritizing protection efforts. Using flood risk management, it became clear that risk could be reduced not only by increasing the probability that the protection system would do the job, but also by taking steps within the protected community to reduce its vulnerability to flooding through use of nonstructural methods including the avoidance of development. While Europe moved ahead with this concept, it was not until Katrina that the US began to examine a comprehensive approach to risk management (Galloway 2008). Now, as USACE and FEMA move to deal with post-Katrina flood vulnerability, they have both adopted a flood risk management paradigm.

WHAT ABOUT THE FUTURE?

With flood damages increasing each decade, the nation's population growing at a high rate and moving to coastal and riverine areas, and climate change promising an increased potential for flooding even in areas where total rainfall may decrease, it became obvious to professionals in the floodplain management business that something needed to be done. In 2007, the ASFPM Foundation decided to conduct a Gilbert F. White Flood Policy Forum, the Foundation's vehicle for addressing critical issues in floodplain management. The Forum was directed to determine what actions needed to be taken to ensure that the flood risk situation that existed at the start of the 21st century would be mitigated by the mid-point of the century.

In November 2007, the Foundation brought 75 national and international flood experts together in Washington to discuss what the floodplain might look like in 2050 if no actions were taken to slow the growth in damages and what it might look like if specific actions were taken to move in the opposite direction. The group quickly agreed that an unchecked 2050 would present the nation with significant problems because it would threaten the lives and property of those living in and near the floodplain and the coasts, and it could endanger the economic viability of the nation as a whole. They also agreed that if the nation was willing to address the challenges it faced in managing the floodplain, future damages could be reduced and the badly damaged ecology of floodplains could be rejuvenated.

> *If the nation is willing to address the challenges in managing floodplains, future damages could be reduced and the badly damaged ecology could be rejuvenated.*

GILBERT WHITE'S THESIS

In defining a broader than "structures-only" approach to dealing with floods, Gilbert White identified eight adjustments that could be made to floodplain use that would reduce the potential for losses and ensure long-term sustainable use of the riverine environment (White 1945):

- *Elevation*: Raising structures above the expected flood level.
- *Flood abatement*: Using measures "taken outside of stream channels with the effect of reducing the crest of flood flows or changing the debris load for a flood event."
- *Flood protection*: Using engineering works to minimize impacts of flooding.
- *Emergency measures*: In areas already occupied, taking actions to mitigate floods that do occur through temporary evacuation, the adjustment of services, and flood fighting.
- *Structural adjustments*: Designing buildings and other structures to reduce losses when floods occur.
- *Land use*: Permanently removing property and services beyond the reach of floods.
- *Public relief*: Using public grants and direct rehabilitation to relieve the impact of flood losses.
- *Insurance*: Mitigating the financial effects of flooding on structure owners and businesses through use of insurance.

During the Forum, participants examined the eight methods of adjustment to determine if White's original list was still relevant, and, where it was not or where it was in need of modification, what changes might be made to increase its 21st century utility. They were also asked to identify new adjustments that might be added to White's list to better address the needs of the future.

A SUSTAINABLE 2050 FLOODPLAIN

Not surprisingly, Forum participants determined that the adjustments posited by White in 1945 largely remain relevant today. They also identified several areas where new adjustments measures could be added to those developed by White. The Forum participants concluded that, should action be taken in accordance with a suite of adjustment measures, the floodplain of 2050 would be far less dangerous, environmentally more suitable, and overall more sustainable than it would be if no action be taken to deal with the impending challenges.

Looking forward to 2050 in light of the White recommended adjustments to floodplain use, participants forecast that the more sustainable floodplain would see:

- Land use in which all states would have comprehensive land-use planning that effectively identified their land and water resources and associated natural hazards, and that permitted development only when there would be no adverse impact on flooding or on the natural and beneficial functions of the floodplain.

- Building and development standards targeted at avoiding new construction in flood prone and residual risk areas behind levees and below dams to reduce the exposure to flood damages. Where structures were built, the nature of their construction would reduce the potential for losses should floods occur. Those who took actions that increased their flood risk would not be rewarded with federal benefits.
- Elevating structures in the floodplain were no longer considered as the best or even desirable solution since structures surrounded by water pose a risk to both those in the structures and the emergency personnel who would be concerned about the welfare of the occupants.
- Mandatory purchase of all-hazard insurance throughout the United States.
- Structural flood protection only used to deal with existing development or where no other alternatives existed. The first choice would be nonstructural.
- Emergency measures based on robust pre-disaster mitigation activities that took full advantage of the lessons learned in previous flooding events.
- Public understanding that disaster relief and assistance would be available only as a backup to other adjustments.
- Watershed planning used to clearly identify the impacts of upstream activities on those downstream and vice versa. Every effort would be made to ensure maximum natural storage of flood waters.

While 21st century consideration of Gilbert White's eight adjustments would certainly go a long way to ensure that the floodplain of 2050 was more sustainable, participants also recommended that four additional adjustments should be considered:
- Providing room for rivers and oceans by choosing not to occupy flood-prone areas and thus avoiding the hazard as well as precluding unintended adverse impacts on ecosystems. This adjustment would ensure that development would routinely place distance between human occupation of the landscape and rivers and oceans.
- Requiring exercise of personal responsibility by the public in recognizing the hazards that are faced, the risks that are taken in dealing with these hazards and the need to become concerned with the sustainability of the environment.
- Recognizing the geographic interdependence of floodplain activities and taking steps to minimize the impacts of these interdependencies. Damages to one community, business, or industry may have significant economic and social impacts at locations far from the flooded area.
- Ensuring national awareness of flood risk and education of the population on flood processes, mitigation and avoidance. Those who are well-educated are far more likely to take appropriate action to reduce their vulnerability to flooding or to totally avoid placing themselves at risk. 21st century information technology offers the rare opportunity for near real-time distribution of hazard information to the entire population.

Attention to the above adjustments would result in a 2050 floodplain where (ASFPM Foundation 2008):

"... in spite of rapidly growing populations and a changing climate, both flood risk and land and water resources are being managed towards more sustainable outcomes. The nation views land and water as precious resources, and therefore protects the natural and beneficial functions of floodplains, wetlands, and coastal areas. Because these areas have been reserved—and in some cases, restored—a maximum amount of natural mitigation of flooding takes place continually. Integrated water management is an accepted practice. All new development is designed and built so that it has no adverse impact on flood levels, sedimentation, erosion, riparian or coastal habitat, or other community-designated values. The market strongly favors sustainable development, which means that floodprone construction rarely occurs. Private and public losses due to floods are indemnified through a government-backed but private system of universal insurance coverage that encourages mitigation. Floodplain management programs are funded from fees charged for development impacts, a highway trust fund, or other secure sources. Risk communication through all levels of government has become advanced enough that local decision making is well informed; policy decisions are based on sound science."

GETTING TO 2050

Change doesn't just happen. Even though flood professionals may strongly endorse modified White-developed adjustments and the addition of other adjustments to deal with the uniqueness of our current situation, these approaches must be understood and accepted by the population at large and they must find their way into clear and holistic public policies that treat land and water as important natural resources. As the Forum report notes, the twin goals of these policies must be "to protect people and property from flooding while also protecting flood prone lands from people." Even with new policies there remains a need for dealing with the nation's fragmented system of water resource management, disaster relief, and mitigation. Efforts must be made to eliminate disincentives to correct action, duplication of programs and minimization of costly and time-consuming litigation. Moving to a safe and sustainable 2050 floodplain will require access to accurate and comprehensive data about our natural resources, the risks we face, and integration of these data with increasingly available data and information about other aspects of society (ASFPM Foundation 2008). A movement to this better floodplain of 2050 will also require adequate funding to support not only proper siting and construction of future development and removal of unwise past development, but also to maintain existing infrastructure that provides protection for many areas.

The Forum report points out that circumstances that surround early 21st century development are unique and represent opportunity for significant change in the way we do business. The report concludes by providing six guidelines that "capsulize the new ways of thinking and operating that will be needed to achieve safe and sustainable relationships with our water resources," and lead to the safe and sustainable floodplain of 2050. These guidelines ask decision-makers and the public at large to (ASFPM Foundation 2008):

- Make room for rivers, oceans, and adjacent lands.
- Reverse perverse incentives in government programs that make it more profitable to act unwisely than to recognize the need for long-term safety and sustainability.
- Restore and enhance the natural, beneficial functions of riverine and coastal areas.
- Generate a renaissance in water resources governance and development of the policies and organization that will support this renaissance.
- Identify risks and communicate them at the public and individual levels.
- Assume personal and public responsibility for their actions in the floodplain.

IMPLICATIONS FOR CIVIL ENGINEERS

According to ASCE's *Vision 2025* (ASCE 2007):

> *"Entrusted by society to create a sustainable world and enhance the global quality of life, civil engineers serve competently, collaboratively, and ethically as master*
> - *planners, designers, constructors, and operators of society's economic and social engine—the built environment;*
> - *stewards of the natural environment and its resources;*
> - *innovators and integrators of ideas and technology across the public, private, and academic sectors;*
> - *managers of risk and uncertainty caused by natural events, accidents, and other threats; and*
> - *leaders in discussions and decisions shaping public environmental and infrastructure policy."*

Moving from where we are today in floodplain and flood risk management to the future described above will require civil engineers to live up to the aspirational expectations of *Vision 2025*. Recognition of Gilbert White's original adjustments to floodplain use, the suggested modifications and additions to his list, and the guidelines proposed in the report of the Gilbert F. White Forum will demand from civil engineers full exercise of the knowledge, skills and attitudes needed to serve the nation in the manner described above. It is important that, as floodplain professionals define a visionary state for 2050, civil engineers are prepared to support this effort and see it through to its fulfillment.

IN SUM

The United States faces major challenges in dealing with flooding. We have learned that we cannot control floods or even focus on simply reducing damages. We must identify and manage our growing flood risks. Damages from disastrous floods are on the rise, and people and property remain at risk. Over the next 40 years, if action is not taken to deal with the problem, it will grow substantially worse. Climate change, population growth, unbridled development in hazardous areas, and a lack of personal responsibility on the part of individuals subject to flooding will lead to an untenable situation by the middle of the 21st century. Gilbert White's seminal work identified what actions could be taken to deal with the flood threat and proposed eight adjustments that have stood the test of time. Those attending the Association of State Flood Plain Managers Foundation 2007 Forum identified four additional areas where human adjustment might result in even better future conditions. With attention to these opportunities, the American floodplain of the future can be far different than it is today. Civil engineers are at the nexus of this challenge and must, along with their many other responsibilities, take on the challenge of ensuring that the floodplain of 2050 is sustainably developed and managed.

ACKNOWLEDGMENTS

The author would like to acknowledge the great efforts of the ASFPM Foundation team that planned and carried out the 2007 Flood Policy Forum, synthesized its results and prepared the report of the Forum: Doug Plascencia, Bruce Baird, Diane Brown, Larry Larson, Dale Lehman, Jackie Monday, and Edward Thomas. Their work made possible this chapter.

REFERENCES

American Society of Civil Engineers (ASCE). (2008). *The New Orleans hurricane protection system: what went wrong and why*. A Report by the ASCE Hurricane Katrina External Review Panel, Reston, VA.

American Society of Civil Engineers (ASCE). (2007). *The vision for civil engineering in 2025*, ASCE Steering Committee to Plan a Summit on the Future of the Civil Engineering Profession in 2025, Reston, VA.

Association of State Floodplain Managers (ASFPM) Foundation. (2008). *Floodplain management 2050*, Report of the 2007 Assembly of the Gilbert F. White National Flood Policy Forum, ASFPM, Madison, WI.

Galloway, G. E. (2008). "Flood risk management in the United States and the impact of Hurricane Katrina." *Int. J. River Basin Manage.*, 4(6), 303-306.

Galloway, G. E, Boesch, D. F., and Twilley, R. R. (2009). "Restoring and protecting coastal Louisiana." *Issues in Science and Technology*, 25(2), 29-38.

Interagency Floodplain Management Review Committee (IFMRC). (1994). *Sharing the challenge: floodplain management into the 21st century*, Report of the IFMRC to the Administration Floodplain Management Task Force, US Government Printing Office, Washington, DC.

Interagency Levee Policy Review Committee (ILPRC). (2006). *The national levee challenge: levees and the FEMA flood map modernization initiative*, Federal Emergency Management Agency, Washington, DC, <http://www.fema.gov/library/viewRecord.do?id=2677> (Dec, 2009).

Interagency Performance Evaluation Task Force (IPET). (2009a). *Volume I –
    Executive summary and overview*, IPET, US Army Corps of Engineers,
    Vicksburg, MS.
Interagency Performance Evaluation Task Force (IPET). (2009b). *Volume VIII –
    Engineering and Operational Risk and Reliability Analysis*, IPET, Vicksburg,
    MS.
National Academy of Engineering/National Research Council (NAE/NRC). (2009).
    *The New Orleans hurricane protection system: assessing pre-Katrina
    vulnerability and improving mitigation and preparedness*, National Academy
    Press, Washington, DC.
National Committee on Levee Safety (NCLS). (2009). *Draft: recommendations for a
    national levee safety program*, A Report to Congress, US Army Corps of
    Engineers, Washington, DC.
    <http://www.iwr.usace.army.mil/ncls/docs/NCLS-Recommendation-
    Report_012009_DRAFT.pdf> (Dec, 2009).
Royal Netherlands Embassy. (2008). *Delta Committee: working with water*, press
    release, The Royal Netherlands Embassy, Washington DC, September 16,
    2008.
White, G. F. (1945). *Human adjustment to floods: a geographical approach to the
    flood problem in the United States*, Research Paper No. 29, University of
    Chicago, Chicago, IL.
Woolley, D., and Shabman, L. (2007). *Decision-making chronology for the Lake
    Pontchartrain and vicinity hurricane protection project*, Final Report for the
    Headquarters, US Army Corps of Engineers, Institute for Water Resources,
    Alexandria, VA.

AUTHOR INFORMATION

Dr. Gerald Galloway is a Glenn L. Martin Institute Professor of Engineering at the
University of Maryland's A. James Clark School of Engineering. This appointment
followed a 38-year career in the US Army Corps of Engineers, retiring as Brigadier
General, and eight additional years of service in the federal government, most of
which was associated with water resources management. In 1993 and 1994 he was
assigned to the White House to lead an interagency study of the causes of the Great
Mississippi River Flood of 1993 and to make recommendations concerning the
nation's floodplain management program.   His federal service culminated as
Secretary and Principal Advisor to the US Section of the International Joint
Commission, Canada and United States. He is a member of the National Academy of
Engineering and an honorary (distinguished) member of the American Society of
Civil Engineers.   He currently serves as a Trustee of the ASFPM Foundation.
Email:gegallo@umd.edu

Chapter 15

Adaptation to Climate Change in Coastal Cities, 2050

David C. Major

ABSTRACT

Coastal cities will be significantly impacted in this century by climate change, including sea level rise, storm surge, inland flooding from intense precipitation events, and droughts. The need for adaptation measures is clear. The past 40 years have seen the development of extensive scientific interest in climate change impacts on coastal cities as well as important advances in the planning framework for adaptation to climate change. The tasks for the next 40 years are to begin and expand applied adaptation planning and to undertake the properly scheduled implementation of adaptations over time. If institutional and other challenges are overcome and resources are made available, it is probable that most US coastal cities can adapt reasonably well to the impacts of climate change, at least over the next 40 years.

"Adapting to climate change has been a challenge."

INTRODUCTION

Coastal cities are impacted in diverse ways by climate change, including sea level rise, storm surge, inland flooding from intense precipitation events, and droughts. Components of water-related systems in coastal cities include distribution systems, sewer systems, wastewater treatment systems, and supply systems (such as aquifers). In addition, coastal cities with upland water supply systems will see effects on quality and quantity in those systems. The natural and human-made environment, the water resources and wastewater treatment systems, and other elements of infrastructure in cities are closely intertwined, so that adaptation to climate change in coastal cities provides one of the most challenging problems facing the engineering, planning, and policy communities. The view taken here is that, at least over the next 40 years, it is probable that most US coastal cities can adapt reasonably well to the impacts of climate change if institutional and other challenges are overcome and resources are made available.

The prospective impacts on coastal cities from climate change are indicated by the Intergovernmental Panel on Climate Change's (IPCC) 21st century estimates for warming: 1.8 to 4.0 °C (3.2 to 7 °F); sea level rise: 0.18 to 0.59 meters (7 to 23 inches, excluding future rapid changes in ice flow); and the expectation of more droughts and intense precipitation events and more intense tropical storms (IPPC 2007a). These changes, which will have substantial impacts on natural and human-made systems (IPCC 2007b), have already begun (IPCC 2008a). Changes in precipitation patterns are also likely, although at present these are challenging to forecast. It is widely expected that the American West will get drier, while the East will have additional precipitation (Lettenmaier et al. 2008; Seager et al. 2007). Even in areas of increasing precipitation, more droughts are likely as the evaporative effects of higher temperature increasingly outweigh additional precipitation as the 21st century progresses.

Many observers now expect that climate changes during the 21st century will be more severe than those foreseen in IPCC (2007a) unless serious efforts to halt emissions can be implemented; there have been some instances of efforts to estimate higher rates of sea level rise than those developed by the IPCC (NPCC 2010). However, even if concentrations of greenhouse gases (GHGs) and aerosols were kept constant at 2000 levels, global temperature and sea level would still rise because of inertia in the system (IPCC 2008a). Thus there is a definite need for adaptation to climate change in coastal cities.

THE PAST 40 YEARS

The past 40 years have seen a dramatic increase in scientific understanding of climate change, from very early research prior to the period, such as the radiative, convective 2-dimensional model of Sellers (1969), through the development of the IPCC and the growth of a large scientific community focused on the need for greater understanding of climate change and the need to develop adequate policy. While the rise of public and stakeholder concern about climate change has been relatively slow in the United States throughout most of this period, in the past few years it has become much more significant. At the same time, scientific work has been earlier to develop than applied adaptations; this scientific interest has been directed in part at the impacts of climate change on coastal cities. A National Research Council report on climate change from 1977 has a chapter on the Northeastern US, an area that includes large coastal cities (Schwarz 1977); an American Association for the Advancement of Science report (Waggoner 1990) and the report of a US Army conference on climate change (Ballentine and Stakhiv 1993) also include material on coastal cities. Hansler and Major (1999) is an early example of specific adaptation proposals for water supply in an urban coastal area.

> *There is a definite need for adaptation to climate change in coastal cities.*

There were also a few isolated examples of actual infrastructure adaptations to climate change in coastal cities in the late 20th century. In New York City, an outlet pipe for City Tunnel #3 on Roosevelt Island was raised above its original design height in response to concern about potential sea level rise (Major and Goldberg 2001). In Boston, an effluent outfall for the Deer Island Wastewater Treatment Plant was raised by 54 cm (1.8 feet) explicitly to deal with sea level rise (Massachusetts Water Resources Authority 1989). However, most existing coastal infrastructure was undertaken without design considerations for climate change.

It is only relatively recently that focused work on climate change and coastal cities has expanded and begun to reach into the area of actual adaptation planning for water supply and other sectors. Among the reports focused on planning are Rosenzweig and Solecki (2001), Greater London Authority (2005), Halifax Regional Municipality (2007), Mote et al. (2008), New York City Department of Environmental Protection (NYCDEP) (2008) and NPCC (2010). IPCC (2008b) focuses on climate impacts and adaptations in the water sector. In Rosenzweig et al. (2007) and other works (including Lim et al. (2005) in international planning), there has been an effort to develop multistep adaptation assessment frameworks for planning. An eight-step procedure has been in use for New York City's critical infrastructure and climate change evaluation:

1. Identify current and future climate hazards
2. Conduct risk assessment inventory of infrastructure and assets
3. Characterize risk of climate change on infrastructure
4. Develop initial adaptation strategies
5. Identify opportunities for coordination
6. Link strategies to capital and rehabilitation cycles
7. Prepare and implement adaptation plans
8. Monitor and reassess.

The extent to which each of these steps has been implemented to date varies—there are fully developed climate scenarios (Step 1--above), and detailed inventory questionnaires (NPCC 2010) have been completed for Step 2, while Steps 3-8 are in progress or in the planning stage. It is of interest that a National Research Council (2009) report includes a discussion of the New York City climate change planning procedures as an appendix.

Another important element that has been developed in recent years is scenarios for local areas for selected benchmark years for planning. The IPCC's projections are for the whole 21st century, and have some regional specificity. However, for practical purposes, scenarios for selected benchmark years for particular areas should be developed to provide guidance for applied adaptation planning. One approach is through downscaling global climate models (GCMs). The results of simulations produced by the models used by the IPCC are deposited at the Program for Climate Model Diagnosis and Intercomparison website at Lawrence Livermore Laboratory (LLNL 2009), and can be accessed by researchers to develop downscaled scenarios (Lettenmaier et al. 2008; NPCC 2010). For New York City's climate work, Columbia University produced scenarios using downscaled simulations from 16 of the GCMs on which the IPCC (2007a) Fourth Assessment Report (AR4) is based, together with 3 IPCC (2000) emissions trajectories. These scenarios are for the 2020s, 2050s, and 2080s, and they have been adopted by the City for its adaptation planning. These scenarios should be revisited at appropriate times as climate science improves and modeling capabilities increase. Because of increasing concern with more rapid climate change, an additional scenario assuming higher melt rates from land ice was included in the NPCC sea level rise projections. The scenario results are presented as ranges so that planners can have an understanding of the model-based and emissions uncertainties in such scenarios. For sea level rise scenarios, 7 AR4 GCMs for which appropriate data are available are used with 3 emissions scenarios to create 21 scenarios in each time frame for sea level rise. However, these downscaling methods are not yet in use in many areas (Lettenmaier et al. 2008), although wider use can be expected.

Extensive approaches with regional climate models (RCMs) have also been undertaken. RCMs focus on smaller areas than GCMs, and are driven by GCM outputs. This work includes a database with monthly precipitation and temperature data/predictions from 1950 to 2099 from 16 climate change models, three future greenhouse gas emission scenarios, and multiple initial conditions statistically downscaled to a spatial resolution of 1/8 degree of latitude and longitude (approximately 13 km by 13 km) (LLNL 2008). Another dynamically downscaled RCM data base is under development (Mearns 2009).

In sum, during the past 40 years there has been extensive scientific interest in climate change impacts on coastal cities, and there have been important advances in planning for adaptation to climate change and the development of climate scenarios. A range of possible adaptations in the areas of management and operations, infrastructure, and policy has been identified (NYCDEP 2008), and there is a recognition of the need for planning over the short-, medium- and long-terms. Frameworks for effective adaptation to climate change in coastal cities are now available. At the same time, extensive design work on adaptations in practice has yet to be undertaken across a wide range of jurisdictions, and this provides a principal task for the future. The present moment is one in which good progress has been made, and a new era of sustained adaptation planning is about to begin. What of the next 40 years?

THE NEXT 40 YEARS: 2050

During the next 40 years, there will be both forces for progress and many challenges. As a result, the next 40 years will see not a quick shift to complete climate change adaptation planning for coastal cities, but rather a trajectory that will see more and more cities confronting climate change in water resources management/operations, infrastructure, and policy. By 2050 there will be a long-established expectation that every city will deal as effectively as it can with climate change. If climate changes are in the middle range of the IPCC forecasts or somewhat above, many US cities will be reasonably well-adapted to climate change for the 2050 period. On the other hand, low-lying cities and those with significant subsidence (such as New Orleans) may find effective adaptation difficult. For national planning, it would be useful to have a typology of coastal cities in terms of the expected effectiveness of adaptation planning over the next decades.

> *It appears that over the next 40 years most US coastal cities can adapt to the impacts of climate change reasonably well, although at possibly substantial cost.*

There are several positive forces that will help to move climate change planning forward in coastal cities in the next decades. One is the development of effective planning frameworks, as noted above, and the second is continued progress in climate science, modeling, and computational capabilities. One of the most striking developments in recent years is the enormous increase in knowledge in the earth and climate sciences. This will continue, and, with modeling and computer advances, will provide the basis for significantly improved planning.

On the other hand, there are factors that present challenges for the implementation of effective climate planning that if not effectively addressed could slow down the planning process. These include:

1. *The need to develop engineering methods that take into account climate change*:   Among the most important changes will be the need to shift methods to non-stationary analyses for water and climate variables (Milly et al. 2008).   This is not a trivial change, as it involves modifying one of the bedrock principles of engineering design, the use of historical data. In addition, more than ever, designs must be varied according to the expected schedule of implementation.   It will no longer be sufficient to design the "best" project and wait for it to be scheduled in a capital plan, because the

definition of "best" will depend on the expected date of implementation. Further, designs for rehabilitation and replacement cycles will need to include climate adaptation planning, a potentially large source of savings in implementation costs as compared to last-minute add-ons.

2. *Integrating planning for climate change with agency procedures*: Agency procedures for planning and implementation often take an unconscionable length of time; more efficient decision processes are required to take climate change effectively into account. This effort will be helped by increased computational power and better planning models, and will assist in making appropriate changes in engineering design practice.

3. *The need to change views of constancy in regulation over time*: For the most part, regulators tend to think of regulations as either fixed or, if anything, suitable for tightening. However, with changing climate, it may be necessary to consider a periodic review of regulations to insure that climate impacts and adaptations are optimally treated by varying regulations over time. This change may be more difficult to implement than engineering design changes due to the fact that there is no discipline of "regulator," as there is, for example, for civil engineering, where there is a set of instructional procedures in place through schools of engineering.

There are some classes of adaptations that may be expected over the next forty years. These include (with reference to whether they relate to management/operations, infrastructure, and/or policy):

1. Revamped coastal wastewater treatment systems, designed or redesigned with increased pumping where needed (infrastructure).

2. Better protection against storm surges. This adaptation may not, however, be large-scale barriers. In many cities, a combination of flood walls, better evacuation plans and improved forecasting should be enough to deal with moderate increases in storm surge (management/operations and/or infrastructure). A discussion of these matters is in Aerts et al. (2009).

3. Better drainage for more intense storms, and separate storm and sewer systems where possible (infrastructure).

4. Better drought management plans both for upland and local supplies (management/operations).

5. Changed reservoir systems operation to maintain quality and quantity (management/ operations).

6. More redundancy in water systems, including links to other systems, backup sources, and increased use of management tools such as water markets and improved pricing (management/operations, infrastructure, policy).

7. Increased efforts to mitigate anthropogenic subsidence in coastal areas.

In 2050, there are two outside possibilities that would be relevant to the need for and success of adaptation. These are:

1. Policy makers confront and seriously reduce the problem of emissions. This would ease the impacts of climate change and reduce, but by no means eliminate, pressures for adaptation to climate change in coastal cities.

2. Global warming and sea level rise occur well above the current IPCC range of scenarios. In this case, not only would the general level of adaptation discussed above be seen by 2050, but also a more urgent effort to integrate then-current efforts into a larger framework of radical climate change would be required.

In sum, from the perspective of the present, it appears that over the next 40 years it is probable that most US coastal cities can adapt reasonably well, although at possibly substantial cost, to the impacts of climate change. Beyond that period it would be hazardous to predict; in any event, there will be much to consider in the next version of this volume, say in 10 years' time.

ACKNOWLEDGMENTS

The author thanks Stephen Estes-Smargiassi, Radley Horton, Alex Ruane, Vivien Gornitz, the editors and anonymous reviewers for sources and comments. All opinions are those of the author.

REFERENCES

Aerts, J., Major, D. C., Bowman, M., Dircke, P., and Marfai, M. A. (2009). *Connecting delta cities: coastal cities, flood risk management, and adaptation to climate change,* VU University Press, Amsterdam, The Netherlands.
Ballentine, T. M., and Stakhiv, E. V., eds. (1993). *Proc., First national conference on climate change and water resources management,* US Army Corps of Engineers, Fort Belvoir, VA.
Greater London Authority. (2005). *Adapting to climate change: a checklist for development*, London Climate Change Partnership, London, UK.
Halifax Regional Municipality. (2007). *Climate change: developer's risk management guide*, Halifax, Nova Scotia.
Hansler, G., and Major, D. C. (1999). "Climate change and the water supply systems of New York City and the Delaware Basin: planning and action considerations for water managers." *Proceedings of the specialty conference*

on potential consequences of climate variability and change to water resources of the United States, D. B. Adams, ed., American Water Resources Association, Herndon, VA, 327-330.

Intergovernmental Panel on Climate Change (IPCC). (2000). *Emissions scenarios 2000,* Special Report of the Intergovernmental Panel on Climate Change, Cambridge University Press, Cambridge, UK.

Intergovernmental Panel on Climate Change (IPCC). (2007a). *Climate change 2007: the physical science basis*, Contribution of Working Group I to the Fourth Assessment Report of the IPCC, Cambridge University Press, Cambridge, UK.

Intergovernmental Panel on Climate Change (IPCC). (2007b). *Climate change 2007: impacts, adaptation and vulnerability*, Contribution of Working Group II to the Fourth Assessment Report of the IPCC, Cambridge University Press, Cambridge, UK.

Intergovernmental Panel on Climate Change (IPCC). (2008a). *Climate change 2007: synthesis report*, IPCC, Geneva, Switzerland.

Intergovernmental Panel on Climate Change (IPCC). (2008b). *Climate change and water*, IPCC Technical Paper VI, IPCC Secretariat, Geneva, Switzerland.

Lawrence Livermore National Laboratory (LLNL). (2009). *PCMDI: Program for climate model diagnosis and intercomparison,* <www-pcmdi.llnl.gov/> (Oct, 2009).

Lawrence Livermore National Laboratory (LLNL). (2008). *Bias corrected and downscaled WCRP CMIP3 climate projections*, <http://gdo-dcp.ucllnl.org/downscaled_cmip3_projections/#Welcome> (Oct, 2009).

Lettenmaier, D. P., Major, D. C., Poff, L., and Running, S. (2008). "Water resources." *The effects of climate change on agriculture, land resources, water resources, and biodiversity in the United States*, A Report by the U.S. Climate Change Science Program and the Subcommittee on Global Change Research, Washington, DC, 121-150.

Lim, B., Spanger-Siegfried E., eds., co-authored by Burton, I., Malone, E., Huq, S. (2005). *Adaptation policy frameworks for climate change: developing strategies, policies and measures*, United Nations Development Programme, Cambridge University Press, Cambridge, UK.

Major, D. C., and Goldberg, R. (2001). "Water supply." *Climate change and a global city: the potential consequences of climate variability and change, Metro East Coast*, Report for the US Global Change Research Program, C. Rosenzweig, and W. Solecki, eds., Columbia Earth Institute, New York, NY, ch. 6.

Massachusetts Water Resources Authority. (1989). *Boston Harbor project, Deer Island related facilities, conceptual design, design package 6, effluent outfall tunnel and diffusers, final design report*, Massachusetts Water Resources Authority, Boston, MA.

Mearns, L. O. (2009). *North American Regional Climate Change Assessment Program (NARCCAP)*, Presentation at Workshop on Water Infrastructure Sustainability and Adaptation to Climate Change, USEPA,

<http://www.epa.gov/nrmrl/wswrd/wqm/wrap/pdf/workshop/A1_Mearns.pdf
> (Oct, 2009).
Milly, P. C. D., Betancourt, J., Falkenmark, M., Hirsch, R. M., Kundzewicz, Z. W.,
Lettenmaier, D. P., and Stouffer, R. J. (2008). "Climate change: stationarity is
dead: whither water management?" *Science*, 319, 573-574.
Mote, P., Petersen, A., Reeder, S., Shipman, H., Binder, L. W. (2008). *Sea level rise
in the coastal waters of Washington State*, Climate Impacts Group and
Washington Department of Ecology, Seattle, WA,
<http://www.cses.washington.edu/db/pdf/moteetalslr579.pdf> (Aug, 2010).
National Research Council. (2009). *Informing decisions in a changing climate*,
National Academy Press, Washington, DC.
New York City Department of Environmental Protection (NYCDEP). (2008).
Climate change program, assessment and action plan, New York, NY.
New York City Panel on Climate Change (NPCC). (2010). *Climate change
adaptation in New York City: building a risk management response*, C.
Rosenzweig and W. Solecki (eds.), New York Academy of Sciences, New
York, NY.
Rosenzweig, C., Solecki, W., eds. (2001). *Climate change and a global city: the
potential consequences of climate variability and change, Metro East Coast*,
Report for the US Global Change Research Program, Columbia Earth
Institute, New York, NY.
Rosenzweig, C., Major, D. C., Demong, K., Stanton, C., Horton, R., and Stults, M.
(2007). "Managing climate change risks in New York City's water system:
assessment and adaptation planning." *Mitigation and Adaptation Strategies
for Global Change*, 12(8), 1391-1409, DOI 1007/s11027-006-9070-5.
Seager, R., Tang, M., Held, I., Kushnir, Y., Lu, J., Vecchi, G., Huang, H.-P., Harnik,
N., Leetmaa, A., Lau, N.-C., Li, C., Velez, J., and Naik, N. (2007). "Model
projections of an imminent transition to a more arid climate in southwestern
North America." *Science*, 316, 1181, DOI: 10.1126/science.1139601.
Sellers, W. D. (1969). "A climate model based on the energy balance of the earth-
atmosphere system." *J. Appl. Meteorol.*, 8, 392-400.
Schwarz, H. E. (1977). "Climatic change and water supply: how sensitive is the
Northeast?" *Climate, climatic change, and water supply*, National Research
Council, Panel on Water and Climate, National Academy of Sciences,
Washington, DC, 111-120.
Waggoner, P. E., ed. (1990). *Climate change and U.S. water resources*, Report of the
AAAS Panel on Climatic Variability, Climate Change, and the Planning and
Management of U.S. Water Resources, John Wiley and Sons, New York, NY.

AUTHOR INFORMATION

Dr. David C. Major is Senior Research Scientist at the Columbia University Earth
Institute's Center for Climate Systems Research. He completed his undergraduate
work at Wesleyan University and the London School of Economics, and received a
PhD in Economics from Harvard. Dr. Major has been a faculty member at MIT and
at Clark University, a Visiting Fellow at Clare Hall, Cambridge, a senior planner with

the New York City Water Supply System, and Program Director for Global Environmental Change at the Social Science Research Council. His principal scientific research focus at Columbia is the adaptation of urban infrastructure to global climate change. Dr. Major is the award-winning author, co-author or co-editor of fourteen books on natural resources planning, environmental management, biography and literary studies. Email: dcm29@columbia.edu

Chapter 16

Agriculture Water Resource Issues in 2050

Michael F. Walter

ABSTRACT

Irrigated agriculture is now and will, in 2050, continue to be the world's largest consumer of water. The diet of the population in 2050 will rely more on meat and less on cereal grains, which will translate to more water needed per calorie of food produced. Expected increases in non-food crops such as cotton and biomass production for the potential growth of the biofuels industry will create even more need for water. There is a growing recognition that irrigated agriculture as now practiced in most countries cannot be sustained without better water management and use of new technologies. However the major thrust to meet agriculture production in the next 40 years is likely to be focused on increasing yields of rain-fed crops. This will surely include emphasis on diversified and intense cropping systems designed and managed to not only be more productive but also to protect the environment and maintain healthy aquatic ecosystems as well. Increased international trade and levels of national food security in 2050 will allow for more efficient use of the world's land and water resources devoted to agriculture production.

"That will be $60 for the two steaks and 7,000 L
of water on your conscience."

THE CURRENT SITUATION

Worldwide agriculture is by far the greatest consumptive use for fresh water of any industry. Agriculture currently uses about 3,000 km³/yr or 70 percent of all water that is withdrawn from streams, lakes, or groundwater, mostly to be used for irrigation (Faurès et al. 2000). Even more impressive is that most of the water withdrawn for agriculture is lost to the atmosphere through evaporation and transpiration. Globally all other industrial and domestic withdrawals of fresh water combined account for the other 30 percent of total water withdrawal, and much of it is returned to streams, lakes or groundwater, but often at a somewhat reduced quality. Most water for cropland is provided directly from rainfall and typically this is referred to as rain-fed agriculture. Water use in this chapter is focused on water that is withdrawn from lakes, streams, or groundwater for agricultural uses. In the recent scientific literature, water withdrawn from lakes, streams, and groundwater is frequently referred to as "blue water" while that resulting directly from rainfall (e.g. soil moisture) is called "green water." While agricultural drainage remains an important water management technology, particularly for shallow groundwater control for rain-fed crops and salinity control for irrigated areas, it is not dealt with in this chapter.

The amount of water that falls annually on all cropland is over an order of magnitude greater than that used for irrigation. However, except for modest efforts at on-farm rainfall harvesting, such as techniques to increase water infiltration, there is currently little effort to control rainfall runoff as a means of increasing water availability to crops. Rain-fed agriculture accounts for about 1.13 billion hectares of cropland while irrigation is used today on over 280 million hectares of cropland. This is more than twice the area of land that was irrigated in 1960 (Browne 2009). In some regions it is possible to grow two crops sequentially in a single year, thus effectively doubling the crop area. In a few places irrigation allows for year-round cropping. The effective irrigation area, which accounts for multiple crops in a single year, is about 400 million hectares. Water used directly by farm animals is relatively small overall compared to irrigation use so it is not a focus of this chapter.

Irrigation for food crops is the primary use of water in irrigated agriculture, although demand for non-food crops (e.g. cotton) is also increasing. Using data reported from several international organizations worldwide, irrigated area in 2003 was estimated at 277 million hectares with water used for irrigation reaching 2,750 km³/yr (Molden 2007). The remarkable increase in irrigation in the decades prior to 2000 was in large part a result of investments in irrigation infrastructure in support of the worldwide initiative to increase crop production in developing countries referred to as the Green Revolution. The success of the Green Revolution was largely due to the increase in yields of corn, wheat, and rice that resulted from development of high-yielding plant varieties. But while these new hybrid crop varieties had the potential for significant improvements in yield, the yields were achievable only when the plants received the required inputs, especially fertilizer, pesticides, and water.

World Bank lending to developing countries increased steadily from US$200 million to US$2.0 billion per year from 1971 to 1979 (Jones 1995). Much of this funding was used to build large storage reservoirs and other irrigation infrastructure. This new irrigation infrastructure was a major factor in the trends of increased crop production and falling crop prices. Irrigation development worldwide continues to increase but in the last few decades much of this development has been increasingly from groundwater, with some development linked to groundwater recharge from surface irrigation systems built in the 1970s.

Going forward, the increased demand for water will not only result from increased population, but also economic growth that is occurring in many countries, which is placing more demand on water, including for agriculture. This trend is apparent, for example, in changing diets of people in countries such as India and China where major economic growth has taken place. Economic growth has led to a demand for more meat in the diet of those who can now afford it. A kilogram of meat not only costs more at the store than a similar amount of grain, such as wheat or rice, but if that meat is from grain-fed animals it also requires much more water to produce. For example, the water required to produce a kilogram of grain-fed beef can take more than 50 times the amount of water needed to produce a kilogram of rice. The potential to increase meat production from range animals that are grass-fed is limited due to scarce grassland resources in some regions such as South Asia, as well as relatively high production costs of grass-fed animals in other places such as the US. Since new animal production systems are often designed for confined grain-fed animals, either more grain crops will need to be grown for animal feed requiring yet more water, or grain crops now used to feed people in the lower part of the economic pyramid will be used for meat production.

Similar to changing diets, the renewed interest in bioenergy is leading to increased use of water in agriculture. Already we have heard concerns expressed from research journals to the popular press about the negative impacts of biofuels on food price and availability, but there will also be an added demand for water to produce the biomass for production of biofuels (Tilman et al. 2009). A liter of ethanol made from corn takes about 170 liters of water and production of a liter of bio-diesel from soybeans requires approximately 900 liters of water (Gerbens-Leenesa 2009). The US Congress has set a target of 1.4×10^{11} liters (36 billion gallons) of ethanol production per year by 2022, some of which will come from cellulosic ethanol (likely rain-fed grass or woody crops), but much of the ethanol will result from an increase in irrigated crops such as corn, soybean, sorghum, or sugar cane. Questions remain unanswered about whether biofuels will be a major fuel source in the future and if so, whether biofuels will continue to be produced using food crops or transition into cellulosic sources.

WHAT ABOUT THE FUTURE?

In 2050 agriculture will continue to be the major industrial user of water, both in terms of withdrawal and consumptive use, but it will likely not be as dominant as it is presently. The need for agriculture to increase production for food and non-food crops will continue. The approach used to meet agricultural production needs over the past five decades that relied on major new development in surface irrigation infrastructure will not work in the future. One reason is that the relatively easily tapped surface water resources appropriate for irrigation have already been developed, leaving only more costly options for surface water or unsustainable approaches using deep groundwater. Already there is an increased use of tube wells that are relatively cheap to develop, but that use groundwater at a rate that in many cases is not sustainable.

The increasing competition for water for both industrial and domestic use is yet another trend that works against an agriculture strategy to increase crop production through the use of more water. In most cases agriculture will not be able to compete with other uses because the unit value of water for most non-agricultural uses exceeds those for irrigation. For example, irrigation water rights are being bought from nearby farmers to meet the needs of Los Angeles, and investors in Texas are buying farmers' rights to the Ogallala Aquifer in anticipation of selling water to Dallas and Fort Worth (Berfield 2008). The challenge for agriculture over the next few decades is daunting, requiring greatly increased production, but with even less water use per unit production than in the past.

Most of the world's population growth will be in developing countries. Estimates by three leading international agricultural development groups (Molden 2007; Wood and Ehui 2005) generally agree on the amount of food needed to feed the world's population by the year 2050: the production of cereal grains must increase by 65 to 70% and meat by at least 100%. To achieve these levels of production, most researchers and analysts suggest a very broad spectrum of solutions including alternatives that will increase irrigated and rain-fed cropland area only marginally while providing a major increase in production per unit area of both irrigated and rain-fed cropland.

> *In 2050 agriculture will continue to be the major industrial user of water, both in terms of withdrawal and consumptive use.*

Irrigation will still be a significant piece of the agricultural strategy to meet future production needs even if at a lower level than in the past. Irrigated crops have about double the yields of rain-fed crops, so some new irrigation will likely be developed if water is available for that use. However, higher-valued industrial and domestic water withdrawals are expected to more than double from 2000 to 2050 (from 900 km^3/yr to 1960 km^3/yr) while withdrawals for agriculture over the same period are expected to increase from 2360 km^3/yr to 3450 km^3/yr (Molden 2007). Therefore even though there is a projected increase of total water withdrawals over this period of about 50%, proportionally less water will be going to agriculture.

Probably more significant than new irrigation development to achieving agricultural production goals in the next 40 years will be modernization of the existing irrigation infrastructure and improved management practices and technologies to increase productivity. Future irrigated agriculture must use water more efficiently both in new and old systems. The focus of the massive irrigation development of the Green Revolution was on infrastructure, especially storage reservoirs and main or large secondary distribution canals. These government managed systems provided water by gravity, often at little or no cost to the farmers. Thus there was little incentive for farmers who could get irrigation water to use it efficiently. Additionally there were few incentives for farmers to pay irrigation water fees and thus little money to maintain the canals. Actual irrigated area from these large systems is often less than half what was planned. The challenge now is to revisit these systems to improve management and water use efficiency through a variety of mechanisms including transfer of management responsibilities to users, finding workable fee structures to finance maintenance, and use of better on-farm water management and crop production technologies. Much of the large surface irrigation infrastructure constructed at the end of last the last century is still maturing as a system. Experience with large-scale irrigation infrastructure in developing countries suggests that the time needed to learn how to manage these systems efficiently and productively requires an evolution of several decades or more. Therefore, many of the large irrigation systems already built are not operating at near optimal productivity, leaving significant potential to increase productivity from existing systems by 2050.

While increased production from irrigated land will continue to be critical, improved yields on rain-fed crops will likely be the primary innovation to meet production requirements in 2050. Better management and biotechnology for rain-fed crops, including use of rainfall harvesting technologies and, where appropriate, subsurface drainage, offers the promise for significantly improved production. Improving soil moisture by proper drainage and increasing water infiltration to the soil not only assures higher yields and reduced probability of crop failure, but also can give farmers the security to invest in higher value crops or more inputs such as fertilizer, herbicides, and new biotechnologies such as genetically modified crops.

> *The challenge now is to improve management and water use efficiency through a variety of mechanisms including transfer of management responsibilities to users, finding workable fee structures to finance maintenance, and use of better on-farm water management and crop production technologies.*

AGRICULTURE'S UNCERTAIN FUTURE

Because of uncertainties in predicting the impact of climate change, effectiveness of new developments in agricultural production technologies, opportunities for international trade of food commodities, and other factors, there is still concern about the ability of agriculture to meet the food and fiber needs of the future, and there is little reason to believe past trends of increasing water to agriculture will continue to be the major part of the solution. Most predictions, barring a world catastrophe, suggest the world population will grow from the current 6.5 billion to 9 billion people by 2050. The daily calories per capita are also expected to go up, but only marginally from about 2770 in 2005 to 3050 kilocalories (FAO 2009). The type of crops and animal products produced to meet those caloric requirements is much harder to predict. The clear trend in some developing countries is toward consumption of more meat, which if produced by feed-grains typical of most beef, swine, and poultry production in the US, requires much more water than cereal grains for the same caloric value. Where appropriate land resources permit, some developing countries could develop their own meat industries that rely more on rain-fed grass to feed animals, but currently much of the international trade in meat products to these countries is from confined grain-fed animals. The most rapid growth in demand for meat products is from China and India, countries with large populations and growing economies, but also with limited unused water and land needed for agricultural expansion. For these countries with relatively limited potential for producing meat products, international trade is likely to grow with countries such as the US that have the relatively abundant water and land resources required.

There seems to be no empirical evidence that demand for more energy will slow over the next forty years. The uncertainty for water use required for energy production is not so much in the confidence in the increasing trend line for energy, but rather how that energy demand will be met. Some new developments in renewable energy, such as wind and solar power, have relatively low water requirements, but energy from oil, natural gas, coal, nuclear sources and bioenergy all have high water needs. The corn, sorghum, soybeans and sugarcane used for some biofuels come from the same total pool as those used for food. Therefore, because these crops are produced from irrigated land, any increase in production will require use of more water. Even non-food crops used for cellulosic-based biofuels that likely will not be irrigated will result in more marginal land being brought into production, which presents another set of environmental concerns such as soil degradation.

Within the scientific community there seems to be acceptance that climate change is coming, but precisely what its impact will be on agriculture remains unclear. Globally temperature and precipitation are expected to increase, which could create an opportunity for greater agricultural production, at least in some regions. However, the variability of the weather is also expected to increase with more extreme events such as longer drought periods and more uncertainty in total rainfall from year to year at any particular location. The impact and response of agriculture to climate changes is being researched, but presently it is not possible to predict how it will impact agricultural use of water. Presumably the ability to control crop water needs by irrigation would reduce part of the uncertainty related to drought.

Historically, projects designed to withdraw irrigation water for agriculture often have been done with insufficient concern for the impact these developments have on other water uses, especially those associated with societal (e.g., equity) or environmental purposes. Over time, even on major rivers, these withdrawals can reach a level where they exceed the amount of renewable water available. Irrigation storage reservoirs, stream diversions and deep groundwater wells can contribute to withdrawing so much water that ecosystem services and environmental flows start to fail. Major rivers such as the Colorado in the US or Krishna in India are now "closed", that is flow at their outlets cease for at a least short period most years. The long-term ecological damage of a river that stops flowing is so significant it cannot be tolerated (Molden 2007).

The development and management of large-scale surface irrigation systems with major water withdrawals (collectively or individually) must be designed to protect relevant environmental flows and ecosystem services. Otherwise, not only will the irrigated agriculture fail, but harm will come to other beneficial uses of the ecosystems. The market system is unlikely to support measures to protect the environment, but the public is largely responsible for developing much of the irrigation infrastructure and must continue to be involved in helping to provide resources to manage and maintain irrigation systems not only for maximum productivity, but also for optimal water allocation to meet societal needs. This will require firm policies and laws. Groundwater development for irrigation is even more difficult because it is often done by private investors, who have economic profitability as their primary if not only motivation. An assessment of the World Bank lending for groundwater related projects shows a very disturbing trend. Of the 10 projects that were most successful at meeting the project objectives, the top projects were those that were focused on drilling wells. Not surprisingly many of these projects have led to non-sustainable over exploitation of the groundwater. At the bottom of the list of the 10 worst World Bank projects in terms of meeting the objectives were generally those aimed at groundwater recharge (World Bank 2010). The Bank must put more emphasis on development projects that will protect the long-term sustainability of the groundwater resource.

The two countries that extract the most groundwater are India and the US. Since 1960 the US withdrawals from groundwater have increased from about 80 to 100 km^3/yr. During that same period groundwater extraction in India, almost exclusively for irrigation, has increased from 25 to over 250 km^3/yr (Shah 2009). India has more irrigated cropland than any country and most of that area is irrigated by groundwater. Groundwater in many Indian states is rapidly falling and groundwater irrigation as being practiced is unsustainable. Unfortunately, in India and the US, neither the legal nor economic systems adequately support approaches to sustainable development that protect the groundwater or the associated environment or ecosystems. US water law, as well as water law in many other countries, views water like any other commodity. As demand for water increases there will be more need to protect the water requirements of the poor and of the environment, neither of which compete well in an economic system with the price dependent on supply and demand.

Water law reform is occurring in some countries with a goal of more social equity and sustainability (Godden 2005). For example, Australia has adopted an approach combining objectives of environmental protection and resource efficiency that is integrated into market based trading mechanisms. In many countries, including the

US, groundwater rights are linked directly to land ownership. Water in the US is a "state subject," meaning the state has the responsibility for water law, so water law reform will likely occur at the state level. There are exceptions. Wetlands are an example of a water-related land use that is, in the US at least, governed by both state and federal governments. Protecting wetlands is seen as a societal need even at the national level. Similar measures applied to wetland controls might be needed to protect sustainability of groundwater or environmental flows that also provide critical ecosystem services.

Global climate change is making clear the need for an international body to guide water development. The World Water Forum in 2000 addressed global water issues related to agriculture and the environment. Since then many groups have come together to look at issues of food and water on a global scale including The Comprehensive Assessment of Water Management in Agriculture and the Consultative Group on the International Agricultural Research Challenge Program. What has come out of the discussions and reports of these and other such groups is the clear need to have a balanced and comprehensive approach to use of water in agriculture that includes sustaining healthy environmental systems. A "comprehensive" approach is one that uses a holistic basin approach that includes not only economic, legal, and political consideration, but also has a much greater focus on the legitimate concerns of the broader societal and ecological issues.

CONCLUSION

In 2050 irrigated agriculture will remain the world's largest industrial consumptive use of water. Water withdrawals for agriculture will increase, but proportionately much slower than many other industries. The diet of the population in 2050 will rely more on meat and less on cereal grains, which will translate to more water needed per calorie of food produced. Water for non-food crops such as cotton is also expected to increase with the potential growth of the biofuels industry based on biomass production creating even more need for water. There is a growing recognition that irrigated agriculture as now practiced in most countries cannot be sustained without more attention given to providing the environmental sustainability including flows needed for healthy ecosystems.

How will the future agriculture system manage to feed an estimated 9 billion people with a diet that requires even more water per calorie to produce than today? Part of the solution will be a modest expansion of irrigated and non-irrigated cropland. Much of the success of the Green Revolution was a result of huge investments made in surface irrigation infrastructure in support of new high yielding crop varieties. But many of these irrigation systems are functioning at a level well below optimal, offering significant opportunity to increase production by investing in better management and new technologies. Increasing international trade could allow for more efficient use of the world's land and water resources for agriculture production. However, the major thrust to meet agriculture production in the next 40 years is likely to be in new developments including biotechnology and water harvesting to increase the yield of rain-fed crops. This will surely include emphasis on diversified and intense cropping systems that are designed and managed to not only be productive but to protect the environment as well.

REFERENCES

Berfield, S. (2008). "There will be water." *Business Week,* June 23, 2008, 40-45.

Browne, P. (2009). "U.N. study urges caution on biofuels." *NY Times*, Oct 22, 2009.

Food and Agriculture Organization (FAO). (2009). Global agriculture towards 2050. High Level Expert Forum - How to Feed the World in 2050. FOA, Rome, Italy, http://www.fao.org/fileadmin/templates/wsfs/docs/Issues_papers/HLEF2050_Global_Agriculture.pdf (Sep, 2010)

Faurès, J., Hoogeveen, J., and Bruinsma. (2000). *The FAO Irrigated Area Forecast for 2030.* FAO, Rome, Italy, <http://www.fao.org/nr/water/aquastat/catalogues/index2.stm> (Aug, 2010).

Gerbens-Leenesa, W., Hoekstraa, A. Y., and van der Meer, T. H. (2009). "The water footprint of bioenergy." *P. Natl. Acad. Sci. USA*, 106 (25), 10219–10223.

Godden, L. (2005). "Water law reform in Australia and South Africa: sustainability, efficiency and social justice." *J. Environ. Law*, 17 (2), 181-205.

Jones, W. I. (1995). *The World Bank and irrigation*, The World Bank, Washington, DC, ISBN 0-8213-3249-X.

Molden, D., ed. (2007). *Water for food, water for life: a comprehensive assessment of water management in agriculture*, Earthscan, London, UK, ISBN 978-1-84407-396-2.

Shah, T. (2009). *Taming the anarchy: groundwater governance in South Asia*, Resources for the Future Press, Washington, DC, 978-1-933-115-60-3.

Tilman, D., Socolow, R., Foley, J. A., Hill, J., Larson, E., Lynd, L., Pacaia, S., Reilly, J., Searchinger, T., Somerville, C., and Williams, R. (2009). "Beneficial biofuels - the food, energy, and environment trilemma." *Science*, 325 (5938), 270-271.

Wood, S., and Ehui, S., eds. (2005). "Food." *Ecosystems and human well-being: current state and trends, Volume 1.* R. Hassan, R. Scholes, and N. Ash, eds., Island Press, Washington, DC, 209-241, ISBN 9781559632287, <http://www.millenniumassessment.org/documents/document.277.aspx.pdf> (Aug, 2010).

World Bank. (2010). *An evaluation of world bank support for water and development 1997-2007*, The World Bank, Washington, DC, ISBN 978-0-8213-8393-3, <http://siteresources.worldbank.org/INTWATER/Resources/Water_eval.pdf> (Aug, 2010).

AUTHOR INFORMATION

Michael Walter is a Professor and past Chair of the Biological and Environmental Engineering Department at Cornell University. He holds a PhD degree in Water Resources Engineering from the University of Wisconsin. His research interests are in hydrology and water quality, with a focus on rural watersheds. Since the early 1980s he has directed and participated in agricultural research programs in the Philippines, Venezuela, Sri Lanka, Indonesia, Honduras, India, Kenya, Rwanda, Niger, Peru, Bangladesh, and Nepal. He served as Irrigation Management Advisor, USAID India, in New Delhi, India from 1984-85 and from 1988-89. Email: mfw2@cornell.edu

Chapter 17

A Vision for Urban Stormwater Management in 2050

James P. Heaney and John J. Sansalone

ABSTRACT

During the past 40 years, urban stormwater management has evolved from a focus on drainage and flood control to inclusion of stormwater quality associated with nonpoint pollution. This chapter projects what the urban stormwater field could look like in the year 2050. The projections are based on our best judgments as to the internal and external drivers that are expected to change the field during the next 40 years. Anticipated changes include increased stormwater reuse, on-site control of stormwater using a variety of low impact development alternatives, generation and accretion of recalcitrant residuals, toxics and chemicals as well as changing temporal and spatial phenomena of the urban hydrologic cycle due to changes in climate and patterns of urban settlement. Key expected drivers of changing attitudes are the greatly increasing relative costs of providing water and energy; greater concern about developing more sustainable green materials and infrastructure systems; and technological advances that will allow proactive management of urban stormwater systems using real time control and including source controls.

"Integrated Stormwater Management"

INTEGRATED STORMWATER SYSTEMS

Clearly the need for stormwater infrastructure is to manage excess runoff from storms so as to prevent or at least reduce flood damage and pollutant discharge into receiving waters. As early as the 1960s, urban water experts were advocating the need to take an integrated systems view of water supply, wastewater, and stormwater (Heaney 2000). Since the 1960s, computational power and models such as the Storm Water Management Model (SWMM) for continuous hydrologic simulations, geographic information systems (GIS) and computational fluid dynamics (CFD), coupled with advances in urban water chemistry and particulate measurements and imaging technology, have helped us to take this integrated view of stormwater system design and management.

The characteristics of sustainable stormwater infrastructure systems include the reduction of stormwater runoff and its impurities by appropriate land cover and retention (groundwater absorption) ponds, the use of cisterns or other collection devices to capture and reuse stormwater for lawn watering and toilet flushing, and the establishment of economic incentives for maintaining stormwater infrastructure (Heaney 2000). Water resource systems of cities are becoming more sustainable by adapting the broader concepts of green cities and smart growth. Future water supply, stormwater, and wastewater systems will likely be managed not separately, but together in a closed loop, and urban landscapes will be hydrologically and ecologically functional (Heaney 2007; Novotny 2006; Novotny and Brown 2007).

An international group of experts affiliated with the IWA/IAHR Joint Committee on Urban Drainage (Marsalek et al. 2007) viewed the "green" option of stormwater management as synonymous with decentralization of urban water systems in order to maximize the reuse of treated wastewater and stormwater. They correctly caution that these green approaches have not yet been implemented on a large scale and significant potential public health issues need to be considered.

USEPA (2007) developed a research plan directed at encouraging innovation and research for water infrastructure for the 21st century. Most of their suggested topics deal with existing infrastructure issues. This plan is somewhat limited by the lack of a federal water agency that can take a holistic view of urban water in general and urban stormwater in particular. For example, the US Environmental Protection Agency (USEPA) deals with urban stormwater quality issues while the US Army Corps of Engineers is responsible for flood control.

URBAN STORMWATER MODELS, SENSORS AND METHODS

Over the past decades the ability to model, simulate and monitor both centralized and decentralized stormwater conveyance and control systems has markedly improved (Elliott and Trowsdale 2007; Heaney and Lee 2006; Lee et al. 2005; Sansalone and Pathapati 2009; Weinstein et al. 2006). However, monitoring and modeling of decentralized low impact development (LID) systems have not developed to a similar extent despite the applicability of existing mechanistic and numerical tools. LID can be more challenging to monitor and model as compared to centralized traditional systems for several reasons including:

- there are many more controls to analyze, e.g., hundreds of small storage-release systems as opposed to a single neighborhood detention pond;
- the reliance on infiltration greatly increases the uncertainty regarding performance;
- control can be exercised anywhere in the stormwater systems, thus blurring the distinction between the transport/storage and control elements in the model;
- there are increased questions regarding liability in the case of system "failures," e.g., allegations that flooding was caused by overland flow from nearby parcels;
- there is increased complexity regarding the expected water quality changes associated with subsurface phenomena;
- there is increased complexity from the non-stationary coupling of water chemistry, variably-saturated phenomena and the fate/transformation of chemicals and particulates in such systems;
- by design, decentralized systems are high surface area systems resulting in systems of higher reactivity and therefore greater temporal and spatial variability;
- measurement practices are adapted from centralized steady flow wastewater treatment systems and applied to decentralized systems, or single/multiple unit operations subject to unsteady runoff loadings (Kim and Sansalone 2008; Ying and Sansalone 2010);
- quantitative operation and maintenance practices and the optimization of such maintenance are subject to competing objectives; and
- there are additional loadings imposed on such systems as a result of urban water reuse.

> *Modeling and monitoring decentralized low impact development systems is more challenging as compared to centralized traditional systems.*

Present and projected computer hardware and software will allow modeling of these more complex decentralized systems. For example, SWMM and CFD can be coupled and validated to predict the fate of chemicals and particulates whether in centralized or newer decentralized systems once the constitutive properties of the system are known (Sansalone et al. 2008). While the hydrologic parameter inputs to such models have developed and matured over the last 50 years, a similar evolution is progressing for rainfall-runoff chemical, thermal and particulate phenomena, in particular with respect to coupling unit operation and process concepts (Sansalone 2005). New sensor and measurement systems and methods are essential to accurately monitor urban stormwater systems and institute proactive adaptive controls. Experimental urban watersheds with state-of–the-art representative monitoring and modeling are an essential element of selected future systems in order to find the optimal mix of centralized and decentralized systems.

Whether our urban water systems are centralized or decentralized, the complexity and uncertainty of rainfall-runoff relationships requires more progress towards continuous simulation that couples hydrology, chemistry and treatment. Beyond intra-event and event-based modeling and design load concepts for unit operation and process (UOP) and LID systems, the long-term performance and viability of such systems is completely unknown. They need to be analyzed using continuous simulation. Longer-term assessments also require the coupling of rainfall-runoff relationships with coupled constitutive relationships for chemical, particulate and thermal regimes. For example, is transport of particulate matter a first-order process (a mass-based first-flush) or a zero-order process as a function of hydrology (Sheng et al. 2008)? Modeling also requires that the signature of a UOP or LID system be generated for rainfall-runoff regimes as well as for chemical, particulate and thermal regimes, recognizing that the signature changes (i.e., is non-stationary) as systems age and are not maintained (Kim and Sansalone 2008). While the hydrologic responses of a UOP or LID system have been effectively modeled under saturated or unsaturated conditions with existing models, modeling of the hydrodynamic, chemical, particulate and thermal regimes is more complex and not as common.

The simple steady-state signature, the more complex event-based signature, or the much more challenging non-stationary signature of a UOP or LID system that includes chemical and thermal transformation, constituent re-mobilization and scour can be developed with CFD. CFD is arguably one of the most powerful tools for assessment of UOP and LID systems since the introduction of continuous simulation modeling. However, as with any powerful tool, CFD has limitations. CFD requires far more representative data and monitoring than what is currently collected. For example, accurate particle size distribution (PSD), whether monitored in-situ or ex-situ is required. As with other models, CFD requires validation. These tools are most commonly utilized as design and analysis tools, for example to examine urban water control by UOPs. However, UOPs and LID cannot be sustained until we use such tools to quantitatively examine maintenance practices and source controls. As we move forward towards 2050, tools such as continuous simulation modeling, SWMM, GIS and CFD modeling will be coupled, providing an even more significant advance for urban water cycle management.

URBAN WATER REUSE AND CHEMICAL CYCLING

Reuse and urban pollutant inventories will continue to grow as we move toward 2050. Pollutant load inventories in urban control systems (including UOPs and low impact development) can be mobile and leachable. Additionally, pollutant inventory in conventional urban conveyance systems and urban land uses requires recovery, quantification and management; otherwise this load becomes part of the urban water cycle. This is particularly important with respect to stormwater and wastewater reuse as a component of the urban water cycle. As we move toward 2050, source controls and pollutant recovery from urban source areas such as pavement cleaning can make a very demonstrable difference in load reduction and in operation and maintenance requirements for centralized or decentralized systems. Load management is required to reduce pollutant leaching from urban load inventories. As our technologies and infrastructure systems are improved to provide more treatment, greater quantitative management and financing for such management will need to be provided. Management of such systems is a critical issue for persistent chemicals, in particular metals, which accrete at the aqueous-particulate interface and have a history of ecological impacts in urban areas. In addition to metals, modern chemicals include xenobiotic and organic chemicals used in the manufacture of materials from asphalt pavement to plastic water bottles, chemicals that are leached into to the urban water cycle and in some cases are incorporated into ecological food webs (Sansalone 2008).

Management of rainfall-runoff requires recognition that hydrology and chemistry are coupled phenomena in urban environments, and it is only with restoration of the hydrologic cycle and management of the urban water cycle that these cycles will be sustainable at the urban interface. The success or failure of reuse is dependent in large part upon our understanding and application of hydrologic processes and treatment controls as an integral part of the urban water cycle. Water reuse is now a critical and important component of the urban water cycle. This reuse is currently dominated by highly treated wastewater but also includes stormwater in selected urban areas. The need for such reuse will continue to increase.

> *Water reuse is now a critical and important component of the urban water cycle and its need will continue to increase.*

Distributing reuse water makes sense on a volumetric basis; however more attention is required for the chemical and microbiological loadings that are cycled back to urban areas by reuse water, thereby becoming part of the hydrologic and urban water cycles. Persistent chemicals in runoff and runoff residuals include metals, organics, endocrine disrupting compounds (EDCs) and nutrients. Unless reuse runoff is specifically treated for the aqueous fraction of these species, such chemicals have the potential to be redistributed back to urban environments. The particulate residual fraction of these chemicals must be separated and also managed due to its potential for leaching or volatilization. Urban runoff contains pathogens and will require disinfection before reuse. While highly treated wastewater may have very low gravimetric levels of TSS and BOD_5 and disinfection residuals, concentrations of nutrients, salts, EDCs and emerging contaminants in urban runoff must also be significantly reduced before re-introduction into the urban hydrologic cycle. States such as Florida and California lead the nation with respect to reuse on a volumetric basis, and it is logical to extend this leadership to urban stormwater chemical management.

FORECASTED CHANGES

Per capita indoor water use is expected to decline from historical levels of about 270 liters per capita per day (lpcd) (70 gallons per capita per day (gpcd)) to as low as 150 lpcd (40 gpcd) with current technology, especially high efficiency toilets (Aquacraft, Inc. 2005). On the other hand, outdoor irrigation usage is increasing in many areas due to larger landscape areas and the use of automatic sprinkling systems that encourages higher application rates. Outdoor water use exceeds indoor water use in many of the warmer, more arid, parts of the country. Outdoor water use also contributes to peak demands. Virtually all indoor water use ends up as wastewater that is treated along with outdoor infiltration and inflow (I/I). Thus, wastewater supply that includes I/I is a fairly steady 300-450 lpcd (80-120 gpcd) year round. This wastewater supply can be expected to decrease to 190-280 lpcd (50-75 gpcd) due to decreased indoor demand and more effective I/I controls. Irrigation demand decreases as precipitation increases so there is a mismatch between irrigation demand and the available supply of stormwater for reuse as irrigation water. A continuous simulation model can be used to estimate the amount of storage that is needed to provide irrigation water from reuse sources (Asano et al. 2007).

The quantity of stormwater per capita increased dramatically during the 20th century due to (Heaney 2000):
- more automobiles which required more streets and parking and created additional pollutant sources
- larger houses on larger lots that increased runoff quantity and pollutant loads
- growth of suburbia and much lower population densities
- more contemporary urban area devoted to parking than to human habitat and commercial activities.
- low density urbanization that has generated over three times as much stormwater runoff per family than did pre-automobile land use patterns.

Major trends during the 21st century can be expected to decrease the demand for urban stormwater systems in the following ways:
- "Green developments" that increase population density and reduce urban sprawl
- Major modifications in our energy policies that increase the relative cost of energy compared to its historically very low costs in the United States (Friedman 2008)
- Reduced demand for larger homes and landscapes due to changing economic conditions and public attitudes towards sustainable lifestyles
- The availability of advanced modeling and data gathering techniques that will enable the direct measurement of stormwater fluxes throughout the urban area and the resultant ability to implement proactive real time control systems that optimize performance for the entire contributing watershed.

The following trends should have a very positive impact on urban water systems:
- Higher gasoline costs will reduce the demand for automobile travel that is the largest source of directly connected impervious areas in cities. This will reduce stormwater runoff generation and the associated pollutant loads.

- Higher energy costs will encourage higher density urban development and reverse the trend over the past 50 years towards lower density urban sprawl that has greatly increased urban stormwater generation.
- Higher density urban development will reduce the irrigated area per person and higher energy costs will reduce demands for irrigation water.
- Higher energy costs will favor the development of decentralized urban water systems because water distribution and collection systems constitute the majority of the cost of urban water systems.

SUMMARY AND CONCLUSIONS

During the past 40 years, urban stormwater management has evolved from focus on drainage and flood control to inclusion of stormwater quality associated with nonpoint pollution and how the demand for off-site stormwater services can be reduced by on-site management, primarily through infiltration. This chapter projects what the urban stormwater field could look like in the year 2050. Anticipated changes include the growing interest in stormwater reuse, on-site control of stormwater using a variety of low impact development alternatives, and changing patterns of urban runoff due to changes in climate and patterns of urban settlement. Key expected drivers of changing attitudes are the greatly increasing relative costs of providing water and energy; greater concern about developing more sustainable green systems; and technological advances that will allow proactive management of urban stormwater systems using real time control. Sustainable green systems will also require management of pollutant loads from reuse and active control and management of recalcitrant or toxic residual inventories generated in urban environs and activities. Source controls and green materials can improve the sustainability of such systems.

REFERENCES

Aquacraft, Inc. (2005). *Water and energy savings from high efficiency fixtures and appliances in single family homes*, USEPA Combined Retrofit Report, <http://www.aquacraft.com/Publications/EPA_Combined_Retrofit_Report.pd f> (Aug, 2010).

Asano, T., Burton, F., Leverenz, H., Tsuchihashi, R., and Tchobanoglous, G. (2007). *Water reuse*, McGraw-Hill, New York, NY, 1570 p.

Elliott, A., and Trowsdale, S. (2007). "A review of models for low impact urban stormwater drainage." *Environ. Modell. Softw.*, 22(3), 394-405.

Friedman, T. (2008). *Hot, flat, and crowded: why we need a green revolution-and how it can renew America*, Farrar, Straus, and Giroux, New York, NY.

Heaney, J. P. (2000). "Principles of integrated urban water management." *Innovative urban wet-weather flow management systems*, J. P. Heaney, R. Pitt, and R. Field, eds., EPA-600-R-99-029, US Environmental Protection Agency, Cincinnati, OH, 2-1 to 2-67, http://www.epa.gov/nrmrl/pubs/600r99029/600R99029prelim.pdf, (Aug,2010).

Heaney, J. (2007). "Centralized and decentralized urban water, wastewater and storm water systems." *Cities of the future: towards integrated sustainable water and landscape management*, V. Novotny, and P. Brown, eds., IWA Publishing, London, UK, 237-250.

Heaney, J., and Lee, J. (2006). *Methods for optimizing urban wet-weather control system*, EPA/600/R-06/034, USEPA, Edison, NJ, <http://www.epa.gov/nrmrl/pubs/600r06034/epa600r06034toc.pdf> (Aug, 2010).

Kim, J. Y., and Sansalone, J. J. (2008). "Hydrodynamic separation of particulate matter transported by source area runoff." *J. Environ. Eng.-ASCE*, 134(11), 912-922.

Lee, J., Heaney, J., and Lai, D. (2005). "Optimization of integrated urban wet-weather control strategies." *J. Water Res. Pl.-ASCE*, 131 (4), 307-315.

Marsalek, J., Ashley, R., Chocat, B., Matos, M., Rauch, W., Schilling, W., and Urbonas, B. (2007). "Urban drainage at cross-roads: four future scenarios ranging from business-as-usual to sustainability." *Cities of the future: towards integrated sustainable water and landscape management*, V. Novotny, and P. Brown, eds., IWA Publishing, London, UK, 338-356.

Novotny, V. (2006). *Cities of the future: creating blue water in green cities*, Wingspread Workshop Report to the National Science Foundation, 30 p.

Novotny, V., and Brown, P., eds. (2007). *Cities of the future: towards integrated sustainable water and landscape management*, IWA Publishing, London, UK, 427 p.

Sansalone, J. (2005). "A perspective on the synthesis of unit operations and process concepts with hydrologic control for rainfall-runoff." *J. Environ. Eng.-ASCE*, 131(7), 995-998.

Sansalone, J. (2008). "Rainfall-runoff management and the urban water cycle." *Florida Water Resources J.*, 1(1), 15-18.

Sansalone, J., Kuang, X., and Ranieri, V. (2008). "Permeable pavement as a hydraulic and filtration interface for urban drainage." *J. Irrig. Drain. E.-ASCE*, 134(5), 666-674.

Sansalone, J. J., and S.-S. Pathapati (2009), Particle dynamics in a hydrodynamic separator subject to transient rainfall-runoff, *Water Resour. Res.*, 45, W09408, doi:10.1029/2008WR007661.

Sheng, Y., Ying, G., and Sansalone, J. (2008). "Differentiation of transport for particulate and dissolved water chemistry load indices in rainfall-runoff from urban source area watersheds." *J. Hydrol.*, 361(1-2), 144-158.

US Environmental Protection Agency (USEPA). (2007). *Innovation and research for water infrastructure for the 21st century research plan*, EPA/600/X-09/003, USEPA, National Risk Management Research Laboratory, Edison, NJ, <http://www.epa.gov/nrmrl/pubs/600x09003/600x09003.pdf> (Aug, 2010).

Weinstein, N., Glass, C., Heaney, J. P., Huber, W. C., Jones, P., Kloss, C., Quigley, M., Stephens, K., and Strecker, E. (2006). *Decentralized stormwater controls for urban retrofit and combined sewer overflow reduction*, WERF 03-SW-3, IWA Publishing, Alexandria, VA, 182 p.

Ying, G. and Sansalone, J. (2010). "Transport and solubility of hetero-disperse dry deposition particulate matter subject to urban source area rainfall-runoff processes." *J. Hydrol.*, 383(3-4), 156-166.

AUTHOR INFORMATION

James P. Heaney, PhD, PE, D.WRE, DEE is a Professor in the Department of Environmental Engineering Sciences at the University of Florida. He holds a PhD in Civil Engineering from Northwestern University. He has extensive experience related to water conservation and overall urban water management including stormwater management and wastewater reuse. Professor Heaney is a member of the Board of Directors of the Alliance for Water Efficiency and of the American Academy of Water Resources Engineers. Email: heaney@ufl.edu

John J. Sansalone, PhD, PE is a Professor in the Department of Environmental Engineering Sciences at the University of Florida. After he completed his PhD from the Department of Civil and Environmental Engineering at the University of Cincinnati he has taught and conducted research at the University of Cincinnati, the Università della Calabria, Louisiana State University, and the University of Genova. His current interests include the interactions of hydrology, chemistry and control/treatment/reuse of rainfall-runoff and snowmelt; green materials and infrastructure systems in the urban environment. Email: jsansal@ufl.edu

Chapter 18

A Vision for Urban Water and Wastewater Management in 2050

Glen T. Daigger

ABSTRACT

Population growth, coupled with increased standards of living and growing resource limitations, is creating water shortages and necessitates changes from the "linear" urban water management approach historically used. Evolving approaches and enabling technologies allow integrated 21st century urban water management systems to be assembled which require the removal of much less water from the natural environment, can achieve energy neutrality and provide significant nutrient recovery. These approaches incorporate increased efficiency, use of local water resources, and much greater recovery and recycling. Further advantages include easier expansion, reduced urban heat island effects, and dramatically increased urban aesthetics. Our existing "linear" systems can be transformed by aggressively incorporating these modern concepts into new developments and when redevelopment occurs. Education and professional practice must be transformed to break down historical barriers between drinking water, stormwater, and wastewater. Economic analysis requires careful consideration of marginal effects.

"I remember the good old days when there was just
a water pipe and a sewage pipe."

INTRODUCTION

The current approach to managing water in urban areas has been used for millennia and was codified in modern cities in the late 19th and early 20th century. It is a "linear" system that involves removing large quantities of water from the environment, transporting it often long distances to the urban area, treating it to potable water standards, distributing it to meet all urban water uses (even those for which lower quality water would be sufficient), collecting used water for treatment to meet water quality standards, and remote discharge. Likewise, urban stormwater is collected and conveyed out of the urban area. This 20th century approach has been highly successful in meeting its original objective of protecting the public from enteric disease and flooding when the population of the planet was less than 2 billion people and the population was mostly rural. However, by 2050 the population of the planet will be approaching nearly 10 billion people, the vast majority will reside in urban areas, and they will be experiencing a significantly elevated standard of living which will place severe strains on the resources of the planet unless current resource consumption patterns are altered (Daigger 2007a; NRC 2003). Under these circumstances the current "linear" 20th century urban water and wastewater management system will no longer be sustainable as it contributes to water stress (the lack of sufficient water supplies to meet human needs), environmental degradation, excessive resource consumption, and the dispersal of nutrients into the aquatic environment (Daigger 2009).

Fortunately, alternate urban water and wastewater management approaches are developing that use water and resources (energy and chemicals) much more efficiently and better manage nutrients (Daigger 2009, 2007b; Daigger and Crawford 2007). These new 21st century approaches include: (1) capturing local water resources through techniques such as rainwater harvesting and distributed stormwater management, (2) reducing net water use through use of water conservation and water reclamation and recycling technologies, (3) becoming energy neutral by both reducing energy use by distributed urban water management and by extracting energy and heat from the wastewater stream, and (4) recovering nutrients. The distribution of potable and non-potable water and separation of wastewater components at the source contribute further to energy and nutrient recovery objectives and offer the potential to significantly improve public health protection. 21st century approaches can also enhance the urban environment by retaining water in the urban landscape and creating natural areas that are not only amenities, but also reduce urban heat island effects.

This chapter outlines the individual technologies and approaches which form the basis for the 21st century urban water (potable and non-potable, waste, and storm) management systems and demonstrates how they can be integrated into more highly performing systems. The year 2050 is especially pertinent for two reasons. First, planning for urban water management systems must be long-term in nature due to the long life of water management infrastructure. Second, the year 2050 represents an expected plateau in the human population, growing through the first half of the 21st century to reach a global population of approximately 10 billion (450 million in the US), and remaining at this level through the second half of the 21st century (Daigger 2007a; UN 2005). Transitioning from the current "linear" system to a more integrated system will require significant changes to infrastructure, urban water management institutions, and professional practice (Daigger 2009; Daigger and Crawford 2007). This transition will require integrated action but can be implemented aggressively in areas where new development is occurring and in existing urban areas as redevelopment occurs. Expanding needs can be met and existing urban areas can be transformed into this higher performing approach to urban water and wastewater management over time.

> *Transitioning to a more integrated urban water management system will require significant changes in infrastructure, institutions, and professional practice*

21st CENTURY URBAN WATER MANAGEMENT

Elements of the 21st Century Approach

Table 18-1 summarizes key approaches and technologies that enable the 21st century approach to urban water management (Daigger 2009; Daigger et al. 2005; Daigger 2003). A wide variety of water conservation technologies are available, and more are expected in the future. Experience in water-short areas indicates that application of these technologies can reduce domestic and commercial indoor water use substantially from over 400 liters/capita-day to between 120 and 150 liters/capita-day. Reduced water use also means significantly reduced used water volumes, which can facilitate added innovations as will be discussed below. Reduced water consumption means that local water sources can become a higher proportion of the urban water supply. One such source is local rainfall, which can be captured by a wide variety of means and stored in either constructed vessels or in local aquifers. Even if rainwater is not reused, infiltration into the local groundwater provides a groundwater source that can replenish local streams and enhance the environment (Strecker et al. 2005).

Of particular note is water reclamation and reuse which produces another local water source that can contribute significantly to meeting urban water needs (Daigger 2007b). Used water can be treated to meet essentially any quality requirement, including for potable consumption or even for industrial applications requiring ultra-pure water. An evolving approach is source separation, which recognizes that different water qualities are appropriate for different uses. This general concept has been used for several decades with dual distribution systems where reclaimed water is distributed for urban irrigation and is now being extended recognizing the small proportion of water which actually needs to meet potable water standards – on the order of 30 to 40 liters/capita-day. If potable water is produced from fresh water sources and non-potable and irrigation water are supplied by rainwater harvesting and water reclamation and reuse, net water removal from the external environment can be reduced by more than an order of magnitude. More extensive treatment, perhaps at a more local level to minimize deterioration in the distribution system (distributed water treatment), can be applied to the small amount of water which must meet potable water standards.

Table 18-1. Approaches and technologies enabling the 21st century approach to urban water management

Approach	Examples of Enabling Technologies
Water conservation	Low-flush toilets, low-volume showerheads, low-volume washing machines, low-volume dishwashers, xeriscape, drip irrigation
Distributed stormwater management	Rainwater harvesting, green roofs, porous pavement, rain gardens, vegetated strips
Water reclamation and reuse	Membrane bioreactors, advanced oxidation, ultraviolet disinfection
Source separation	Dual distribution systems, urine separating toilets
Distributed water treatment	Membranes, advanced oxidation, ultraviolet disinfection
Heat recovery	Heat pumps
Organic management for energy production	Anaerobic treatment, microbial fuel cells
Nutrient recovery	Crystallizers, struvite, calcium phosphate

Source separation can be extended further to the collection of used water from domestic and commercial sources. Grey water is relatively uncontaminated, and consequently can be treated without chemicals and with relatively little energy to produce non-potable water that is usable for a variety of purposes. Importantly, this is the largest proportion of domestic and commercial water use. Further separation of black water (feces) from yellow water (urine) segregates the majority of the organic matter (which can be used for energy production) from the nutrients in the waste stream. Due to the higher concentration, the organic matter stream can be subject to direct anaerobic treatment with biogas collected for energy production, rather than being treated aerobically which requires energy. In the future it may be possible to directly produce electricity from the organic matter contained in this waste stream using microbial fuel cells (Logan et al. 2006). The concentrated yellow water can be separately treated to recover nutrients and to remove pharmaceuticals.

Not only can energy be produced from the organic matter contained in the waste stream, the thermal mass of the water and waste stream can also be used productively. Heat exchangers and heat pumps can be used to extract heat from the waste stream for space heating, and heat can also be rejected to this stream for cooling. These approaches represent a significant departure from the traditional linear approach and can be further combined into integrated systems with additional enhanced performance characteristics.

Integrated 21st Century Urban Water Management Systems
When developing integrated urban water, organic matter, and nutrient management systems it is necessary to recognize the appropriate scale for various activities.

Development of the stormwater, water treatment, and wastewater reclamation technologies listed in Table 18-1 allows water management to be accomplished on a more distributed basis. This offers at least two advantages. First, transmission distances (and consequently pumping energy requirements) are minimized when rainwater is captured and reclaimed water is produced closer to its use. Second, high quality reclaimed water facilitates extraction of heat from or rejection of heat to the waste stream is produced to meet local needs. At the same time, economical energy production and nutrient recovery from the waste stream requires relatively large quantities of organic matter and nutrients, suggesting that these functions are best accomplished on a more centralized basis.

Integrated urban water management systems must also comply with a set of guiding principles and constraints, as summarized in Table 18-2. The guiding principles lead to systems alternatives, while the constraints must be complied with for any alternative.

Table 18-2. Integrated urban water management systems guiding principles and constraints (from Daigger 2009)

Guiding Principles	Constraints
Protect and use local water resources	Maintain water balance under dry and wet conditions
Mimic local hydrogeology	Maintain salt balance
Provide multiple barriers to protect public health	Maintain nutrient balance
Minimize resource consumption and maximize recovery	Collect and manage residuals

Consider an integrated 21st century urban water management system intended to use only local water supplies. Potable water is supplied by local water resources, in this case a potable water aquifer which will provide suitable capacity due to the relatively small amount of truly potable water required. Non-potable water supply is secured by rainwater harvesting and water reclamation and recycling. Non-potable water storage (to balance demand with production) is provided by another local aquifer.

Consider another integrated 21st century urban water management system intended to minimize energy requirements and maximize nutrient recovery. Potable and non-potable water supplies are separated to minimize pumping distances and pumping energy for potable and non-potable water distribution. Local water supplies (rainwater, grey water wastewater reclamation) are used for non-potable water supply because of the lower resulting energy consumption. Separate collection of black water and yellow water allows the concentrated black water stream to be treated anaerobically for biogas production and nutrient recovery from yellow water. The thermal mass of the waste stream is used locally as a heat source for space heating and to reject heat for cooling, depending on the season.

Analysis of systems such as these demonstrates that they can significantly reduce net water use, which makes water available to meet growing needs based on population and economic growth, and achieve energy neutrality (no net energy input required) and significant nutrient recovery. They provide further benefits to the urban area, including reduced heat island effects (due to the increased vegetated cover), greatly improved aesthetics, and easy expansion. The monetary value of these benefits is often not reflected in cost-benefit analysis, but they are real.

> *If non-potable and irrigation water are supplied by rainwater harvesting and water reclamation and reuse, net water removal from the external environment can be reduced by more than an order of magnitude.*

Transition to 21st Century Systems

When high efficiency, closed loop 21st century integrated urban water management systems are compared to our current, linear 20th century systems, one may ask "How can we transform our existing systems?" Said another way, what will we do with our "legacy" systems? The answer is obvious as we have significant experience in many contexts dealing with legacy systems and phasing them out while phasing in new generation approaches. We do it by aggressively incorporating 21st century approaches into new developments and also when we redevelop existing urban areas. Recognizing that the US population is expected to grow 50 percent by 2050 from the current 300 million to about 450 million, simply incorporating 21st century approaches into new development will result in one-third penetration of the new approaches into the urban water management infrastructure that will exist in 2050. Further recognizing the urgent need for repair and replacement of much of our existing urban water management infrastructure, aggressively incorporating 21st century approaches as this infrastructure is redeveloped will result in significant conversion of our entire infrastructure. The key is to begin now, as it will provide two benefits. Accelerating the transition from 20th to 21st century approaches will allow us to capture the benefits of these new approaches as quickly as possible. Aggressively incorporating these approaches will provide practical knowledge that will allow "fine tuning" of these new approaches and drive a research and development agenda, leading to their further advancement. The modular nature of 21st century infrastructure is an important feature as it can be easily added and expanded in response to demand, thereby facilitating financing.

Institutional arrangements are certainly a key to accelerating the transition to 21st century approaches (Daigger 2009; Daigger and Crawford 2007). Urban drinking water, wastewater, and stormwater are often managed by separate utilities, and even when managed by the same utility they are often not managed in an integrated fashion. Though actual integration of water, wastewater and stormwater utilities is not necessarily a requirement as indicated by the numerous examples of separate utilities that successfully cooperate, coordinated planning and activities are a necessity. One constraint to this holistic viewpoint is the structure of our historic educational approaches and our professional organizations which emphasize the separate management of drinking water, wastewater, and stormwater. Better integrating our approaches to education and expanded cooperation by our professional organizations can create an integrated vision for urban water management, which can carry into professional practice.

Economics is key to enabling rapid transition to 21st century integrated urban water management approaches (Daigger 2009; Daigger and Crawford 2007). The benefits of integrated approaches can be broad and must be evaluated properly. For example, the costs and benefits of options that reduce net water demand (e.g., water conservation, rainwater harvesting, and water reclamation and reuse) should not be compared to the average cost of delivering potable water. Reduced demand will allow the most expensive water supply option to be retired or implementation of the next most expensive water supply option to be avoided. In other words, the marginal cost, rather than the average cost must be considered in the evaluation. Multiple benefits can also be generated by these measures – for example, a reduction in both water supply and waste management costs – and all of these benefits must be considered in the evaluation. Thus, we must be careful to perform a "global" rather than "local" optimization. We must also include broader benefits such as reductions in heat island affects and greenhouse gas emissions in the overall evaluation.

At the same time, the costs and benefits for various options may not be uniformly distributed between the responsible parties. Such issues can be dealt with through inter-agency or inter-departmental charges. It may also be necessary to change the basis for financing urban water management utilities. In many instances urban drinking water and waste management utilities are financed based on the volume of water sold or wastewater generated. Obviously, this penalizes utilities for reducing water use and wastewater generation, steps which are contrary to our general objectives. Moreover, utility costs do not go down in proportion to the volume of water sold or wastewater processed. This challenge has been faced by many electric utilities and has been solved by at least partially separating the revenue that the electric utility receives from the quantity of electricity it sells. This more enlightened approach compensates electric utilities for causing increased efficiency of electricity use, along with the total amount used. The same approach could be applied to urban water management utilities.

CONCLUSIONS

The traditional, 20th century approach to urban water management may be described as "linear" and involves removing large quantities of water from the environment, transporting it long distances to the urban area, treating all to potable water standards, distributing it to meet all urban water uses (even those for which lower quality water would be sufficient), collecting used water for treatment to meet water quality standards, and remote discharge. While this linear 20th century approach has successfully protected public health, several factors are creating the need to transform our approach to urban water management, including global and national population growth, urbanization, increased living standards, and resource availability. As a result, widespread water stress is developing both globally and within the US.

Fortunately, higher efficiency, closed loop approaches are available which can:
- Dramatically reduce the quantity of water urban areas remove from the external environment.
- Achieve energy neutrality (i.e., no net energy input).
- Achieve significant nutrient recovery.

These 21st century approaches incorporate (1) increased water conservation and efficiency, (2) distributed stormwater management which captures and uses rainfall, (3) source separation, (4) water reclamation and reuse, (5) distributed water treatment, (6) heat recovery, (7) organic management for energy production, and (8) nutrient recovery. To achieve full benefit, these approaches must be developed into integrated urban water management systems where a variety of qualities of water are produced and used and collected for reuse. The transition from linear 20th century to closed loop 21st century approaches can be implemented by aggressively incorporating 21st century approaches into new development and as redevelopment occurs. The modular nature of these technologies facilitates incremental additions in response to growing demand. Changes in professional practice and our educational system are required to develop practitioners capable of developing and implementing these integrated systems. Economics must be carefully examined, often considering marginal cost impacts. Collaboration between utilities will be required, including approaches to financing them.

REFERENCES

Daigger, G. T. (2009). "State-of-the-art review: evolving urban water and residuals management paradigms: water reclamation and reuse, decentralization, resource recovery." *Water Environ. Res.,* 81(8), 809-823.

Daigger, G.T. (2007a). "Wastewater management in the 21st century." *J. Environ. Eng.,* 133(7), 671-680.

Daigger, G. T. (2007b) "Creation of sustainable water resources by water reclamation and reuse." *Proc., 3rd International Conference on Sustainable Water Environment: Integrated Water Resour. – New Steps,* Sapporo, Japan.

Daigger, G. T. (2003). "Tools for future success." *Water Environ. Technol.,* 15(12), 38-45.

Daigger, G. T., and Crawford, G. V. (2007). "Enhanced water system security and sustainability by incorporating centralized and decentralized water reclamation and reuse into urban water management systems." *J. Environ. Eng. Manage.,* 17(1), 1-10.

Daigger, G. T., Rittman, B. E., Adham, S., and Andreottola, G. (2005). "Are membrane bioreactors ready for widespread application?" *Environ. Sci. Technol.,* 39(19), 399A-406A.

Logan, B. E., Hamelers, B., Rozendal, R., Schroder, U., Keller, J., Freguia, S., Aelterman, P., Verstraete, W., and Rabaey, K. (2006). "Microbial fuel cells: methodology and technology." *Environ. Sci. Technol.,* 40(17), 5181-5192.

National Research Council (NRC). (2003). *Cities transformed: demographic change and its implications in the developing world*, The National Academy Press, Washington, DC.

Strecker, E., Huber, W, Heaney, J., Bodine, D., Sansalone, J., Quigley, M., Leisenring, M., Pankani, D., and Thayumanavan, A. (2005). *Critical assessment of stormwater treatment and control selection issues*, Report No. 02-SW-1, Water Environment Research Foundation, Alexandria, VA.

United Nations (UN). (2005). *World population prospects: the 2004 revision*, Economic and Social Affairs, United Nations. <http://www.un.org/esa/population/publications/WPP2004/wpp2004.htm> (Oct, 2009).

AUTHOR INFORMATION

Glen T. Daigger is Senior Vice President and Chief Technology Officer for Civil Infrastructure with CH2M HILL, a global project delivery company. He holds BSCE, MSCE, and PhD degrees from Purdue University. A recognized expert in biological wastewater treatment, water management, and urban sustainability, he is the author of four books, several manuals, and more than 200 publications. Dr. Daigger has received awards from ASCE and WEF and is a member of the National Academy of Engineering. He is currently President of the International Water Association. Email: gdaigger@ch2m.com

Chapter 19

Water Resources and Sustainable Aquatic Ecosystems: A Vision for 2050

N. LeRoy Poff and Brian D. Richter

ABSTRACT

Failure to include the goods and services provided by freshwater ecosystems in the design, development and operation of water infrastructure results in the degradation of these ecosystems. Human societies and governments must act with urgency to more comprehensively incorporate robust principles of ecosystem science into planning and management of freshwater resources if long-term sustainability of freshwater ecosystems is to be secured for the 21st century. Absent this, we can expect the state of freshwater ecosystems in 2050 to be massively diminished, perhaps irretrievably so, with unforeseen economic consequences to human populations that depend on the self-sustaining nature of functional freshwater systems. The foundations for integrating ecosystem sustainability principles into water resources planning, development and management already exist. We identify four major pathways forward for achieving a new water management paradigm that will be able to ensure the viability and robustness of freshwater ecosystems for posterity. However, implementing them will require substantial political will, in addition to sustained efforts from the technical community needed to devise water management strategies that meet both human and ecosystem needs.

INTRODUCTION

Sustaining healthy, functioning aquatic ecosystems in the face of increasing human population growth and accelerating climate change is one of the greatest societal challenges facing water resources management now and in the coming decades. Early in the 21st century, water has already become a limiting resource for population growth and poverty alleviation in many areas of the world (WWAP 2009). Further, water scarcity is of growing concern in industrialized countries, particularly when drought cycles coincide with expanding populations. While humans clearly derive benefits from out-of-stream diversions, removing too much water from freshwater ecosystems impairs ecosystem function and diminishes many ecosystem services and goods upon which humans depend (Postel and Richter 2003; Richter 2009). Water resources decision-making typically fails to account for this loss of natural goods and services, making it a hidden cost (Emerton and Bos 2004). Indeed, one unintended consequence of this failure to balance the costs and benefits of water infrastructure is global scale degradation of freshwater ecosystems (Dudgeon et al. 2006; Strayer and Dudgeon 2010).

Human societies and governments must act with urgency to more comprehensively incorporate robust principles of ecosystem science into planning and management of freshwater resources if long-term sustainability of freshwater ecosystems is to be secured for the 21st century. Absent this, we can expect the state of freshwater ecosystems in 2050 to be massively diminished, perhaps irretrievably so, with unforeseen economic consequences to human populations that depend on the self-sustaining nature of functional freshwater systems. The foundations for integrating ecosystem sustainability principles into water resources planning, development and management already exist (Petts 2009; Poff 2009; Richter 2009). However, implementation of meaningful "solutions" presents a major social challenge that will require substantial political will, in addition to sustained efforts from the technical community needed to devise water management strategies that meet both human and ecosystem needs (O'Keeffe 2009).

OUR VISION

Our vision for 2050 is a new paradigm for water management planning, development and management, one that aims to explicitly "balance" the economic and ecological costs, benefits and tradeoffs associated with water extracted from freshwater ecosystems vs. water that remains within the ecosystem. By recognizing that freshwater systems must be managed *both* for the needs of people and ecosystems, a policy of sustainability can be rationally and consistently pursued. Historically, and even today, the balance scale has been grossly tipped to out-of-stream or out-of-lake benefits, which are typically directed to agricultural enterprises and urban populations, while ecosystem-dependent rural populations such as those living downstream of dams bear the brunt of negative impacts of water development (Richter et al. 2010). Joint human-ecosystem sustainability requires that certain management, engineering, scientific and social challenges be addressed. Meeting these challenges requires both immediate and long-term actions to build a foundation that provides the flexibility that will be required to sustainably manage water resources in the future, as human populations grow and climate change introduces new uncertainties in water allocation.

A fundamental principle of freshwater sustainability is that human alteration of natural variability of water chemistry and hydrologic processes must be constrained within specified limits that support natural riverine processes (Poff et al. 1997; Richter 2009). Social decisions will not necessarily converge on the "natural" as the most desirable management goal, because competing uses or alternative visions of desirability for ecosystem states (e.g., caused by use of dams) will be desired for different places (Jowett and Biggs 2009; Poff 2009; Poff et al. 2010). But to achieve a vision of "balancing" economic and ecological costs in order to attain desired and sustainable freshwater ecosystems, planning and management must occur at two different scales, both of which are of social and ecological relevance. At the *local* scale, stakeholders and scientists focus on the upstream watershed and the management strategies required to maintain the desired ecosystem condition for a particular site or river. At the *regional* scale, some evaluation of cumulative instream-outstream tradeoffs associated with placement and management of all existing and proposed infrastructure and water extractions is needed to accommodate regional "optimization" of watershed-scale ecosystem performance and freshwater sustainability (Krchnak et al. 2009). This process will need to be replicated for all regions within a governance domain (e.g., individual states, entire US) to account for geographic variation in ecosystem structure and function and for human cultural contexts that differ in socially-desired levels of sustainability for individual projects and for distributed projects in river networks (Poff 2009). This process can succeed only when decision-making and priority-setting take place through transparent, inclusive, and well-informed stakeholder engagement (Richter 2009).

In order to achieve this vision, a new "integration" is required, one that brings scientists, engineers, managers, policy makers and stakeholders together to develop and work cooperatively toward a common set of goals. But there are numerous challenges that must be addressed and overcome for this to happen.

CHALLENGES TO ACHIEVING FRESHWATER SUSTAINABILITY

Management/Policy Challenges

Our existing policy and management system is often dominated by adversarial positions and camps that generally lack a common vision or have asymmetrical political power and who often hold different perspectives on the "value" placed on environmental amenities and natural processes. The challenges of achieving freshwater sustainability are perhaps epitomized in the arid western US, where existing water law greatly favors historical uses of water and fails to provide adequate water for ecosystem sustainability (MacDonnell 2009a,b). In the western US, future demands for water resulting from population growth coupled with a drying climate are projected to be severe (Lettenmaier et al. 2008). However, constraints are rapidly arising in wetter regions of the country as well, such as in the Apalachicola-Chattahoochee-Flint River basin, where urban growth in Atlanta and increasing irrigation demands intersect with drought cycles to create shortages for both humans and ecosystems. Indeed, projections of future conflict and likely impairment of freshwater ecosystems has led to collaborative, stakeholder-driven visioning for state-wide water development and management in Georgia (Georgia Environmental Protection Division 2008).

> *Scientists, engineers, managers, policy makers and stakeholders must work cooperatively together to identify and develop strategies to sustain largely ignored ecosystem values.*

Water resource policy in the US has largely ignored ecosystem values and has fostered a management culture that is too often reactive in nature. Typically, ecosystem needs are not incorporated in the planning phases of water resources design, in no small part because the goods and services provided by ecosystems are not easily placed into an economic valuation context (Emerton and Bos 2004). Post-hoc resource degradation often leads to reactive legal intervention in a narrow regulatory context to stem gross degradation in water quality (e.g., Clean Water Act) or prevent extinction of rare species (e.g., Endangered Species Act) of societal concern.

Climate change and other environmental changes are inevitable in the coming decades at unprecedented geographic scope, and these changes will likely overwhelm the capacity of regulatory systems to manage them. We know natural systems will respond in complex ways and severe degradation of these systems is likely if proactive and adaptive planning and management are not embraced (Palmer et al. 2009; Poff et al. 2002, 2010; Strayer and Dudgeon 2010). The most rational avenue open to us is to recognize that freshwater systems are currently in a stressed state, to anticipate the impacts of new stressors on freshwater ecosystems (including the human reactions to climate change), and to fully explore the range of options for managing water resources in a more sustainable fashion. Thus, the active, coordinated management of existing and future water infrastructure can and must be used to help achieve the balance between human and ecosystem needs for fresh water. Adopting this perspective provides a foundation for climate change adaptation (Matthews and Wickel 2009; Poff 2009).

Achieving a balanced human-ecosystem management ethos will require a more democratic process of broad stakeholder involvement in envisioning the future states of managed ecosystems. Efforts are underway to develop such a process, as for example the strategic environmental planning approach championed by The Nature Conservancy (Richter and Thomas 2007) or stakeholder-driven process captured in the "ecological limits of hydrological alteration" approach (Poff et al. 2010). Having ecosystems represented in the planning and management of water infrastructure requires adoption of a framework on the ecological side for evaluating relative risks to ecosystems under proposed water resources development and management and projected climate changes, and it requires definition of some ecological "currency" that can be appropriately valued in the larger socio-economic models that guide investment in water infrastructure and management.

Engineering/Technical Challenges
In the broadest sense, there are three major "technical" challenges to realizing sustainable water management by 2050. The first is significant improvement of irrigation efficiency and agricultural productivity on both irrigated and rain-fed croplands. This will serve to keep more water in streams and rivers and thus provide more management flexibility. The second is overcoming the energy and brine disposal barriers to desalination for urban water supplies. With the projection of more than half the human population in 2050 living within 100 kilometers of a coastline, desalination could greatly alleviate current pressures on inland water sources. Third, for inland waters it is critical that the siting and operation of water infrastructure (i.e., dams, and particularly hydropower dams) be done in the most ecologically compatible manner possible to avoid and mitigate ecological and social impacts at local to regional scales.

On this third front, much progress has been made in recent years. Reservoir management tools have been developed that better "optimize" environmental flow needs given the project design and goals (Dittman et al. 2009; Hughes and Mallory 2008; Suen and Eheart 2006; Vogel et al. 2007). The US Army Corps of Engineers (USACE) has entered into a cooperative program with The Nature Conservancy to provide environmental flows below USACE dams for downstream ecosystem benefits. Results from these actions can be used to adaptively manage larger river systems that have dams on them (Richter et al. 2006; World Commission on Dams 2000). There is much effort to develop scientifically-based flow-ecology relationships that can be regionalized based on flow regime typologies to afford some guidance for environmental flow management required to sustain freshwater ecosystems in some desired state (Arthington et al. 2006; Poff et al. 2010). All these activities suggest a self-organizing nexus of planners, engineers, hydrologists, scientists and managers working to achieve some targeted degree of ecosystem health in the face of human demands for fresh water. Continuing efforts along these lines are essential to reach our vision of 2050 water management.

Scientific Challenges
A fundamental scientific challenge is to be able to specify the spatial and temporal scales needed to understand and manage for ecosystem resilience and sustainability. Focused effort on better articulating the relationships between flow regime, its alteration, and ecosystem dynamics is increasing rapidly (Arthington et al. 2010; Poff et al. 2010), but identifying the "bounds" on ecosystem sustainability (Postel and Richter 2003; Richter 2009) remains a research goal.

Scientists now understand that local ecosystems exist in a regional context, where movement of water, nutrients, individual organisms and genetic information is critical to sustaining the interconnected elements in a landscape setting (Fausch et al. 2002;

Poff et al. 2007; Pringle 2001; Strayer and Dudgeon 2010). This growing scientific perspective is feeding into conservation planning, where the location of dams and other water infrastructure has to be viewed both in terms of local effects and how the structure(s) will influence broader regional connectivity and sustainability. This poses an additional political challenge because environmental impacts of water infrastructure are typically viewed only at the local scale. In the future, local-scale planning will become increasingly ineffective as a viable strategy to sustain freshwater ecosystems if river basins or networks become increasingly fragmented by water infrastructure placement and management.

Another key scientific challenge is to understand ecosystem responses and adaptation to rapid global change, i.e., how human activities (land use modification, climate change, spread of invasive species) variously alter hydrologic and biological processes and thus diminish ecological resilience and sustainability. Developing this understanding is challenging due to massive alteration of earth surface processes (water, sediment and nutrient flux) over the last few hundred years. These changes have created transient (or non-equilibrium) states for the majority of freshwater ecosystems we currently observe, impairing even "reference" sites that are often used to gauge ecosystem health (Humphries and Winemiller 2009; Wohl 2005).

> *Management decisions to sustain freshwaters must be made in the face of considerable scientific uncertainty.*

The inescapable reality is that management decisions to sustain freshwaters must be made in the face of considerable scientific uncertainty. This uncertainty need not cripple the process of securing a more balanced allocation of water for people and nature, in part because we know that "no action" is not an acceptable path if freshwater sustainability is to be taken seriously. Even in the face of uncertainty, scientists are reasonably able to bound management scenarios and thus offer a risk-based assessment that can guide critical management decisions needed to promote freshwater ecosystem resilience and sustainability (Poff et al. 2010).

An additional challenge facing scientists is the human dimension of freshwater sustainability. Freshwater ecosystems are complex social-ecological systems (Berkes and Folke 1998), meaning that human desires must be taken into account and stakeholders will decide the desired ecosystem endpoints based on cultural value systems. Human preferences have to be articulated in order to frame the tradeoffs that are faced in water management decisions (Baron et al. 2003). A more integrated effort between social scientists, ecological scientists and water managers is beginning to develop (Krchnak et al. 2009; Richter 2009), but rapid progress in this area is sorely needed.

FOUR STEPS TOWARDS A NEW WATER MANAGEMENT PARADIGM

The fundamental challenges described above stand in the way of creating a regulatory and management framework that efficiently promotes long-term sustainability of freshwater ecosystems for the benefit of nature and humans. We see four major pathways forward for achieving a new water management paradigm that will be able to ensure the viability and robustness of freshwater ecosystems for posterity.

Actively Incorporate Ecosystem Principles into Management

A major step toward sustainability is to regularly and more fully include ecosystem needs in the process of integrated watershed planning and management (Bernhardt et al. 2006). Management of water infrastructure must rapidly move away from simple rules such as minimum allowable flows to more actively incorporate ecosystem principles of dynamic flow variability. The science of environmental flows is rapidly advancing and should form the basis for managing toward sustainability (Poff et al. 2010; Richter 2009). Simultaneously, a broader watershed-scale perspective must be adopted that actively seeks to promote connectivity of sites within a river network to promote freshwater ecosystem sustainability. This recognition requires that the planning and design of new water infrastructure examine both the local and regional impacts on freshwater sustainability (Opperman et al. in review; Poff 2009; World Bank 2009).

Integrate Social and Ecological Sciences into Sustainability Management

A science-based management of freshwater systems requires a more sophisticated integration of the social and ecological sciences to provide a common framework for finding sustainable solutions to the threats of water scarcity and ecosystem degradation. This is essential given the projected future demand for water by an expanding human population under the potential high uncertainties of climate change. Protecting ecosystems against unnecessary degradation will be greatly aided by development of techniques of ecosystem valuation that account for the economic benefits and costs of water resources planning and development. More effort is needed to develop an ecosystem services framework that articulates both ecological and social benefits from leaving water in freshwater ecosystems.

> *More effort is needed to develop a framework that defines the ecological, economic and social benefits of freshwater ecosystems.*

Coordinate Regulatory and Management Authorities Over Water

Attaining suitable water quality for biological integrity is federally regulated; however, little federal authority exists to require water flow regimes in freshwater ecosystems to be managed toward long-term integrity (sustainability). Therefore, federal agencies with water science and/or management missions (US Bureau of Reclamation, USACE, US Geological Survey, US Forest Service, US Fish and Wildlife Service, etc.) should engage in a collaborative program to assess the sustainability of freshwater ecosystems under their jurisdiction. Some efforts to examine water supply have already been collaboratively undertaken by agencies in the federal government with respect to climate change (e.g., Brekke et al. 2009). All federal and state dam managers should be required to reassess the operations of their facilities to identify opportunities for restoring ecosystem benefits. Federal and state agencies should cooperate to undertake vulnerability assessments for freshwater ecosystem sustainability at local to regional to national scales. Existing data on physical and biological characteristics of the nation's surface waters should be assembled and viewed through the lens of ecosystem vulnerability. This baseline information is a critical foundation for sustainable management planning at regional to national scales.

Interdisciplinary Education and Research
A key need is the education for individuals who will be the technical experts in the various aspects of water resources management. Certainly, training workshops for the current generation of technical experts can be valuable. More fundamentally, a serious commitment to interdisciplinary graduate training is needed to break down the narrow disciplinary barriers between ecology, environmental science, resource economics, political science and engineering that fragment the multiple elements required for sustainable freshwater resources planning and management.

From a research perspective, the attainment of viable solutions for water management that meet both the needs of people and ecosystems is surely a grand challenge (National Academy of Science 2001). Focused efforts are needed to bring together life scientists, physical scientists, social scientists and economists, resource managers, and engineers to pursue solutions. Initiatives modeled after the National Science Foundation's cross-cutting Dynamics of Coupled Natural and Human Systems would provide one option. This should be pursued on regional scales that reflect natural differences in climate, water infrastructure and freshwater ecosystems.

THE WATER RESOURCES WORLD OF 2050?

What will the water resources planning and management world of 2050 look like? If the above key challenges confronting freshwater sustainability can be addressed, we would hope to see a full integration of ecological, physical and social sciences to provide a unified framework for sustainable management of limited freshwater resources. In 2050 we would expect research to be explicitly and comfortably interdisciplinary. Engineering, physical scientists, ecologists and social scientists will all be well versed in each other's fundamental principles and understanding. Mid-career professionals will have facility in more than one disciplinary field due to their graduate training and their professional collaborative experiences. The link between these disciplines will be tight and highly functional.

From a regulatory standpoint, water quality and water quantity, and the management of surface water withdrawals, groundwater pumping and dam operations will be fully integrated at the whole watershed scale. The water needs of freshwater ecosystems (and the social and environmental tradeoffs) will be included in the planning and development phases of water infrastructure, contributing to a truly integrated water resources planning and management.

At local to regional to national scales, water resources planning and management will explicitly account for environmental needs. The provisioning of water for freshwater ecosystems will be part of an open discourse wherein the "value" of limited water will be publicly debated and the optimal allocation of water for people and the environment will be based on social values and the best available scientific information. The unifying goal of water management will be to balance human and ecosystem needs so that freshwater ecosystems can be sustainably managed for the benefit of future generations.

REFERENCES

Arthington, A. H., Bunn, S. E., Poff, N. L., and Naiman, R. J. (2006). "The challenge of providing environmental flow rules to sustain river ecosystems." *Ecol. Appl.*, 16, 1311-1318.

Arthington, A., Naiman, R. J., McClain, M., and Nilsson, C. (2010). "Preserving the biodiversity and ecological services of rivers: new challenges and research opportunities." *Freshwater Biol.*, 55, 1–16, doi:10.1111/j.1365-2427.2009.02340.x.

Baron, J. S., Poff, N. L., Angermeier, P. L., Dahm, C. N., Gleick, P. H., Hairston, N. G., et al. (2003). *Sustaining healthy freshwater ecosystems*, Issues in Ecology, No. 10, Ecological Society of America, Washington, DC, 18 pp., <http://www.epa.gov/owow/watershed/wacademy/acad2000/pdf/issue10.pdf> (Aug, 2010).

Berkes, F., and Folke, C., eds. (1998). *Linking social and ecological systems: management practices and social mechanisms for building resilience*, Cambridge University Press, Cambridge, UK.

Bernhardt, E., Bunn, S. E., Hart, D. D., Malmqvist, B., Muotka, T., Naiman, R. J., Pringle, C., Reuss, M., and van Wilgen, B. (2006). "Perspective: the challenge of ecologically sustainable water management." *Water Policy*, 8, 475–479.

Brekke, L. D., Kiang, J. E., Olsen, J. R., Pulwarty, R. S., Raff, D. A., Turnipseed, D. P., Webb, R. S., and White, K. D. (2009). *Climate change and water resources management—a federal perspective*, US Geological Survey Circular 1331, US Geological Survey, Reston, VA, 65 p., <http://pubs.usgs.gov/circ/1331/> (Mar, 2010).

Dittmann, R., Froehlich, F., Pohl, R., Ostrowski, M. (2009). "Optimum multi-objective reservoir operation with emphasis on flood control and ecology." *Nat. Hazards Earth Sys.*, 9, 1973–1980.

Dudgeon, D., Arthington, A. H., Gessner, M. O., Kawabata, Z. I., Knowler, D. J., Lévêque, C., et al. (2006). "Freshwater biodiversity: Importance, threats, status and conservation challenges." *Biol. Rev. Cambridge Philosophical Society*, 81, 163–182, doi:10.1017/S1464793105006950.

Emerton, L., and Bos, E. (2004). *Value: counting ecosystems as an economic part of water infrastructure*, IUCN, Gland, Switzerland and Cambridge, UK. 88 pp. <http://data.iucn.org/dbtw-wpd/edocs/2004-046.pdf> (Aug, 2010)

Fausch, K. D., Torgersen, C. E., Baxter, C. V., and Li, H. W. (2002). "Landscapes to riverscapes: bridging the gap between research and conservation of stream fishes." *BioScience*, 52, 483–498.

Georgia Environmental Protection Division. (2008). *Georgia comprehensive state-wide water management plan*, The Water Council, Atlanta, GA, <http://www.georgiawaterplanning.org/pages/technical_guidance/state_water _plan.php > (Mar, 2010).

Hughes, D. A., and Mallory, S. J. L. (2008). "Including environmental flow requirements as part of real-time water resource management." *River. Res. Appl.*, 24, 852–861.

Humphries, P., and Winemiller, K. O. (2009). "Historical impacts on river fauna, shifting baselines, and challenges for restoration." *BioScience*, 59, 673-684.

Jowett, I. G., and Biggs, B. J. F. (2009). "Application of the 'natural flow paradigm' in a New Zealand context." *River Res. Appl.*, 25, 1126-1135.

Krchnak, K., Richter, B., and Thomas, G. (2009). *Integrating environmental flows into hydropower dam planning, design, and operations*, World Bank Water Working Notes No. 22, World Bank Group, Washington, DC.

Lettenmaier, D., Major, D., Poff, L., and Running, S. (2008). "Water resources." *The effects of climate change on agriculture, land resources, water resources, and biodiversity*, A Report by the US Climate Change Science Program and the subcommittee on Global Change Research, US Department of Agriculture, Washington, DC, 121-150, <http://www.climatescience.gov/Library/sap/sap4-3/final-report/default.htm> (Mar, 2010).

MacDonnell, L. J. (2009a). "Return to the river: environmental flow policy in the United States and Canada." *J. Am. Water Resour. As.*, 45, 1087-1089.

MacDonnell, L. J. (2009b). "Environmental flows in the Rocky Mountain West: a progress report." *Wyoming Law Review*, 9(2), 335-396.

Matthews, J. H., and Wickel, A. J. (2009). "Embracing uncertainty in freshwater climate change adaptation: a natural history approach. *Clim. and Development*, 1(3), 269-279.

National Academy of Sciences. (2001). *Grand challenges in environmental science*, National Academy Press, Washington, DC, ISBN: 978-0-309-07254-0.

O'Keeffe, J. (2009). "Sustaining river ecosystems: balancing use and protection." *Prog. Phys. Geog.*, 33. 339, DOI: 10.1177/0309133309342645.

Opperman, J. J., Apse, C., Banks, J., Day, L. R., and Royte, J. In review. "The Penobscot River (Maine, USA): a basin-scale approach to balancing power generation and ecosystem restoration." Submitted to *Ecol. Soc.*

Palmer, M. A., Lettenmaier, D. P, Poff, N. L., Postel, S., Richter, B., and Warner, R. (2009). "Climate change and river ecosystems: protection and adaptation options." *Environ. Manage.*, 44(6), 1053-1068, DOI 10.1007/s00267-009-9329-1.

Petts, G. E. (2009). "Instream flow science for sustainable river management." *J. Am. Water Resour. As.*, 45, 1071-1086.

Poff, N. L. (2009). "Managing for variation to sustain freshwater ecosystems." *J. Water Res. Pl.-ASCE*, 135, 1-4.

Poff, N. L., Allan, J. D., Bain, M. B., Karr, J. R., Prestegaard, K. L., Richter, B. D., Sparks, R. E., and Stromberg, J. C. (1997). "The natural flow regime: a paradigm for river conservation and restoration." *BioScience*, 47, 769-784.

Poff, N. L., Brinson, M., and Day, J. B. (2002). *Freshwater and coastal ecosystems and global climate change: a review of projected impacts for the United States*, Pew Center on Global Climate Change, Arlington, VA, 44 pp., <http://www.pewclimate.org/docUploads/aquatic.pdf> (Aug, 2010).

Poff, N. L., Olden, J. D., Merritt, D., and Pepin, D. (2007). "Homogenization of regional river dynamics by dams and global biodiversity implications." *P. Natl. Acad. Sci. USA*, 104, 5732-5737.

Poff, N. L., Richter, B., Arthington, A. H., Bunn, S. E., Naiman, R. J., Kendy, E., Acreman, M., Apse, C., Bledsoe, B. P., Freeman, M., Henriksen, J., Jacobson, R. B., Kennen, J., Merritt, D. M., O'Keeffe, J., Olden, J. D., Rogers, K., Tharme, R. E., and Warner, A. (2010). "The ecological limits of hydrologic alteration (ELOHA): a new framework for developing regional environmental flow standards." *Freshwater Biol.*, 55(1), 147-170, DOI: 10.1111/j.1365-2427.2009.02204.x.

Postel, S., and Richter, B. (2003). *Rivers for life: managing water for people and nature*, Island Press, Washington, DC.

Pringle, C. M. (2001). "Hydrologic connectivity and the management of biological reserves: a global perspective." *Ecol. Appl.*, 11, 981–88.

Richter, B. D. (2009). "Re-thinking environmental flows: from allocations and reserves to sustainability boundaries." *River Res. Appl.*, 25, 1-12.

Richter, B. D., Postel, S., Revenga, C., Scudder, T., Lehner, B., Churchill, A., and Chow, M. (2010). "Lost in development's shadow: the downstream human consequences of dams." *Water Alternatives*, 3(2), 14-42, <www.water-alternatives.org> (Mar, 2010).

Richter, B. D., and Thomas, G. A. (2007). "Restoring environmental flows by modifying dam operations." *Ecol. Soc.*, 12(1), 12.

Richter, B. D., Warner, A. T., Meyer, J. L., and Lutz, K. (2006). "A collaborative and adaptive process for developing environmental flow recommendations." *River Res. Appl.*, 22, 297-318.

Suen, J.-P., and Eheart, J. W. (2006). "Reservoir management to balance ecosystem and human needs: incorporating the paradigm of the ecological flow regime." *Water Resour. Res.*, 42, W03417.

Strayer, D. L., and Dudgeon, D. (2010). "Meeting the challenges of freshwater biodiversity conservation." *J. N. Am. Benthol. Soc.*, 29, 344-358.

Vogel, R., Sieber, J., Archfield, S., Smith, M., Apse, C., and Huber-Lee, A. (2007). "Relations among storage, yield and instream flow." *Water Resour. Res.*, 43, W05403.

Wohl, E. E. (2005). "Compromised rivers: understanding historical human impacts on rivers in the context of restoration." *Ecol. Soc.*, 10(2), 2.

World Bank. (2009). Convenient solutions to an inconvenient truth: ecosystem-based approaches to climate change, Environmental Department, The World Bank, Washington, DC, 91pp.

World Commission on Dams. (2000). Dams and development: a new framework for decision making, Earthscan Publications, London, UK.
World Water Assessment Programme (WWAP). (2009). *The United Nations world water development report 3: water in a changing world*, UNESCO and Earthscan, Paris, France, and London, UK.

AUTHOR INFORMATION

N. LeRoy Poff is a Professor in the Department of Biology and Graduate Degree Program in Ecology at Colorado State University. Dr. Poff is a stream and river ecologist who studies the role of natural environmental variability (especially in flow regime) and its modification by humans on ecosystem structure and function. He received his MS in Environmental Sciences from Indiana University and his PhD from Colorado State in 1989. Email: poff@lamar.colostate.edu

Brian D. Richter is Director of Global Freshwater Program at The Nature Conservancy. He has been involved in river conservation for more than 20 years and has provided scientific or technical consultation on more than 90 river projects worldwide. Email: brichter@tnc.org

III EDUCATION

Chapter 20

Facing the Challenges in Educational, Technological and Social Change Leading to 2050

Jeff R. Wright

ABSTRACT

The evolution of the field of environmental and water resources engineering over the next half century will both shape and be shaped by changes in our natural and man-made environment, changes in society and what it expects from professionals, changes in technology, and changes in how we educate tomorrow's professional and technical workforce. While predicting *anything* 40 years into the future is initially daunting and ultimately humbling, this chapter presents a framework for anticipating the changes that will be needed in the way we educate environmental engineers. Particular attention is given to the expectation for new and emerging information and computational technologies, and opportunities and challenges for developing new educational pedagogies.

"Global Learning Community"

PERSPECTIVE

Evaluating attempts to predict the future with respect to important societal concerns, Princeton physicist Gerard K. O'Neill observed that forecasters tend to underestimate the rate of technical change, and overestimate the rate of social change (O'Neill 1981). This appears to be consistent with the rapid pace at which engineering innovation over the past several decades has provided technologies and methodologies that can improve water resources assessment and management, as well as the sluggishness with which widespread incorporation of such advances are mandated for use within comprehensive resource management programs. Slower still is the rate at which this innovation has motivated substantial changes in the undergraduate engineering curriculums.

Here I offer a number of prognoses of *technological change*, *social change*, and *educational change* that will challenge, and provide opportunities for, water resources professionals and educators between now and 2050.

> *Forecasters tend to underestimate the rate of technical change, and overestimate the rate of social change.*

TECHNOLOGICAL CHANGE

Sustainable Distributed Energy Sources
Recent attention to concerns of energy independence, sustainability, and global warming will drive massive research and development investments in renewable energy sources and dramatically improve distribution and control systems (Sayigh 2008). This investment will produce cost-effective, modular and scalable sources of high-quality energy that will enable increasingly reliable water monitoring, assessment, management and control systems. Improved efficiencies, reliability, and maintainability of these systems will reduce the overall relative cost of providing sustainable water resources to all sectors of our economy. New technologies for energy storage will enable much more efficient load shifting and balancing that will in turn allow enhanced optimization of production and delivery systems.

Ubiquitous Environmental Sensor Technologies
New sensor technologies and methodologies for their use are being created at an ever increasing rate (Kanoun and Trankler 2004). Advances in modern sensor technology across all spatial and performance scales will continue and accelerate over the next 40 years. Smaller and more efficient sensors will be adaptable to widespread environmental and water resources monitoring systems, and will be more readily integrated into physical infrastructure to monitor performance and condition, which will improve service and reduce the cost of systems maintenance and operation. Sensor networks will become increasingly energy independent and able to collect and transmit data reliably and continuously as needed.

Remote Sensing and Earth Observation
Remote sensing and related earth observation technologies will advance quickly with much higher resolution and reliability. High resolution technologies will enable daily image capture from all populated areas with higher frequency data collection from sensitive or critical areas. Custom image capture perspectives and schedules will be readily available to engineers, scientists, and water authorities. Large scale data storage and central repositories will enable widespread access to these data.

Intelligent Visualization and Image Analysis Systems
New and continuously improved intelligent and adaptive systems will be created to perform real-time analyses of images and sensor signals. The information from the analyses of these images will be combined seamlessly with data from distributed sensor networks to provide immediate and reliable measurements of the condition and health of environmental and water resource systems. Autonomous learning agents and adaptive systems will form the structure for intelligent scene-driven data analysis algorithms, providing opportunities for the development of more cost effective and responsive early warning systems.

Adaptive Modeling Systems
Modeling will remain an important component of water resources planning and management and environmental engineering (Loucks 2008). While innovation will continue in the design and development of next generation modeling technologies and methodologies, major advances must be made in the use of this innovation. New development environments for model applications will emerge rapidly over the coming decades that will enable new opportunities for rapid prototyping of water resources models using fully emerging computing architectures including virtual distributed client-server networks and grid computers. Prototyping will enable rapid integration of state-of-the-art simulation and optimization algorithms as well as inferential algorithms. New gigapixel hardware output display devices such as 3D powerwalls, caves, and other immersive media systems (including networked systems supporting multiple users across space and time) will emerge, enabling exploratory evaluation of complex images for use by systems managers as well as water resources engineers and scientists (Wallace et al. 2005). These modeling and systems technologies will greatly expand the rate at which modern shared vision modeling environments can be developed for, and used by, water resources stakeholders (Perez and Viessman 2009).

Commonplace Open Information Management Systems
The interactive access and use of water resources models and data will be facilitated greatly by Open Information Management Systems (OIMS) which will become widely available and commonplace, enabled by explosive growth in the development and use of free and open source software. Transparent interfaces for the spectrum of input and output devices will enable systems to be designed and implemented by engineers and administrators without the need for extensive and expensive computational support staffs.

SOCIAL CHANGE

Increased Public Awareness of Water Issues

Expanded pressures on water resources from continued population growth (Table 20-1) and environmental pressures will become much more visible to the general public, with growth in size and number of better informed citizens action groups. These groups will hold municipalities and water authorities much more accountable for sharing information and water resources forecasts, and for providing regular updates on water-related and environmental issues. Daily water reports will become commonplace in print, broadcast and online media, and other public forums.

Table 20-1. Projected growth and change in US population demographics

Year	2005	2050
Population (millions) [1]		
World	6,426	9,309
United States	296	438
Shifts in U.S. Racial/ethnic groups [2]		
Foreign-born	12%	19%
White	67%	47%
Hispanic	14%	29%
Black	13%	13%
Asian	5%	9%

[1] U.S. Census Bureau (2008)   [2] Passel and Cohn (2008)

Increased Public Pressure for Water Sustainability

Due in part to the increased availability of water resources information and public awareness, society will demand improved stewardship of this valuable resource to meet its needs for sustainable and reliable high quality water supplies. The decisions by water agencies and public officials responsible for water resources will be under increased scrutiny because of a larger and better informed citizenry. Water-related public expenditures and the stewardship of public infrastructure will be more visible and will provide the basis for citizen choices in public elections.

EDUCATIONAL CHANGE

Universal Technical General Education

The perspective on general education by most of our universities is that technical students must have broader backgrounds in the arts, humanities, and the social sciences. While certainly true, in this increasingly technical and complex society it will become increasingly important for non-technical students to obtain, through their formal education, a deeper understanding of technologies and sciences that impact their lives. This is nowhere more true than in areas of public welfare such as health care, environmental sustainability, and water reliability and quality assurance.

Universities will be under increasing pressure to provide technically-based learning experiences to all students, driven by the country's need to attract more K-12 students into technical careers, or careers that involve the management of technology. Stronger and more effective linkages and networks will be created between universities, community colleges, and K-12 institutions to improve the seamless transition of students into career paths that are more compelling for them because of the impact they will have on society.

> *Technical students must have broader backgrounds in the arts, humanities, and the social sciences and non-technical students must obtain a deeper understanding of technologies and sciences.*

Technical Workforce Diversification

The next 40 years will experience not only rapid world and US population growth, but also dramatic demographic shifts (El Nasser 2008; Passel and Cohn 2008) as reflected in Table 20-1. Most dramatically, the US will no longer have a majority Caucasian population, with the fraction of White citizens dropping from 67% to 47%, while the Hispanic population will increase from 14% to 29% over the same period. With the Hispanic representation in the current US engineering workforce at less than 5.5% and the current enrollment in engineering undergraduate degree programs at fewer than 3.5% of total engineering students (NSF Engineering Task Force 2005), increasing Hispanic participation in engineering will be a top priority in the coming decades. Doing so will result in an influx of new talent and important new perspectives into the engineering workforce at the time when this is essential for the country. Strong and targeted recruitment pipeline facilitation efforts will emerge nationally, particularly in the US southwest.

Standard 5-Year Requirement for Engineering

By 2050 the majority of engineering programs in the US, particularly those disciplines that address most directly engineering problems in the public sector (e.g. civil engineering, environmental engineering, etc.) will transition to 5-year programs, many offering streamlined Bachelor of Science in Engineering/Master of Science emphasis programs. For water resources and environmental engineering students, this will enable broader exposure to information management and networking communications technologies, modeling and model development tools and techniques, data and database development technologies, and collaboration systems. Valuable internship and co-op experiences will become a formal and required component for most of these programs.

Global Learning Communities

Recent interest in the development of national and international learning communities will continue (Palloff and Pratt 2007; Smith et al. 2004) and become commonplace within the engineering community. These collaborations will include educational/research universities at multiple locations working as appropriate with leading private sector firms and government organizations. Curricula will become increasingly experiential learning-based, and be configured in a manner that will reduce the overall cost and redundancy of staffing and equipping more narrow, but higher quality programs. Courses will consist of flexible module choices within a connected theme, and will adapt most directly to specialized learning needs rather than teaching needs. The resulting curricula for a particular degree or certification will be offered by the very top faculty and professionals in the area regardless of physical location.

Lifeline Learning
Universities and learning communities will become an increasingly important part of a student's formal professional development throughout one's career. With improved networked communications methodologies and infrastructure, students will be able to remain linked to their formal education continuously and formally. Academic programs will transition from being a foundational experience for formal engineering education to one that is viewed explicitly as part of one's *lifeline learning* (Wright 2000); students will stay "connected" with their learning roots, and will nourish, as well as be nourished by that foundation.

REFERENCES

El Nasser, H. (2008). "U.S. Hispanic population to triple by 2050." *USA Today*, February 12, < http://www.usatoday.com/news/nation/2008-02-11-population-study_N.htm> (Sep, 2010).

Kanoun, O., and Trankler, H. R. (2004). "Sensor technology advances and future trends, instrumentation and measurement." *IEEE T. Instrum. Meas.*, 53(6), 1497-1501.

Loucks, D. P. (2008). "Water resource management models." *The Bridge*, 28(3), 24-30, <http://www.nae.edu/Publications/TheBridge/Archives/V38N2.aspx> (Sep 2010).

National Science Foundation (NSF) Engineering Task Force. (2005). *The engineering workforce: current state, issues, and recommendations,* The National Science Foundation, Washington, DC, 48 p., <www.nsf.gov/attachments/104206/public/Final_Workforce.doc> (Sep, 2010).

O'Neill, G. (1981). *Year 2081: a hopeful view of the human future*, Simon and Schuster, New York, NY.

Palloff, R. M., and Pratt, K. (2007). *Building online learning communities: effective strategies for the virtual classroom*, Jossey-Bass, San Francisco, CA.

Passel, J. S., and Cohn, D. (2008). *U.S. population projections: 2005-2050*, Pew Research Center, Washington, DC, 55 p., <http://pewhispanic.org/reports/report.php?ReportID=85> (Sep, 2010).

Perez, E. M., and Viessman, Jr., W., eds. (2009). *The role of technology in water resources planning and management*, American Society of Civil Engineers, Reston, VA.

Sayigh, A., ed. (2008). *Renewable energy 2008*, Sovereign Publications, London.

Smith, B., MacGregor, J., Mathews, R., and Gabelnick, F. (2004). *Learning communities: reforming undergraduate education*, Jossey-Bass, San Francisco, CA.

US Census Bureau. (2008). "Projections of the population and components of change for the United States: 2010 to 2050." *U.S. population projections*, <http://www.census.gov/population/www/projections/summarytables.html> (Sep, 2010).

Wallace, G., Anshus, O. J., Bi, P., Chen, H., Chen, Y., Clark, D., Cook, P., Finkelstein, A., Funkhouser, T., Gupta, A., Hibbs, M., Li, K., Liu, Z., Samanta, R., Sukthankar, R., and Troyanskaya, O. (2005). "Tools and applications for large-scale display walls." *IEEE Comput. Graph.*, 25(4), 24-33.

Wright, J. R. (2000). "Internetworking and lifeline learning." *J. Water Res. Pl.-ASCE*, 126(1), 1-2.

AUTHOR INFORMATION

Jeff Wright is the Dean of Engineering of the School of Engineering at the University of California in Merced, California. He holds a PhD from the Johns Hopkins University, and MS and BS from the University of Washington. Research interests include the use of advanced modeling and information technologies to improve water resources and environmental management and the design and implementation of computer-based spatial decision support systems for civil infrastructure, transportation, water resources, and land resources engineering and management. Email: jwright@eng.ucmerced.edu

Chapter 21

A Vision of Interdisciplinary Graduate Education in Water and Environmental Resources in 2050

Laurel Saito, Fritz Fiedler, Barbara Cosens, and Derek Kauneckis

ABSTRACT

The science and management of environmental- and water-related issues requires an interdisciplinary approach, but many academic institutions remain focused on disciplinary training and traditional, narrowly defined dissertation topics. This chapter summarizes issues facing academic institutions in implementing interdisciplinary education for water and environmental issues. Three case studies of emerging interdisciplinary efforts are presented, followed by our vision of interdisciplinary graduate education in water and environmental resources in 2050.

"This interdisciplinary education really keeps us on our toes!"

INTRODUCTION

This chapter addresses a vision of interdisciplinary graduate education in water and environmental resources in 2050, as well as challenges faced in achieving that vision. In this context, the term interdisciplinary refers to activities that involve interactions between multiple disciplines within courses, across degree programs, and at the institutional level. Challenges in education overlap with those faced in solving real-world interdisciplinary problems, but academia has challenges of its own.

To appropriately address environmental- and water-related issues can require input from disciplines as varied as law, hydrology, atmospheric science, water quality, geochemistry, public policy, sociology, economics, engineering, and ecology. Funding agencies, consulting firms, and public organizations have recognized this and increasingly ask interdisciplinary teams to tackle cross-cutting projects (Tansel 2008). The National Research Council's (NRC) examination of the role of research in addressing water problems in the United States advocated integrated approaches that spanned the physical, chemical, biological, and social sciences over strictly discipline-based approaches (NRC 2004). Institutions of higher education are often training grounds for future researchers and managers, but most academic institutions remain primarily focused on disciplinary training (Lele and Norgaard 2005; Loucks 2008; NSF 2000; Nicolson et al. 2002) and traditional, narrowly defined dissertation topics (Moslemi et al. 2009). However, Brint et al. (2009) noted that there was a substantial increase in interdisciplinary degree-granting programs between 1975 and 2000 in nine program areas, including Environmental Studies. The National Science Foundation's (NSF) Integrative Graduate Education and Research Traineeship (IGERT) program has been successful in encouraging graduate education and research that cross disciplinary lines (Morse et al. 2009; Moslemi et al. 2009).

Applying interdisciplinary approaches involves challenges such as
- differences in temporal and spatial scales of issues of interest across disciplines,
- theory and models of causation, and tolerance of measurement error and data uncertainty (Nilsson et al. 2003; Saito et al. 2007),
- different "cultural" perspectives of related issues that may make communication and interaction difficult between disciplines (Cullen 1990; Eigenbrode et al. 2007; Nicolson et al. 2002; Nilsson et al. 2003), and
- lack of awareness and training in interdisciplinary approaches (NSF 2000; Nicolson et al. 2002).

Institutions of higher learning are well-poised to address the issue of improving awareness and training in interdisciplinary approaches, but current academic environments make interdisciplinary education especially challenging. Issues facing interdisciplinary education for water and environmental resources include 1) challenges in addressing real-world problems in an education context; 2) challenges at the course level; 3) challenges at the programmatic level; and 4) challenges at the institutional level.

Issue 1 - Challenges in Addressing Real-World Problems in an Education Context
Addressing real-world problems often requires multidisciplinary inputs. The more disciplines involved, the greater the difficulty in exposing students to interdisciplinary approaches in sufficient depth in an academic environment. Ideally, students are exposed to the same hurdles they will face as practitioners in both a theoretical and an experiential manner. Developing realistic interdisciplinary educational experiences is difficult due to faculty availability and experience, stakeholder interaction, and the mix of students available to compose interdisciplinary teams. Given the transitional state of academia, many faculty may not have the experience (or even an interest) in addressing problems outside their traditional discipline.

Issue 2 – Challenges at the Course Level
Attracting an interdisciplinary student body that meets course pre-requisites is a primary challenge (Saito et al. 2007). Having instructors from different disciplines provides students with the opportunity to observe interdisciplinary dialogue and faculty interaction, but requires more coordination and commitment from these instructors. Expectations about depth/breadth, workload, and grading vary among students and instructors depending upon their disciplinary background. In particular, there is tension between the desire to cover material in each discipline, and the need to focus on methods of working across disciplines. Furthermore, the lack of existing interdisciplinary course material requires a greater time investment on the part of instructors to develop such materials.

> *There is tension between the desire for depth in each discipline, and for breath across disciplines.*

Issue 3 – Challenges at the Programmatic Level
We define interdisciplinary programs as those that grant degrees and include faculty from more than one academic department. Consistency in courses and curricula is difficult to maintain for reasons discussed under issue 4, and because the degree of interdisciplinary interaction may vary depending on the program and mix of faculty involved. While students are often attracted to interdisciplinary degree programs because of the breadth of courses and collaborative research opportunities, university faculty and students often have difficulty in evaluating relative quality of interdisciplinary programs. Being involved in interdisciplinary programs may be perceived by faculty to harm promotion potential and by students to harm job searches (Golde and Gallagher 1999). Rhoten and Parker (2004) noted that while graduate students found interdisciplinary work challenging and of interest, they had concerns about professional costs associated with focusing on interdisciplinary work.

Issue 4 – Challenges at the Institutional Level
Brint et al. (2009) found that interdisciplinary programs tended to be at larger, wealthier universities, possibly due to greater organizational capacity to support such programs, as well as having a critical mass of student participation. In smaller

institutions, departments and colleges can be protective of their faculty, students, and resources, and hence, less supportive of interdisciplinary programs. Faculty lines are typically controlled by departments in which faculty are appointed. Thus, faculty may be directed to reduce participation in interdisciplinary programs, and key positions in a program may not be replaced. Faculty who do participate in interdisciplinary courses and programs often volunteer their time, adding to the "regular" home-program load. Many disciplines also have curricula that discourage the addition of courses considered "outside" of disciplinary training. Evaluation of faculty and promotion are often still tied to departments and colleges, and there may not be the means or criteria to evaluate interdisciplinary publication and teaching by tenure and promotion committees. Indirect cost returns from interdisciplinary research grants obtained by faculty in interdisciplinary programs generally go to colleges or departments rather than to the interdisciplinary program.

EXAMPLES OF CURRENT INTERDISCIPLINARY ACTIVITIES

There are different perspectives on what constitutes a well-designed interdisciplinary program. Programs rest on a continuum of shallow to deep expertise within a discipline as well as a continuum of theoretical to applied focus. Both continua can involve tradeoffs in breadth, depth and expertise necessary to satisfy expectations of hyper-specialization in an academic environment and practical multifaceted skills of applied problem-solving. Interdisciplinary education that focuses on moving beyond the narrow scope of academic disciplines and attempts to transcend traditional disciplinary boundaries risks creating graduates that do not have the depth of training in any specific discipline to be considered an expert. Those that focus on problem-solving skills on the other hand run the risk of becoming too applied and losing the important foundation of theory on which all pragmatics rests. An interdisciplinary program that serves the purpose of both preparing specialists as well as practitioners needs to generate students that are able to fully engage their own disciplines as well as communicate with those examining similar practical and theoretical challenges from other disciplinary perspectives.

We briefly highlight three example activities: 1) the Graduate Program of Hydrologic Sciences at the University of Nevada Reno (UNR); 2) the Waters of the West interdisciplinary graduate program at the University of Idaho (UI) and an interdisciplinary methods course taught in that program; and 3) an inter-institutional graduate level course on interdisciplinary modeling for water-related issues.

Graduate Program of Hydrologic Sciences

The Graduate Program of Hydrologic Sciences at UNR was created in 1962 and offers MS and PhD degrees in Hydrology and Hydrogeology. The program includes faculty from 7 departments at UNR, several divisions of the Desert Research Institute (DRI), and adjunct faculty from agencies such as the US Geological Survey. Funding for the program is provided by UNR, DRI, and private sources and covers costs for a part-time Program Director, an administrative assistant, teaching assistantships, a colloquia series, recruitment, and some operating costs (GPHS 2008). Participating faculty are fully appointed within their respective departments and the program is not directly involved in their hire, evaluation, or promotion and tenure. Strengths of the program include its visibility and recognition, the quality and diversity of published work associated with the program, and the success of program graduates. The lack of control of faculty lines and course scheduling and coordination affect the strength of the program (Bahr et al. 2005). In 2005 the feasibility of converting the program into an academic department was explored. However, the university decided the strengths of the interdisciplinary program outweighed the advantages of creating a new department and the program has remained as an interdisciplinary entity.

Waters of the West Graduate Program and Interdisciplinary Methods Course
The Waters of the West graduate program at UI draws on expertise of 56 faculty members in seven colleges to integrate aspects of law, natural resources, engineering, political science and more. The program has three overlapping degree focus areas: 1) Water Resources Engineering and Science; 2) Water Resources Science and Management; and 3) Water Resources Law, Management and Policy. The program partners with the UI College of Law to allow students to seek a concurrent Juris Doctorate in any focus area. An interdisciplinary thesis is required.

Faculty developed a team-taught introductory interdisciplinary methods class that serves as a foundation to all focus areas. A cross-college course of this nature should be written into faculty position descriptions to assure coverage. Faculty have designed the course to address barriers to effective interdisciplinary research and applied problem solving by addressing differences in language, methodology, values, and goals across disciplines and misperceptions about those factors in other disciplines. The course begins with an introduction to interdisciplinary theory (e.g., Newell 2001) and the terminology and methodology of key water resource disciplines. Students are taught conceptual methods for working across disciplines, including: problem definition, discipline selection, communication, identification and reconciliation of conflicts between disciplinary insights, finding common ground, and integration (Eigenbrode et al. 2007; Repko 2008). Tools employed for working across disciplines include systems conceptualization and modeling and use of GIS.

Students apply these methods and tools to three prepared problems derived from existing faculty/student team-based research and designed to focus student time and learning specifically on interdisciplinary aspects of problems. An example problem deals with conjunctive management of ground and surface water along the Snake River in eastern Idaho and focuses on the interrelationship between the legal doctrine of prior appropriation and technical difficulties of determining the relationship between groundwater pumping and river flows to the degree of specificity required to curtail junior groundwater pumpers to protect senior surface water users. Another typical problem addresses steelhead recovery in a tributary to the Clearwater River within the Nez Perce Indian Reservation and focuses on the different datasets and approaches needed to understand endangered species recovery from the viewpoints of a biologist, a lawyer, and a tribal government seeking to satisfy tribal elders. A third problem addresses management of water supply for a community relying on the declining Palouse Basin aquifer and employs a systems approach to compare costs of conservation and new source development over a fifty year timeframe.

Interdisciplinary Modeling for Water-Related Issues Course

A graduate-level course developed at UNR introduces students to models in different disciplines (Saito et al. 2007; www.cabnr.unr.edu/saito/Classes/nres730/nres730.htm) using multiple instructors with different backgrounds. Students learn that if they collaborate with others in other disciplines, they may be able to combine and apply models from different disciplines to address particular problems. The course addresses: 1) advantages and limitations of using models; 2) different discipline-specific spatial and temporal scales; 3) differences in uncertainty; 4) interdisciplinary modeling options; 5) communication between disciplines; 6) education and training of scientists and modelers about applying interdisciplinary approaches; and 7) interaction with stakeholders, the public and policy-makers. The objective is to engage students in interdisciplinary discourse addressing these issues. The course has been taught as a three-credit graduate level course jointly with other institutions over 15 days in the summer. Students are assigned a faculty-developed group modeling project. A wiki has been used as a virtual textbook to post material about the course before, during, and after the course. Implementation challenges for the course include finding faculty who can commit for little or no compensation or course credit, recruiting an interdisciplinary set of students, and coordinating and designing lectures and exercises. Student evaluations have been very positive and cited interdisciplinary interaction among students and instructors as one of the best features.

OUR VISION FOR 2050

We have two visions of interdisciplinary graduate education in water and environmental resources in 2050. Either model of graduate education will require implementation of interdisciplinary or collaborative dissertations (such as that described in the UI case study) as a means of furthering student experiences in interdisciplinary research and education.

Vision 1: Nested Cluster of Expertise

In our first vision, a typical graduate program offers a nested cluster of expertise that roughly corresponds to disciplinary areas combined with one or more courses on integration and thesis or dissertation requirements for integration. There are three areas of study: the built environment (including disciplines such as engineering, architecture, design, etc.), the social environment (including economics, law, political science, sociology, policy studies, anthropology, etc.), and the natural environment (including ecology, hydrology, soil science, limnology, etc.). Students are required to train within a particular discipline and select a small number of courses outside their area of study. For example, a political science student focused on collective action problems in lake system management could develop a level of competence in hydrology that would allow them to communicate and collaborate with natural sciences. Likewise a hydrology student could take courses in policy analysis to be better able to understand the tools and methods of program evaluation toward improving the integration of hydrological modeling.

The crux of the interdisciplinary nature of this program is that all students are required to work on an interdisciplinary project directed towards a problem that develops new approaches through integration of theoretical approaches from more than one discipline. In one scenario, students work in an interdisciplinary team to develop project reports on the topic of their choosing. Thus, a project on "solutions to transboundary water disputes in the Middle East" would be presented by a water engineer, a student of international water law and a political science student specialized in international relations. Similarly, a project on "designing optimal water conservation strategies for rural western communities" would be presented by students of economics, civil engineering, psychology and design. Another scenario could involve a single student integrating two or more disciplines to address a particular practical or theoretical problem. Through interaction with other disciplines, students learn to develop a common lexicon for discussing similar issues, understand the perspective of other disciplines and their specific approach to problem definition and the formulation of solutions, and learn the common boundaries and limits of cross and interdisciplinary research.

> *Interdisciplinary graduate education in water and environmental resources in 2050 will require implementation of interdisciplinary or collaborative dissertations.*

Vision 2: Broad Interdisciplinary Education

Our second vision involves a graduate program that provides training for people with a broad education in water and environmental resources who are not considered to be an "expert" in any particular discipline. Such educated people can play the role of integrators in a world of ever-increasing complexity. This is not to say that we would attempt to educate "Renaissance People" who are truly experts in several subject areas; only those of genius caliber might live up to that title. If we can work past the societal need to categorize, label, or otherwise market ourselves and others to fit a particular well-known, traditional profession in society (engineer, lawyer, scientist, economist, etc.), then people with breadth and people with depth may be able to work together to more effectively integrate across traditional disciplines to solve both applied and theoretical problems. A description of such a program might be: "It's not either disciplinary or interdisciplinary, it's both." The program could consist of a series of courses that are initially team-taught so that students all have at least one course in water/environmental policy, water chemistry, aquatic ecology or limnology, economics, hydrology, and modeling. The courses would have to be team-taught initially as instructors transition from those who have been trained in a disciplinary sense (as current education models are), to those who have been broadly trained who would be able to teach a whole class on interdisciplinary topics alone.

For both visions we see the concept of life-long learning having an interdisciplinary focus in 2050. In the past, universities have attempted to instill a desire for life-long learning, but in the context of learning more and more about a particular discipline.

In fact in some cases discipline-specific continuing education is required by law to maintain licensure (e.g., engineering, law). In 2050, continuing education has been recast as a need to continue learning about a particular thematic area such as water resources, and professional licensure requirements have been revised to recognize the value of having a professional engineer benefit from professional development in social sciences. This transition from educating primarily in particular areas to learning more about other areas important to the field has over time increased interdisciplinary knowledge and skills among the practicing professional community as well by 2050.

Achieving our vision for 2050 will not be possible without a change in the traditional structure of higher education. In an article in the *NY Times*, Taylor (2009) calls for abolishing departments and structuring curriculum as more of a "web or complex adaptive network" as opposed to the traditional disciplinary silos. Criticism of this approach does not address the merits of the basic concept, but the fact that many universities attempting this approach through a top-down restructuring have used it as an excuse to cut support structure and smaller departments (Adamson 2010). The UI and UNR case studies are examples of approaches generated from the bottom up. Nevertheless, these approaches will require some high-level restructuring to assure sustainability. Designing that restructuring to remove obstacles to a thriving faculty/student-led program should address many of the concerns identified with top-down restructuring.

> *Achieving our vision for 2050 will not be possible without a change in the traditional structure of higher education.*

In the current climate of 2010, recent widespread budget challenges have exposed the vulnerability of interdisciplinary efforts. At many institutions, departments and colleges are being asked to increase faculty productivity by focusing on increased class sizes within departments, and departments and colleges compete with interdisciplinary programs for scarce funding resources. This may cause some to doubt that our visions for interdisciplinary education in 2050 are achievable. However, two factors will keep interdisciplinary efforts alive and growing. The first is the influence of young faculty. Recent studies have shown that many graduate students, the next generation of faculty, are interested in interdisciplinary research (Rhoten and Parker 2004; Tress et al. 2009). Rhoten and Parker (2004) noted that interdisciplinary faculty role models tended to be non-tenured more than tenured. By 2050, tenured faculty with interdisciplinary commitment should reach a critical mass to sustain interdisciplinary efforts. The second factor is funding agencies and organizations that will ultimately hire graduates. Such organizations will likely continue to value interdisciplinary education and skills, so there will be demand for courses and programs that produce such students (Ewel 2001).

REFERENCES

Adamson, M. (2010). "Graduate education is the Dubai of higher learning. *Academe*, 96(1), 25-27.

Bahr, J., Burges, S., and Wilson, J. (2005). *Report of the external reviewers on the interdisciplinary graduate program of hydrologic sciences, University of Nevada, Reno*, University of Nevada Reno, Reno, NV, 18 p.

Brint, S. G., Turk-Bicakci, L., Proctor, K., and Murphy, S. P. (2009). "Expanding the social frame of knowledge: interdisciplinary, degree-granting fields in American colleges and universities, 1975-2000." *Rev. High. Educ.*, 32(2), 155-183.

Cullen, P. (1990). "The turbulent boundary between water science and water management." *Freshwater Biol.*, 24, 201–209.

Eigenbrode, S. D., O'Rourke, M., Wulfhorst, J. D., Althoff, D. M., Goldberg, C. S., Merrill, K., Morse, W., Nielsen-Pincus, M., Stephens, J., Winowiecki, L., and Bosque-Perez, N. A. (2007). "Employing philosophical dialogue in collaborative science." *BioScience*, 57(1), 55-64.

Ewel, K. C. (2001). "Natural resource management: the need for interdisciplinary collaboration." *Ecosystems*, 4, 716-722.

Golde, C. M., and Gallagher, H. A. (1999). "The challenges of conducting interdisciplinary research in traditional doctoral programs." *Ecosystems*, 2, 281-285.

Graduate Program of Hydrologic Sciences (GPHS). (2008). *Program review*. University of Nevada Reno, Reno, NV, 5 p.

Lele, S., and Norgaard, R. B. (2005). "Practicing interdisciplinarity." *BioScience*, 5(11), 967-975.

Loucks, D. P. (2008). "Educating future water resource managers." *J. Contemp. Water Res. Educ.*, 139, 17-22.

Morse, W. C., Nielsen-Incus, M., Force, J. E., and Wulfhorst, J. D. (2009). Bridges and barriers to developing and conducting interdisciplinary graduate-student team research. *Ecol. Soc.*, 12(2), 8, <http://www.ecologyandsociety.org/vol12/iss2/art8/> (Sep, 2010)

Moslemi, J. M., Capps, K. A., Johnson, M. S., Maul, J., McIntyre, P. B., Melvin, A. M., Vadas, T. M., Vallano, D. M., Watkins, J. M., and Weiss, M. (2009). "Training tomorrow's environmental problem solvers: an integrative approach to graduate education." *BioScience*, 59(6), 514-521.

National Research Council (NRC). (2004). *Confronting the nation's water problems: The role of research*, National Academy Press, Washington, DC.

National Science Foundation (NSF). (2000). *Environmental science and engineering for the 21st century: The role of the National Science Foundation*, NSB 00-22, National Science Foundation, Arlington, VA, <www.nsf.gov/pubs/2000/nsb0022/reports/nsb0022.pdf> (May 29, 2009).

Newell, W. H. (2001). "A theory of interdisciplinary studies." *Iss. Integrat. Stud.*, 19, 1-25.

Nicolson, C. R., Starfield, A. M., Kofinas, G. P., and Kruse, J. A. (2002). "Ten heuristics for interdisciplinary modeling projects." *Ecosystems*, 5, 376–84.

Nilsson, C., Pizzuto, J. E., Moglen, G. E., Palmer, M. A., Stanley, E. H., Bockstael, N. E., and Thompson, L. C. (2003). "Ecological forecasting and the urbanization of stream ecosystems: Challenges for economists, hydrologists, geomorphologists, and ecologists." *Ecosystems*, 6, 659–74.

Repko, A. F. (2008). *Interdisciplinary research: process and theory*, Sage Publications, Inc., California.

Rhoten, D., and Parker, A. (2004). "Risks and rewards of an interdisciplinary research path." *Science*, 306, 2046.

Saito, L., Segale, H. M., DeAngelis, D. L., and Jenkins, S. (2007). "Developing an interdisciplinary curriculum framework for aquatic ecosystem modeling." *J. College Sci. Teach.*, 37(2), 46-52.

Tansel, B. (2008). "Changing the status quo in environmental engineering education in response to emerging markets." *J. Prof. Iss. Eng. Ed. Pr.*, 134(2), 197-202.

Taylor, M. C. (2009). "End the university as we know it. *The New York Times: Late Edition*, April 27, 2009.

Tress, B., Tress, G., and Fry, G. (2009). "Integrative research on environmental and landscape change: PhD students' motivations and challenges." *J. Environ. Manage.*, 90, 2921-2929.

AUTHOR INFORMATION

Laurel Saito is an Associate Professor in the Department of Natural Resources and Environmental Science at the University of Nevada Reno (UNR). She is also Deputy Director of the Graduate Program of Hydrologic Sciences at UNR. She obtained her PhD and MS in Civil Engineering from Colorado State University, and a BS from the University of California at Davis in Civil Engineering. Her research and teaching focuses on interdisciplinary modeling for aquatic ecosystems and international issues for water development. Email: lsaito@cabnr.unr.edu

Fritz Fiedler earned his BS and MS from the University of New Hampshire in Civil Engineering/Water Resources, and a PhD from Colorado State University in Civil Engineering/Hydrologic Science and Engineering. He has worked as an environmental consultant and water resources engineer. Dr. Fiedler joined the University of Idaho (UI) in 2000. His research interests include monitoring and modeling complex hydrologic systems, and water resources sustainability. He was one of the core developers of the interdisciplinary graduate program Waters of the West at UI. Email: fritz@uidaho.edu

Barbara Cosens is an Associate Professor at the UI College of Law and Waters of the West Program. She holds an LLM in Environmental Law from Lewis and Clark Law School, a JD from UC Hastings School of Law, an MS in Geology from the University of Washington, and a BS in Geology from UC Davis. Her research interests include Native American water rights, interactions between law and science in water resources, and application of resilience theory to multi-agency, multi-jurisdictional response to water resource problems. Email: bcosens@uidaho.edu

Derek Kauneckis is an Assistant Professor at UNR in the Department of Political Science. He received an MS in International Development from the University of California at Davis and a PhD in Public Policy from Indiana University, Bloomington. Dr. Kauneckis' research interests are focused on the development of institutional arrangements for environmental management, property rights theory, and public policy analysis. Email: kauneck@unr.edu

Chapter 22

Two Big Issues for Water Resources Systems: Advances in Educational Technology and Changes in Valuation

Jared L. Cohon

ABSTRACT

In this chapter, I examine two big issues with implications for the teaching and practice of water resource systems. Recent and future advances in educational technology will fundamentally transform learning. The university of 2050 may barely resemble the institution with which we are familiar today. Even with more modest institutional change, we can expect to see much more inter-institutional and international collaboration and a dramatically enhanced ability to educate citizens about water issues. The other big and classically fundamental issue is how we value natural resources. This age-old question is at the heart of sustainability and whether and how we achieve it.

THE UNIVERSITY OF 2050

HOME STUDY PERIOD
To learn the academic subjects

CAMPUS LIFE PERIOD
To experience dorm and Greek life,
team sports, parties and controlled drinking

EDUCATIONAL TECHNOLOGY

Advances in learning science and technology will transform higher education and the way people learn over the next several years. This is an assertion easily made because the transformation has already started.

In 2002 MIT initiated the Open Courseware project to place all of the Institute's course materials on the web, making it available to anyone with access to a computer connected to the internet (see http://ocw.mit.edu/index.htm). Yale and other universities put courses on the web some years ago (see, for example, open.yale.edu). These early attempts to make educational materials widely available are admirable and valuable. Now, by using advances in learning science, the Open Learning Initiative (OLI) at Carnegie Mellon has taken online education to the next level with profound implications for higher education (see oli.web.cmu.edu/openlearning/).

Based on the results of cognitive science research on learning, OLI courses use artificial intelligence and sophisticated techniques from human-computer interaction to create an active and high-quality learning environment. Pilots with the OLI introductory statistics course have shown that OLI students perform as well or better than the students in the traditional lecture course. As impressive as OLI courses are, their developers still think of them as relatively primitive. In 2050 we will have 40 more years of advances in cognitive and brain science and our understanding of the learning process, as well as several more generations of computers, human-computer interfaces and internet technology. It seems a certainty that all this technology will transform access to education, the delivery of education and the institutions that deliver it in dramatic ways.

The dream of the open learning movement is to make education available anywhere, anytime. Imagine what this might mean for organizing effective watershed associations or, in general, for engaging the public in the water issues of 2050. Note, that I said making _education_ available, not data or information. So, now imagine again what you could achieve if everyone could _learn_ enough hydrology, economics and engineering to be as knowledgeable as we'd like them to be about water issues that they face. The educational and communications technology will certainly exist; all it will take is one of us (or, more likely, one of our students' students) to invest the time to create the course content (or maybe it'll be a game) at a level that an average, educated citizen can manage (and, note that the average education level will be higher because of OLI and its descendents).

> *Imagine what you could achieve if everyone could learn enough to be as knowledgeable as we'd like them to be about water issues that they face.*

Imagine what the advances in educational technology will mean for water resource systems programs and the institutions in which they are located. This is not a new topic. Since the mid-1990s, when it was predicted that the internet would change the world (it has and will but it's just taking longer than we thought), education experts have been debating what this will mean for colleges and universities (see for example, Brown and Duguid (1996; 2000)). There are those who believe that colleges and universities will go the way of the drive-in movie theater. The simple version of this is: Why would anyone pay $40,000 per year (or $200,000 per year in 2050) when they can learn just as well online from home or from another location? Of course, there are still drive-in movie theaters, and they're even growing in some places. So, too, one can argue, there will continue to be a demand for residential institutions whose campuses provide the benefits of socialization and personal development. But is that sufficient reason for colleges to continue to exist in their current form and with their high cost structure?

Research universities present a particularly complicated picture because of their twin mission of knowledge creation and dissemination. The disassociation of teaching from location is one thing; separation of researchers is quite another. To date, and for many years to come, co-location with colleagues and students has been and will be a compelling argument for keeping the model of the residential university. This is especially so for interdisciplinary fields like water resource systems. Will we feel so strongly about this with the communication and telepresence technology of 2050?

The advances in educational technology are playing out against a backdrop of shifts in society that will put great pressure on colleges and universities. The willingness and ability of society to pay for American institutions of higher education are challenged to an unprecedented degree. Many of us feel that the financial crisis of 2008 and the recession of 2009 and their impact on state and federal budgets – impacts that are far from being fully realized – will have long-lasting, perhaps permanent implications for universities. There is a sense that "doing more with less" will be an ongoing challenge, forcing universities to rethink their basic models. This is the case for all universities, but especially public universities which are dependent on state budgets.

While American universities have been struggling to get by, the rise of universities in other countries has been very rapid, and it will accelerate in the years to come. We are kidding ourselves if we don't think America's universities, which have enjoyed pre-eminence for many decades, will be equaled and perhaps surpassed. Other countries are investing massively to make that happen.

Add together cost pressures, fierce competition and disruptive technology and you're likely to get significant institutional change. In the medium term, say the next decade, I expect we will see the emergence of the three-year residential bachelor's degree program in which four years of material are crammed into three by using online courses. We may see totally or predominantly virtual community colleges emerge using online courses to prepare students for acceptance by four-year institutions, thereby effectively creating a two-year residential bachelor's degree program. These are not heroic predictions; there are already many Master's programs and some undergraduate programs taught entirely online, and that's with pretty clunky and inferior technology.

In the longer term one may see a real disassociation of the traditional university structure. In one future scenario, "faculty" become independent contractors, selling their content to universities or online publishers or perhaps directly to students (iCourses instead of iTunes) and their research skills to clients, which might be universities. In this view, the universities would become system integrators for research and credential grantors for students.

> *In the longer term one may see a real disassociation of the traditional university structure.*

Physically, universities would be reduced to places for socialization and extracurricular activities – finishing schools for teenagers – and locations for experimental equipment. All we would need are fraternities and sororities, a football stadium and labs (as well as administration buildings, of course).

The above is an extreme view, but it serves to help us imagine new institutional forms and structures. For example, and of great potential significance for water resource systems, we can expect to see much more inter-institutional collaboration. This is both enabled by the sort of technological advances noted above and a natural result of tighter cost constraints. When one considers the great regional variability of characteristics of water systems, it is especially appealing to contemplate inter-institutional programs. Imagine a joint PhD program offered by universities in the Northeast and the Southwest United States or by a group of universities in China, India and the United States.

In 2050, our ideas about learning will have changed significantly due to the advance of educational technology. The institutions of higher education will change as well, perhaps dramatically. The teaching and practice of water resource systems will also be transformed – in positive ways if we seize the opportunities these shifts present.

VALUING NATURAL RESOURCES

In 2050, the notion of value and how we measure it will have shifted significantly from today's framework, and the implications for society and water systems will be profound.

Capitalism and the power of markets underpin all global economic activity. Centrally planned economies are a thing of the past – in 2050 the demise of the Soviet Union will have occurred 60 years ago – and they will be as relevant to contemporary society as the old maharajahs of India are today. Even China has embraced capitalism as the central driving force of its economy, with spectacular results, both positive in terms of economic development and negative in the state of its environment.

As water resource people know well, free market economies have their limits when it comes to valuing and allocating natural resources. There has been much work on monetary evaluation of non-market effects, e.g. the value of a human life and ecosystem services, but not much has changed in any fundamental way and it won't until we change the basic economic model, which makes some heroic assumptions. Chief among these is the assumption that our individual utility, which each of us seeks to maximize, is a function only of our consumption of goods and services. There is no room in the model for natural or environmental resources unless they are consumed directly or as part of a production process.

What is true for water is true for every other natural resource which falls outside the market system. And, even those for which markets exist, e.g. North Atlantic fisheries, our capitalist system has failed to create conditions that lead to sustainable use of the resource.

The "tragedy of the commons," so dramatically displayed in ocean fisheries, and externalities like water pollution both represent market failures. As such, there is a compelling case to correct them through regulation, taxes or other policy instruments. The current political scene in the United States makes it hard to imagine effective regulation ever being implemented. And, of course, the political and policy problem is even more complicated – by at least an order of magnitude – by the international nature of problems like fishery management and transboundary water systems, not to mention climate change.

I believe that achieving sustainability will require fundamental changes in the basic economic model and how it and we put value on our natural and environmental resources. Changing the model is one thing – and something economists can debate ad infinitum; making change in the real world is quite another. I have no clear prescriptions for how this can or will happen, but I do have some thoughts about the role of governments, corporations and universities in effecting this change.

In trying to imagine the economic scene of 2050, it's useful to put yourself in 1970 and to contemplate whether you could have imagined today's main economic drivers. There have, of course, been large shifts along many dimensions. I'll just focus on one of these: the remarkable emergence of companies that make money purely by providing access to information and to other people. Google didn't exist even ten years ago, let alone 40 years ago. Yet, in terms of market capitalization and revenues, it swamps most of the corporations that dominated the American economy in 1970.

Google's success is fascinating from a technical and economic perspective, but does it say anything about a shift in society and what it values? We have to be cautious here. After all, Google's main revenue source is advertising, which is entirely familiar and traditional – maybe even depressing from the perspective of social value. Still, our use of Google and Facebook and other similar sites does say something about how we elect to use our time, which is itself an expression of value.

In focusing on Google and similar companies, my interest is in detecting shifts in what we value. Might it be that consumers in 2050 will value natural resources in a way that allows companies to make money without exploiting them? Will there be a Google of 2050 – maybe Google itself – that converts the existence value of a resource into monetary value for its shareholders? I suppose ecotourism is a step in that direction, but I'm talking about something more fundamental from a value point of view: our willingness to pay for the continued existence of something without any need or expectation of using it or seeing it.

> *Achieving sustainability will require fundamental changes in the basic economic model and how it and we put value on our natural and environmental resources.*

If this is going to happen, there will have to be a massive shift in the average person's understanding and valuation of the environment, as well as our understanding of national wealth. The idea of broadening gross national product to include environmental and natural resources has been around for a long time (see for example, Repetto et al. 1989). It's hard to say that the notion is getting traction, and maybe it won't until the average person embraces the idea that their standard of living is a result of more than their direct consumption of traditional goods and services. Here, as with policy interventions to correct price signals, government and political leadership will be crucial. In 2010, it's hard to imagine any politician embracing this agenda, but perhaps things will look different after we've experienced a sufficient number of water shortages, water-borne disease outbreaks, devastating floods and other catastrophes.

We should not forget or discount the important role that universities have to play. Political leaders, policy makers and corporate CEO's are, after all, our alumni. So too, are average, well-educated citizens. How many of them graduate from our universities with anything that we in water resource systems would call hydrologic or environmental literacy?

REFERENCES

Brown, J. S., and Duguid, P. (1996). "Universities in the digital age." *Change*, 28(4), 10-19, also in *The mirage of continuity: reconfiguring academic information resources for the 21st century*, (1998), B. L. Hawkins, and P. Battin, eds., Council on Library and Information Resources, Washington, DC, 39-60, <www.johnseelybrown.com> (Dec, 2010).

Brown, J. S., and Duguid, P. (2000). *The social life of information*, Harvard Business School Press, Boston, MA.

Repetto, R., Magrath, W., Wells, M., Beer, C., and Rossini, F. (1989). *Wasting assets: natural resources in the national income accounts*, World Resources Institute, Washington, DC.

AUTHOR INFORMATION

Jared L. Cohon, PhD, is President of Carnegie Mellon University. Dr. Cohon formerly served as dean of the School of Forestry and Environmental Studies and professor of environmental systems analysis at Yale University and in various roles including vice provost for research at The Johns Hopkins University. He was appointed by President Clinton to chair the Nuclear Waste Technical Review Board, and was appointed by presidents G. W. Bush and Barack Obama to the Homeland Security Advisory Council. Dr. Cohon was named a distinguished member of ASCE in 2005. He earned his BS in civil engineering from the University of Pennsylvania and his PhD from the Massachusetts Institute of Technology. Email: jaredcohon@cmu.edu

IV SCIENCE AND TECHNOLOGY

Chapter 23

The Science, Information, and Engineering Needed to Manage Water Availability and Quality in 2050

Robert M. Hirsch

ABSTRACT

This chapter explores four water resources issues: 1) hydrologic variability, hazards, water supply and ecosystem preservation; 2) urban landscape design; 3) non-point source water quality, and 4) climate change, resiliency, and nonstationarity. It also considers what science, technology, and engineering practice may be needed in the coming decades to sustain water supplies and ecosystems in the face of increasing stresses from a growing demand for water. Dealing with these four water resource issues in the highly uncertain future world will demand predictive models that are rooted in real-world data. In a non-stationary world, continuity of observations is crucial. All watersheds are influenced by human actions through changes in land use, water use, and climate. The focus of water planning and management between today and 2050 will depend more than ever on collection and analysis of long-term data to learn about the evolving state of the system, understanding ecosystem processes in the water and on the landscape, and finding innovative ways to manage water as a shared resource. This includes sharing water resources with our neighbors on the landscape, sharing with the other species that depend on water, and sharing with future generations.

"Sorry I'm late guys - walking is not my thing."

INTRODUCTION

The science and engineering that are the foundation of national and global water resources management changed substantially over the twentieth century due to population and resource pressures. The approaches we use to plan, design, and operate our water resource systems have improved as a result of achievements in science and engineering. At the beginning of the twentieth century, the primary focus of scientific investigations was describing the system (e.g., how much water is flowing in our rivers and how much dissolved or suspended material is moving with them). As time passed, the science and engineering turned more to questions of how to exploit the resource for drinking water, hydropower, irrigation water, and for waste disposal. The questions revolved around how much water one can extract from a river or aquifer to obtain the desired economic benefit. Or, how much waste can be discharged to the river without causing unacceptable levels of harm to people or the biota in the river? As we arrived in the final two decades of the twentieth century and first decade of the twenty-first century, the questions shifted from those focused on how to exploit the resource to those focused on how to restore and sustain the resource. As we move into this era of sustainability, the types of questions posed move away from "how much water is there?" or "how much water can we extract?" to questions like "how much water do we need to leave in the river and what kind of habitat will it provide?"

This chapter will explore the evolution of four water resources issues and consider what science, technology, and engineering practice may be needed in the coming decades to sustain water supplies and ecosystems in the face of increasing stresses from a growing demand for water.

HYDROLOGIC VARIABILITY, HAZARDS, WATER SUPPLY, AND ECOSYSTEM CONDITION

The history of water resources development is about "trimming the tails" off the probability distribution of flow (Shabman 2008). Dams store water from wetter periods and deliver it to users and to the downstream channels during dry periods. They do this to increase reliable water supply, to decrease flood magnitudes, or both. Regardless of their purpose, dams end up changing the frequency distribution of river flows and this can have significant impacts on aquatic ecosystems (Collier et al. 1996; Poff et al. 1997; Richter and Postel 2003). Prior to the past two or three decades, the science community did explore this issue but primarily focused on setting constraints on the minimum flow. The analysis focused on requirements for the fish to migrate, live, or propagate in a particular river reach. This was based on a minimum amount of streambed that stays wet, or water velocity that is sufficient to flush sediment and aerate the streambed. The regulatory response was to set a "minimum instream flow" that is expected to be sufficient to support the species of concern.

What we now know is that it is not only important to keep flows above that minimum, but to assure some amount of variability. This variability is important to maintaining the right kind of channel and bed characteristics and to facilitate movement of organic matter between riparian zone, stream banks, and the water in the stream to sustain the health of the stream and the riparian corridor. The new paradigm for instream flows for aquatic habitat aims at achieving patterns of variation that are functionally similar to those before flow regulation and water withdrawals began. The new paradigm also recognizes that groundwater is critical to aquatic habitat because it provides the baseflow of the stream during critical dry periods. If that groundwater is depleted, the baseflow may be significantly reduced. Also, the temperature and chemistry of surface water are highly influenced by the amount of this baseflow, which typically has a cooling effect on the stream in the hot, dry months of the year. We have now moved from the question of "How much water can we take from this river?" to "How much water must we leave in the river and how much variability should we attempt to maintain?"

> *We have moved from the question of "How much water can we take from this river?" to "How much water must we leave in the river and how much variability should be maintained?"*

In the past, the design and operations of water resource systems revolved around questions of the net economic benefits of the system. These include benefits from water supply (for cities, farms, power plants, and factories), benefits from decreased economic losses from floods, and benefits from instream uses (recreation, navigation, waste assimilation), which were all balanced against the cost of the project. Today and in the coming decades, all of these factors will still be important, but added to them will be questions of prediction of ecological outcomes and the value that should be associated with these outcomes. The paradigm for the future must be one of selecting a desired and feasible state of the watershed/stream system and managing the system through wet and dry periods in a manner that is consistent with approximating that desired future state.

This process presents several major challenges. The first is that of attaining a consensus on what the desired state is. It will generally be some compromise between the pre-development condition and a management scenario that delivers all of the water to off-stream users or prevents all flood damages. Working out the trade-offs between water supply, flood control, and ecological uses of the water requires a predictive model that can translate a management change into a set of population characteristics for the species of interest. These populations are subject to many other forces including changes in water quality, changes in harvesting pressure, and introduction of disease or invasive species. For each of these types of pressures, there is great uncertainty about the future state of the pressure and about how those pressures acting together will affect the species of interest. The water resources management community needs several science products and tools to deal effectively with this issue. The needs include: 1) data on the ever-changing state of the physical system (flows, temperatures, water quality) and on the status of the ecological community that depends on the physical system; 2) the predictive tools that will produce meaningful statements about the changes in the ecological community that may result from the management changes; and finally, 3) the communications ability to tell the stakeholders what we think about how the ecosystem will respond to the changes and to help them understand our very limited ability to predict the future state of the system. These limitations arise because of process-uncertainty and the role of randomness and surprise (due, for example, to a major flood, a major drought, or an invasive species). We must help the public and decision-makers to embrace an adaptive management approach that involves on-going measurements, predictive models, and actions, cycling back to measurement, prediction, and new actions. Water resource systems design and operations in the coming decades will involve as much biological insight as it will engineering expertise.

URBAN LANDSCAPE-DESIGN PRINCIPLES

Our cities (including the suburbs) depend on a set of engineering design concepts focused on getting water off the landscape rapidly in a manner that minimizes the potential for flood damages and water quality degradation. This has led to urban stormwater design and to the use of sanitary sewers connected to large regional wastewater treatment plants. These design concepts lead to decreased recharge of aquifers in the urban area, which can lead to an increased need to import drinking water over long distances and to declines in the groundwater levels in urban areas. Such declines in groundwater levels, driven both by pumping and by reduced recharge, can have serious consequences for instream habitat conditions (see Charles River Watershed Association 2008). The new paradigm for urban design will be focused on keeping water on the landscape, but doing it in a manner that is consistent with public safety and health. These new designs will have to balance urban flooding risks against the cost of providing sufficient capacity for infiltration such that extreme precipitation will not cause an excessive amount of flooding of streets or basements. It will also involve a balance between the benefits to water supply (for humans and ecosystems) versus the potential threats to water quality from contaminants in storm water and in treated effluents.

Architecture and planning departments at the universities are moving in the direction of designs that are much more "green" than the traditional designs. University engineering departments must be fully engaged in the following: development and testing of urban drainage systems that foster reduced dependency on public supplies and all the energy and chemical use that is entailed in that process; systems for enhancing the safe recharge of stormwater and wastewater to local groundwater; on-site wastewater treatment (rather than treatment in large regional wastewater treatment plants); and finding ways to use the nutrients in wastewater as a resource to foster photosynthesis and production of biomass energy rather than allowing these nutrients to become an economic "bad" that either degrades water bodies or consumes massive amounts of energy to remove them from the wastewater stream. This issue of transforming wastewater from an environmental "bad" to a valued resource (a "good") should be applied not only to waste from human communities but also to waste from "communities" of domestic animals (in confined feeding operations). The successful implementation of these "green" designs will require all of the following: innovative design (around principles of conservation of water, energy, nutrients, and other aspects of the chemistry of the water); data collection and testing of these systems and their external effects; training engineers in using these new technologies; and a focused political process led by engineers, aimed at modifying building and land-development codes, and water-related regulations and law, particularly at the local level.

WATER QUALITY ISSUES BEYOND THE POINT-SOURCE ERA

The water quality issues at the time of enactment of the Clean Water Act in 1972 were driven by point sources. They dealt with bacteria, dissolved oxygen, and toxic levels of metals and organic compounds. We have improved water quality since that time by dealing with point sources at publicly owned treatment works and industrial sources, but point sources are not the only sources. The problems that remain are much more difficult to deal with. They are primarily driven by non-point sources (including nutrients, pesticides, and sediment from urban or agricultural lands) or from very low concentrations of compounds that our treatment systems were not designed to control. In spite of our efforts, we see around us many water bodies that do not live up to our goals in terms of the health of aquatic ecosystems. The list of possible causes of these impairments is a long one. It includes factors such as: changes in flow, increases in water temperature or salinity, natural or anthropogenic chemical contaminants (including those at concentrations that are not lethal, but that may have adverse effects on humans or aquatic life through changes in reproduction or development), invasive species, riparian disturbance, and physical barriers to species migration. If we are going to make the politically and economically difficult decisions that will fix these issues, we will need a higher level of scientific certainty about the causes of the impairment and the predictive power to make meaningful statements of how our costly actions, if taken today, will affect ecological outcomes tomorrow.

The problem of describing the changes in water quality and ecosystem conditions is made particularly difficult by the fact that normal variations between wet and dry periods easily overwhelm human influences. The general public and public decision-makers reasonably want to know how human actions are degrading or improving the condition of the ecosystem and whether investments in environmental restoration are yielding results. Unfortunately, the relationships are less than obvious. They are fraught with large amounts of temporal variability and time lags. For example, in many watersheds, the movement of nitrogen from the land surface (where it is introduced by urban and agricultural fertilizers, through septic systems, or through atmospheric deposition) to its destination in a stream, lake, or estuary, can include time traversing the soil, unsaturated zone, and the shallow groundwater system. This process can easily take a decade or more (Phillips and Lindsey 2003). For phosphorus, the transport process is often dominated by episodic movement of phosphorus attached to sediment particles that may move only infrequently in large storms, then go into sediment storage in floodplains, streambanks, and reservoirs. A major consequence of these time lags is that even the best set of actions on the landscape, designed to reduce these forms of pollution, may lead to improvements in ambient water quality that happen only a decade or more after the action. In addition to these time lags, water quality in the river, reservoir, lake, or estuary of interest can be strongly affected by year-to-year variation in streamflow. Thus, real improvements can easily be masked by the natural "noise" while the positive "signal" of actions taken in the watershed is difficult to identify.

The scientists and engineers involved in guiding the actions to improve water quality will need data collection, data analysis, and communication skills to give decision-makers a realistic picture of the anticipated, as well as the actual, progress. Although we live in an age of instant gratification, these problems of water quality took more than a half century to develop and will not be resolved overnight. The scientists and engineers involved will need to be honest and skillful in conveying this message. Systems of data collection and analysis must be in place to track the progress of water quality and the ecosystem. What is needed are: long-term data, models that can predict the biological end points, and clear interpretation about progress that is, or is not, being made towards more healthy aquatic ecosystems.

CLIMATE CHANGE, WATER RESOURCE RESILIENCY, AND THE "DEATH OF STATIONARITY"

The accepted approach to water resources planning and design in use today derives from the work of the Harvard Water Program (Maass et al. 1962). It strives to find an optimal tradeoff between the cost of a project and the benefits that it can deliver to society. The calculation of these trade-offs depends on a characterization of the statistical properties of the hydrologic system that is at the heart of the project. The implicit assumption is that the hydrologic system is stationary. We recognized that we know its properties imperfectly, but until recently we still believed that those properties did not change over time. We now recognize that entirely natural phenomena (such as El Niño or Pacific Decadal Oscillation) are responsible for a high degree of persistence in the hydrologic system and that human-driven forces, particularly the enrichment of atmospheric greenhouse gases, may be adding a long-term trend on top of a highly persistent process. This has led to the idea that "stationarity is dead" (Milly et al. 2008) and that a successor concept for water planning and management needs to be found.

Hydrologists and water resource planners and managers will need to find new approaches that recognize that hydrologic processes are not stationary and that also recognize that reliable predictions of future hydrologic conditions are very limited. Although we are not yet in a position to describe the "successor" to stationarity, a few things are clear. One is that we must be sure we are making full use of the hydrologic data that are available. Because of persistence, it is important that we look well into the past to see what kinds of changes the system is capable of making. We must also look to the recent past, in recognition of the possibility that conditions may be changing and that we want our expectations about the future to consider the ever evolving state of the system. In short, the death of stationarity means we must increase our attention to the continuity of monitoring and to the frequent repetition of data analysis as new data are collected.

> *In a nonstationary world, continuity of observations is crucial.*

A second aspect for a successor approach to water planning is that, more than ever, we need to consider resiliency and flexibility as key elements in planning. Water supply planning has traditionally been based on building of surface water reservoirs to capture streamflows during times of abundance, storing them for months or years, and then using the stored water during times of low flow. In some instances the design has been based on development of groundwater wells (the ultimate natural reservoir) that yield a relatively constant supply over time. In the coming years, water supply options will involve greater use of a "diversified portfolio" of sources. There are several dimensions to diversification. One example is the combination of surface water and groundwater as major sources of supply ("conjunctive use"). Another example is the use of multiple reservoirs in multiple watersheds. The benefit of diversification of sources stems from the fact that no two sources of supply will ever behave the same. The differences in timing and severity of shortage among multiple sources can be exploited to improve the reliability of the overall yield of the system. This phenomena is known as "synergistic gain" (see Hirsch et al. 1976) and the underlying principle is that the yield of the sum of several water sources will likely be greater than the sum of the yields of individual sources.

Groundwater supplies are highly resistant to drought, so if they are allowed to recharge during wetter periods, they can provide for a plentiful supply during drought periods when surface water reservoirs are low. Depletion of groundwater results in a loss of resiliency in water resource systems, because groundwater is less affected by drought conditions than surface water. If groundwater has been depleted, this element of resiliency is lost. Aquifer storage and recovery is a strategy that takes this principle of groundwater as a source to be used in times of shortage, and amplifies it, by purposefully putting water into underground storage during times of plenty, to withdraw it during times of drought. This technology holds great promise for water management, but it is not without its science and engineering challenges (NRC 2007).

There is an important institutional aspect to this concept of synergy and that is the idea that different jurisdictions have access to different supplies (watersheds, reservoirs, aquifers, pipelines, pumps, etc.). The natural tendency of jurisdictions is to attempt to maintain sovereign rights to those supplies and not to give up any control over water supplies in times of shortage. However, it can be shown that by operating their supply jointly with other jurisdictions, they can increase the reliable yield of all the participants (provided that there is some degree of flexibility in the pathways along which water can be delivered from source to user). An important goal for water professionals in the coming decades is to demonstrate to water managers and communities that developing and sharing a diverse water supply system can have great benefits. When the benefits of shared resources are demonstrated by water resource professionals, the motivation to cooperate can be enhanced sufficiently to bring about the necessary agreements. Sharing resources with neighboring and downstream communities and with future generations is critical to the sustainability of water resources. Scientists and engineers collectively have an obligation to educate the public to these ideas.

> *Sharing resources with neighboring and downstream communities and with future generations is critical to the sustainability of water resources.*

Currently, many water managers are searching for "actionable science" that will tell them how the hydrologic system 40 years from now will be different from what it is today due to greenhouse-gas-driven climate change. They are likely to remain frustrated because the ability to develop reliable models of future precipitation and runoff patterns is very limited. The scale, boundary conditions, and representations of key processes in the models are simply not suited to the task at hand. The strategy that must be developed and taught to the next generation of water planners and managers is one of dealing with uncertainty through adaptation and flexible designs and institutions.

CONCLUSION

Dealing with these four water resource issues in the highly uncertain future world will demand predictive models that are strongly rooted in theory but also rooted in real-world data. We must not only collect the data, but we must continuously analyze it to understand the changing world we live in. Ralph Keeling (2008) stated it well: "The only way to figure out what is happening to our planet is to measure it, and this means tracking changes decade after decade, and poring over the records." Milly et al. (2008) stated "Modeling should be used to synthesize observations; it can never replace them. In a non-stationary world, continuity of observations is crucial." Hydrologists and engineers will need to jettison the notion that watersheds are natural systems responding to a set of stable drivers and adopt a view that all watersheds are influenced by human actions through changes in land use, water use, and climate. They will also need to recognize the limitations of predictability. The focus of water planning and management between today and the year 2050 will depend more than ever on collection and analysis of long-term data to learn about the evolving state of the system, understanding ecosystem processes in the water and on the landscape, and finding innovative ways to manage water as a shared resource. This includes sharing water resources with our neighbors on the landscape, sharing with the other species that depend on water, and sharing with future generations.

REFERENCES

Charles River Watershed Association. (2008). "Water budgets." *Charles River Watershed Association projects*, <http://www.crwa.org/projects/waterbudgets.html> (November 13, 2009).

Collier, M., Webb, R. H., and Schmidt, J. C. (1996). *Dams and rivers, a primer on the downstream effects of dams*, US Geological Survey Circular 1126, US Geological Survey, Denver, CO, 94 p.

Hirsch, R. M., Cohon, J. L., and ReVelle, C. S. (1976). "Gains from joint operations of multiple reservoir systems." *Water Resour. Res.*, 13(2), 239-245.

Keeling, R. (2008). "Recording the Earth's vital signs." *Science*, 319, 1771-1772.

Maass, A., Hufschmidt, M. M., Dorfman, R., Thomas, Jr., H. A., Marglin, S. A., Fair, G. M. (1962). *Design of water-resource systems: new techniques for relating economic objectives, engineering analysis, and government planning*, Harvard University Press, Cambridge, MA.

Milly, P. C. D., Betancourt, J, Falkenmark, M., Hirsch, R. M., Kundzewicz, Z. W., Lettenmaier, D. P., and Stouffer, R. J. (2008). "Stationarity is dead: whither water management?" *Science*, 319, 573-574.

National Research Council (NRC). (2007). *Prospects for managed underground storage of recoverable water*, National Academies Press, Washington, DC, 350 p.

Phillips, S. W., and Lindsey, B. D. (2003). *The influence of groundwater on nitrogen delivery to the Chesapeake Bay*, US Geological Survey Fact Sheet-091-03, US Geological Survey, Baltimore, MD, <http://md.water.usgs.gov/publications/fs-091-03/html/index.html> (April 16, 2010).

Poff, N. L., Allan, J. D., Bain, M. B., Karr, J. R., Prestegaard, K. L., Richter, B. D., Sparks, R. E., and Stromberg, J. C. (1997). "The natural flow regime: a paradigm for river conservation and restoration." *BioScience*, 47, 769-784.

Richter, B. D., and Postel, S. (2003). *Rivers for life: managing water for people and nature*, Island Press, Washington, DC, 220 p.

Shabman, L. (2008). "Water resources management and the challenge of sustainability." *Perspectives on sustainable resources in America*, R. Sedjo, ed., Resources for the Future, Washington, DC, 104-132.

AUTHOR INFORMATION

Robert M. Hirsch is currently a research hydrologist with the US Geological Survey (USGS). He formerly served as Chief Hydrologist where he was responsible for the water science programs of USGS. In 2008, Dr. Hirsch transitioned to the USGS National Research Program to rededicate himself to advancing the science on critical issues of climate change and long-term trends in water resources. He holds a PhD from The Johns Hopkins University from the Department of Geography and Environmental Engineering. Email: rhirsch@usgs.gov

Chapter 24

Hydrologic Modeling in 2050: Knowledge Requirements in a Multi-Nonstationary Environment

Richard H. McCuen

ABSTRACT

The design hydrologist of 2050 will need to address problems that are more complex than those of 2010. However, improved models and databases will be available. This includes coupled models, such as those based on those atmospheric – hydrologic – ecologic processes. Anthropogenic forces will introduce multi-nonstationarity into data, so the hydrologist of 2050 will need more advanced methods of model calibration. Questions relevant to engineering design and sustainability in 2050 are posed and related viewpoints are presented.

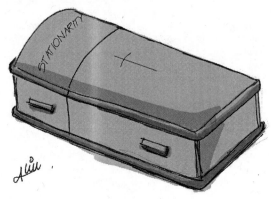

INTRODUCTION

Anthropogenic forcing, which affects hydrologic processes, has been an issue for decades. Urbanization has been a dominant research issue with respect to urban flooding. Deforestation for purposes of agricultural development has been another major concern, in terms of sediment generation and pollution transport. Modeling of such issues has been a research staple and will continue to be in the future. Urbanization, deforestation, and agricultural development have introduced nonstationarity into runoff time series. Even the installation of many small urban stormwater detention structures can influence the flood record of a watershed. Climate change is a more recent anthropogenic concern that will introduce more nonstationarity into measured hydrologic data, thus increasing the complexity of modeling for decades to come. In fact, Milly et al. (2008) define stationarity as "the idea that natural systems fluctuate within an unchanging envelope of variability" and say that anthropogenic change has rendered stationarity dead. Rind (1999) indicated that the degree of chaotic behavior introduced into data in the past is unknown so its importance is speculation. Because of the nonstationarity of physical processes, greater chaotic behavior should be expected in data collected over the next few decades. There is every reason to believe that more complex data requires more complex methods of analysis and interpretation.

Changes to the physical watershed cause runoff processes to change. Measurements of runoff reflect the watershed changes and include trends that reflect the physical changes to the watershed. Thus, the measured data seem chaotic and to be from a non-constant population. Where a watershed experiences deforestation, urbanization, the growth of stormwater control structures, and climate change at different times, each factor introduces a measure of nonstationarity into the measured data, with each affecting a record over different time periods and to differing extents. This situation represents multi-nonstationarity. Models developed for stationary systems and parameters calibrated from stationary data will not accurately reflect the response of a changing system. This seems to be the environment in which the hydrologic design engineer must now practice. The problem is especially difficult when data records are short. More complex modeling techniques are required to analyze data from multi-nonstationary physical systems.

> *Watershed deforestation, urbanization, stormwater control structures, and climate change all lead to nonstationarity of measured data.*

As the physical environment is subject to more nonstationary forces, hydrologic modeling will become exceedingly more challenging, yet more important. We will need a greater knowledge base, starting with a better understanding of the effect of changes on the physical processes. Improved modeling methods will be needed, including ways of reliably separating the total variance in a data set, calibrating models that reflect multi-nonstationary effects, and addressing added complexity as sustainability requirements are added to design requirements.

QUESTIONS AND VIEWPOINTS ON THE DIRECTION OF MODELING

Numerous concerns arise because of the interlocking issues of anthropogenic-caused nonstationarity, modern data collection methods, and increasingly complex models. This increased complexity in problems, data, and models will create a need for changes to water resources education and require significant research in the coming decades. Consider, for example, the following questions:

What are the implications of nonstationarity to the hydrologic design engineer?
Nonstationarity whether due to climate change or urbanization is not currently addressed in most hydrologic design methods. Stationarity is assumed. The

hydrologic design process will need to be more complex as the effects of nonstationarity become more significant. Projection of nonstationary trends will need to be made and addressed in the design. Greater computational power will be available to the design engineer of the future and advances in technology will partially compensate for the complexity of nonstationary data, but the designer will require greater knowledge, a better understanding of resource limitations, greater vision, and an acute awareness of his or her ethical responsibilities.

The state of information technology and artificial intelligence will have advanced significantly by 2050, and hydrologic design will likely require their use. Therefore, the design engineer will need to know the underlying algorithms, not just how to input the required data. Input data for design methods will be more voluminous, hopefully more accurate, and more readily available. However, nonstationarity will render the data to be more complex. Advanced sensor systems will provide spatially and temporally distributed data at any scale needed, but the design engineer will need to understand the effect of scale on the design. Climate, land use, and other watershed changes will likely not have stabilized by 2050, so the designer will need to have the vision to consider the adequacy of a design over the projected life of the project, specifically as the nonstationarity of the hydrologic processes increases beyond 2050. As pointed out by Goldenfeld and Kadanoff (1999), complexity demands a change in attitude, one that moves away from systems in equilibrium to one that shows variation in time and space.

A design engineer currently has ethical responsibilities to public safety, sustainability, resource use, and many environmental issues. This is true now and it will be just as true in 2050. Balancing these ethical responsibilities to public welfare, sustainability, and others will require a knowledge of values and value decision making, especially how to balance the ethical concerns with economic, legal, and public policy aspects of a project. Water resource education will need to become more diverse over the next 40 years in order for the design engineer to respond effectively to all of these concerns. Specifically, issues such as policy and value sensitive topics will play a greater role in water resource education.

Will improved sensing and measurement assist in the detection of the effects of multi-nonstationary trends?
Studies have shown that the spatial variability of hydrometeorological data affects prediction accuracy (Chang 2007). This is true of rainfall input based on radar rainfall analyses and on soil moisture studies. Sensors will continue to advance and provide a massive database from which many aspects of water distribution throughout a watershed can be measured. However, some portion of the added variability will not be fully explainable and part of the added variance will contribute to increased random variation. The exact separation of the variability in the data collected from advanced sensing methods into systematic and random components will determine the worth of the data and its ability to help quantify the effects of nonstationarity. As our sensing capabilities improve, we will need advances in methods of analysis. Specifically, we will need to improve upon the techniques

currently used to identify individual effects in multi-factor data sequences. Without this, improved sensing will contribute less to our ability to model nonstationary systems.

Will sustainability be an issue relevant to hydrologic design in 2050?
Sustainability will continue to be an important issue to the engineering profession in the future. The general focus of sustainability is the preservation of resources and the environment for future generations. Obviously, water resources are central to sustainability. Sustainability metrics related to water resources include stream stability, groundwater quality, the diversity of flora and aquatic life in water bodies, and the aesthetic characteristics of a watershed, each of which are resources that need to be sustained. Water quality and low-flow levels, which are affected by design, are also important elements of water resource sustainability.

Many current hydrologic design models focus on hydrologic characteristics such as peak discharge or runoff volume. These computed values indirectly relate to sustainability metrics but sustainability metrics are not currently a direct criterion in hydrologic design. To achieve sustainability goals, direct connections will need to be made between sustainability goals and hydrologic design metrics. For example, peak discharge rates are based on a return period. Therefore, resource use and sustainability metrics affected by decisions such as the selection of the return period of a design flood should be assessed. A hydrologic design based on design criteria unrelated to sustainability may protect or damage the sustainability characteristics of a river or the quality of an aquatic habitat. While sustainability factors are generally not presently assessed when completing a hydrologic design, they will likely become part of the decision process by 2050.

How can variation in a nonstationary flood series associated with climate change be identified when other nonstationary effects such as urbanization, deforestation, or channel cross section changes are also present and confounding the ability to detect individual effects?
The problem of identifying trends in multivariate data has long plagued data analysts. Even in a relatively simple modeling exercise such as a regression analysis with many watershed characteristics, the issue of identifying individual effects is widely debated. For example, is the standard partial regression coefficient, the bivariate correlation coefficient, or the coefficient of separation determination the best indicator of individual effects? With data subjected to forces that introduce nonstationarity at different times in the flood record, the task of identifying the effects is difficult, at best. Agreement on the detection procedure among hydrologists is unlikely, but an accurate estimate of the trend effect depends on finding a solution that has a reasonable level of accuracy.

Resolution of the issue of multiple nonstationary effects has implications for public safety, resource allocation, making decisions about corrective action, assessing risk, and developing public policies. If too much or too little emphasis is incorrectly assigned to one of the factors (e.g., climate change, urbanization, etc.), resources may be inefficiently allocated. It is sufficiently difficult to model one source of nonstationarity, but in 2050 multi-nonstationary effects will need to be modeled.

Will the model calibration methods of 2010 be adequate for calibrating the models of 2050?

Least squares, both analytical and numerical, are currently staples for calibrating hydrologic models. Numerical search methods are used for more complex models such as HSPF. However, search methods have had limited success with complex models (Duan et al. 1992). Blasone et al. (2006) indicated the problems of existing search methods and the need for global procedures, and Gupta et al. (1998) discussed the growth in the need for multiobjective calibration. Some multicriterion methods are used in research but rarely in practice. Model calibration is assessed using goodness-of-fit statistics such as the correlation coefficient, the Nash-Sutcliffe index, or the root mean square error. However, studies have shown that very similar goodness-of-fit measures can be achieved using quite different parameter sets and input sequences. For example, Andreassian et al. (2004) showed that model efficiency was not overly sensitive to sequences of potential evapotranspiration obtained in different ways. This indicates that model quality goes beyond goodness-of-fit statistics as the parameter values are intended to reflect the physical processes being modeled. Future hydrologists will need to rethink what constitutes model calibration and optimal solutions, as methods that include parameter rationality and accuracy will be needed to ensure a unique set of parameters that reflect the physical processes.

In 2050, will hydrologic design require coupled models?

Most hydrologic design work today uses a model that is based solely on a representation of relevant hydrologic processes (e.g., HEC programs and TR-55/TR-20). Hydrologic models in 2050 are likely to be coupled with a broader set of physical processes, as this will enable the effects of a hydrologic design on other parts of the natural world to be investigated. For example, a hydrologic model may be coupled with an atmospheric model to provide more realistic rainfall input and an ecological model that reflects stream habitat quality. This represents a much more complex modeling environment. Additionally, a coupled model will allow, for example, the ecological processes to guide the calibration of the parameters of the hydrologic model. Calibrating the models separately may yield a hydrologic model that does not reflect ecological processes. The simultaneous calibration of ecological and hydrologic models will yield a more accurate reflection of the effect of the hydrologic response on stream aquatic life. With data for the ecological processes used in calibration, the coupled model will provide more realistic estimates of the hydrologic model parameters. However, if either of the coupled models is poorly structured, complexity frustration (Binder 2008) may prevent the identification of the correct parameter set. Singh and Woolhiser (2002) commented on the growing importance of integrated environmental management, which will create a demand for coupled models.

How will nonstationarity introduced by climate change influence the upper tail of the distribution of flood peaks?

Univariate frequency analysis remains an important method of hydrologic analysis and will likely remain so for decades. Given the projected increases in extreme meteorological events due to climate change, the return period of design work is being increased to reflect increases in expected damages. For example, designs based on 500-yr flood magnitudes are now being considered, whereas the 100-yr return period was widely used as the design criterion in the past. However, the longer return period requires making estimates of flood magnitudes further out in the tail of the assumed flood distribution. Flood estimates are of limited accuracy even for the more frequent events from stationary systems. Magnitudes of extreme events (e.g., 500-yr peak) estimated from analyses of nonstationary flood records will be much less accurate, both because of the rare exceedence probability and because of the nonstationarity of the data record.

Given the lower expected accuracy of the extreme flood estimates, more complex methods of analysis will be needed to estimate flood magnitudes from nonstationary series. The traditional rank-order flood frequency analysis using the log-Pearson distribution will not be sufficient, as many of its basic assumptions will be violated. One approach would involve including a trend component into the flood analysis such that the data represent a stationary condition. A second alternative would be to develop multiplier coefficients that reflect the degree of nonstationarity. Third, the probability function that is used to represent the processes could be modified to have statistical characteristics that vary with the nonstationarity. Many other alternatives could be proposed. Regardless of the method developed, improvements in accuracy will be necessary in 2050 in order to reduce design risk and uncertainty.

What educational requirements will be needed for those using the complex hydrologic methods of 2050?

Design engineers currently use an array of hydrologic models that range in complexity from very simple models like the Rational equation to moderately complex unit hydrograph models like TR-20 to more complex models like HSPF. Geographic information systems have enabled spatially varied data to be used as input to more complex analyses, and new developments in data collection such as radar rainfall data will enable even more complex, physically realistic models to be applied in hydrologic design. We should then expect that the hydrologic sensor systems of the future will enable even more complex models to be developed and used in design work.

Will hydrologic engineering education advance fast enough to prepare design engineers to properly use more complex models? The knowledge and experience needed to apply simple models such as the Rational equation or peak discharge regression equations is minimal. To properly apply complex models like HSPF, the user needs greater knowledge of physical processes, an educational background in model calibration, and an understanding of both the characteristics of hydrologic data (e.g., handling outliers, temporal and spatial correlation effects) and the use of multiple fitting criteria (as opposed to least squares, which only seeks to minimize the sum of the squares of the differences between computed and measured values). All of these facets of modeling will be necessary in 2050, but the user of the coupled, sensor-driven models will need to have even more knowledge of both the physical hydrologic processes and calibration of models with massive spatio-temporal data bases. This will require an educational background with more exposure to statistical methods, physical hydrology, and decision theory. Without this broad exposure, narrowly focused modelers may yield models developed with diverse theories that provide similar goodness of fit but universally poor extrapolations (Klemes 1986).

> *Hydrologic sensor systems of the future will enable even more complex models to be developed and used in design work.*

CONCLUDING THOUGHTS

Over the last few decades the trend has been for increasing model complexity. Satellite and other remotely sensed data as well as GIS have provided modelers with a more complex database. This trend towards greater complexity is likely to continue as societal problems become more complex, risks increase, and hydrologists seek a more physically realistic model representation of the hydrologic processes. Modeling methods will, therefore, need to improve. A number of issues that relate to modeling of complex systems have been touched upon in this chapter. Each of these issues points toward needed research and changes in water resources education. Modeling in 2050 will not be successful if 2010 modeling methods are used. General areas where research is needed include:

- The design hydrologist of 2050 will face more complex problems that will require more complex models.
- Water resources education will need to have a broader foundation, with advances in modeling techniques as well as the inclusion of topics in water policy, law, and human values.
- Methods of calibration will need to be more complex, including multi-criterion fitting.
- Measured data will likely include the effects of multi-nonstationarity influences, which will require new, more complex methods for separating variation associated with the different factors.
- Because we will want to assign physical meaning to model parameters, a method of incorporating parameter rationality with goodness-of-fit criteria in model calibration will be needed.
- New methods of data collection based on sensors will be developed and ways of incorporating such data with the traditional data will be needed. The spatio-temporally correlated nature of a voluminous amount of data will need new methods of analysis.
- Methods of defining the upper tail of a flood distribution when nonstationarity is embedded in the data are needed.

The complexity of water resource problems is increasing. Changing watershed conditions, nonstationary time series, and limitations of the modeling process will increase the difficulty in making decisions. Will the chasm between the problems and the ability of models to provide solutions increase or decrease in the time between now and 2050?

REFERENCES

Andreassian, V., Perrin, C., and Michel, C. (2004). "Input of imperfect potential evapotranspiration knowledge on the efficiency and parameters of watershed models." *J. Hydrol.*, 286, 19-35.

Binder, P.-M. (2008). "Frustration in complexity." *Science*, 320, 322-323.

Blasone, R. S., Madsen, H., and Rosbjerg, D. (2006). "Comparison of parameter estimation algorithms in hydrologic modelling." *Calibration and reliability in groundwater modelling: from uncertainty to decision making*, Proceedings of ModelCARE'2005, M. F. P. Bierkens, J. C. Gehrels, and K. Kovar, eds., IAHS Publication 304, 67-72.

Chang, C.-L. (2007). "Influence of moving rainstorms on watershed responses." *Environ. Eng. Sci.*, 24(10), 1353-1360.

Duan, Q., Sorooshian, S., and Gupta, V. (1992). "Effective and efficient global optimization for conceptual rainfall-runoff models." *Water Resour. Res.*, 28(4), 1015-1031.

Goldenfeld, N., and Kadanoff, L. P. (1999). "Simple lessons from complexity." *Science*, 284, 87-89.

Gupta, H. V., Sorooshian, S., and Yapo, P. O. (1998). "Toward improved calibration of hydrologic models: multiple and noncommensurable measures of information." *Water Resour. Res.*, 34(4), 751-763.

Klemes, V. (1986) "Dilettantism in hydrology: transition or destiny?" *Water Resour. Res.*, 22(9), 177S-188S.

Milly, P. C. D., Betancourt, J., Falkenmark, M., Hirsch, R. M., Kundzewicz, Z. W., Lettenmaier, D. P., and Stouffer, R. J. (2008). "Stationarity is dead: whither water management?" *Science*, 319, 573-574.

Rind, D. (1999). "Complexity and climate." *Science*, 284, 105-107.

Singh, V. P., and Woolhiser, D. A. (2002). "Mathematical modeling of watershed hydrology." *J. Hydrol. Eng.*, 7(4), 270-292.

AUTHOR INFORMATION

Richard H. McCuen is the Ben Dyer Professor of Civil and Environmental Engineering at the University of Maryland, College Park, where he has taught since 1971. He has authored many articles and books on mathematical modeling, probability and statistics, and their applications to engineering, hydrologic sciences and water resources management. He has a BS from Carnegie-Mellon University and MS and PhD from the Georgia Institute of Technology. Email: rhmccuen@eng.umd.edu

Chapter 25

Hydroelectric Power and the Future

Charles D. D. Howard and Jery R. Stedinger

ABSTRACT

A hydropower plant and the machinery inside today look much like they did a century ago. So, does hydropower, a 130-year-old technology, have a long-term future? A few small dams have been removed to open up streams to fish and outdoor recreation. Do such environmental concerns threaten the future of hydropower? Maybe, but hydropower's positive contributions to water and energy system management are essential ingredients of electric power systems around the world, and of the industrial societies they support. Hydropower's ability to generate revenue and pay for dams is an important factor for associated irrigation, flood management, navigation, and urban water supplies. Thus, hydropower's future lies within the future value of water as a natural resource to produce benefits for society. Hydropower's future value is also intimately linked to the future of electrical energy generation by other means and for its transmission, regulation, and the growing initiatives for improved electrical generation, transmission, and environmental protection. In this chapter, hydropower's future is discussed in the context of the future of electrical energy and the growth of related technologies and environmental concerns. Improvements in design and operations management will enhance the future value of hydropower resources within expanding networks of electrical power systems.

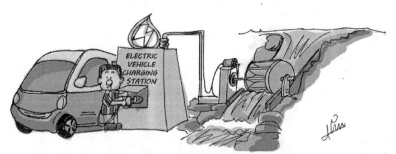

"Hydropower - it still works!"

INTRODUCTION

Hydropower is a renewable energy source that harnesses the energy lost to friction in flowing water. This is not some hydraulic version of perpetual motion – here is how it works: As rivers flow over the landscape, most of their flowing energy is dissipated in the heat and sound of friction that goes into the atmosphere and the surrounding earth and rock. This loss of energy is greatest where rivers are swiftly flowing and turbulence is high. Deep slow-moving reservoirs replace a reach of river, and the energy formerly lost as friction is converted to pressure (described as head) that spins turbines as water from behind the dam exits through the power house. Below the dam and power station the river continues on downstream driven as before by the force of gravity and the slope of the landscape. Hydropower is driven by the river's waste heat. The result is not only renewable energy, but also energy recycled! So what is the future of hydropower, and what do we need to do to get ready for that future?

HISTORY

In 1880, Michigan's Grand Rapids Electric Light and Power Company lit up 16 brush-arc lamps using electricity generated by a dynamo belted to a water turbine at the Wolverine Chair Factory. City street lamps in Niagara Falls, NY were powered by hydropower in 1881. By 1886 about 45 electric plants were powered by hydropower in the US and Canada, and by 1889 there were some 200 electric plants in the US that used water power for some or all of the power they generated (USDOE 2008a). According to the Niagara Falls Thunder Alley (2009) website, the City of Buffalo, NY on November 15, 1896 joined the power grid of Niagara Falls, making it the first long-distance transmission of electricity for commercial purposes.

In 1920 hydropower provided 25 % of electric generation in the US and by 1940 the percentage reached 40% of the nation's electricity (INL 2005). Currently about 7% of US electricity comes from about 80,000 MW of conventional hydroelectric capacity. There is an additional 18,000 MW of pumped storage that supports thermal generation. In little more than 100 years, hydroelectric power has reached full technical maturity from the original concept of dam, penstock, turbine, generator, switchyard, transmission line, and consumer.

Hydropower technology development has been evolutionary rather than revolutionary. As an example, by 1927 the development of hydro projects had become relatively standardized, as outlined in the *Hydroelectric Handbook* (Creager and Justin 1927). However, there have been significant changes as technologies evolved and new uses emerged. Pumped storage, a new use that took advantage of hydropower's flexibility, was adopted to offset nuclear energy generation's difficulties in matching changes in load and the desire to avoid daily cycling of such plants. Operation of hydropower projects, as reflected in the use of water, has become more effective as efficiencies increased for individual generating units, for sets of units in multi-unit plants, and across all generating units in integrated hydro-thermal power systems. As a result, in closely integrated systems, individual generating units now operate near their most-efficient settings more of the time. As these considerations of hydropower design, construction and operation roll through our mind's eye, we can see that hydropower's future will continue to be tweaked by improvements in river flow forecasting, materials and maintenance methods, hydraulic and structural design, types of turbines, low head applications, and more and better data for the computer and information systems that control hydropower facilities with increasing sophistication.

Hydropower's role in water and environmental management is still evolving. In the future, the value of hydropower may be closely tied to the expansion of alternative methods for generating and managing electricity. Hydropower, as both energy and reserve capacity, will certainly remain one of the valuable economic services provided by large reservoir systems. Large reservoir storage systems support irrigated agriculture, provide flood control, and meet industrial, municipal, transportation, recreational and a host of ecosystem and environmental demands. They also provide head and regulated flows that when used for hydropower operations bring revenue and benefits that pay much of the cost of construction, operation, and rehabilitation.

THE FUTURE OF HYDROPOWER AND THE ENVIRONMENT

Environmental sensitivities will probably increase in parallel with the costs of energy. The emphasis on environmental pragmatism will give way to a premium on site-specific scientific understanding for what a healthy ecosystem requires. Hydropower utilities currently buy solutions. In the future, hydropower utilities will find it profitable to actually do ongoing research and seriously take on the role of "steward of the river." Science-based data will support hydropower operating decisions on river flows that improve opportunities for a mix of species and life stages to adjust to changes in flows and water levels.

> *In the future, hydropower utilities will find it profitable to actually do ongoing research and seriously take on the role of "steward of the river."*

The global desire to reduce carbon dioxide (CO_2) is currently generating an interest in constructing expensive "green" generating facilities of marginal energy benefit, and in the case of small hydropower, no environmental benefit. Wind, photovoltaic, osmotic (Statkraft 1999), and kinetic hydropower turbines cannot replace the nuclear, oil and coal-fired thermal generating facilities that provide most of the electricity to the world. The only currently viable alternative of significant scale is massive investments in energy conservation, increased efficiency of cleaner coal-fired generation, and more widespread application of nuclear power. In some locations, reservoirs of existing large hydropower facilities will become more important in managing the flow of cooling water that supports large-scale expansion of efficient clean thermal generation.

Green energy (wind and solar) are notoriously unreliable and require matching kilowatt-hour for kilowatt-hour energy reserves to operate within a power grid. Hydropower is particularly well-suited to provide such reserve capacity without adding CO_2 in the atmosphere. Use of hydropower to provide capacity reserves may increase the risk of spills from reservoirs which are kept fuller to provide energy reserves to back up unreliable wind and solar energy resources. The cost of spilled hydropower energy is a cost against the value of green energy. Sophisticated electrical demand and supply management are essential or green energy generation facilities will continually burden system power generation and transmission. The challenge is to use all of the power system's resources in a coordinated manner to minimize the overall cost of electric power, and to reduce CO_2 emission and environmental impacts.

Rising temperatures are a contentious emerging issue as climate changes. There is unlikely to be a climate change problem for hydropower if energy is generated at plants that do not depend on upstream storage for head. The situation is different if storage is synonymous with generating head; in this case, a rising snow line forces a trade-off. High reservoir levels can maximize generating capacity for short bursts of high output, while low reservoir levels can maximize hydropower energy by reducing spill and capturing more of the anticipated higher and flashier winter inflows. Low levels also support better flood management.

In the Sierra Nevada mountains the snow line has been higher in recent years (less water stored as snow) resulting in greater winter runoff and lower late summer flows. To compensate, the operation of storage must be changed. In Manitoba, which receives water for hydropower from mountains half a continent to the west, there has been no detectable change in runoff behavior and no required change in storage operation. Thus, is climate change a problem for operation of hydropower systems? It would appear to be both yes and no, depending on site specific factors.

Environmental operation, a driving factor for innovation, will become more important, and in some cases dominant, as hydropower evolves further as a peaking resource in highly integrated systems. Future turbines may appear essentially unchanged, but the operation of hydropower systems will become more challenging. As hydropower units are operated more aggressively to meet new requirements, there will be rising requirements for maintenance and replacement as circuit breakers, generator windings, and other facilities are cycled more frequently.

THE FUTURE OF HYDROPOWER IN ELECTRICAL POWER SYSTEMS

A change in the way electricity is supplied and used would change the value of hydropower. Revamped electricity supply and demand could integrate generation into local grids that are supported by a greater diversity of distributed generation. Possibilities include efficient and economical household photovoltaic generation backed up by domestic fuel cells or energy storage. Advances may occur in cogeneration linked to industrial production along with increased use of small combustion turbines serving local loads. Mass-produced small nuclear power reactors could be used to provide a distributed base load capability. Tom Sanders of Sandia National Laboratories claims that such small reactors can produce 100-300 MW of thermal power, supplying energy in remote areas and developing countries (SNL 2009). Such reactors would need to be refueled only every couple of decades, and their small size and reactor core configuration reduces nuclear proliferation concerns. Future generation sources will move "ahead to the past" and locate economically close to loads, as was done when hydropower was first developed before high-voltage AC transmission became viable (Niagara Falls Thunder Valley 2009).

In addition to providing energy, hydropower also provides the most economical method for managing the timing of that energy flow to consumers. The current paradigm is "generation follows fluctuations in load." A significant part of the variability in system loads originates from domestic consumers whose pocket books would quickly respond to incentives in new technologies. As various devices and cost incentives make demand management more viable, the varying electrical load on power systems may become more uniform during the day. This would create a profound response to many cost, power, and environmental issues that arise from rapidly fluctuating loads, including dependence on hydropower generation for meeting temporary peaks in power demand. Conversely, hydropower's ability to support transmission stability will become more important where power systems become larger and transmission becomes more extended.   Hydropower's rapid response to voltage changes and pumped storage at hydropower facilities provides dispatchable loads that contribute to transmission network stability.

EVOLVING TECHNOLOGIES

Long established conventional wisdom will be challenged by closer integration of new technologies as recent scientific information enters the realm of practice. Superconducting generator windings operating at temperatures in the range of -290 degrees C will allow current densities 50 to 100 times that of conventional copper windings. The result will allow smaller and lighter generators. Lighter generators will improve the economics of hydropower, especially for remote small hydropower construction projects that can only be reached by helicopter. Turbines will operate at peak efficiency under all heads and flow rates by using electronic frequency control systems that permit variable speed generator operation. This will add efficiency and corresponding generating capability to existing facilities.

GPS receivers at existing seismic and other geologic monitoring sites currently can monitor snow depth accurately to a few millimeters. Consequently, runoff forecasting in mountain areas will improve as the number of these inexpensive monitoring stations with associated telemetry (already in the 1000's in the US and Canada) multiply and the analysis software becomes generally available. Similar technologies will monitor real-time environmental parameters related to river discharges, water quality parameters, and temperature as ecologists better understand the aquatic environment and the needs of aquatic ecosystems over the course of a day or a week.

The currently evolving Smart Grid initiatives will monitor flows and voltages on the grid many times each second, allowing real-time corrections to create new energy by minimizing electrical losses (USDOE 2008b). Distributed energy generation like hydropower within the Smart Grid will become more important for voltage and frequency control, spinning reserve, and network stability control. New loads, like battery and inertial powered automobiles, will reflect feedback between timely demand and the cost of delivering energy on the grid (Howard 1999). Hydropower's role will increase in completely interconnected and integrated transmission and generation systems.

> *Hydropower's role will increase in completely interconnected and integrated transmission and generation systems.*

Complete integration to achieve benefits will have its institutional price in terms of heightened central control of locally owned hydropower resources. New markets, and interstate and international agreements, will be required to compensate hydropower owners for using their resources as tools dedicated to overall system effectiveness instead of their own maximum efficiency and revenue. Smart Grid initiatives will coordinate delivery and demand for energy while smart environmental and hydropower control sensors and models provide information on generating rates, river flows and levels below run-of-river plants.

More and better remote sensing from space will open the door to new data and near real-time adaptive methods for managing hydro projects. Precipitation coverage will improve dramatically as the proposed "string of pearls" satellite system becomes a reality and precipitation is reported everywhere on earth every 10 or 15 minutes (NRC 2007). Runoff forecasting will continue to improve with more and better precipitation data and as satellite sensing provides reports of soil moisture, water stored in snow and lakes, and water levels that are converted to river discharge.

Improvements in sensors coupled with computer systems, better communication, and better computer coordination will provide opportunities for improved and more sophisticated reservoir management, both long-term and short-term. Dynamic probable maximum flood forecasts determined dynamically during severe runoff events will allow more flexible operating guidelines for storage. This will determine event-specific maximum reservoir levels for flood management, reduce spill, and increase generation. More and better data, and the software to use it effectively, will increase the water management benefits from hydropower dams. Of course, hydrology is not the only uncertainty in hydropower system operation; deregulation and the evolution of volatile hourly, next-day and longer-term energy and capacity markets associated with regional Integrated Systems Operation centers have greatly complicated hydropower systems operating and marketing decisions.

The transmission network in the eastern US is heavily loaded and efforts are underway to make it smarter by adjusting the capacity of local legs to reroute currents in response to shifts in the center of the loads. This procedure has been practiced for many years in the water distribution systems of major cities (e.g., Denver) by adjusting valve settings and pumping station operations to reroute flows during periods of heavy water demand. Hydropower generation flexibility can be an important component in determining how network flows are directed away from transmission bottlenecks. Under present deregulation rules the transmission and generation functions are kept separate from one another. This institutional barrier may have to be removed to optimize generation in support of transmission capacity.

FUTURE ADVANCES IN RELICENSING AND RATE CASES

A recurring concern is the time-consuming and expensive hearing process employed for electricity rate changes and relicensing of hydropower projects. Technologies will lighten the load and make these processes more productive. Web-based meetings are now commonplace in businesses and among private citizens and it is only a matter of time until on-line computer support of these virtual meetings becomes commonplace. An entirely possible step for software will be virtual human communication solely among computers (Stedinger and Howard 1993). Pre-programmed responses to anticipated issues will play off within computers before people get involved and emotions sidetrack negotiations. The factual data and scientific issues will be cleared away in a common database. Personal and group preferences then will attach values to alternatives developed in computers independently from the stakeholders and the power utilities. Software will bring up likely acceptable compromises and then call in the actual people on-line with the regulatory authority. Resolution will be swift, and documents embodied in the software will draft the agreement.

CONCLUSIONS

Hydropower has a long history of valuable service to economic growth and in providing funding for water management to produce food, navigation, flood management and water supply. Hydropower's future is assured as a clean and renewable source of energy without an ongoing carbon footprint. Hydropower's ancillary role in electrical supply will continue to be important in stabilizing power transmission networks, in reducing fluctuations in load, and in leveling intermittent power supplies from other renewable energy sources. How best to schedule and market hydropower operations to maximize its value will be a challenge. The basic ideas behind hydropower are mature, but technology developments will provide incremental improvements in the design of hydropower facilities, reduce their cost, and improve the power system benefits from hydropower. The challenge to water and hydropower managers is to continue to pursue improvements in plant efficiency, efficient unit operations, system efficiency through system-wide coordination, better forecasting of water flows and environmental parameters, operations that address environmental objectives, and more effective regulatory and public forums. Overall, given advances in related technologies, anticipated increases in demand and thermal generation, constraints on transmission systems, evolution of energy and capacity markets, and the intermittent character of green energy generation facilities, the value of hydropower will be greater in the year 2050 than it is today.

REFERENCES

Creager, W. P., and Justin, J. D. (1927). *Hydroelectric handbook*, John Wiley and Sons, New York, NY.
Howard, C. D. D. (1999) . "'Imagineering' the future of hydro and water resources." *Hydro Review*, 18(4), 38-43.
Idaho National Laboratory (INL). (2005). "Hydropower's historical progression" *Idaho National Laboratory*, <http://hydropower.inel.gov/hydrofacts/historical_progression.shtml> (Feb, 2010).
National Research Council (NRC). (2007). *Earth science and applications from space: national imperatives for the next decade and beyond,* Committee on Earth Science and Applications from Space: A Community Assessment and Strategy for the Future, National Academies Press, Washington, DC, 456 p., <http://www.nap.edu/catalog/11820.html> (Nov, 2009).
Niagara Falls Thunder Valley. (2009). "Niagara Falls history of power." *Niagara Falls Thunder Valley*, <http://www.niagarafrontier.com/power.html#Origins> (Nov, 2009).
Sandia National Laboratories (SNL). (2009). "Sandia team developing right-sized reactor." *Sandia news releases*, August 25, 2009, <http://www.sandia.gov/news/resources/news_releases/sandia-team-developing-right-sized-reactor/> (Nov, 2009).
Stedinger, J., and Howard, C. D. D. (1993). "The control room of the not-so-distant future." *Hydro Review*, 12(5), 78-83.
Statkraft. (2000). "Osmotic power." *Energy sources,* <http://www.statkraft.com/energy-sources/osmotic-power/> (Nov, 2009)
US Department of Energy (USDOE). (2008a). "History of hydropower." *Energy efficiency and renewable energy*, US Department of Energy, <http://www1.eere.energy.gov/windandhydro/hydro_history.html> (Sep, 2010).
US Department of Energy (US DOE). (2008b). *The Smart Grid: an introduction,* US Department of Energy, Office of Electricity Delivery and Energy Reliability, Washington, DC, < http://www.oe.energy.gov/SmartGridIntroduction.htm> (Nov, 2009).

AUTHOR INFORMATION

Charles D. D. Howard is an independent consulting engineer in water resources management, hydraulic engineering and development of innovative water management software. He provided senior level technical advice to water and power utilities, provincial, state, and federal governments in Canada and the US, and in many countries under the United Nations Development Program and for the World Bank. He has served on many committees of the US National Academy of Sciences

(National Research Council) and as an external examiner for the US National Science Foundation's research program on semi-arid hydrology. He received the 1998 Julian Hinds Award of ASCE for leadership and technical achievement in advancing the state of the art in water resources management. He is a registered engineer in British Columbia and Washington, and holds civil engineering degrees from University of Alberta (BS and MS) and from Massachusetts Institute of Technology (MS). Email: CddHoward@shaw.ca

Jery Stedinger received a BA in Applied Mathematics from the University of California at Berkeley in 1972, and a PhD in Environmental Systems Engineering from Harvard University in 1977. Since that time he has been a professor in Cornell's School of Civil and Environmental Engineering. His research has focused on statistical and risk issues in hydrology, and the optimal operation of water resource and hydropower systems. Jery was a 1989 ASCE Huber Civil Engineering Research Prize winner, and the 1997 winner of the ASCE Julian Hinds Award. In 2004 he received the Prince Sultan Bin Abdulaziz International Prize for Water for the Surface Water Branch for his work on flood risk management. He has spent sabbaticals with the US Geological Survey, the US Army Corps of Engineers, and Pacific Gas & Electric Company. Email: jrs5@cornell.edu

Chapter 26

Water Distribution Systems in 2050

Walter M. Grayman, Mark W. LeChevallier, and Tom Walski

ABSTRACT

Water distribution systems provide the mechanism for conveying and distributing finished water to customers. Early systems in Greece, the Middle East and Rome date back several millennia and back to the early 19th century in the US. Over the past 40 years, both structural changes in distribution systems and significant advances in operations and water quality considerations in distribution systems have been seen. Climate change, increasing population and water demand, limited water resources, and aging infrastructure will put significant demands on water distribution systems over the coming decades. Advances in pipe technology, operations, monitoring, asset management and design over the next 40 years could result in very significant improvements in water distribution systems by 2050. These changes are predicated on an increasing research and investment strategy and the need for a longer-term view of needs by the water industry.

"We're upgrading our water system.
I'll take 200 miles of those smart pipes."

243

BACKGROUND

Water distribution systems serve as the primary mechanism for distribution of finished water to customers. They are typically composed of pipes, pumps, valves and storage facilities to store and convey the water from the treatment plant or source to the customers. The use of distribution systems dates back many millennia. Cisterns, wells, water supply lines, pressure pipe and siphons were all used in water distribution in ancient Greece, Asia Minor and the Middle East in the centuries and even millennia BCE. Further advances in water distribution and sanitation were made during the Roman Empire period in the first and second century AD. Philadelphia dedicated the first large-scale water works and municipal distribution system in the US in 1801 (APWA 1976). Though today's technology associated with water distribution has progressed from these early systems, many of the basic design and operational principles remain the same. The primary emphasis of this chapter is on water distribution systems in the US, but many of the concepts, historical developments and predictions for future systems are also applicable to other countries.

LOOKING BACK 40 YEARS

Before looking 40 years into the future to predict what water distribution systems may look like (or should look like) in 2050, it is instructive to look back over the previous 40 year period to see what progress was made over that time period. Changes can be categorized as structural, operational, analysis and management, and emerging areas of interest.

There have been some significant structural changes in water distribution systems over the past 40 years, though changes have not been as sweeping and widespread as is the case in many other industries. New pipe materials have evolved, including plastic (PVC and HDPE) pipe and ductile iron pipe that have replaced cast iron and asbestos cement pipes of earlier eras. Pumps have become more efficient and versatile, and improved variable speed pumps and controls have been introduced. Elimination of lead piping and joints has reduced exposure to lead in distribution piping. Trenchless technology methods such as pipe bursting and horizontal directional drilling have been introduced in the water industry. Dual water systems that convey water of different quality such as potable water and reclaimed water have been the subject of much discussion and some implementation in the past 40 years (Okun 1976). Regionalization is a continuing trend as smaller water systems are merged into larger ones with the goal of increasing reliability and efficiency. Many cross connection control programs have been implemented in the past 40 years, reducing the incidence of contamination in distribution systems. Much wider use of fire sprinkler systems combined with improvements in fire-fighting technology has reduced peak water demands.

The primary innovation in the operation of water systems in the past 40 years is the introduction and widespread use of Supervisory Control And Data Acquisition

(SCADA) systems. First introduced in the water industry in the late 1960s, SCADA systems have become widely used in the control, operation and monitoring of water systems of all sizes.

Growth in use of computer based analysis and management tools for water distribution systems have followed the phenomenal growth in computer technology over the past 40 years. Tools such as computer-based water distribution system modeling, mapping (CAD, GIS, AM/FM), maintenance management and asset management were essentially non-existent 40 years ago and are now commonly used throughout the water industry.

The past 40 years has also seen the emergence of several areas of interest within the water distribution system field. Widespread concerns about the environment and conservation in general, and water quality in our drinking water systems in particular were in their infancy in 1970. Since then, the formation of the US Environmental Protection Agency (USEPA), promulgation of the Safe Drinking Water Act and its amendments, and extensive research programs sponsored by the Water Research Foundation (formerly AwwaRF), the USEPA and other organizations have influenced how water systems are designed and operated. Water security has emerged as a critical issue as a result of the events of September 11, 2001.

In summary, the past 40 years has seen some actual structural changes in water distribution systems, and extensive changes in computer-based operational and analysis support systems, greater emphasis on water quality, and an active research program in many areas related to water distribution. This sets the stage for the potential for very significant changes and improvements in water distribution systems in the coming 40 years.

DISTRIBUTION SYSTEMS TODAY: ISSUES AND NEEDS

If the overall objective of effective water distribution systems was delivering an adequate quantity of water at an acceptable pressure and water quality at a reasonable price so that it can be used with confidence, most water supply and distribution systems in the United States would pass that test. However, this does not fully address the current needs and risks associated with water distribution, and certainly does not mean that all distribution systems meet today's minimum standards nor will be able to meet the concerns of the future. The National Research Council (NRC) recently assessed and identified the risks associated with water distribution systems (NRC 2006). Based on the NRC report and other sources, some of the issues facing distribution systems today and in the future include:

- *Degraded infrastructure.* In its 2009 infrastructure report card, the American Society of Civil Engineers (ASCE) gave drinking water infrastructure a score of D- and concluded that "America's drinking water systems face an annual shortfall of at least $11 billion to replace aging facilities that are near the end of their useful life and to comply with existing and future federal water regulations. Leaking pipes lose an estimated seven billion gallons of clean drinking water a day" (ASCE 2009). This has resulted in a shift from new construction to rehabilitation/renewal of piping components to maintain service.

> **Leaking pipes lose an estimated 26.5 billion liters (seven billion gallons) of clean drinking water a day.**

- *Climate change, resource depletion and increasing demands for water.* Together these will all tax the ability of many water supply systems to deliver adequate water in the future.
- *Using highly treated water to satisfy lower quality needs.* Water distribution systems typically deliver high quality water for a variety of uses by customers. However, more than 80% of the water supplied to residences is used for activities other than human consumption such as sanitary service and landscape irrigation.
- *Providing adequate standby fire-flow needs.* To satisfy this need, most distribution systems use standpipes, elevated tanks, storage reservoirs, and larger sized pipes. This results in higher capital costs and longer transit times.
- *Preventing contamination in distribution systems.* Distribution systems are the remaining components of public water supplies yet to be adequately addressed in national efforts to eradicate waterborne disease. Most of the reported outbreaks associated with distribution systems have involved contamination from cross-connections and back-siphonage.
- *Reducing energy requirements.* Distribution system pumping can account for more than 90% of energy use for many water systems and therefore a significant portion of the greenhouse gas emissions generated (direct or indirect) by water utilities. A focus on maintaining pump efficiency is important not only for economic reasons, but also for environmental stewardship.
- *Providing centralized systems in developing regions.* Population continues to increase in many less-developed countries and the shift from community wells to central water distribution systems puts a premium on the development of cost-effective and easily implemented systems.
- *Reducing vulnerability to terrorism.* Concern over terrorist attacks since 2001 has directed attention to potential vulnerabilities of the nation's water systems (including cyber-systems) as targets of malicious attacks.

A 2050 VISION

The real purpose of this chapter is to identify areas where changes are needed or desirable in the future of water distribution systems and to propose how the water distribution systems in the year 2050 could address these issues.

Control and Operation of Distribution Systems

Following the lead of the food and chemistry industry in the area of process control, the movement of water in water distribution systems will be far better controlled, tracked and operated by the year 2050. Elements of the 2050 system will include an integrated central automated operating system, SCADA systems, monitors, real-time automated meter reading (AMR) systems, leak monitors, real-time hydraulic models, and automated valve and pump systems that together can both track and control the flow of water from treatment plants to the customer.

> *Water will be fully monitored, tracked and controlled from treatment plants to the customer.*

These elements will provide computerized operating systems with real-time information on the flow (rates, velocity, water quality, calculated water age) and leakage of water throughout the distribution system and forecasts of water use in order to determine optimal short-term operating rules. These systems will also facilitate real-time pricing for water usage that will help control demand during periods of water shortage. Both the water system components and their associated cyber-systems will be better designed and operated to protect from malicious attacks. Advances in water quality and transient flow modeling in distribution system piping and tanks will result in improvements in design and operations of water systems.

Pipe Technology

New pipe technology will include new pipe materials and associated construction techniques that result in a longer life expectancy, is stronger, resists water quality deterioration and biofilm formation, and virtually eliminates leakage and intrusion of contaminants due to cracks and small breaks in the pipes. Smart pipe sensor technology embedded within the pipes will continually monitor the integrity of the pipe and notify the operating system of any problems. Trenchless installation technology will reduce the cost of installation of new pipes and rehabilitation of existing pipe. Improvements in rehabilitation technology will extend the life of existing infrastructure.

Dual or Multiple Water Systems

Many water distribution systems in 2050 will be composed of multiple parallel systems that will convey water of different levels of quality commensurate for their ultimate use. Ultra high quality water will be delivered in smaller pipes for consumption. Grey-water systems will convey and use recycled water for lower quality needs. Fire-fighting needs, a primary driver for the present day design of water distribution systems, will depend much more heavily on conventional and self-contained chemical sprinkler systems and fire-fighting equipment that will reduce the need for oversized water delivery pipes and hydrants.

Distribution System Design

The objectives associated with the design of water distribution systems in 2050 will go beyond the current objectives of minimizing capital costs, increasing reliability and providing adequate capacity to meet fire-fighting needs. Water quality, water security, new fire-fighting technology and increased levels of water conservation will all be considerations in the design and rehabilitation of water distribution systems. The water quality objective will result in designs that minimize the water age and use pipe materials that minimize the deterioration of water quality during the delivery process. Water security concerns will drive designs that reduce the spread of contamination throughout the distribution system and facilitate control if a contaminant is detected in the system. New fire-fighting technology will largely eliminate the need for delivery of water for fire-fighting, resulting in smaller diameter pipes. Water conservation will result in dual (or multiple) pipe systems, and use of new pipe material and monitoring to reduce leakage. This will lead to smaller storage requirements resulting in lower water age and improvements in water quality.

Pumping Systems
Because a) energy for pumping is one of the largest operating costs for many water utilities, b) the cost of energy is increasing, and c) awareness of carbon footprints is increasing, water suppliers will minimize energy usage. This will be accomplished through more vigilant analysis of new pump selection, existing pumping efficiency, new pump station design, and improved pump scheduling. Operators will be able to link their SCADA data with hydraulic analysis to better support pump operation decisions.

Monitors in Distribution Systems
The development of new technology for monitoring the water quality and hydraulic conditions and its availability at low costs will result in a many-fold increase in monitoring in distribution systems. Smart pipe sensor technologies based on nanotechnology and wireless transmission will continuously assess water quality and hydraulic conditions at key locations in the distribution system and transmit information and warnings to the central operating system (Lin et al. 2009). Inexpensive point-of-use monitors installed on the service lines of all customers will detect both a wide range of contaminants and the presence of backflow into the distribution system and immediately transmit a warning to both the central operating system and the customer.

Asset Management
With the cumulative value of distribution systems across the United States in the trillions of dollars, these assets will be far better managed in 2050. Asset management systems will track the history, condition and operation of each individual component. Integrated leak monitors will detect when pipes first begin to leak and immediately report the information to the operator. Sealants will be used to fix the pipes without excavation. As soon as a new pipe or valve is added to a system, the asset management system updates the inventory and mapping systems instantly. With linkages to the smart pipe technology and the SCADA system, the asset management system will also know the condition of the asset and its current status. Valve status (open or closed) will continually be updated in the asset

management system, facilitating repair of pipe breaks and avoiding incorrectly operated valves that inhibit flow through the system.

Computers in Operations and Maintenance
Computer technology will increasingly find its way into the hands of operation and maintenance personnel. Evidence of this is the increased use of computers to bring up-to-date maps into the field digitally, instead of relying on paper maps which may be significantly out of date. The ability to turn map layers on and off and link maps with global positioning systems will make field work more efficient.

Water Quality
The water industry will better understand the contribution of the distribution systems to deterioration in water quality. On-line analyzers including disinfectant residual analyzers, microbial monitoring stations, chemical labs on-a-chip and other advanced monitoring methods developed in the coming 40 years will provide near real-time data on any deteriorations in water quality. Automatic shut-off valves built into water meters and controlled through the automatic metering infrastructure can be activated to protect customers from any detected contamination. A better understanding of the nature of microbes in the biofilms and their potential health impacts will lead to strategies for producing biologically stable drinking water, managing water stagnation (which leads to water quality degradation), and optimization of disinfectant residuals.

Premise Plumbing
Premise plumbing, the portion of the potable water distribution system associated with the customer, "can magnify the potential public health risk relative to the main distribution system and complicate formulation of coherent strategies to deal with problems" (NRC 2006). In the future, premise plumbing will be designed, operated and regulated in concert with and consistent with the public distribution system in order to reduce public health impacts such as increased water age, bacterial growth, backflow and contamination.

Paradigm Shifts
Two future potential paradigm shifts affecting water distribution system design and operation are described above: widespread use of dual or multiple pipe systems, and changes in fire-fighting technology that will free water systems from delivering high quality water for fire fighting. In an even more drastic potential paradigm shift, LeChevallier (2009) suggests the following scenario that would have obvious profound impacts on water distribution:

> "*We are on the verge of a paradigm shift to a hydrogen economy within the next century, and a by-product of energy generation from hydrogen is water. This is not a far-fetched scenario. Drinking water is already produced from the hydrogen fuel cells on the Space Station. What will happen when all of the electricity in the US is generated from hydrogen fuel cells? What would*

we do with molecular pure water? Could this be an alternate water delivery system?"

Hristovski et al. (2009) elaborate on this potential paradigm shift in their discussion of the production of drinking water from hydrogen fuel cells. Over the coming 40-year period, major technological developments emanating from other fields could be transferred to the water industry resulting in other significant paradigm shifts.

NEEDS AND BARRIERS TO ACHIEVING THE 2050 VISION

Many of these predictions for 2050 are very likely to occur and in some cases may come to pass well before the target date. Generally, these predictions fall into the computer-related areas that are the subject of ongoing research and development. The predictions that will be more difficult to implement are those that require either significant breakthroughs in research or require wholesale changes to the actual distribution system assets.

The water industry as a whole has not spent much money on long-term research. Most major breakthroughs in the water industry have been derived from other industries such as the food and chemical industries. Private research and development tends to emphasize research that will provide payback within reasonably short periods (5 to 10 years). In order to make some of the advances that are predicted, greater investments in long-term research must be made. Additionally, greater cooperation between academic, government and water industry groups is needed to focus the research program towards the short-term and long-term needs. With a customer base for the water industry in the US of over a quarter of a billion people (and a worldwide customer base in the billions), it is not unreasonable to expect sufficient funding to support a very vibrant research program.

A second barrier to large-scale changes in water distribution systems is the quantity of pipe and other facilities within water systems in the US. There are nearly 1.6 million kilometers (1 million miles) of water pipe and over 150,000 water storage tanks nationwide (NRC 2006). At the current annual rate of approximately 0.5% for replacement of drinking water pipe in the US, it would take about 200 years to replace the entire current inventory of pipe (Buchberger 2009). Therefore, even if there were a major breakthrough in pipe material or construction, it would take centuries to replace the pipe inventory at the current replacement rate or an order of magnitude increase in spending to accomplish this within a few decades.

> *It will take centuries to replace the pipe inventory at the current replacement rate, let alone meet future increasing demands for water.*

CONCLUSION

There are many areas of improvement that are possible in the area of water distribution systems, and improvements are needed just to keep up with the stressors and risks that will be faced in the coming 40 years. However, if we consider the actual progress and implemented advances of the past 40 years in water distribution system technology and components, then we cannot be overly optimistic that the needed progress will be made. On the other hand, if we examine recent research results and assume an even more vibrant research and development program in the coming years, then most or all of the predictions made in this chapter are possible within the 40 year timeframe leading up to 2050. This assessment has concentrated on the needs and future for water distribution systems in the United States. Much of this analysis is also applicable to other developed countries. However, with the continuing shifts in population towards less developed countries and the expected widespread shift from community wells to central water distribution systems by the year 2050, future mechanisms for transferring and adapting technology and advances in water distribution systems are needed.

REFERENCES

American Public Works Association (APWA). (1976). *History of public works in the United States 1776-1976*, American Public Works Association, Chicago, IL.

American Society of Civil Engineers (ASCE). (2009). Report card for America's Infrastructure. <http://www.asce.org/reportcard/2009/grades.cfm> (Oct, 2010).

Buchberger, S. (2009). "Climate change readiness assessment and planning for the nation's drinking water and wastewater utilities." *Proc., First national expert and stakeholder workshop on water infrastructure sustainability and adaptation to climate change*, US Environmental Protection Agency, Washington, DC.

Hristovski, K. D., Dhanasekaran, B., Tibaquira, J. E., Posner, J. D., Westerhoff, P. K. (2009). "Producing drinking water from hydrogen fuel cells." *J. Water Supply Res.T.*, 58(5), 327-335.

LeChevallier, M. W. (2009). "Drinking water: challenges and solutions for the next century." *Proc., Conference on your drinking water: challenges and solutions for the 21st century*, Yale University, New Haven, CT.

Lin, Y.-F., Lui, C., and Whisler, J. (2009). "Smart Pipe – nanosensors for monitoring water quantity and quality in public water systems." *Proc., 11th Water distribution systems analysis symposium, World environmental and water resources congress 2009*, American Society of Civil Engineers, Reston, VA.

National Research Council (NRC). (2006). *Drinking water distribution systems: assessing and reducing risks*, National Academies Press, Washington, DC.

Okun, D. A. (1976). "Drinking water for the future." *Am J Public Health*, 66(7), 639-643.

AUTHOR INFORMATION

Walter Grayman, PhD, PE, D.WRE is an independent consulting civil/environmental engineer specializing in computer applications in water resources and water supply. For the past quarter of a century he has been involved in research, development, teaching and application of water distribution system modeling and monitoring of water systems. Dr. Grayman has received awards from AWWA and ASCE for his work. Email: grayman@fuse.net

Mark LeChevallier, PhD is the Director of Innovation and Environmental Stewardship at the American Water Corporate Center in Voorhees, NJ. In this capacity he directs the research program and environmental compliance for American Water, the largest waster and wastewater utility in the US serving over 15 million people in 32 states and in Canada. Email: mark.lechevallier@amwater.com

Tom Walski, PhD, PE, D.WRE is senior product manager for Bentley Systems. Among his previous positions, he was engineering manager for Pennsylvania American Water, associate professor of environmental engineering at Wilkes University and manager of water distribution operation for Austin, TX. He has published numerous books and articles on water distribution (including receiving the J AWWA award for best Distribution and Plant Operation paper on three occasions). He is a licensed water and wastewater operator in Pennsylvania. Email: Tom.Walski@bentley.com

Chapter 27

Sensing for Improved Water Infrastructure Management in 2050

David A. Dzombak, Jeanne M. VanBriesen, James H. Garrett, Jr., and Lucio Soibelman

ABSTRACT

Ubiquitous sensing of water infrastructure is under development in 2010 and will be critical to sustainable urban water infrastructure systems of 2050. Sensed water infrastructure coupled with data management systems for rapid data analysis and visualization will enable improved asset management as well as real-time operational control for a higher level of infrastructure performance. The water infrastructure renewal challenge of 2010 derives in part from the fact that our current water infrastructure cannot self-monitor, adapt to changing conditions, or self-repair and regenerate. In 2050, urban water infrastructure will need to have these characteristics to be more sustainable, and this will be achieved in part through creation of a cyber-physical infrastructure.

"Self-repairing Pipes"

INTRODUCTION

The urban water and wastewater infrastructure in the US of 2010 reflects the basic designs established in the late 1800s and early 1900s, when rapidly increasing urbanization and the rise of sanitary engineering led to modern approaches to wastewater management and drinking water treatment and distribution (Melosi 2000; Tarr 1996). The basic design goals established in those formative years remain the same today: treat water from a relatively clean source to remove pathogenic microorganisms, distribute it via piping systems throughout urban communities, and convey wastewater from community users to treatment and discharge locations away from the source of water supply. In the 130 years since the first installation of the current US urban water infrastructure, the list of water contaminants of interest has steadily expanded and new water and wastewater treatment technologies have been developed and deployed. More recently, the electronic age has brought the development and implementation of new kinds of monitoring and control systems, with a primary focus on treatment facilities. However, the water distribution and wastewater conveyance systems have changed little in design or method of operation over this period.

In 2010, the US is faced with a large challenge of aging water and wastewater infrastructure, with renewal of the subsurface water distribution and wastewater/stormwater conveyance systems representing the largest portion of this challenge. In many communities, the subsurface infrastructure has not been adequately maintained, and system failures are occurring at increasing rates.

The US Environmental Protection Agency (USEPA) performed a study of the nation's drinking water and wastewater/stormwater infrastructure challenges (USEPA 2002). This assessment confirmed the existence of aged water infrastructure in many older urban areas, with some system components exceeding 100 years in age. It described the current challenges for renewal considering years of deferred maintenance and inadequate capital investment. It also noted the need for new infrastructure in some growth areas, and the challenge of dealing with underused, "stranded" infrastructure in areas of decreasing population. In the report, the USEPA developed estimates totaling more than $500 billion needed for repair and upgrade of drinking water and wastewater/stormwater infrastructure through 2020. A follow-on study by USEPA, the *Drinking Water Infrastructure Needs Survey and Assessment* (USEPA 2009a), found that 60% of the needs projected through 2027 were related to the distribution system.

An August 2002 GAO report echoed the concerns raised by USEPA, indicating that one-third of water utilities had significant deferred maintenance and more than 20% of their pipes were at the end of useful life (GAO 2002). A more recent GAO analysis estimated water infrastructure needs of $485 billion to $1.2 trillion over the next 20 years (GAO 2008). Similarly, the 2009 infrastructure report card of the American Society of Civil Engineers (ASCE) cited an annual $11 billion shortfall for drinking water infrastructure over the next 20 years, and cited a USEPA estimate of a

$390 billion investment need over the same period to update or replace existing wastewater collection and treatment systems and build new ones to meet increasing demand (ASCE 2009).

As the USEPA and states and communities across the US work on the water infrastructure renewal challenge, there is growing recognition of the importance of developing a more sustainable urban water infrastructure and improved systems for water infrastructure asset management. We need to aim for a water infrastructure of 2050 that can be maintained at reasonable cost, and that provides a higher level of performance than the system of 2010. Ubiquitous sensing of water infrastructure is coming and will be critical to sustainable urban water infrastructure systems of 2050.

> *We need to aim for a water infrastructure of 2050 that can be maintained at reasonable cost, and that provides a higher level of performance than the system of 2010.*

SUSTAINABLE WATER INFRASTRUCTURE

Infrastructure systems are not static; we grow them. Infrastructure is expanded to meet new needs, replaced, rebuilt, modified, adapted, and upgraded. Infrastructure is designed and then re-designed to meet changing needs for human civilization.

The scale and cost of water infrastructure naturally constrain the rate of renewal, but as the US experience demonstrates, public interest can accelerate or slow the rate of renewal. In the US we are entering an era of great need for water infrastructure renewal and expansion (AWWA 2001), and also an era of greater public interest in, and higher expectations for, water infrastructure. At the same time, the amount of funding that the public is willing to provide will increase only modestly.

Achieving higher performance at the same cost will require new approaches to the design and management of water infrastructure. Improved asset management and operation will be important for improved performance and to avoid the financial and operational problems that accrue with deferred maintenance. In short, a more operationally and economically sustainable water infrastructure is needed. Hassanain et al. (2003) proposed an asset management process in which data acquired at the beginning of the process will be managed and assessed in order to provide support to decisions regarding daily operations and capital investments.

The water infrastructure renewal challenge of 2010 derives in part from the fact that our current water infrastructure cannot self-monitor, adapt to changing conditions, or self-repair and regenerate. In 2050, urban water infrastructure will need to have the following characteristics to be more sustainable:

- *Self-monitoring* is critical to enable management and prediction of system behavior. Currently the day-by-day status of the infrastructure systems that enable our modern life is largely unknown. Water distribution system pipes routinely fail, but no system of sensors predicts or even reports these failures. The water distribution system is open to intentional attack, but no sentinel system would detect an accidental or intentional water quality incident. Thus, sensors are needed to generate enough data to allow better understanding of failure patterns, understand cause and effect for system failures, predict failure, remove root causes of potential failures, and make possible more reliable and less expensive operation.

- *Self-adaptation* is needed to allow systems to respond to conditions with changes that improve performance or prevent failure. Adaptation within the water infrastructure of 2010 is human-controlled. Managers respond to customer calls, monitor source water or water in the distribution system, and make expert decisions on changes to system operations. The dependence on key personnel with long-term, deep understanding of an individual system is particularly concerning given the low number of engineers electing to be trained in water infrastructure.

- *Self-repair* is needed to fix small problems before they become bigger problems. Our current infrastructure, while constantly being altered and intensively managed, is not able to self-repair or proactively fix small problems before they cascade to larger failures. Detection and classification of leaks is the first step in managing proactive repairs prior to cascading failures. Sensor systems and associated data analysis tools have been developed to assist in these classifications (Mounce et al. 2003; Stoianov et al. 2007). Water infrastructure is largely buried and even small repairs require extensive disruption to human activities. Systems of in-situ repair and maintenance are critically needed to reduce social disruption and cost of repairs.

Many of the physical components of water infrastructure systems that will be in service in 2050 are in place now. Water infrastructure has a long service life, with cast iron pipe expected to last 100 years or more. Process modifications are common, but plant expansion or replacement occurs very infrequently. The infrastructure of 2050 is therefore expected to be built on the same platform as the infrastructure of 2010. However, our 2050 infrastructure must be able to self-monitor, adapt to changing conditions, and self-repair and regenerate. This can only be achieved by changing the relationship between the physical infrastructure and 1) a newly evolving cyber infrastructure, and 2) a reorganized management system for integration, maintenance and operation. Implementation of critical changes in cyber infrastructure and system management will enable the transformation of our water system.

> *Our 2050 infrastructure must be able to self-monitor, adapt to changing conditions, and self-repair and regenerate.*

SENSED WATER INFRASTRUCTURE

Advances in sensing technology are rapidly changing what is possible in monitoring and managing water infrastructure systems. For example, deployable, *in situ* water quality sensors are now available to collect "real-time" data at second to minute to hour intervals, a significant improvement over traditional "grab and take to the lab for analysis" time intervals. These sensors are just beginning to be placed in the natural and built environment and their data collected for human analysis (USEPA 2009b). At present, the information that sensors can collect is limited to a few parameters and they generally require frequent calibration and maintenance in the field. Eventually, networks of these (and improved) sensors will be widely deployed, producing a wealth of data. Sensors will allow us to understand how water management systems like cisterns and green roofs reduce the loading to storm sewers. Sensors in our drinking water distribution systems will track changes to our drinking water quality that could indicate problems with treatment or even an intentional attack on our water distribution system. This type of real-time data acquisition in our water infrastructure systems will revolutionize our understanding of the systems and improve our ability to manage these systems to improve human and ecosystem health, even as we put increasing pressure on these systems.

The use of real-time sensors for water flow and some water quality parameters has improved understanding when coupled with distribution system modeling and sensor placement algorithms (see, for example, Isovitsch and VanBriesen (2008) and Xu et al. (2008)). Sensor networks within distribution systems are increasingly being proposed and deployed to enhance security (Ailamaki et al. 2003; Krause et al. 2008).

As an example of the potential of sensors for improved operation and performance in drinking water distribution systems, on-line sensors for measuring chlorine residual have already been installed in many water distribution networks. Chlorine sensors, usually in conjunction with other sensors, can be used to detect events (accidental or intentional contamination) as well as to monitor chlorine residual during normal operation. Coupled with booster stations to deliver chlorine at additional locations, sensors allow better control of chlorine residuals and the formation of disinfection by-products in the system. Further, chlorine booster stations can be activated in response to an event to disinfect the water in transit to the consumer. Control of chlorine boosters and interpretation of sensor data is currently done by water engineers, but in the future this will be done by using cyber infrastructure to model, evaluate and control the system autonomously.

Another example of the potential for sensors is the use of advanced ultrasonic testing technologies for condition assessment of pipeline systems, including discrete ultrasonic testing, continuous ultrasonic testing (i.e., guided wave techniques) and ultrasonic profiling or sound navigation and ranging (sonar). Advances in microelectronics, computers and piezoelectronics have led to the development of innovative sensors and ultrasonic technologies that allow for the rapid inspection and monitoring of pipelines. Unlike the typical ultrasonic pipeline inspection systems that require specially-designed transducers to reduce the coherent noise, new approaches using guided-wave based time reversal methods can relax restrictions on excitation frequency and signal bandwidth (Harley et. al. 2009) and allow the deployment of monitoring systems. Time reversal has been demonstrated to effectively compensate for complex wave modes and dispersion behaviors in pipes, and to enhance signal level and the ability to detect small defects (Harley et. al. 2009).

In addition to the technology to make measurements rapidly in water infrastructure systems, we will need technology that receives these data in real-time and enables extraction of relevant information from the raw data to present it in such a way that it is intelligible to our much slower human senses. The general problem of pattern discovery in a large number of co-evolving groups of data streams is the focus of extensive study (Papadimitriou et al. 2005), and direct application to drinking water data streams has been undertaken by research teams (Faloutsos and VanBriesen 2006; Sun et al. 2006) and by groups within government agencies (USEPA 2009c). In order to use these real-time data to manage our infrastructure systems in real time, we will need the extracted relevant information to be organized in ways that enable us to make decisions, to understand, and to act.

Research and development is in progress to create water infrastructure sensor technology and networks, as well as the signal and data handling, processing, and analysis systems for improved human decision-making capability for water infrastructure management. Integration of these various components is critical to developing sensed water infrastructure for 2050. This integration requires water system experts who know what to measure in water and why; sensor and sensor network experts who understand how signals and data are measured, collected, stored, transmitted, and processed; and information technology experts who are able to transform streaming data into information useful for human decision-making about design, operation, and maintenance of water infrastructure systems.

CAPABILITIES OF SENSED WATER INFRASTRUCTURE

Implementation of ubiquitous sensing integrated with real-time data collection and processing capability will make possible improved condition assessment, operations, and asset management, which will be the path to higher system performance at reasonable cost. Some examples of the capabilities that can be expected of sensed water infrastructure in 2050 are discussed below.

Inspection and Maintenance

Increased efficiency in inspection and maintenance operations required to maximize asset life will be enabled by sensor-based inspection tools that increase the accuracy and speed of acquisition of inspection data. For example, Soibelman et al. (2006) have explored the automatic detection of defects using computer vision algorithms to expedite the inspection process and improve the quality of inspection data collected. Multi-sensor inspection technologies will provide the measurements of distribution and conveyance systems needed for condition assessment and system maintenance, e.g., structural integrity and flow measurements. The data obtained will be normalized and stored in a manner that will enable baseline benchmarking for analysis of data obtained in subsequent inspections.

Rapid Detection and Response
The capture and rapid analysis of streaming data from sensors in distribution and conveyance systems will enable rapid detection of and response to problems and situations that develop. The data management system will be able to process the multiple sensor data streams and detect changes from a continuously-updated baseline in real time without revisiting of stored data.

Macro-Level Trend Analysis and Compliance Stress Testing
The computerized framework for collection and analysis of sensor data will allow integration with data and relevant, non-system data, e.g., weather and urban development data, making possible macro-level trend analysis, regulatory compliance stress testing, and optimization of capital and operation and maintenance investments. De Oliveira et al. (2009) have illustrated the value of exploratory data analysis using geospatial clustering algorithms to extract preliminary insights from a data set for such purposes as developing deterioration models by determining the attributes that might be correlated with deterioration. Examples of optimization of capital investment in infrastructure are provided by Abraham et al. (1998) and Morcous and Lounis (2005). By creating a complete view of the system that combines all real-time monitoring, weather, flooding, inspection, and geographic information data, trends and patterns can be identified, and system operation and maintenance activities can be prioritized and optimized. It will be possible to characterize long-term in addition to short-term risks.

Prediction of System Performance
The data record obtained through continuous monitoring and the subsequent automated data analysis will provide the system-wide measurement base needed for frequent calibration of system performance models, enabling the use of such models in routine forecasting of system performance. This capability will be useful for responding to rapidly evolving situations such as intense rainfall in part of the sewershed, an unusual contaminant in the water supply, an intrusion in the drinking water system, or other events that require a rapid response to maintain desired system performance.

CONCLUSIONS

The sensed water infrastructure of 2050 will enable much more insight and control of treatment, distribution, and conveyance systems than is currently possible. These capabilities will, in turn, make possible more efficient operation and maintenance, a higher level of system performance, and more sustainable operation. The life of subsurface assets will be extended by improving maintenance performance. The increased knowledge of the system will make possible more effectively deployed capital investments, and system modifications aimed at continuous increase in system performance and resilience. All of these characteristics will move urban water infrastructure in the US to a more operationally and economically sustainable state.

REFERENCES

Abraham, D. M., Wirahadikusumah, R., Short, T. J., and Shahbahrami, S. (1998). "Optimization modeling for sewer network management." *J. Constr. Eng. M. ASCE*, 124(5), 402-410.

Ailamaki, A., Faloutsos, C., VanBriesen, J. M., Small, M., and Fischbeck, P. (2003). "An environmental sensor network to determine drinking water quality and security." *SIGMOD*, 34(2), 47-52.

American Society of Civil Engineers (ASCE). (2009). "Report card for America's infrastructure." *American Society of Civil Engineers*, Reston, VA, <http://www.infrastructurereportcard.org/index> (Sep, 2009).

American Water Works Association (AWWA). (2001). *Dawn of the replacement era: reinvesting in drinking water infrastructure,*" American Water Works Association, Denver CO, <http://www.win-water.org/reports/infrastructure.pdf> (Sep, 2009).

de Oliveira, D. P., Soibelman, L., and Garrett, Jr., J. H. (2009). "Exploratory spatial data analysis (ESDA) of drinking water pipe break events: an overview." *Proc., 2009 NSF Engineering Research and Innovation Conference*, Honolulu, HI.

Faloutsos, C., and VanBriesen, J. M. (2006). "Sensor mining at work: principles and a water quality case-study." *Proc., Knowledge Discovery in Databases (KDD)*. Philadelphia, PA.

Government Accounting Office (GAO). (2002). *Water infrastructure: information on financing, capital planning, and privatization*, United States General Accounting Office, Washington, DC.

Government Accounting Office (GAO). (2008). *Physical infrastructure: challenges and investment options for the nation's infrastructure*, United States General Accounting Office, Washington, DC.

Harley, J., Donoughue, N., States, J., Ying, Y., Garrett, Jr., J. H., Jin, Y., Moura, J. M. F., Oppenheim, I. J., and Soibelman, L. (2009). "Focusing of ultrasonic waves in cylindrical shells using time reversal." *Proc., 7th International Workshop on Structural Health Monitoring*, Stanford, CA.

Hassanain, M. A., Froese, T. M., and Vanier, D. J. (2003). "Framework model for asset maintenance management." *J. Water Res. Pl.-ASCE*, 17(1), 51-64.

Isovitsch, S. L., and VanBriesen, J. M. (2008). "Sensor placement and optimization criteria dependencies in a water distribution system." *J. Water Res. Pl.-ASCE*, 134(2), 186-196.

Krause, A., Leskovec, J., Guestrin, C., VanBriesen, J., and Faloutsos, C. (2008). "Efficient sensor placement optimization for securing large water distribution networks." *J. Water Res. Pl-ASCE*, 134(6), 516-526.

Melosi, M. C. (2000). *The sanitary city: urban infrastructure in America from colonial times to the present*, Johns Hopkins University Press, Baltimore. MD.

Morcous, G., and Lounis, Z. (2005). "Maintenance optimization of infrastructure networks using genetic algorithms." *Automat. Constr.*, 14(1), 129-142.

Mounce, S. R., Khan, A., Wood, A. S., Day, A. J., Widdop, P. D., and Mahcell, J. (2003). "Sensor fusion of hydraulic data for burst detection and location in a treated water distribution system." *Information Fusion*, 4(3), 217-229.

Papadimitriou, S., Sun, J., and Faloutsos, C. (2005). "Streaming pattern discovery in multiple time series." *Proc., 31st International Conference on Very Large Data Bases*, Trondheim, Norway, 697 - 708.

Soibelman, L., Guo, W., and Garrett, Jr., J. H. (2006). "Automatic visual data interpretation for pipeline infrastructure assessment." *Proc., International Association for Bridge and Structural Engineering (IABSE) 2006 Symposium - Responding to Tomorrow's Challenges in Structural Engineering*, Budapest, Hungary.

Stoianov, I., Nachman, L., Madden, S., and Tokmouline, T. (2007). "PIPENET a wireless sensors network for pipeline monitoring." *Proc., 6th International Conference on Information Processing in Sensor Networks*, Cambridge, MA, 264-273.

Sun, J., Papadimitriou, S., and Faloutsos, C. (2006). "Distributed pattern discovery in multiple streams." *Proc., Pacific-Asia Conference on Knowledge Discovery and Data Mining (PAKDD)*, Singapore.

Tarr, J. A. (1996). *The search for the ultimate sink*, University of Akron Press, Akron, OH.

US Environmental Protection Agency (USEPA). (2002). *The clean water and drinking water infrastructure gap analysis*, EPA-816-R-02-020, Office of Water, US Environmental Protection Agency, Washington, DC.

US Environmental Protection Agency (USEPA). (2009a). *Drinking water infrastructure needs survey and assessment*, EPA 816-R-09-001, US Environmental Protection Agency, Washington, DC, <http://www.epa.gov/safewater/needssurvey/index.html> (Sep, 2009).

US Environmental Protection Agency (USEPA). (2009b). *Distribution system water quality monitoring: sensor technology evaluation methodology and results*, EPA-600-R-09-076, US Environmental Protection Agency, Washington, DC, <http://www.epa.gov/nhsrc/pubs/600r09076.pdf> (Sep, 2009).

US Environmental Protection Agency (USEPA). (2009c). *CANARY user's manual, version 4.2*, EPA-600-R-08-040A, US Environmental Protection Agency, Washington, DC, <http://www.epa.gov/NHSRC/pubs/600r08040a.pdf> (Sep, 2009).

Xu, J., Fischbeck, P., Small, M., VanBriesen, J., and Casman, E. (2008). "Identifying sets of key nodes for placing sensors in dynamic water distribution networks." *J. Water Res. Pl-ASCE*, 134(4), 378-385.

AUTHOR INFORMATION

David Dzombak is a professor in the Department of Civil and Environmental Engineering at Carnegie Mellon University where he teaches and conducts research in water quality engineering. He is also director of the Steinbrenner Institute for Environmental Education and Research at Carnegie Mellon. He holds a PhD in Civil Engineering from the Massachusetts Institute of Technology and is a Fellow of ASCE. Email: dzombak@cmu.edu

Jeanne VanBriesen is a professor in the Department of Civil and Environmental Engineering at Carnegie Mellon University where she teaches and conducts research in water quality engineering and environmental biotechnology. She is also director of the Center for Water Quality in Urban Environmental Systems (WaterQUEST) at Carnegie Mellon. She holds a PhD in Civil Engineering from Northwestern University, and is a Member of ASCE. Email: jeanne@cmu.edu

James Garrett is professor and Head of the Department of Civil and Environmental Engineering at Carnegie Mellon University where he teaches and conducts research in advanced infrastructure systems. He is also co-director of the Center for Sensed Critical Infrastructure at Carnegie Mellon. He holds a PhD in Civil Engineering from Carnegie Mellon University. He is a Fellow of ASCE. Email: garrett@cmu.edu

Lucio Soibelman is a professor in the Department of Civil and Environmental Engineering at Carnegie Mellon University where he teaches and conducts research in information technology, data management and mining, and sensing for infrastructure systems. He is the co-chief-editor of the ASCE *Journal of Computing in Civil Engineering*. He holds a PhD in Civil Engineering from the Massachusetts Institute of Technology and is a Member of ASCE. Email: lucio@andrew.cmu.edu

Chapter 28

Visions of Green Technologies in 2050 for Municipal Resource Management

Scott D. Struck

ABSTRACT

By the year 2050 many system resources will be integrated into every plan and design from the smallest projects to the largest. Green technologies will be applied through holistic systems approaches. Project teams will be multidisciplinary with professionals that spend as much time understanding the relationships with the other project systems (e.g., water supply, wastewater stormwater, electrical, heating and cooling, transportation, climate, air quality) rather than individual systems in isolation. In response to this, green technologies in all resource areas will push the envelope of recognizing and using all aspects of potential energy production, waste elimination, and the development of professionals that are adept at examining the linkages and interactions between project elements as well as providing expertise in at least one of the green technology components. As such these technologies will no longer be considered "green" but will simply be "technologies" that are widely recognized to have environmental, economic, and social benefits. Management of these systems will require cross collaboration between many traditionally recognized departments, forcing integration and organizational communication with a resultant shift in traditional roles or the development of completely new roles.

"And they said green roofs would never catch on."

INTRODUCTION

To understand the future of green technologies, especially those within water resources and drainage engineering, one must first recognize and understand changes in the recent past. The drainage of stormwater from urban areas has traditionally been accomplished by constructing storm sewers, through which the urban runoff is conveyed directly to the receiving water. Urban drainage before the 1970s was designed to transport stormwater away as quickly as possible. However, during the 1970s more attention was drawn to the quality dimension of urban runoff. The pollution content in stormwater and its impact on the receiving waters became a major concern. Measures were taken to protect receiving waters from polluted urban runoff. In the 1990s the concept of sustainable development was introduced. In this concept the social dimension of the urban drainage came into focus (Stahre 2008).

The transition from traditional to sustainable urban drainage can be viewed as a sequence of steps, from the consideration of only quantity prior to 1975, to both quantity and quality through 1995, the addition of amenity values through 2005, and from 2005 to now, the inclusion of integrated water management as well. What was "traditional urban drainage" prior to 1975 has now become "sustainable water management" (Stahre 2008). The characteristic feature of sustainable urban drainage is that quantity and quality aspects of the runoff are handled together and included with social aspects of the drainage. For instance many drainage approaches can be incorporated into the urban form to provide aesthetic and artistic amenities such as creative downspout scuppers and landscaped stormwater runoff storage and treatment features (e.g., eco/green roofs, and rain gardens).

However, there are more differences that may be less recognized. The sustainable water management approach also views all water systems as a whole, including drinking water, wastewater, and drainage management (stormwater) as a collective system that should be managed together to be truly efficient and sustainable (i.e., integrated water management; Biswas 2004). In the sustainable water management approach, all water systems are looked upon as a positive resource in the urban landscape with multiple supplies for use or in many cases, reuse. This is idealized presently. The question is, will it be possible in the future?

IN THE YEAR 2050

All built environments in the year 2050 will reduce urban runoff by meeting pre-development hydrologic conditions using technologies such as green roofs, bioretention system, porous pavers and similar technologies. However, many of these technologies will incorporate recycled materials such as crushed glass, recycled, washed aggregate concrete and other deconstruction debris instead of virgin materials. By using these materials, resources previously considered as waste streams and deposited in landfills will result in reduced costs of recycled materials (closer in proximity to reuse locations), reduced transportation impacts, and an increase in the lifetime for a landfill to reach capacity. In systems such as porous paver technologies, heat exchangers will be installed within these systems to provide maximum benefit of solar heat conductance as a geothermal energy source. Similarly, technologies to recover useful nutrients such as nitrogen and phosphorus will be outfitted on systems that have larger concentrations of these nutrients.

Water collection systems for both potable (on-site treatment devices) and non-potable uses will be a requirement for every building in 2050. Water reuse will influence building design, with nearly every household and commercial building containing cisterns internally (mostly on upper levels to increase gravity fed systems). In areas with plentiful, distributed rainfall, cisterns will provide all non-potable uses such as toilet flushing and landscape irrigation. Most potable needs will also be met in these areas with public water supply used for supplementing additional needs and during drought periods. In more arid regions, rainfall capture and reuse provides potable and non-potable water needs during wet periods and supplements public water supply for water needs during drier periods and drought conditions.

> *Water collection and treatment systems for both potable and non-potable uses will be a requirement for every building in 2050.*

Both water distribution and water treatment systems have significant energy requirements. Technologies that collect by-products (biogas, heat, steam) and convert them into energy for local use will be an essential part of these systems in 2050. *Every* wastewater treatment facility will be designed to use anaerobic digesters to convert organics from biosolids and other organic sources (e.g., food waste, yard trimmings, applicable construction or deconstruction debris) into methane to maintain facility temperatures, pumps, electrical systems, and other energy needs. If incineration is used, insulators and heat collectors will be employed to capture heat/steam to convert to energy. Digesters will also be used at all water supply systems to provide similar energy needs.

Urban drainage systems will be more visible in the urban environment, e.g. as open drainage corridors (swales), wetlands, and small ponds in 2050. In the design of sustainable drainage facilities a variety of other aspects other than simply conveyance will be part of planning and design. As sustainable drainage facilities constitute an integrated part of the city environment, they will be included at every level of planning. Other resource systems and recovery operations will be co-located (e.g., food waste recycling and composting centers) with water supply and wastewater treatment facilities. In addition, many of the storage systems can potentially offer locations for urban rooftop or similar gardens, creating small but centralized sources of locally grown food (Mentens et al. 2006). Collectively, these systems may be optimized on a more distributed fashion, where appropriate, with small systems servicing smaller areas and centralized systems serving larger urban and suburban needs.

When considering the availability of resources in 2050, water, both clean and non-potable, would be only two of many resource components looked upon as potential requirements for sustainable resource management. Other resources such as open space, land acquisition costs, transportation, utilities, and landfills will also be considered. Similarly, the particulates and gases released will be considered in every decision-making process, including those from metals and solids in exhausts to carbon dioxide and other greenhouse gases (GHGs).

Using many of the resources traditionally thought of as waste and using available potential energy, such as recovering biogas from biosolids (liquid and solid) and other organic food waste as an energy source, will minimize carbon emissions while reducing the use of imported fuels (and associated transportation costs), providing multiple advantages over dispersal to the atmosphere. Likewise, recovering and reusing nitrogen or phosphorus to offset imported fertilizer use is preferable to dispersing it into the water environment. Through these means GHGs and carbon footprints will be substantially smaller in 2050.

> *There will be a transition from the "sustainable water management" of today to an integrated "systems and holistic total resource management" approach by 2050.*

In short, there will be a transition from the "sustainable water management" of today in 2010 to an integrated "systems and holistic resource management" approach by 2050. This systems and holistic resource management approach includes the explicit consideration of air, amenities, energy, integrated water management involving water quantity and quality, solid waste, transportation, and urban development. It allows the capture of added aesthetic, ecological, economic, educational, energy production and conservation, recreational, social, and other benefits in ways never realized by those advocating sustainable water management back in 2010. Approaches that consider these benefits are necessary early in the planning stages to allow adequate resources and resource distribution to realize these benefits.

Therefore, management and organization of systems will include different disciplines in the planning and design of these facilities. Examples of such expertise are planning architects, landscape architects, drainage engineers, civil (street and traffic engineers), ecologists, biologists etc.

With this in mind, it has become increasingly evident that the water (and other valuable resource) problems in 2050 can no longer be resolved by water professionals and/or water agencies alone. Water problems have become far too large, complex, and inter-connected with other resources to be handled by any one single institution. The problems with water and other resources are increasingly more interconnected with other development and redevelopment-related issues and also with social, economic, environmental, legal, and political factors at local, national and international scales.

As the management of multiple resources through systems approaches engages a variety of utilities within the typical municipal infrastructure, funding for facilities, capital improvements, design, and operation and maintenance must rely on funding from multiple sources. As such, organization of departments within a municipality may be best represented through a lateral structure (e.g., each department having equal footing and equal representation). While this is a departure from typical current models, especially when considering funding, departments will be required to plan as one entity to provide the most benefit with the most efficient capital outlay (cost and labor) to achieve the necessary multi-departmental objectives and realize the numerous outcomes expected of the municipality.

Multi-objective criteria will be the norm with integrated department planning and execution at crossover points to tackle similar or overlapping criteria (e.g., codes and ordinances). Technologies that support each of the criteria will be planned in combination to achieve the objectives and goals. Decision support tools will be developed to assist in complex decision-making and in the identification and evaluation of water management alternatives that benefit the economy, the environment, and society as a whole.

CONCLUSION

Green technologies in 2050 will no longer be considered "green." With every decision process including a multitude of outcomes, including environmental benefits, such designation will be outdated. Systems management of all resources will be commonplace, with new federal, state and local entities represented with lateral collaborative structures rather than single resource stove pipes. Professionals within these departments will form teams with multi-disciplinary backgrounds that use decision support tools to evaluate complex alternatives with multi-criteria objectives. These objectives will focus on treating all materials as potential resources including heat and other materials now considered as waste products. With more efficient use of these resources, greenhouse gases will be reduced, landfills will last longer (or be eliminated as we get to zero waste) and carbon footprints will be smaller or carbon neutral. Efficient use of water resources will close the loop in many urban water cycles making water and other resource systems more efficient. In the year 2050, the world society will have a better understanding of water needs and uses, placing a higher value on all facets of water including water supply, treatment, and recreation.

REFERENCES

Biswas, A. (2004). "Integrated water resources management: a reassessment." *Water Int.*, 29 (2), 248–256.
Mentens, J., Raes, D., and Hermy, M. (2006). "Green roofs as a tool for solving the rainwater runoff problem in the urbanized 21st century?" *Landscape Urban Plan.*, 77, 217–226.

Stahre, P. (2008). *Sustainable urban drainage: blue-green fingerprints in the city of Malmö, Sweden*, VA SYD, Malmö, Sweden, <www.vasyd.se/fingerprints> (Dec, 2009).

AUTHOR INFORMATION

Scott Struck is a senior environmental scientist and policy analyst with Tetra Tech in Golden, Colorado. Before his current position, he worked with USEPA's Office of Research and Development within the National Risk Management Research Laboratory. He holds a PhD in environmental science from Indiana University, a MS in environmental science, a MPA in environmental policy and natural resource management from Indiana University, and BS and BA from the University of Washington in zoology and psychology, respectively. For the past decade, Dr. Struck has been involved in research, development, teaching and application of integrated water resource management. Email: scott.struck@tetratech.com

Chapter 29

Irrigation in 2050

Marshall J. English

ABSTRACT

Irrigation technology has to change during the coming decades if we as a society are to meet our food production needs. Extraordinary changes on a scale comparable to the electronics revolution of the last generation seem inescapable. While we may not be able to predict exactly how irrigated agriculture will change by 2050, it seems certain that by 2050 irrigators will necessarily be fully embracing deficit irrigation strategies, and will rely to a greater extent on reuse of wastewater because of decreases in per capita water availability and increasing water demands. Ecological engineering will become an integral part of the process of irrigation system design and management. Irrigation engineers in 2050 will need to deal with multidisciplinary issues and challenges rarely considered by today's engineers. Newly emerging technologies for irrigation management will make today's most advanced technology look primitive. And finally, attacking the challenges of 2050 effectively will require institutional partnerships unlike any we see today.

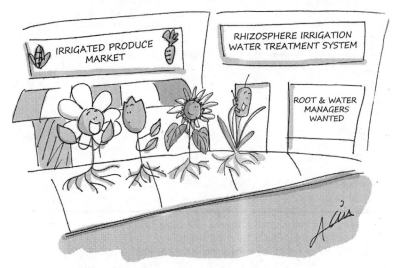

"The job market's looking pretty good for us!"

INTRODUCTION

Irrigation is the overwhelming dominant factor in global water use. We have all heard that water will be the new oil. In fact, it is a resource even more critical and less amenable to substitution than oil. Sandra Postel, in a seminal 1996 article in *Science*, made the argument that by 2025 the world demand for fresh water may be approaching the limits of readily accessible supplies (Postel et al. 1996). In 2003, at a UN-sponsored conference on water demand management in the Near East, representatives from about 35 countries in that region each summarized their national water resource situation. Most delegates said their countries had reached the limit of renewable supplies of fresh water and reusable wastewater, but in every case demands for water were forecast to increase substantially, with projected increases in irrigation to feed expanding populations in the next few decades. What Sandra Postel forecast for the world in 2025 is already reality in the most water stressed parts of the world.

Since irrigation takes about 70% of all water diversions world-wide, and 90% in the most water-short countries, the developing water crisis will profoundly affect irrigated agriculture. The biggest challenges and the greatest potential for change will be in irrigation management. Efficient use of irrigation water is determined by the intrinsic efficiency of the application system and the effectiveness of irrigation management. I am one of the many who see irrigation management as the weakest link by far.

A few years ago I had a conversation with some students who were questioning the future of engineering in agriculture. Talking about irrigation, their impression was that the big engineering advances have already been made. I disagree; the intersection of irrigation and engineering is one of the places to be for the next generation. The 2050 horizon is not as far away as it sounds, roughly the length of a career. Let's talk about what a young person, just starting a career in irrigation engineering, will be witness to.

PERSPECTIVE

I actually started my career as an electrical engineer. That was at a time when industry was still designing circuits with vacuum tubes, and electronics only came in big boxes – appliances, large radios and TVs and computers that occupied entire buildings. That was forty years ago, and during the intervening years, electronics have moved through transistors, circuit boards, plug-in circuit modules, and then to a progression of chips that continue to increase in power and decrease in size relentlessly. And the applications now pervade every aspect of our lives: iPhones and iPads, pacemakers the size of a quarter, automatic braking systems … embedded processors all around us. It is fascinating to think that when the first commercial transistor products began to appear, virtually no one imagined the impending technological transformation of our world. It has been astounding.

Pondering the challenges for irrigation in the not very distant future, extraordinary changes on a scale comparable to that electronics revolution seem inescapable. We may not be able to predict exactly how irrigated agriculture will change by 2050, but let me offer a few propositions:

1. Irrigators of the future will necessarily adopt deficit irrigation management strategies, and will rely to a greater extent on reuse of wastewater.
2. Ecological engineering will become an integral part of the process of irrigation system design and management.
3. The scope of issues to be dealt with by irrigation engineers will expand to encompass issues and challenges that we have given little thought to in the past.
4. Newly emerging technologies for irrigation management, some already in early stages of development, will make today's most advanced technology look primitive.
5. Attacking the challenges of 2050 effectively will require many institutional partnerships unlike any we see today.

Let me elaborate further on each of these propositions.

Deficit Irrigation
Today the conventional management paradigm is to apply sufficient water to prevent crop stress in order to maximize yields, and to do so with a minimum of applied water. Good stewardship also requires that we keep water use to a minimum and minimize the environmental impacts of irrigation. The management paradigm of 2050 will be quite different: we will seek to maximize net benefits of irrigation water use, a fundamentally different thing from yield maximization. Benefits will be defined more broadly, encompassing such multiple objectives as farm profitability, food security, risk avoidance and water quality preservation.

> *In 2050 we will seek to maximize net benefits of irrigation water use, a fundamentally different thing from maximizing yield.*

Basic economics indicates that net benefits derived from a limited irrigation water supply will be maximized by applying something less than maximum crop water requirements, i.e., by *deficit irrigation*, the deliberate under-irrigation of crops. Consequently, water stress will need to be managed rather than avoided, demanding a much higher level of precision in root zone moisture management than is attainable today.

Ecological Engineering
Ecological engineering is a new field, I know of only one engineering school now offering a degree program with this title. However, it will become increasingly important in relation to irrigation management. A good example, one that attracts little interest today but which has important implications for the future, will be using

the rhizosphere processes going on in the root zone to achieve distributed, low cost, tertiary treatment of irrigation return flows. By enhancing rhizosphere processes we can mitigate and even reverse the water quality degradation associated with irrigation. To that end, the irrigation engineer of tomorrow may be managing irrigation to insure sufficient root zone dwell time and root system contact to take advantage of processes that break down organics, sequester heavy metals and capture excess nutrients within the rhizosphere. If done effectively, return flows can be of higher quality than the original diversions.

Twenty or thirty years from now irrigation engineers may routinely incorporate ecosystem processes into their designs. In the above example the ecosystem was the soil rhizosphere. In other cases it might be a wetland or an aquacultural system linked synergistically with an irrigation system.

Increased Scope
Irrigated agriculture is one of the most significant of all human activities, and increasing demand for food, coupled with the accelerating competition for water will only increase its importance and amplify its consequences. As world populations become more tightly connected we will need to address the consequences of irrigation development that are largely ignored today.

As an example, let us consider managing irrigation to protect public health. It is a truism that not having enough to eat is a public health problem, and many of the poorer countries of the world are moving aggressively to expand irrigation to deal with this problem. But development of irrigation schemes often involves a series of other public health issues. The water often provides a medium for movement of pathogens and creates an environment for vector-borne diseases. Outbreaks of malaria, filaria, encephalitis and bilharzia often follow new irrigation development. Pesticides are often used to control the disease vectors -- the mosquitoes in the case of malaria. But in poorer economies the residues of pesticides often end up mixed with domestic water supplies, creating another public health problem. To further complicate matters, mosquitoes are becoming increasingly resistant to pesticides, so malaria may still persist.

Finding water management-based interventions to control these problems could become a prominent issue in coming decades. To illustrate the point, the International Water Management Institute (IWMI) has declared it a research priority to determine how irrigation management can help control malaria. Controlling disease vectors may require that irrigation schedules include significant intervals when irrigation will be stopped altogether for strategic periods of time.

Other new issues that may increasingly influence future irrigation planning and practice could include such public policy objectives as employment and land redistribution (both of which are already objectives of irrigation projects in some countries today) or mitigation of climate change.

Technologies for the Next Generation

Irrigation management today generally employs a simple decision rule: irrigation should commence when soil moisture reaches a stipulated "management-allowed depletion." But we all know that soil moisture can vary dramatically throughout a field, and determinations of soil moisture based on either cumulative evapotranspiration (ET) or soil moisture measurements are actually quite uncertain. When water supplies are not limited, the problem of uncertainty can be avoided by maintaining soil moisture content well above critical levels and keeping some soil moisture in reserve as a hedge against uncertainty. But deficit irrigation, the paradigm of the future, must be managed differently. Crops will be subjected to managed levels of stress, with no reserves of soil moisture to prevent unintended stress.

A more appropriate decision rule for 2050 may be to irrigate when a specified fraction of the field has reached an allowable level of depletion with a specified probability. For example, we might call for irrigation when there is a 25% probability that 50% of the field has reached 60% depletion. For such a decision rule to be effective we must quantify the variability of soil moisture and uncertainty of soil moisture determinations.

Implementing such a decision rule will not be possible without new supporting technologies. The term "technologies" here refers to the full spectrum of tools for irrigation management, ranging from instrumentation and science-based modeling to decision support software. Managing deficit irrigation will require monitoring and controlling spatially variable patterns of soil water content in heterogeneous fields, anticipating the spatial distribution of water stress in fields and estimating how crop yields will be affected by the resulting patterns of stress. Rhizosphere filtration will depend upon carefully controlled movement of water through the root zone. Rather than simply applying water at or below the infiltration rates of soils, irrigators will need to virtually *titrate* the water at rates designed to achieve desired dwell times and root system contact.

The next generation of irrigation management will need a corresponding new generation of analytical tools and field instrumentation designed specifically to support deficit irrigation management. New decision support algorithms to deal with uncertainty and risk associated with deficit irrigation will be needed. Perhaps the biggest and most important challenge will be reliable modeling of crop responses to applied water. It is still very difficult to predict or explain water use and yields under deficit irrigation, even for sophisticated scientists working with familiar crops in a familiar environment.

> *Irrigation management in 2050 will need new analytical tools and field instrumentation.*

Three examples below, all involving technological developments that are in early stages of testing today, illustrate the nature of the needed new technologies.

Irrigation advisory programs for deficit irrigation

Scientific irrigation scheduling appeared on the scene during the 1970s. Though the principles of irrigation scheduling had been well-established long before that, the development of computer-based programs linked to weather station data and using instruments for measuring soil moisture was a transformative event in irrigation management. Such programs were predicated on the conventional management paradigm, meeting crop water demands to maximize yields, and that is still the case with virtually all advisory programs today.

Decision support programs of the next generation will be an order of magnitude more sophisticated and complicated. Principal features needed for such programs include:

- explicit modeling of spatial variability, surface water accumulation and redistribution, and spray losses, which collectively determine how application efficiencies vary with irrigation strategies;
- analytical procedures to support conjunctive management of multiple fields that share a common water supply in order to facilitate allocations of limited water;
- reliable modeling of crop response to water;
- algorithms for quantifying uncertainties in the distributions of soil moisture, crop water use and crop yields, coupled with algorithms for analyzing the risks associated with chosen irrigation strategies; and
- an interface that permits individual managers to incorporate their own experience, awareness of constraints and individual preferences in a search for feasible, quasi-optimal irrigation management strategies.

One prototype of such an irrigation advisory program is Irrigation Management Online (IMO) developed at Oregon State University in conjunction with other research teams around the country. IMO is a decision support system for use in planning and scheduling irrigation operations. The system downloads weather data from local weather stations and uses those data in combination with farm-specific information about fields, crops, and actual irrigation practices provided by irrigators to estimate soil moisture conditions and to forecast irrigation schedules (http://oiso.bioe.orst.edu/RealtimeIrrigationSchedule/index.aspx).

Distributed measurements of soil water content

A pioneering application of fiber optic technologies is being used to monitor soil moisture at different depths throughout an irrigated field. The system uses fiber optic cable to monitor thermal response of soils at three depths for several hundred points in an irrigated field. A heat pulse heats soil near the cable, then the fiber optic cable monitors the rise and fall of soil temperatures. Because thermal response of the soil is a function of water content, the cable system can be calibrated to measure soil water content at intervals along the cable. Rather than measuring soil moisture at a few discrete points, it will be possible to represent the statistical distribution of soil moisture throughout the entire field with this system, increasing available information for assessing irrigation requirements by an order of magnitude.

An algorithm for decision-making under uncertainty
ET-based estimates of soil moisture and field measurements of soil moisture are both subject to significant error. Neither can be relied upon completely, but both embody useful information. Rather than arbitrarily dismissing one in favor of the other, a more rational approach is to estimate the uncertainty of each, and then derive a hybrid estimate that weights each of these estimators according to its characteristic uncertainty. Bayes theorem provides a way of integrating the information about each estimator to derive an estimate of depletion that is both more precise (reduced variance) and more accurate. This approach is being built into the Irrigation Management Online (IMO) program.

Institutional Cooperation
During the past few decades effective irrigation management tools were often developed by dedicated individuals or small research teams. Such independent, pioneering efforts will not be adequate for the challenge of building advanced irrigation advisory programs such as outlined above. Close coordination of shared efforts among multiple institutions will be required if we are to attain the level of sophistication needed in the next 40 years. As an example of this new way of doing business, the IMO program has been configured explicitly to integrate the work of other research teams. To that end it is designed to be flexible and adaptable so that individual components of the program can be readily replaced as the underlying science, engineering and modeling evolve, and research teams develop new and better algorithms for the various elements of the program. Additionally, an open source release of IMO will enable local users to adapt the system for the circumstances, scientific observations and preferred practices unique to their own individual circumstances.

EBEY'S PRAIRIE: A LOOK INTO THE FUTURE

A project now in a conceptual stage of development offers some perspective on what irrigated agriculture might look like when that young engineer retires in 40 years. The project involves reuse of wastewater on Ebey's Prairie, an agricultural area on an island in Puget Sound. The island gets surprisingly little rainfall for that region, about 50 centimeters (20 inches) a year, and very little of that occurs during the summer months. Farmed since about 1850, Ebey's Prairie is considered such a scenic and historic treasure that Congress created the first National Historic Trust in the US here, and invited the farms to deed development rights to the trust to preserve the agricultural nature of the prairie for all time.

While most of the prairie is now preserved as farmland in perpetuity, changing circumstances have made it difficult for these farms to survive economically. However, the farmers on the Prairie will tell you that if they had irrigation water they could make it.

Adjacent to the Prairie is a small city on the south shore of Penn Cove, an inlet that is famous for its mussels. The city's discharges of treated wastewater into the cove are impacting mussel production. The city would like to divert their treated wastewater away from the cove and deliver it to the farming community, and the farms would be happy to have it. Most of the wastewater is produced during months when the farms have no use for it, so a plan is being developed for aquifer storage between irrigation seasons. Before injection into an aquifer, the water must go through tertiary treatment, which is expensive. There is also a concern that irrigation, by its very nature, could result in non-point source pollution from return flows to Puget Sound.

Nevertheless, imaginative people have come up with a two-part plan that illustrates where irrigated agriculture is headed in the next generation. The first element of the plan will involve rhizosphere filtration in poplar plantations and other selected fields, carefully filtering water through an active root mass at a rate that provides sufficient dwell time for denitrification and root system sequestration of heavy metals and breakdown of pharmaceuticals and toxic compounds. The combination of rhizosphere filtration and mechanical filtration through the soil will provide distributed, low cost tertiary treatment that will render the wastewater fit for aquifer injection. A strategy of regulated deficit irrigation on the Prairie will preclude return flows to the Sound and maximize economic returns to the farming community from the still very limited supply of water.

The goals of this scheme are to mitigate pollution of Penn Cove and preserve the economic viability of the agricultural community. The techniques to be used will involve ecological engineering and deficit irrigation. The engineering challenges are very different, and much more complex, than a conventional irrigation scheme. This is an excellent example of the kind of irrigation management that will be commonplace in 2050.

REFERENCES

Postel, S. L., Daily, G. C., and Ehrlich, P. R. 1996. "Human appropriation of renewable fresh water." *Science*, 271 (9), 785-788.

AUTHOR INFORMATION

Marshall J. English, PhD, PE is a Professor Emeritus and an Irrigation Extension Specialist in the Biological and Ecological Engineering Department at Oregon State University. His areas of specialization include irrigation optimization, irrigation advisory services, and systems analysis and modeling. He was awarded the prestigious Royce J. Tipton Award by ASCE in 2009 in recognition of his contributions to the advancement of irrigation and drainage engineering. He was a Fulbright Fellow involved in irrigation management research in sub-Saharan Africa from 1991-1992, and a Senior Research Fellow, New Zealand Ministry of Agriculture and Fisheries involved in modeling efficiency of irrigation systems from 1984-1985. He received his MS and PhD in Civil Engineering from the University of California, Davis, and his BS in Electrical Engineering from San Jose State College. Email: englishm@engr.orst.edu

Chapter 30

Groundwater Hydrology in 2050

George F. Pinder

ABSTRACT

Informed husbanding of groundwater resources is critical to the survival of people in many parts of the world. Even where surface water supplies exist and are used, groundwater provides the base flows in rivers and streams which, in turn, are often critical for water supplies and the maintenance of aquatic ecosystems. This chapter reviews the current status of groundwater exploitation and use, groundwater contamination, and factors that will influence how groundwater quantity and quality will be modeled and managed as we move toward 2050. By 2050 groundwater will be recognized as more valuable than it is today. Management of aquifer depletion, especially in arid areas, will continue to require use of groundwater quantity models. Estimating the effectiveness of measures to reduce groundwater contamination will require improved groundwater quality models. Currently the complexity of groundwater quality models ranges from the relatively simple non-reactive solute transport case to that of very complex slightly miscible, multiphase fluid transport with biological contaminant degradation. The period between now and 2050 could be one in which groundwater flow and transport models find vastly wider application in addressing issues related to geothermal energy, carbon sequestration, and long-term storage of high-level radioactive material from nuclear power plants and other sources.

"Well, well, well,
what do we have here?"

PAST DEVELOPMENTS AND CURRENT PERSPECTIVES

Water Supply and Water Wells

Spring water is, in essence, groundwater that has made its way to the surface. As such, it has a history of use that precedes that of recorded time. The technical advance allowing humans to exploit *in situ* groundwater was the invention of the well. The first drilled wells in the United States were completed in 1806 and used to obtain brine. By the mid-1820s drill rigs were used to obtain water in the United States. With the success of bored wells came the ability to access water at considerable depths. No enormous conceptual leaps in drilling technology have been realized in nearly a century.

Water Quality

Naturally occurring compounds

Groundwater, in general, did not suffer from the type of gross contamination identified with the open sewers of the middle-ages. Rather, the primary groundwater quality concern until the early 1970s was attributable to naturally occurring compounds, especially objectionable components that form "hard water." At the present time, it is generally believed that the most important problems associated with the chemical evolution of naturally occurring waters have been addressed, although how one acquires the geohydrological information needed to understand a particular groundwater system remains a challenge.

Two naturally occurring compounds that do impact human health and are therefore of considerable importance are sodium chloride (common salt) and radioactive elements. Saline water, especially that associated with salt-water intrusion in coastal aquifers and irrigation return water, make over-exploited coastal aquifer waters unusable for some domestic and industrial applications. Thus considerable effort has been expended in investigating the physical-chemical nature of salt movement, particularly in coastal aquifers (Kohout 1960). Of the radioactive constituents of groundwater, the element radium, which disintegrates into daughter isotopes of radon with the release of radiation, is of considerable concern. The resulting collision of alpha particles with living cell tissue is known to cause tissue damage that can lead to cancer. Both of these concerns, salt-water intrusion and the evolution of radioactive compounds, have been carefully examined and, while solutions to these problems can be expensive and in some instances unattainable, from a scientific perspective, few open issues remain.

Anthropogenic compounds

Widespread use of agrochemicals, leaking sewers, septic tanks, pit latrines, and careless use and disposal of industrial chemicals can give rise to groundwater contamination. Agriculture is the primary source of elevated nitrate levels, although in some rare cases certain geologic units can be the source of the nitrate. The use of nitrogen fertilizers is the primary source of high nitrate levels in groundwater although wastes from livestock and poultry farms can also be a source. Nitrates are known to be a public health concern, especially for infants. Phosphorus is also a common constituent of agricultural fertilizers as well as occurring in organic wastes in sewage and in industrial effluents. Excess phosphorus discharging to water bodies can cause eutrophication. The development of a strategy for addressing nitrogen and phosphorous contamination remains an open problem.

> *The development of a strategy for addressing nitrogen and phosphorous contamination remains an open problem.*

Organic compounds, especially hydrocarbons, have contaminated many groundwater supplies. Hydrocarbons of the greatest concern in groundwater pollution come in two main flavors, petroleum hydrocarbons and chlorinated hydrocarbons. The compounds of concern in petroleum hydrocarbons are primarily benzene, toluene, ethylbenzene and xylene (BTEX) as well as an additive to gasoline called methyl tert-butyl ether (MTBE). Benzene is a known carcinogen and ethylbenzene is possibly carcinogenic. Petroleum contamination is widespread due to the wide use of petroleum in transportation and the challenges associated with its effective storage. If there is a silver lining in the case of petroleum hydrocarbons, it is that they are amenable to biodegradation.

Chlorinated hydrocarbons are hydrocarbon molecules that have atoms of the element chlorine chemically bonded to them. DDT (dichlorodiphenyltrichloroethane) is possibly the best-known chlorinated hydrocarbon. Beginning in the World War II years chlorinated hydrocarbons were the industrial solvent of choice. Careless handling and disposal of these compounds led to widespread soil and groundwater contamination. Unfortunately, unlike petroleum hydrocarbons, chlorinated hydrocarbons are not biologically degraded quickly, and the daughter products of biodegradation as well as the parent compound can be dangerous to human health. At this time, contamination by chlorinated compounds is one of the more serious groundwater contamination problems and effective strategies to deal with this problem are still being sought.

Simulation of Groundwater System Behavior
Advances in the simulation of groundwater system behavior can be subdivided into those associated with groundwater flow and those associated with groundwater transport. The former are used to determine the fluid potential and in some instances the velocity of groundwater. The latter use the flow model results as input and then determine a concentration or temperature distribution.

Groundwater flow simulation
Simulation of groundwater flow determines the state of the groundwater system given specified information about it. Simulation can be done using exact-solution or numerical-solution mathematics, electrical analog models, or physical models. The transition from analytical models and analog models (resistor-capacitor models) to computer-based models occurred in the mid 1960s (Remson et al. 1965). Numerical methods were used to solve the flow equations. The numerical approach could accommodate the flexibility found in the analog models, but in addition the numerical

models could be constructed much more quickly than the time required to fabricate the resistor capacitor network. Moreover, they could be quickly changed so calibration was faster and easier. Numerical methods also allowed for the simulation of more complicated systems such as those involving multiphase flow, fracture flow, coefficients described by random fields and connections with surface-water bodies. Groundwater flow modeling is a mature area of investigation and development, although the solution to the multiphase equations remains challenging.

Groundwater transport simulation
The solution of the equations that describe transport in a groundwater system does not have the long history of those associated with flow. Today numerical methods can handle complicated transport problems and geometries. Multiple species transport models, fractured media transport models, bacterial transport models and coupled multiphase flow and species transport models are available. Unlike flow models, transport models still have open questions to be addressed. The convective term in the equations causes problems as do nonlinearities that often characterize these equations.

Model applications
The predictive capability of groundwater flow and transport models can be integrated into other algorithms identified with parameter estimation (sometimes referred to as inverse modeling), risk analysis, optimal remediation design, plume search, contaminant source identification and long-term monitoring. In each of these cases, higher-level software uses the model interactively to achieve one of the above-defined goals. In the case of risk analysis, the model employs a random-field representation of hydraulic conductivity to determine the probability that a particular species concentration at a particular point at a particular time will be encountered. The other examples mentioned above may use this capability but also employ some aspect of optimization. The use of models in this setting is currently an active research area.

The Physical System
In some sense, the evolution of simulation techniques mirrors the evolution in the type of problems being addressed. More flexible simulation tools allowed more complex systems to be considered. In addition, changing water resource and other priorities also played a significant role. Until the early to mid-1960s groundwater professionals focused on the quantity of water available to supply municipal, industrial and agricultural needs. Some attention was paid to water quality issues, especially degradation of quality due to salt-water intrusion and groundwater contamination by toxic metals. However, it was the recognition of the widespread occurrence of organic compounds, especially BTEX and chlorinated hydrocarbons used in industry, and the determination that some of these compounds could possibly be carcinogenic, that caused water quality, rather than water quantity to come to the forefront.

Today groundwater transport modeling is a relatively commonly used geohydrological tool in groundwater contamination investigation, analysis and remediation (plume containment and aquifer rehabilitation). It is more challenging to model transport than flow in part because additional physical parameters, such as dispersivity, are needed. Moreover, since groundwater flow velocities are required as input to the transport equation, an accurate transport model requires an existing accurate flow model. The complexity of models ranges from relatively simple non-reactive solute transport types to very complex slightly miscible, multiphase fluid transport models with biological contaminant degradation. Very complex models require an enormous amount of parametric input and considerable modeling skill to be used effectively, and consequently, their use is not widespread.

While the above-described physical systems have been the focus of hydrogeological activity, there are others that have been and continue to be of interest. The storage of high-level radioactive waste in a permanent underground repository requires assessment of the risk of exposure to humans and the environment. Because of the enormous time periods over which containment must be demonstrated (e.g., plutonium has a half-life of 24,000 years), there is no practical way to demonstrate the efficacy of the containment strategy aside from modeling. The evaluation of the efficacy of carbon dioxide sequestration is a problem that lies somewhere between petroleum reservoir engineering and groundwater engineering. Forecasting land subsidence due to groundwater extraction is a problem that spans the disciplines of soil mechanics and groundwater hydrology. In summary, the history of problems addressed by groundwater professionals reveals that new challenges emerge that are triggered by events very difficult to anticipate.

> *There is no practical way to demonstrate the efficacy of radioactive containment strategies aside from modeling.*

Geothermal simulation enjoyed a brief period of support in response to the OPEC oil embargo in 1973-1974. Geothermal reservoirs, including their very complex thermodynamics and chemical reactions, were modeled for a number of fields worldwide. However, the support for this area of activity did not last more than a decade. The current rise in the cost of petroleum may resuscitate interest in the geothermal industry. Perhaps more probable is the wider use of low temperature, near-surface geothermal energy resources for heating and cooling. At this point relatively little effort has been expended on understanding the groundwater flow and transport issues surrounding this potentially important energy source.

PROJECTIONS TO THE YEAR 2050

Water Supply and Water Wells
As noted, drilling technology is a mature field and in 2050 it is probable that water-well drilling will be largely as it is today. Completion of wells (i.e., installation of well casing, screens, and multiple port sensors) may change, but not fundamentally.

On the other hand, the use of groundwater will probably change substantially. Part of that change will reflect the fact that much of the groundwater use in the arid west is not sustainable. The misconception that one can safely remove, without resource degradation, an amount equal to the net infiltration from rainfall ignores the fact that water continues to discharge into surface water bodies irrespective of rainfall such that, unless that discharge is reduced or the effective recharge is increased, aquifer water level elevations (piezometric surfaces) in the long term will decline. It is likely that municipal and industrial needs will ultimately be met at the expense of agricultural needs, which in turn could result in significant changes in land use.

Conjunctive use, the strategy by which surface water and groundwater are exploited in concert, will almost certainly be more widely used. The factor that is difficult to forecast is the degree to which public sector capital will be available to move water overland from areas of abundance to areas of need and the degree to which areas of abundance will permit such transfers.

It is probable that by 2050 groundwater will be recognized as more valuable than it is today. It is unclear if this increased value will be reflected through increased costs to consumers or through government subsidy, but it will become more evident that 1) water in general, and groundwater in particular, cannot be replaced by an alternative resource, as can energy supplies; 2) the supply of groundwater is not easily augmented through engineering structures (although some strategies such as recharge basins and water reuse may be helpful); and 3) once contaminated, groundwater is very difficult to return to drinking water quality.

Water Quality

Enhanced understanding of the source of, movement of, and strategies for protecting groundwater from naturally occurring contaminants, such as salinity, chromium and radon has already resulted in actions taken to reduce their impact. Unlike point-source contaminants that can be ameliorated through elimination of the source, most natural contaminants cannot be easily contained or significantly reduced. Rather, practical, cost-effective approaches are needed to minimize their impact. Improved understanding of the occurrence of contaminants, their transport behavior, and strategies to minimize their occurrence in groundwater used for the public good are needed and will be revealed through ongoing research.

An example of a very important non-point anthropogenic source of contamination, as noted earlier, is that created by the use of excess fertilizer and animal waste associated with agricultural activity. Surface runoff and groundwater discharge containing such compounds provide nutrients for algae blooms in freshwater and saltwater bodies. In spite of efforts to reduce the flow of nutrients, particularly phosphorous, to surface water bodies, the problem continues. By 2050, this source of contamination will be of greater concern than it is today because there is a significant lag time between the implementation of intervention strategies and observable results.

To decrease groundwater contamination by point sources, it is probable that there will be a continuing trend towards resource protection. Industry, responsible for many point source contamination occurrences, is likely to put more financial resources into groundwater protection not only to protect the resource but also to minimize company liability. Similarly, public concern will require that government entities, such as military bases and national laboratories, step up to the plate and invest in groundwater protection and remediation. Until 1996, three excise taxes levied on petroleum and chemical companies and a special income tax on corporate profits provided the primary source of revenue for the US Environmental Protection Agency's (USEPA) Superfund branch to clean up so-called "orphan sites." The Superfund Tax reauthorized by Congress in 1990 expired at the end of 1995, and as a result, the Super "fund" dwindled to essentially nothing by 2003. Two bills to reauthorize the Tax were recently introduced in the House of Representatives, and a companion bill in the Senate is likely to follow (MacCurdy 2009). How this legislation pans out will significantly determine how rapidly and effectively point source-contaminated sites are addressed. The complex interplay between public health concerns and the sensitivity of people to economic recovery makes it difficult to characterize the legislation likely to emerge from Congress in the short term. It is probable, however, that some form of private-sector financial support will be realized to continue efforts to address existing and yet to be identified Superfund sites.

Underground storage tanks, especially those used by gas stations, are ubiquitous. Many have been investigated, evaluated and in some cases replaced to preclude new or additional contamination by petroleum hydrocarbons and their associated additives. This trend is likely to continue until existing storage tanks, especially those in areas particularly susceptible to being impacted by released contaminants, are secured or replaced. Note that concerns about these and other volatile compounds are not limited to water exploited for domestic use, but extend to concerns about contaminant vapor intrusion into homes from volatilization from subsurface plumes.

The vexing problem of long-term high-level radioactive waste storage remains unresolved. The current hiatus in the pursuit of a suitable storage facility will not last indefinitely. There is general agreement that the only viable strategy for long-term storage is burial in deep, relatively impermeable geological formations augmented by engineered barriers. Both irretrievable and retrievable strategies have been considered worldwide. In spite of vocal opposition, the Department of Energy submitted a license application to the Nuclear Regulatory Commission (NRC) on June 3, 2008, seeking approval to construct a repository for radioactive waste at Yucca Mountain in Nevada. The NRC may take several years for its license application review. The demonstration of compliance at Yucca Mountain depends in large part on a groundwater transport model that predicts concentration levels to be expected near the site at periods in excess of 10,000 years into the future. The uncertainty associated with modeling contaminant transport so far into the future is very great, so reducing the uncertainty of parameters and other hydrogeological factors is an important challenge. By 2050, the need for a permanent storage facility will be sufficiently pressing that a compromise that depends upon geological sequestration and enhanced engineered barriers and effective monitoring is probable.

Carbon dioxide sequestration in geological formations does not necessarily fit in the category of groundwater contamination, but it is an important issue and deserves consideration in this chapter. The idea is to emplace carbon dioxide at very great depth in suitable geological formations. Eventually, it is anticipated that the carbon dioxide would react with the host rock and become mineralized. While several design options are being considered, the two most pertinent here are sequestration in saline aquifers and in oil reservoir formations that are no longer productive. The primary concern is the migration of the sequestered carbon dioxide to the surface via naturally occurring dislocations such as geologic faults or by way of abandoned wells used in years gone by for production or exploration. The importance of this topic will depend upon the level of commitment of governments to the reduction of carbon dioxide in the atmosphere and the advent of new technologies that can capture and indefinitely retain carbon dioxide without geological sequestration. It is probable that geological sequestration of carbon dioxide will see an intensive level of financial investment and concomitant scientific investigation in the short term. The long-term forecast is difficult since the concept is still very new.

Simulation of Groundwater System Behavior
Groundwater flow simulation

I stated earlier that groundwater flow simulation is a mature field. By mature I imply that modeling techniques and software designed for relatively straight-forward saturated flow in porous media are available and are being used by groundwater professionals. However there are extensions of these models that are needed to address a range of problems. Among these are a) unsaturated flow (passive air, flowing water), b) multiphase flow (two or more dynamic phases such air, water and non-aqueous phase liquids), c) single and multiphase flow through fractured media and d) single and multiphase flow with uncertain coefficients (especially the random field representation of hydraulic conductivity). In addition, the numerical algorithms used for the popular MODFLOW model are in need of upgrading to more flexible finite element or finite volume numerical algorithms that do not depend upon rectangular meshes.

While I opine that there is a need for these improvements in flow modeling, I am not sure they will materialize by 2050. Existing codes for standard simulations are well-established and can be applied by professionals with a minimum of mathematical training. The more advanced models itemized above are less tolerant of user abuse and it is not clear that the practicing groundwater professional will embrace their use. Rather there may be a limited number of specialists to whom general groundwater modeling practitioners may go to have more challenging flow problems addressed.

Flow modeling is facilitated by the use of a graphical user interface (GUI) where information can be input easily. Although progress has been made in the development and distribution of groundwater modeling GUIs, they are still relatively primitive. By

2050 there should be robust, user-friendly GUIs available for groundwater models, perhaps coupled to a more flexible set of groundwater flow codes.

Groundwater transport modeling
Groundwater transport models are less accessible than flow models to practicing groundwater professionals because they are more difficult to use and are less robust. Consequently, users of such models should have numerical methods as well as groundwater flow and transport training to achieve consistent success.

The quantification of mass transfer between phases, chemical reactions and biological growth require significant parametric information that must be obtained from laboratory or field experiments. Such information is scarce and expensive to obtain. As a result I do not see widespread use of simulators with these attributes in field applications by 2050.

As should now be evident to the reader, available models span the spectrum from relative simple to very complex. A modular code that would permit the accommodation of problems of different levels of complexity without necessarily carrying the computational and data input burden of a very general simulator is needed and probably will be available by 2050. Should, as is probable, interest in geothermal energy, carbon sequestration, and high-level radioactive disposal increase, transport models dedicated specifically to these problem classes will be developed.

Modeling applications
The period between now and 2050 could be one in which groundwater flow and transport models find vastly wider application than we see today. The foundation for this opinion lies in the growth in the use of models in higher-level applications. Groundwater flow and transport models in combination with optimization algorithms provide a very important technology. The estimation of groundwater parameters, such as permeability, uses an optimization formulation that minimizes the error between simulated and measured values of piezometric head. Flow and transport models imbedded in linear and non-linear optimization algorithms can provide cost-effective strategies for containing plumes or achieving goals of acceptable risk due to remaining contaminants. Finding designs for data collection in long-term monitoring of contaminant migration can be viewed as an optimization problem where the algorithm determines the minimum number of water samples taken in time and space that must be collected to achieve a specified level of certainty. Search algorithms that combine optimization and modeling capability can be used to define a contaminant plume perimeter or identify the contaminant source with the minimum number of sampling events. All of these applications are based on the fundamental idea of using models in conjunction with other mathematical algorithms to achieve a desired practical goal at minimum cost, or alternatively maximizing the amount of information garnered for a given level of investment.

The Physical System

The increase in demand for water will result in a redistribution of the resource between competing interests. As noted earlier, it is probable that agricultural use will be reduced, especially in arid regions, and much of the water resources now used for agriculture will be redirected to municipal and industrial needs. In addition more effort will be focused on using water more efficiently and effectively. Conjunctive use is one strategy that has been used in the past and will probably become more popular in the future. The basic idea is to withdraw needed water from fluvial aquifers during low stream discharge and let the aquifer be recharged by the river when the river stage is high. It is also likely that greater water-reuse will be practiced, perhaps realized through an increased use of recharge basins and similar facilities.

The sensitivity to protection of groundwater as its value increases will motivate municipalities, government and industry to rehabilitate those aquifers where rehabilitation is possible and to protect aquifers in general from further contamination. By 2050 most of the existing Superfund sites will still be problematic, but significant progress towards cleanup will have been made. Most important, new occurrences of groundwater contamination will be relatively rare.

> *By 2050 new occurrences of groundwater contamination will be relatively rare.*

A strategy for radioactive waste disposal will be generally accepted by 2050 although it may not have been implemented. Some form of geological isolation is the probable strategy of choice.

Carbon dioxide sequestration in geological formations is actively being considered, but to forecast the degree to which this methodology will be used is very difficult, not only because of technical issues, but also because of the political dimensions of the carbon dioxide reduction concept in general. If significant carbon dioxide reduction in the United States is implemented, geological sequestration probably will be employed.

The history of groundwater hydrology has been one in which the unexpected becomes the rule. Organic contamination, geothermal power production, radioactive waste disposal and carbon dioxide sequestration are all unanticipated additions to the family of groundwater problems. It is very probable that there will, by 2050, be new unanticipated problems.

The assessment of risk due to groundwater related activities, whether to public health or to the environment, will play an increasingly important role by 2050. The benefits of reduced risk versus the costs of risk reduction will become more apparent as methodology to quantify such risk becomes available.

SUMMARY

To forecast the state of knowledge of, and nature of applications in, groundwater hydrology in 2050 requires an assessment of current conditions. The breadth of the topic takes one from the practical application of drilling technology to the more abstract use of modeling and optimization. Some methodologies are mature while others are emerging. New problems drive the development of new enabling technologies and new enabling technologies in turn allow for the solution of new and existing problems. History shows that groundwater hydrology is not a static discipline but rather is continually evolving as unanticipated problems arise.

REFERENCES

Kohout, F.A. (1960). "Cyclic flow of salt water in the Biscayne Aquifer of Southeastern Florida." *J. Geophys. Res.*, 65, 2133-2141.

MacCurdy, M. (2009). "Reinstatement of Superfund tax proposed in congress, presumed in President Obama's budget." *Marten Law*, April 22, 2009, <http://www.martenlaw.com/news/?20090422-superfund-tax-reinstated> (Nov, 2009).

Remson, I., Appel, C. A., and Webster, R. A. (1965). "Ground-water models solved by digital computer." *J. Hydr. Div.-ASCE*, 91 (HY3), 133-147.

AUTHOR INFORMATION

George Pinder is a Professor of Civil and Environmental Engineering with secondary appointments in Mathematics and Statistics and Computer Science at the University of Vermont, in Burlington, VT. He holds a PhD from University of Illinois and a BS from the University of Western Ontario. His principal area of scholarly activity is the development and application of applied mathematics, especially numerical mathematics to solve groundwater contamination and supply problems using computers. Dr. Pinder has received numerous awards, is a member of the National Academy of Engineering, and has held national leadership positions in professional societies. Email: pinder@uvm.edu

Chapter 31

GIS for Water Resources 2050

Robert M. Wallace

ABSTRACT

Geographic Information Systems (GIS) have been important tools used by the water resources community for over forty years. GIS have primarily been used in this context by engineers and scientists to perform complex analyses and for integration with, and visualization of, computational models. However, GIS technology has recently made a transition from a niche "supportive" technology into a mainstream "must-have" tool useful for a variety of industries. This change will naturally lead to an increase in attention which will spur development that will increasingly transform the technology. These changes will increasingly impact the use of GIS within the water resources community. This chapter will first present a brief history of GIS and its application toward water resource engineering. It will then present a few of the technology trends that are currently transforming geographic information systems. Finally, it will present visions of what GIS in water resources could look like in 2050.

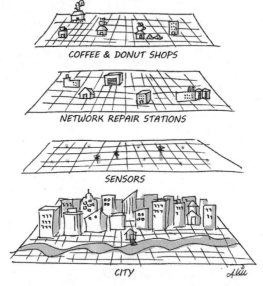

COFFEE & DONUT SHOPS

NETWORK REPAIR STATIONS

SENSORS

CITY

"Water Network Repair Crew GIS"

INTRODUCTION

Electronic geography is everywhere. The usability and effectiveness of geographic information systems (GIS) tools is changing so rapidly that it has moved from a sideline technical niche in the engineering community to a primary data delivery method for integrated decision support. GIS is now moving beyond engineering and has become so ubiquitous that it follows (and can be used to track) our daily routine; it powers the navigation systems found in our cars, it is pervasive on a new generation of smart-phones and it has even found its way into popular culture. Popular television shows like NCIS, CSI and other technology-driven shows utilize GIS frequently as the television characters chase down bad guys, find terrorist bombs and solve the world's problems with touch technology. GIS has truly revolutionized the use of positional information in many aspects of everyday life and commerce.

This recent "mainstreaming" of GIS is producing a torrent of changes that mark the first wave in a technological transformation that is sweeping across the GIS industry. As with any technology that becomes "mainstream" the rate at which change and innovation occurs will only increase. While no one can accurately predict the true impact that a more popular GIS will have on the water resources community, we are starting to see those technologies that will drive innovation and change for the next ten to twenty years, and we can therefore begin to assess their impact. This chapter will first present a brief history of GIS and its application toward water resource engineering. It will then present a few of the technology trends that are currently transforming GIS. Finally, it will present a vision of what GIS in water resources might look like in the future leading up to 2050.

FOUR PARADIGMS OF GIS

Before looking toward the future of GIS, it is instructive to look back over the origins of GIS technology and its application to water resource engineering. GIS evolved from a variety of tools developed for separate disciplines including computerized mapping, surveying, photogrammetry, design, and planning (Males and Grayman 1992). Early applications reflected these specific disciplines and included overlay analysis and suitability analysis in the planning area (McHarg 1969); civil engineering programs such as COGO, digital terrain models, and computer-aided design (CAD) in the photogrammetry, surveying and design area (Weisberg 2008); and early GIS mapping systems. This first paradigm of GIS included command line and digitizer tablets for data input, limited computer graphics, vector plotters for data output and separate programs for raster and vector analyses (Loucks et al. 1985).

It was during this first wave that GIS technology started to be adopted within the water resources community. This involved the linkage of the analysis, mapping and storage capabilities of GIS to engineering models. Early examples included integration of hydrologic models and GIS (Thirkill 1991), and water quality management planning models and GIS (Grayman et al. 1975). Extensive spatial databases became available in the 1970s for use in water resources analysis including the LANDSAT satellite land cover data base and the US Environmental Protection Agency's (USEPA) Reach File, a nationwide river index system (Horn and Grayman 1992). Despite these early model integration efforts within a GIS context, the linkages required significant manual interaction.

The second paradigm of GIS corresponded with the combination of raster and vector analysis within the same computational framework and a distinctively more "user-friendly" interface with the ability to print high-quality maps using raster plotters. It also corresponded with the first personal computers with windowed operating systems and improved graphics used for visualization. These new tools significantly increased the usability of the systems and they started gaining widespread acceptance within many communities, especially water resources. While GIS tools previously provided a viable method to integrate and display the myriad of data layers required to perform a detailed water resources investigation, it was still difficult to obtain the data. Another aspect of this second paradigm of GIS was the standardization of data sources and tools that ingested them for analysis. Systems such as USEPA's BASINS (USEPA 2010) and the Watershed Modeling System (Aquaveo 2010) provided a GIS framework for creating a conceptual model from which a computational model was derived (Nelson and Jones 1996).

The third paradigm of GIS corresponded with the full adoption of the Internet as an integral part of the GIS process and its use for more than just "surfing" for data. GIS tools embraced the web and became a vital part of a distributed decision support system where data, models and users are no longer required to be co-located (Wallace et al. 2000). This era was also highlighted by the adoption of extensible data models and standards such as ArcHydro (Maidment 2002) and KML (http://code.google.com/apis/kml/documentation/). There was also a large push to develop web services (e.g. Google Earth; http://earth.google.com/) where data were supplied by authoritative data sources at the moment they were required rather than replicating large geospatial databases at every office or worksite. In addition, there was an increase in the understanding and use of appropriate data projections. The impact of these changes on water resources has been profound. GIS has become a primary tool used to ingest data and prepare it for computational analysis using such tools as WMS and HEC-GeoRAS. GIS also provides fundamental tools used by water resource professionals for data dissemination using electronic methods.

> *The advances in GIS over the past 40 years have truly been astounding but will pale when compared to what will happen over the next 40.*

The advances in GIS over the past 40 years have truly been astounding but will pale when compared to what will happen over the next 40. This is because GIS tools have undergone an extensive popularization and adoption of the tools into the mainstream. The increased interest in geospatial analysis will bring attention and resources that will dramatically transform the industry. This change represents a fourth paradigm of GIS and will ultimately drive a more robust and profound toolset available for use by the water resources community. The primary characteristic of this paradigm is the use of complete cartographic maps rapidly delivered as a web service and available for use as a base map. This frees the user from the primary cartographic responsibility and standardizes the look and feel of map products. It is also characterized by the adoption of collaborative tools that allow communities of users who work cooperatively to modify and improve map quality and accuracy. The water resources community is just now identifying and implementing new capabilities that take advantage of the fourth paradigm of GIS. However, it is clear that the advancement of technology is rapidly increasing and a new transformation is already underway. The following section will identify the enabling technologies that are poised to move GIS into a fifth paradigm.

ENABLING TECHNOLOGIES

What are the technologies that are going to fuel this new transformation? The primary driver of change in the GIS community for the past decade has been web-based mapping. First popularized by MapQuest (http://www.mapquest.com/), the ability to obtain base maps from a dedicated service and overlay local information is a transformational capability that has morphed the mapping industry. More recent technologies such as Google Maps (http://maps.google.com), Google Earth, and Bing Maps (http://www.bing.com/maps/) provide a rich set of aesthetically pleasing base maps that can be delivered to any user with an Internet connection. Maps consisting of both vector and high-resolution raster images are now routinely delivered using this same methodology. The impact of this technology has been tremendous to many industries. In relation to the water resource community, it frees an agency or company from the task of cartography and provides a common operating picture where decision information can be displayed. In essence, this is the new face of mapping.

Community map collaboration is another distinctive technology that is changing how GIS impacts water resources. Furthering the concept of the web-based generic map background, community map systems allow custom mapping products to be developed by and shared within a community of users. The "community" can build web-delivered map services that are specific to a group, company or project. These communities take advantage of the generic backgrounds but add to them data layers that are specific to the group and can be shared by all registered members. This dramatically increases the functionality of a mapping system by allowing multiple users to work in parallel. Each user can focus on their responsibility and the final product is created faster and with greater completeness. Further, the system can be re-used by other members who add additional data layers that are specific to another purpose.

The Global Positioning System (GPS) is another technology that has seen phenomenal growth and adoption over the past decade. Going from a mere idea when Sputnik was first launched in 1957 to a fully functional constellation of satellites, GPS technology has changed the way humans conduct their activities. We now know where we are and hence our relationship to places around us. This is very powerful, especially in a personal decision environment where location can play a significant role (i.e., where will we eat and sleep while traveling). The impact of this technology will only increase as broader adoption and improved accuracy occurs over the next twenty to thirty years. Further, additional satellite navigation constellations such as GLONASS (NASA 2010) and Galileo (ESA 2010) will only accelerate the impact of satellite-based location services.

Another influential change that has dramatically impacted GIS is the advent of ubiquitous wireless data communications. According to AT&T, 90% of the entire US is covered with cellular data communication capability. While the quality of the coverage is debatable, the rise in wireless availability is not. According to the FCC in 2009, 98.1% of the US population is served by one or more mobile broadband providers (FCC 2010). By 2050, it is not unreasonable to assume that the entire world population will be covered by broadband wireless capability. Other technologies such as the satellite-based iridium data communications network allow wireless data communication from most regions on the planet. Newer and faster data communications technology will further increase the speed and reduce the cost of this ubiquitous wireless capability.

> *By 2050, it is not unreasonable to assume that the entire world population will be covered by broadband wireless*

In concert with the rise of cellular and other wireless technologies has been the rapid adoption of miniature, portable, Internet-capable computing devices, or smart-phones. These devices are more powerful computing devices than the PCs of 1995. For instance, the iPhone 3GS has a LINPACK (http://www.netlib.org/linpack/) average score of 28 Mflop/s (LINPACK for iPhone) while the Apple Power Macintosh 9500/132 from 1995 had a LINPACK score of 19 Mflop/s. These powerful new devices provide a new paradigm for delivering and processing personalized information. Most devices also include GPS receivers that provide location information as well as extremely fast networking capability. The combination of a powerful computing device with superb graphics, a high-speed network connection and location information from a GPS sensor create the perfect platform for a mapping device. Background map information is delivered through the network connection while positional information is delivered directly from the GPS receiver, all of which are displayed and manipulated using the powerful CPU found in the smart device.

Display technology is also advancing at a rapid pace and new technologies are changing how data are viewed and interpreted. Among the more exciting technologies is the idea of augmented reality visualization. This technology is similar to the oft-touted virtual reality where special eyeglasses with GPS and gyroscopes accurately track the location and orientation of the user. The difference is that whereas virtual reality brings the user into a 3D computational world, the augmented reality system brings the 3D computational world to the user. An example of augmented reality devices that have been around for decades are the Heads Up

Displays (HUDs) found in many fighter and other military aircraft. These devices project the horizon and other vital information into the line of sight of the pilot so he/she can keep their eyes focused on what matters. Technological advances have miniaturized and reduced the cost of these systems so that now they are being developed as a navigation and safety aid in automobiles.

Extreme parallelization of computing devices may not appear to be as impactful on GIS and its adoption within the water resources community, but this technology is rapidly changing the way decisions are modeled. Most computers are now equipped with at least two processing cores that provide a parallel path for computational activity. Workstations routinely have eight or twelve processing cores. By 2050, it is not unreasonable to assume that a single workstation class computer will have hundreds if not thousands of processing cores. Further, advances in cloud computing architecture will make available millions of processing cores for modeling. The impact of this exponential increase in computational power is that the accuracy and utility of computational models will be dramatically improved, first by providing access to high resolution, physics-based computational models that more precisely mimic the natural environment, and secondly by being able to run hundreds or thousands of simulations that provide a range of model solutions for better stochastic representation of the variance in boundary conditions. More accurate models that work in near real-time will be the hallmark of computing for water resources in 2050.

Each of the technologies listed above have been transformational without any interaction with the other. However, by combining these technologies, truly revolutionary ideas are beginning to emerge, especially in the area of online or web-based mapping. The next section will explore how combinations of these technologies could provide dramatic changes to the field of water resources over the next 40 years.

GIS FOR WATER RESOURCES 2050

To illustrate the ways in which GIS will change the way water resources will be managed and developed, the following four scenarios are presented. They are not intended to be prophetic but to illustrate visions of how the new advances mentioned before may impact water resources. Some of these scenarios are likely to come to pass within a few years while others may truly be 2050 visions.

Scenario 1 – Water Distribution Network Repair
It's 2050 and at the operations center of a municipal water utility an alarm goes off indicating that a reduced pressure reading has been detected. Because of the dense network of miniature, induction powered, wirelessly connected pressure sensors that roam through the pipe network, the exact location of the system failure is pinpointed immediately. This information is transmitted through the sensor network without the use of SCADA and the location and other parameters of the problem are displayed on a wall-sized map of the network. With the location of the problem known, automated

procedures send a series of commands to the control valves that isolate the degraded portion of the network, stopping the flow of water to the affected area.

The GIS system at the water works headquarters locates the closest repair crew based on their active GPS and geo-location equipment. The location of the degraded section is wirelessly sent to the closest repair crew and the on-board navigation system in their utility truck provides turn-by-turn directions to the site. Once on-site, visual inspections are conducted using camera, ground-penetrating radar or other active sensors with the results collected and relayed back to the command center for archival purposes.

The crew on-site unloads their equipment and begins repairs. One of the primary tools used is a set of augmented reality goggles. The goggles have a GPS sensor to know their location within millimeters as well as an inertial navigation system that measures the direction and orientation of the wearer. The goggles are wirelessly connected to a three-dimensional as-built diagram of the subsurface infrastructure that contains the water distribution network, any subsurface electrical distribution conduit, telephone and cable systems, and any other underground system that could impact the repair. When the workers look into the augmented reality glasses, they see all of these sub-surface features. As they turn their heads, the view of what is underground is super-imposed over the natural view as if they were looking through the earth and seeing the infrastructure below. This allows the workers to avoid any pipes and wires, prevents unintended degradation of other services, and provides direct access to the affected water distribution network.

Scenario 2 – In-Car Navigation Warning of Impending Flood

A family is driving home from a long vacation across a relatively flat section of west Texas. The car is kilometers away from any storms but the driver notices in the distance a large cumulonimbus cloud that could support rain. The driver doesn't worry about it because the cloud is very far away and not in the direct line of their travel. What the family does not realize is that this area of Texas is known as "flash flood alley" and that more deaths related to flooding happen here than anywhere else. They also don't realize that the National Weather Service (NWS) has issued a flash flood warning directly on their route and an accompanying polygon indicated the expected areas of inundation. While they continue to drive, the sun goes down and a major disaster is looming in their path. The family is engaged in many of the entertainment options available in their vehicle and is not aware of the flash flood warnings being broadcast on the news networks being received by the ever-evolving information communication technologies in their fancy new car.

During the previous five years, the state water resource agency has conducted a state-wide inventory of potential "low" spots that flood frequently. Using a combination of extremely high resolution LIDAR and a community-based mapping system, the state has identified hundreds of locations that can be dangerous during certain rain conditions. This high-resolution information is made available to the community and in conjunction with advanced spatial hydrology programs that take advantage of extreme computer parallelization; the NWS can predict, in near real-time, the depth, velocity and spatial extents of flash floods in the impacted areas.

In addition to the improved prediction capabilities of the NWS, the automobile this family recently purchased is equipped with a Road Hazard Warning System. Their car is in constant communication with the central servers of the road hazard company and is receiving the locations of disasters and warning areas. The Road Hazard servers communicate with the NWS servers and obtain the location of the expected area of inundation. The car receives this information and initiates an analysis to recognize that it is near the danger area. A secondary set of analysis algorithms is initiated. The system begins comparing the actual programmed navigation route with the actual route traveled and guesses where the car is traveling over the next 15 minutes. Based on this information, the car determines that it will intersect the expected flood polygon and begins to initiate a warning. An alarm sounds and the driver receives a message on the in-auto HUD indicating that the car is traveling toward a potential danger area and that they should think of taking alternative routes. The navigation automatically computes a new route and the system asks the driver if they accept the new route. The family changes their direction of travel and completely avoids the area of potential danger.

Scenario 3 – Water Resource Regulatory Staff
A staff member of the Division of Water Quality is performing water quality inspections downstream of a local chemical manufacturing plant. Using the latest *in situ* testing equipment, the tests indicate that the receiving water may be out of compliance with USEPA water quality standards. This information is automatically input into the agency's water quality database and flags a warning. Another field agent who is working nearby receives a notice that a field sample needs to be taken upstream of the chemical plant and is given navigation routes to the appropriate test location. This information is also sent directly to the state water quality database and the GIS system at the agency headquarters begins to query both historical as well as spatial records in this area to determine if a full violation has occurred. The system pulls in the real-time water quantity data being collected by other agencies and runs an analysis to identify if any flora and fauna will be impacted by the current conditions.

After the system identifies a problem, the agent in charge of violations is sent a full report that was developed by the automated system. The report includes a map showing the results of the water quality sampling activity. The map allows users to scroll through time to see previous water quality sampling results. The agent reviews the information, approves the conclusions of the report, and an official violation report is sent to the chemical facility. This all occurs within a single working day.

Scenario 4 – Location Aware Early Warning Systems
Currently, there a number of commercial and government systems that send text messages to warn individuals of impending storm weather alerts (http://inws.wrh.noaa.gov). However, utilizing GPS-equipped smart phone

technology combined with higher precision modeling, it may be possible to create a weather warning system that only contacts impacted individuals. For example, with higher precision flood forecasting models, it may be possible for the alert system to recognize that one device is near but not directly in the path of an impending flood event while another device is directly in harms way. The messages could vary in intensity and could be continuously sent until the device clears the impacted area. If no motion is detected, a message could be sent to emergency personnel with the last known location of the device so search and rescue operations can more rapidly be implemented.

CHALLENGES AND ISSUES IN ACHIEVING THE 2050 VISION

Data Availability
One of the major advances in 2050 in the GIS/spatial data field will be the availability and use of huge spatial databases. In the past decade we have seen exponential growth in the amount of data that is widely available and that growth is likely to continue over the coming years and decades. Spatial data will come from many sources, will be available in near real time and will be ubiquitous. Even today, "four million surveillance cameras are in use in the UK at any given time, making the British one of the most heavily monitored societies on earth. The average person is captured on camera 300 times a day" (Maser 2010).

In order to use the large data banks, data from all sources will be stored in a form such that it can be integrated and used together. In conjunction with the huge database, there will be sophisticated ways in which the data will be processed and analyzed. Raw data coming from different sources will be subject to a quality control analysis to eliminate or adjust data to ensure its quality. Sophisticated analysis techniques will be in use so that data will not be viewed as individual packets of information but rather will be woven together to form a near-continuous (in both time and space) picture. A glimpse of this type of data integration can be seen in the "Photo Tourism" system (http://phototour.cs.washington.edu/) described by Snavely et al. (2006).

> *Will privacy concerns limit the development and availability of spatial data banks in 2050 or will the public be more accepting of living in a fish bowl?*

Another important issue associated with the availability of these vast amounts of data is privacy. Even today, many people object to Google Map's "Street View" and use of automated cameras for detecting speeding and red light violations. Will privacy concerns limit the development and availability of spatial data banks in 2050? Will mechanisms be in place to protect privacy or will the public be more accepting of living in a fish bowl?

NEEDS AND BARRIERS TO ACHIEVING THE 2050 VISION

To achieve this 2050 vision of the future of GIS applied to water resources, a number of advances will need to be achieved. Primary among them are cost-saving pressures on federal and state budgets. In 2010, the US Geological Survey estimated that 278 out of 7600 (or 4%) stream gages within the US are in jeopardy of closing (USGS 2010). Increasing pressure to reduce costs will only exacerbate this problem. The only thing that will alleviate this threat will be a drastic reduction in the cost and a corresponding increase in capability of the sensors. Current research indicates that many of the cost and accuracy issues will be overcome using a network of extreme low power sensors. Such systems are already being deployed in refineries and other industrial sites (http://www.dustnetworks.com) and experience has indicated that this technology will eventually disseminate into other applications.

Another barrier to achieving this vision is the ability to develop extremely detailed as-builts of subsurface infrastructure required for the water distribution network repair scenario. Currently it is extremely difficult to obtain these with enough accuracy to perform the detailed augmented reality exercise described, especially for the hundreds of thousands of kilometers of existing subsurface infrastructure. However, newer technologies, including Ground Penetrating Radar (GPR), Magnetic Induction Tomography and other geophysical technologies are rapidly improving the capability to "see" underground. These technologies will improve with the result of high quality underground surveys.

CONCLUSION

The future is bright for the use of GIS technologies within the water resources industry. This technology has recently made the transition from a niche technology used primarily by engineers and scientists into a mainstream "must-have" tool useful for a variety of industries. This change will naturally lead to an increase in attention and development that will increasingly transform the technology. These changes are already on the horizon and their impacts on the use of GIS in water resources brings exciting prospects for what might be.

ACKNOWLEDGMENTS

Dr. Walter Grayman contributed information relative to GIS history in water resources over the previous 40 years, as well as editorial review. Dr. Richard Males provided feedback and review during the development of this chapter. Dr. Phillip Hendrix provided additional insight into the various scenarios of the future. Tusen takk (a thousand thanks) to Sheri Wallace who provided editorial assistance as well as moral support.

REFERENCES

Aquaveo. (2010). "Watershed modeling system overview." *The watershed modeling solution*, Aquaveo, <http://www.aquaveo.com/wms> (Aug, 2010).

European Space Agency (ESA). (2010). "What is Galileo?" *About Galileo*, European Space Agency, <http://www.esa.int/esaNA/GGGMX650NDC_galileo_0.html> (Oct, 2010).

Federal Communications Commission (FCC) (2010). FCC 10-81. <http://hraunfoss.fcc.gov/edocs_public/attachmatch/FCC-10-81A1.pdf> (Oct, 2010).

Grayman, W. M., Males, R. M., Gates, W. E., and Hadder, A. W. (1975). "Land-based modeling system for water quality management studies." *J. Hydr. Eng. Div.-ASCE*, 101(5): 567-580.

Horn, C. R., and Grayman, W.M. (1992). "Water quality modeling with the EPA reach file system." *J. Water Res. Pl.-ASCE*, 119(2), 262-274.

Loucks, D. P., Taylor, M. T., and French, P. N. (1985). "Interactive data management for resource planning and analysis." *Water Resour. Res. – AGU*, 21(2),131-142.

Maidment, D. (2002). *Arc Hydro: GIS for water resources*, ESRI Press, Redlands, CA.

Males, R.M. , and Grayman, W.M. (1992). "Past, present and future of geographic information systems in water resources." *Water Resources Update*, 87, 5-11.

Maser, M. (2010). "Big Brother watching British 24 hours a day." *Global Times*, March 7, 2010, <http://opinion.globaltimes.cn/foreign-view/2010-03/510361.html> (Aug, 2010).

McHarg, I. (1969). *Design with nature*, Natural History Press, Garden City, NY.

National Aeronautics and Space Administration (NASA). (2010). "GLONASS." *International Laser Ranging Service*, National Aeronautics and Space Administration, <http://ilrs.gsfc.nasa.gov/satellite_missions/list_of_satellites/g102_general.html> (Oct, 2010).

Nelson, E. J., and Jones, N. L. (1996). "Using the ARC/INFO data model to build conceptual models for environmental/hydraulic/hydrologic simulations." *Proc. 1996 ESRI User Conference*.

Snavely, N., Seitz, S.M., Szeliski, R. 2006. "Photo tourism: exploring photo collections in 3D." *Comp. Graph.*, 25(3), 835-846.

Thirkill, D.L. (1991). *Application of a geographic information system to rainfall-runoff modeling*, Research Document No. 36, US Army Corps of Engineers Hydrologic Engineering Center, Davis, CA, < http://www.dtic.mil/cgi-bin/GetTRDoc?AD=ADA273431&Location=U2&doc=GetTRDoc.pdf> (Aug, 2010).

US Environmental Protection Agency (USEPA). (2010). *BASINS (Better assessment integrating point and non-point sources)*, US Environmental Protection Agency, <http://water.epa.gove/scitech/datait/models/basins/index.cfm> (Aug, 2010).

US Geological Survey (USGS). (2010). "Streamflow information program – 2010 update." *USGS national streamflow information program*, US Geological Survey, <http://water.usgs.gov/nsip/status.html> (Aug, 2010).

Wallace, R. M., Zhang, Y., and Wright, J. R. (2000). "Distributed system for coastal infrastructure modeling and assessment." *J. Comput. Civil Eng.*, 15, 67-73.

Weisberg, D.E. (2008). *The engineering design revolution*, <http://www.cadhistory.net/> (Aug, 2010).

AUTHOR INFORMATION

Robert M. Wallace, PhD, PE, is Chief of the Computational Science and Engineering Division at the US Army Engineer Research and Development Center. He leads a team of over 80 federal engineers, computer scientists and technicians in developing state-of-the-art software solutions to support the US Army Corps of Engineers, the Department of Defense and other federal agencies.
Email: Robert.M.Wallace@usace.army.mil

Chapter 32

Information Technology in 2050

A. Charles Rowney, Theodore G. Cleveland, and James G. Gerth

ABSTRACT

The evolution of applied information technology (IT) over four decades is not predictable except in the most general ways, but some current trends and issues will likely persist and these can be identified and their outcomes hypothesized. A subset of such trends is considered in this discussion. IT trends that are expected to continue include increasing computational capability, improved interoperability, expanding storage capability and extending connectivity, as well as a profound evolution of software and data norms. Obvious positive consequences will include the ability to more perfectly represent the real world in analysis and simulation tools, revolutionizing engineering practice by enabling fine-grained representation of physical problems. Negative consequences may include the loss of information, quality implications associated with the spread of "grey" literature, and the inaccessibility of engineering computations to engineers. Responses to these negative consequences may include a shift in the notion of information accreditation, a drive towards formal accreditation of common engineering tools, changes in the fundamental precepts of engineering education, and the forced evolution of a paradigm shift of the notion of professionalism in IT services sectors. The picture that emerges is one of changes in practice, not just in speed and scale, but in kind.

A STARTING POINT

While we don't believe IT progress over decades is predictable, there are some groundswell changes in IT that we are experiencing today which will echo long into the future, and it is interesting to identify some of these and to speculate on where they will bring us. The constraints of space sharply limited what we could address even partially in this chapter, so we have explored some issues that are of interest to us and are as yet undecided, and suggested some outcomes that might follow. This should not be taken as an attempt at prediction, but simply as a speculation as to what might come – or might not.

It is tempting to delve into the speed and capability of computing machinery as a part of this exploration, because this is a core consideration in our day-to-day decisions as to which new piece of hardware we should buy, or which software we should load. The speed and capability evolution in both hardware and communications has driven the IT world from the time-sharing concept on mainframes to the work-station file-server model, and now to the cloud computing model (which can be viewed as essentially time-sharing re-visited). A cyclic "revolution" of computing paradigms, as a response to hardware and communications acceleration and other pressures, could repeat, and we have little doubt that "faster, better" will be a continuing theme in this sector. However, on the time scale we are now considering we suggest that this kind of change is for the most part not really a major interest area, because it is the *uses* of that machinery that are important in engineering, not their nature. So let's simply stipulate that over the time span we are considering, our hardware will be blindingly fast, physically tiny, ubiquitous and affordable. Let's assume that memory and storage are vast, cheap and robust. Let's assume that connectivity is for practical purposes limitless in space and speed. Let's even dare to hope that over this time span we will evolve a dominant operating system that is stable, dependable, and secure to the point where it isn't of much interest.

This perspective doesn't end the list of underlying technical changes we will face. There is also a range of other technical areas that will deliver fascinating extensions to present practice by 2050. There will be new ways to input data and interact with computers, including direct neural interfaces, and computer-aided problem solving will become a different experience. There will also be new ways to render results. Even now, three-dimensional renderings are possible, and this kind of technology will no doubt continue in ease of use and effectiveness. Truly photo-realistic renderings of structures and engineering works will be the expectation, not the exception, well before 2050. In this chapter, we have avoided exploring these kinds of extensions of present capability because they will tend to make what we already do faster and more effective, but will not by themselves change professional practice. Instead, we have focused on some of the larger technical trends that have the clear potential to markedly affect the practice of professional engineering.

Reluctantly, we have also decided to exclude the societal and engineering practice changes that will continue to be experienced as social networking technologies progressively drive an evolution in the way engineers interact as communities. The notions of leadership, mentoring, peer group definitions and other facets of human interaction that are fundamental to engineering practice and are being affected by IT will evolve profoundly by 2050. So will the evolution of regional and/or systematic censoring of internet connectivity, the potential for fracturing of communities based on differing computational platforms, the long-term implications of ceding data housing to generic third party service providers, the potential reconsideration of specific technologies in the face of IT-centric disasters, and others.

Processing speed is not just a consequence of hardware evolution, but of evolving practice and understanding, and we posit that this too will increase computational and application capabilities through 2050 and beyond, even though a multitude of technical, production and business challenges will be faced along the way. Some aspects of the recent acceleration in processing speed (circa 2000 – 2010) are explained less in hardware and more in how hardware is being used. Identification of parallel structures in how we cast a problem lets us attack computational problems in parallel, with enormous acceleration of throughput (apparent as "fast" to humans) without demanding a fundamental advance in actual hardware speed. Database look-up has also benefited from intellectual progress in how problems are presented to our machines, with vastly improved search algorithms and filing systems, so that speed is conferred not by faster machines, but by application of greater intellect.

Unfortunately, there is also a factor that seems to be an inevitable collateral factor to the development of faster computing capability. The bloat that bogs down our hardware is staggering. An often-cited example can be found in our word processing software. Fifteen years ago the file sizes, application sizes and requirements of our basic word processing hardware required a fraction of the capability that our massive word processing products demand today, yet the benefit of the escalation in requirements for the newer products seems to be questionable. We wonder if this bloat will ever be managed. An informal poll taken by the author amongst his colleagues found that virtually no one saw benefits to a recent release of a common word processing product, yet market forces have demanded that it be adopted nevertheless.

At the end of the day, we believe it is fair to conclude that processing power will continue to evolve and that applications will keep pace with this evolution, but much of this evolution will be enabling but not fundamental in its impact. It is the expression of IT in engineering in other ways that will have a material impact on engineering practice.

> *IT processing power will continue to evolve and applications will keep pace with this evolution, but it is the expression of IT in engineering in other ways that will have the greatest impact on engineering practice.*

LOSS OF INFORMATION

For information to be of meaning, it must be accessible and in a format that can be interpreted. The problem we now face is that accessibility and interpretation have new dimensions as a result of the IT revolution.

As things stand, information retained from centuries past can still have meaning. Much may be lost as fragile manuscripts decay or are destroyed over the centuries, but the manuscripts that survive can be made available, whether or not the content has current value. Data persistence in the electronic information age is similar in some ways and different in others, sometimes blatantly and other times subtly.

What changes in the electronic world is largely a shift in the degree of the problem, not the essential nature of the problem. The format of electronic information changes far more rapidly than its "paper" counterpart. While written documents may be readable over centuries, many electronic formats can become useless over decades for several reasons.

Media change, as anyone with a library of 5-¼ inch floppies knows, or anyone with a camera based on XD chips has learned. Even where they don't change, media themselves can degrade over time. Current CD-R technology is largely a photographic technique and the dyes in the disks, like those in a Kodachrome photograph, decay with time. Manufacturer estimates of CD/DVD life are on the order of 70 years or less. Magnetic tape has a lifespan measured in decades, paper has proven to be a multi-century medium, and burned CD/DVD lifespan has been reported as limited to possibly a few years (e.g. 2 to 5 years for burned CDs) depending on the manufacturer and storage conditions (Blau 2006). Surely storage conditions matter, but the potential for loss is not diminished with different media; in fact, because the outer "shell" in CDs or DVDs appears robust to the casual observer, we speculate that such media are more likely to be mistreated than some more visibly sensitive storage options.

Even if media are compatible, base formats can become unreadable, or readable only with difficulty or at cost. Although still widely understood, the ASCII and EBCDIC formats that provide a representation of familiar readable characters as a set of numerical values are nearing their 50th anniversary. These 8-bit encodings have evolved to form the basis of much data encoding today, and they are still "readable," decodable and translatable between each other. Although some more recent data formats are built upon these standards, some formats are proprietary enough that decoding without the manufacturer's software is practically impossible. A change in format could render in a single keystroke decades of information, collective knowledge, financial transactions, etc. unreadable. If we also in some way lose the ability to interpret older formats, then the unreadable data becomes nothing more than digital clutter, perhaps resolvable only through the equivalent of decryption methods.

Some of these issues are problematic over the long term, and some more immediately. If data are published in a proprietary format, a sometimes-costly proprietary tool may be required simply to access the data. Over the long term, the tools to access the data may no longer be available, and the prospect of reverse engineering an obsolete format emerges. This outcome can be an issue even if the agency responsible for maintaining the data has the national interest at heart. At the time of writing, the US Geological Survey (USGS) National Geospatial Program Standards website states: "Standards set the criteria and specifications to ensure that all products prepared by the USGS under the National Geospatial Program (formerly the National Mapping Program) are accurate and consistent in style and content. Most of these standards are historical and apply to products no longer produced by the USGS..." (USGS 2010). A further review of standards in the National Mapping Program Technical Standards document *Standards for Digital Elevation Models* (USGS 1998) reveals five change notices between 1993 and 1998, beginning in 1993 when the determination was made to store content on ANSI labeled 9 track magnetic tape. The USGS runs an excellent and carefully managed program, so we infer that the trail of actions by this agency speaks to the magnitude of the problem of information maintenance in the technical context. Taken together, it is fair to conclude that our electronic tools have added many complexities to the problem of information storage, and eliminated few.

What of the future, then? A likely scenario is that we will continue to progressively lose content even though much of the foregoing is generally known. A number of factors lead to this end point. Continually migrating data to new media, preserving standards and maintaining continuity of content is an expensive and demanding requirement. Public agency funding is stressed, and is likely to continue that way for some time. Some are beginning to attach costs to content they have gathered or developed, presumably in an effort to defray or recoup operating costs. Proprietary interests offer apparent solutions, but it is arguable whether the interests behind those solutions will meet future needs. Beyond this, emerging national security needs may impact the availability or access requirements for some kinds of information. A likely end point is that in contrast to the ready availability of information that we currently experience, we will enter a time of increasingly complex access problems.

This trajectory has several implications. One is that there will be a period where content access will be more complex. Another is that there will be a permanent loss of information, because for some kinds of content, records lost are records permanently gone. The extent of this erosion remains to be seen, but it can be considered for convenience in two contexts, namely data that represent primary physical phenomena, and data that are derived (designs, plans, models and so on).

Primary physical data, such as rainfall, temperature, and other meteorological data, are generally made available by public entities that have an interest in long-term data preservation and resources to properly manage that content. Although there are likely to be issues along the way, we see no inherent reason why management of these types of data in 2050 will be fundamentally different from what is experienced now. There will be a generally standard format for information, but also a constant pressure as technology changes to migrate historical content to newer forms. A danger after such migration is that there will be an incentive to destroy the original source.

For example, let's consider the Google Books project. Copyright and revenue issues aside, scanning all known literature into referenced and searchable files is indeed a worthy endeavor, and a great service to mankind, perhaps one of the best yet conceived. The activity may preserve documents from antiquity to present and the associated information. But what of the original sources, once the electronic content is fully converted and available? Perhaps many will be destroyed to make shelf space for more physical volumes, but years later we may discover a single missing page in the electronic image. If the original is long destroyed then so is that knowledge, either lost forever or, if important enough, requiring re-constitution. Such total loss of knowledge is unlikely, but no one knows what is needed in the future, so we cannot make perfect value judgments now about what must be preserved and what can be sacrificed. It may be that this loss can be slowed, not only by consciously selecting media and behaviors that emphasize durability, but by maintaining reference copies of content as long as possible, thereby reducing the need to make copies of copies along the way. Hence this is a compelling argument that electronic content should be considered working material and somewhere a physical archive should be maintained on a medium with long lifetime and in a language that will be decipherable to future generations.

We cannot comment on how likely it is that this need will be met, but we note that the prospects seem dim. The National Aeronautics and Space Administration (NASA) may well represent one of the pinnacles of human accomplishment in their role in sending humans to the moon. They are presumably not only technically inclined but aware of the transcendent importance of the records surrounding their history of accomplishment. However, it has been reported in the popular press (Kaufmann 2007) and by NASA (2009) that they have had difficulty finding video footage of the moon landing, and had to overcome obstacles accessing and playing back footage because of the need to address obsolete recording formats and equipment. If this is the case, what hope is there that less exalted but still critical records will be maintained by agencies or owners with a lesser technical pedigree?

> *Electronic content should be considered working material and somewhere a physical archive should be maintained on a medium with long lifetime and in a language that will be decipherable to future generations.*

Another concern is indications that some agencies may be inclined to vest the data for which they are responsible in proprietary frameworks, which in some cases could imply that they must be managed and accessed through software or services of a third party. We concur with the need to set effective standards, but note that there are implications to this kind of stance that range from added cost to the potential that data ownership is in an extreme case effectively ceded to a private entity. If that happens, the potential for a negative outcome is substantial. Future data users may have to pay a third party for access to information they need. Beyond that, the ultimate decisions for the continued maintenance of data are *de facto* ceded to that third party. Thus, in the 2050 scenario, basic data are no longer freely available, but constitute a profit-making commodity. Further, depending on the vendor, the data could in some cases disappear entirely either through a market based vendor decision or perhaps through the disappearance of the vendor and their infrastructure.

The second data context, derived data, is also problematic. Current state-of-practice puts little limitation on engineering firms or other enterprises as to how derived data are preserved and maintained. Enterprises have developed solutions based on a range of proprietary and locally developed solutions, in a range of formats and using a range of tools. In the long run, several issues may have to be addressed. One is the value of the content. Even though the system itself may save images of data dependably, the value of the images may be nil if the software it serves is obsolete and no migration pathway exists. It is not known how many enterprises have a program to refresh data in their care so that it remains viable as technology changes, or have taken steps to store the data in a format that is likely to be at least viewable in the long term. Engineering practice has not faced this issue in quite the same way in the past, because the "flat files" that were so characteristic of traditional engineering record-keeping in the past did not have the same kinds of long-term problems. They may have been susceptible to water damage, rodents, fire or other catastrophes, but they were at least viewable and generally understandable if found. Even substantially damaged physical drawings may still convey some remnant portion of the original design intent, whereas it's unlikely that a partial portion of an electronic design file in an undocumented proprietary format will retain any of the design information.

A complicating factor in this situation is the metadata an enterprise may choose to associate with the data in their care. Often identified by keys such as project names or numbers, they may or may not be easily located in the future. The chosen metadata may not be suitable for arbitrary future searches, and may not lead to confident recovery or provenance in the event that the data are needed. Prudent practice in metadata selection and effective search engines are a remedy to part of this problem, but do not solve all things. For example, distinguishing between two similar source documents in the longer term may be difficult, so it may be relatively easy to get "close" to the right data with a suitable search engine, but impossible to find the "right" data if the associated metadata are inadequate.

A related danger in metadata-referenced information (with no solution offered by the authors other than awareness and vigilance) is that the metafile index (the pointers to the actual data) can be moved or migrated, but the source data left in-place or moved into a location that the pointers cannot find. In this situation, which we anecdotally have heard happens with regularity in small system upgrades if the loss of path is not detected early, the metadata index is no longer useful, and simply a memory that at some time in the past certain data existed somewhere.

The overall picture is that there is a reasonable likelihood that some categories of information will persist in the future reasonably well but other categories will prove to be problematic. The information equivalent of thermodynamic entropy is always at work, and the degradation of information is inexorable and progressive. If this degradation acts faster than the degradation of the physical works, an outcome could be infrastructure documented only by the infrastructure's existence, not by a reliable or accessible set of "as-builts" or other documentation. We believe that by 2050, the calculations behind and origins of many features in the ground today will have become a mystery. We hope that by 2050 the lessons learned surrounding this entropy will have led to dependable truly long term archiving of engineering information, but we don't assert that this is likely.

> *The information equivalent of thermodynamic entropy is always at work, and the degradation of information is inexorable and progressive.*

A rather different direction emerging in information lies in the sources of general technical content. Traditional sources of content, such as journals and other publications, are now supplemented with a wide range of on-line resources. Wikipedia, user groups and other alternatives publish content that purport to be accurate. More than an expanded offering, electronically offered content is becoming a primary delivery vehicle.

As traditional sources of content shift to on-line formats, they tend to become more available. However, we expect that physical technical publications as we have known them will all but disappear as 2050 approaches. The multiple pressures of environmental stewardship and cost, as well as the inherent physical limitations, will eventually eliminate traditional publications except in special circumstances.

Unfortunately, we don't believe that a massive shift to e-delivery will be an unalloyed positive change. Even now, many reputable journals are not available to second generation users (those who were not initially subscribers or purchasers) for free. They are accessed either directly or through third parties for a fee that can be quite substantial. The ability to browse back through years of a journal in a library and select related content from seemingly unrelated titles is rapidly disappearing, and changes in access are evident. Even physical libraries are choosing all-electronic holdings, and new profit avenues are emerging. Consider abstracting, once a modestly lucrative sideline that is becoming more crucial as a primary way to communicate content prior to access. Abstracts don't always provide a useful indication of content and we speculate that in the near future the display of content for a short time (say a few hours) with some mechanism to prevent screen capture and printing could provide a mechanism to browse holdings rather than browse abstracts. A clever entrepreneur might be able to profit from a mechanism based on charging a connection time fee for browsing content fully rather than a per-document fee based on an abstract that may or may not provide a useful indication of content.

Whatever happens, we have no doubt that the profit motive will be present in some form, and that through 2050 there will be endless attempts to restrict or control information access and to implement ways to visit further fees on those looking for information. Whether this profit focus will benefit the originators of content or merely the incidental third party "owners" of that content remains to be seen.

Counterpressures to the attempts to assert ownership of third party information exist, and will no doubt continue. A person searching for information is therefore likely to find many answers for free from the "grey" on-line literature using a basic search engine. Finding reputable content from a more formal repository requires a different set of search skills and a willingness to spend possibly significant amounts of money to obtain content. The result, compounded by generations accustomed to finding content for casual purposes from ubiquitous on-line sources, may be a tendency to rely on "grey" sources rather than more credible content. This tendency will likely be more pronounced in professional practice than in academic contexts or agency offices where direct and free (at least to the individual) access to the formal literature is facilitated. The question that emerges is whether or not a groundswell recognition of and response to this situation of reliance on "grey" sources will emerge.

We define "content accreditation" as a term for some agreed and formal mechanisms that could credibly constitute a substantiation that a particular item of information is factual and as cited without purporting to defend or endorse that information other than speaking to its authenticity. There are instances that parallel this kind of endorsement now. For example, the US Environmental Protection Agency (USEPA) has a practice of requiring specific quality control checks on secondary data (e.g. data cited in a research report but not generated as a part of that report; USEPA 2006). As the decades pass and content (all of it easily searchable) continues to accrue on a world-wide basis, the value of content accreditation will become more apparent. The attachment of an institutional endorsement to a publication will have increased value, as it will become a primary filter for what we now refer to as "refereed" or otherwise "proven" content. We suggest that the value of association of content with an accrediting institution, coupled with the shift away from traditional publication models for revenue generation, is likely to push entities that previously relied on hard-copy publication for revenue towards new profit paradigms. Will we see charges levied for naming a source, rather than for access to content?

IMPACTS ON PROFESSIONALISM

Similar to the data issues we face, there will be pressures on engineering as technical software applications evolve. In its first emergence in this profession, software tended to be the result of professional engineering efforts and was freely available. It didn't take long for profit makers to enter the field, and a rich set of proprietary tools now exists for use by engineers. The available software is commonly closed source (i.e., the code is unavailable) and sometimes even the data formats used by the software are proprietary and opaque to the user. Even where software is open to the user, knowledge of programming in the engineering profession is under downward pressure and the ability to read and understand code is increasingly limited in the profession. The concurrent increase in sophistication of engineering software means that the effort to truly understand it becomes increasingly difficult over time. Many new graduates are well versed in the use of some technology or software, but less skilled in the basic computations and principles that those tools embody. Thus, as 2050 approaches, we wonder if hands-on understanding of the theory behind the software will prevail, or not. Efforts to increase engineering education standards are underway and will likely address some of this, but the basic opacity of the tools does not seem to have a remedy.

We suggest, therefore, that in the future we will see a time where engineers will pervasively use software tools that they can't truly understand or verify in detail. The results of such tools will perforce be accepted as authoritative, perhaps backed up by simple calculations or parity checks, but otherwise accepted as-is. One then must question whether engineering will truly be practiced in a professional way, at least as understood today. There are arguments for and against the implications of software on professional functions, but their resolution is beyond the scope of this chapter. What is of interest here is how the profession will respond to the reality that some aspects of engineering functionality and judgment will be subsumed by software.

Another major change agent will be failures arising from software limitations. Today, software that is inherently flawed is tolerated to a degree we find astonishing, much more than would be accepted in humans undertaking the same function. Computational errors in water resources software have been observed and accepted for years; we accept this as a reasonable consequence of the early evolution of this field, when many lessons about numerical methods and software development were being learned. This acceptance persists. Vendors, for example, are understandably reluctant to accept liability for their products (for examples read typical End User License Agreements addressing damages arising from use of software), and users routinely sign and accept agreements for software that in turn accept that denial of liability. At some point, however, we may see an evolution in thinking, where software flaws are less accepted and where consequences are recognized as tied to the apparently inevitable use of software taken past the point where an engineer can truly control all aspects of the computation. If and when this happens, there may be a move towards accreditation of software on a par with accreditation of engineers. Steps in this direction are evident. Many entities express preferences or adopt *de facto* standards by encouraging the use of particular software packages. The US Army Corps of Engineers publishes a list that indicates which software is acceptable, preferred or mandatory. Some vendors seek peer review in an attempt to validate their offerings and promote their use. It seems a reasonable leap to consider software accreditation on a professional basis in cases where the software is linked to the professional practice of engineering.

> *In the future we will see a time where engineers will pervasively use software tools they can't understand or verify.*

What emerges is a question as to how this would be regulated, monitored and pursued on a continuing basis. The groups that regulate the professional practice of engineering are not equipped to do this. We anticipate there will also likely be resistance to this evolution on the part of vendors, who have little to benefit by implicitly accepting greater risk as their products are used and in some cases may have concerns about their code being made visible or otherwise audited in ways they may not be able to control. The USEPA Environmental Technology Verification (ETV) program targeting software for verification was excellent, but some vendors absented themselves from the table even though circumstances were designed to respect their interests in privacy and protection of intellectual property.

Despite the complexity of the problem, given the increasing reliance on software, the increasing substitution of software for human judgment and the eventual need to associate liability with more than the engineer, we feel it is inevitable that the hurdle of software accreditation will be faced by 2050, if not resolved by then.

REAL WORLD REPRESENTATION

Another change in capability driven by IT that has the potential to profoundly affect professional practice can be found in the convergence of several factors related to the way we define the physical world around us. Two of them are a radical increase in the ability to address and access locations around the earth, and an evolution in the ability to deploy sensing devices to the point where they are cheap enough to deploy, in quantity, as elements of any physical project.

Addressing is fundamental, because the ability to resolve elements of the physical world is dependent on the ability to locate and monitor them. We have stipulated that internet connectivity and speed will not be limiting, so the question is whether or not fine-grained addressing is stressed in 2050. The currently dominant addressing scheme for the internet has served well, but it will be exhausted (saturated) well before 2050, not long from the time of writing this chapter. It will be replaced by a successor that has a vastly greater ability to uniquely identify locations around the earth; this process is under way now. Continued evolution over the next decades makes it clear that it is realistic to expect that by 2050, every conceivable physical item of interest to engineers at a gross physical level will be addressable. We note that this may occur not through the application of internet technology, but rather through the application of other connectivity mechanisms, and it is moot as to which option eventually emerges. At the same time, sensing technology is increasing rapidly in its ability to identify locations and conditions at a location. Satellite technology, airborne sensing, Radio Frequency Identification (RFID) technology (www.rfidjournal.com), and many other evolving sensing methods point to a future ability to sense conditions at any point and time to a degree that makes the essentially perfect knowledge of the state of a physical system a realistic possibility.

Coupling processing speed, storage, sensing and addressability, it is possible to foresee the construction of engineering applications by 2050 that are today only concepts and possibilities. Rather than the often somewhat crude systems that currently characterize practice, the potential exists that large-scale systems will be manageable based on real-time sensing, processing and intervention at a highly accurate level. Rule-based planning will be reduced in significance, and methods that rely on physical prediction will become the norm. Rather than static assumptions, dynamic behaviors will be accommodated in engineering analyses of physical systems. Feed-forward control capabilities that have hitherto only been possible by engineers in plants and factories will be extended to natural systems. Numerous other examples of paradigm changes will accompany pervasive communication coupled with connectivity and sensing, but the essential point is the impact on routine engineering practice will be substantial. This evolution has only just begun, but by 2050 it has the potential to dominate engineering practice.

We note that the value of real-time control of natural systems is predicated on the ability to predict the responses of a system to human intervention, and that many biological systems have response times that are measured in years or decades. Given the number of variables and the complexity of scientific research before these responses are fully understood, we expect that there are decades of research into natural systems that must occur before real time control can be perfected. It is our speculation that by 2050, the IT infrastructure to accomplish this will be fully available, but the natural sciences basis for physically based interpretation and prediction will still be evolving. We therefore expect that real-time control will be pervasive and unencumbered by IT limitations, but still developing where long period natural system responses (multiple years or decades) are concerned.

CONCLUSION

The future of IT is impossible to predict except perhaps to note that it will expand in speed and capacity and decrease in cost very substantially between the time of writing and 2050. This expansion will bring with it both enhancements and losses in engineering practice. Many currently available sources of information will be lost, and there may be a consequent shift in the notion of information accreditation. Fees for basic data, either direct or as a result of the need to purchase applications to access those data, may be common and significant. Engineering software will continue to evolve and there may be a drive towards formal accreditation of common engineering tools and a limitation of the ability to independently (i.e. without using certified tools) practice engineering. The ability to fully represent the real world in analysis and simulation tools will undergo a change that revolutionizes engineering practice in this area by enabling fine-grained representation of the real world, perhaps limited only by the rate of increase in scientific knowledge as opposed to engineering capability. We will therefore experience changes in practice not just in speed and scale, but in kind. The human skill sets required to manage and work effectively in this changing environment will evolve; syntax, sources and organizational models will change, but the ability to apply intellect and propositional logic will not. Knowledge workers of the future will require much of the fundamental skills of today, but will extend their abilities to encompass specific needs that result from the evolution in pervasively used information technology.

Some of these hypotheses are troubling, and some exciting. Whatever the case, the likelihood of many of them rests on our willingness to accept a particular outcome. In this regard, the future is ours to determine. Perhaps the greatest value of these speculations is that if we don't like the look of where we might end up, we can be inspired to forestall some of the more negative future histories in favor of better ones.

ACKNOWLEDGEMENTS

We wish to express our appreciation for the careful review and comments provided by Adrian Goulding, Andrew Marks and Richard Males. Their time and attention was supportive and was valued as we grappled with the massive issues surrounding the central theme of this chapter, and we were delighted to respond to their suggestions and thereby improve the end result.

REFERENCES

Blau, J. 2006. "Storage expert warns of short life span for burned CDs." *Computerworld*, January 10, 2006, <http://www.computerworld.com/s/article/107607/Storage_expert_warns_of_short_life_span_for_burned_CDs> (Sep, 2010).

Kaufmann, M. 2007. "The saga of the lost space tapes." *The Washington Post*, January 31, 2007, <http://www.washingtonpost.com/wp-dyn/content/article/2007/01/30/AR2007013002065.html> (Sep, 2010).

National Atmospheric and Space Administration (NASA). 2009. "NASA releases restored Apollo 11 moonwalk video." *Press release archives*, July 16, 2009, <http://www.nasa.gov/home/hqnews/2009/jul/HQ_09_166_Apollo_11_Moonwalk_Video.html> (Sep, 2010).

United States Environmental Protection Agency (USEPA). 2006. *Guidance on systematic planning using the data quality objectives process*, EPA/240/B-06/001, USEPA, Washington, DC.

United States Geological Survey (USGS). 2010. "National geospatial program standards." *United States Geological Survey*, < http://nationalmap.gov/gio/standards/> (Sep, 2010).

United States Geological Survey (USGS). 1998. *Standards for digital elevation models*, USGS <http://rmmcweb.cr.usgs.gov/nmpstds/demstds.html>

AUTHOR INFORMATION

A. Charles Rowney is an independent consultant (ACR, LLC). He serves as a board member for EWRI, and has a long history of involvement in the development, testing, use and integration of software applications in engineering problems. He also has a strong background in knowledge management and information management applied to enterprise problems in collaboration and interoperability. He obtained his BS, BA, MA and PhD at the University of Ottawa. Email: acr@rowney.com

Theodore G. Cleveland is an Associate Professor at Texas Tech University and formerly an Associate Professor at the University of Houston. His teaching and research interests are in hydrology, emerging statistical methods in engineering, and computing. He has worked in information management, communications, and computation in support of his research and teaching activities. He received his BS in Environmental Resources Engineering from Humboldt State University and his MS and PhD in Civil Engineering from the University of California, Los Angeles. Email: ted.cleveland@gmail.com

James G. Gerth is a Senior Engineering Designer with WilsonMiller Inc. in Tallahassee, Florida, and he has worked in a leadership and management capacity at various civil engineering firms. He has been intensively involved as a user and a trainer with design and drafting software from multiple publishers for 25 years, and has a strong interest in the formats, portability, archivability, and recovery of design data. Email: james.gerth@stantec.com

Chapter 33

Creativity: An Important Problem-Solving Tool for Water Resources in 2050

Richard H. McCuen

ABSTRACT

Many complex water problems of 2050 will not be solved using the decision processes of 2010. More creative decision-making will be helpful. The changes needed for more creative problem solving are discussed. Advancements in computer technology, especially algorithms based on the neurological processes of discovery, will be required. The algorithms in the form of artificial intelligence will incorporate emotional thinking with cognitive processes. Success in advancing creative thinking will also require attitude changes and broader thinking skills such as those emphasized in the ASCE Body of Knowledge.

"Holy smokes! You've solved it!"

INTRODUCTION

Consider the year 2050. The global community faces many water resources problems that affect large populations in many parts of the world. In addition to issues related to inadequate water quantity and quality within countries, the conflict between countries sharing common water resources add to the complexity of these problems. The economic growth within nations conflicts with efforts to minimize environmental damage. Sustainability issues are more critical now than in 2010 because of the rise in human population. The continued use of nonrenewable natural resources still causes conflict between meeting current needs and preservation of the resources for future generations; however, now (2050) the amount of nonrenewable resources has declined since 2010 while the demand has increased. The increase in weather extremes, such as extreme hurricanes, due to the inability to control climate change creates a conflict between those wanting to use public monies for disaster prevention and relief and those favoring the use of the funds for everyday infrastructure needs. Traditional approaches to problem solving and decision making cannot resolve these significant water conflicts, in part because of the wider range of interests by stakeholders. As the breadth of problems increases, traditional approaches will be less efficient.

Adapting to climate change, achieving greater sustainability, restoring and maintaining infrastructure, and increasing energy efficiency are major challenges for the current generation, but these issues were hardly discussed two scores of years ago. We can only speculate as to their place in the array of challenges that society will face in 2050. Will global water policy, megacity water supply, and hydroterrorism be among the issues that water professionals will be addressing in 2050? We can argue about which issues will be of major importance, but there is little doubt that the problems will be more complex and more critical to the larger global population in 2050 than are the issues that we face today. The increased complexity will be the result of more political and environmental constraints, more diverse cultural considerations, more rapidly changing technologies, and a larger population with a greater variety of wants and needs.

The focus here is not on which problems water professionals will face in 2050, but on the way that the problems will be solved. Traditional problem-solving methods currently taught are unlikely to be sufficient to address the complex problems of the future, so it seems reasonable that the breadth of problem-solving skills will need to broaden as the complexity of the problems increases. Specifically, current methods generally use only objective criteria and avoid value based criteria. One problem-solving approach that is often discounted is creativity because parts of the creative process emphasize emotional involvement at the expense of cognitive processes.

Just as the major water-related issues will change between now and 2050, the methods of creative thinking will need to change to better address the broader, more complex issues of 2050. To make the necessary advancements in creative thinking, computer technology, our understanding of neurological processes, and the recognition of the importance of emotions in the creative process will need to be addressed. Educational programs on creativity will need to be expanded, and attitudes that promote the use of creativity rather than inhibit its use will need to be the norm. These issues are the subject of this chapter.

TECHNOLOGY AND CREATIVITY

Brainstorming, synectics, and the Pugh method (Lumsdaine and Lumsdaine 1995) are among the techniques currently available to foster creative thinking. These methods have served problem solvers well, but before 2050 we will need to reorient our problem-solving direction and develop new methods that will be better able to help solve the complex problems of 2050. Pencil-and-paper methods may still play a role, but creative efficiency (i.e., creative output divided by input) will be improved by incorporating technology into the idea generation effort. To make significant advances in technology-assisted creative thinking, we will need vastly more sophisticated technologies, a more complete understanding of the brain processes related to discovery, and the ability to represent these processes with algorithms.

Initial attempts at using computers began more than a quarter of a century ago. Bradshaw et al. (1983) used computer simulation to study scientific discovery. Using measured data as input, they were able to infer the concept of specific heat and show that Black's law of temperature equilibrium was valid. Programs such as these were tested for their inductive reasoning capabilities. Computer simulation for discovery and creative thinking can only be as effective as the algorithms on which the programs are based, and current algorithms cannot accurately mimic human brain processes.

Computers could be a means of facilitating creativity in 2050. The creative efficiency of a brainstorming or synectic session depends in part on the ability of the facilitator. The role of the facilitator is to suggest ideas, encourage the group to identify add-on ideas, and even create a competitive environment that encourages subgroups to propose wilder ideas than other subgroups in the audience. The facilitator should be sufficiently glib that momentum can be recovered following lulls in idea generation. If computers are to fulfill the role of facilitators in 2050, they will need to have creative capabilities at least to the level of the participants.

Computers could act alone as facilitators or serve as a co-facilitator with a human. They could be very helpful in each of the facilitator tasks. For example, as computer programs become better representations of human emotional and cognitive processes, algorithms could be designed to act as idea thesauri. As those in the audience volunteer ideas, the computer could generate supplemental ideas, even new ideas. These could then motivate the audience to generate even more unique ideas. An idea thesaurus of the future would not be limited to a list of related words. The underlying algorithm could be designed to mimic the emotional processes of the human brain from which many wild-and-crazy ideas could be generated.

KNOWLEDGE PRODUCTION IN THE CREATIVE PROCESS

For now the creative process can be viewed as the series of mental activities that produce new knowledge. In each human and in each problem, the series of activities in creative discovery used may not be the same; however, based on different perceptions of the creative process, it seems reasonable to imagine the creative process as including the following activities: inspiration, preparation, illumination, and actualization. In each of the four activities, knowledge is produced. Table 33-1 summarizes the knowledge production for each part of the creative process and the way that computers of 2050 might influence knowledge production in each activity. The creative process is not considered complete unless new knowledge has been developed, communicated, and put into use.

It is instructive to compare the creative process with the steps of the noncreative mental process: observation, recollection, reasoning, and decision. In the observation step, facts are collected and observations made on the system. In the recollection step, past experience is reviewed and solutions to similar problems of the past are identified. Then the pros and cons of the possible decisions are identified and the implication of each alternative stated. In the decision step, the best alternative is selected. It is important to note that in the traditional approach new knowledge is not developed or communicated.

Table 33-1. Knowledge Production in the Creative Process

Step	Action	Role of Thinking Computers	Knowledge Production
Inspiration	• observation • analysis • problem identification	• recall, analyze, and incorporate past experiences • learn from experiences of others	Understand the problem
Preparation	• application of creative methods	• make remote connections • make multiple combinations and add-ons	List of alternatives/ideas
Illumination	• incubation • evaluation of ideas	• develop complex relationships • relate to inspiration	Insight into a workable solution
Actualization	• communicate • verification • finalize solution	• compose more effective communications • useful relationship	Creative knowledge production

ARTIFICIAL INTELLIGENCE

Artificial intelligence (AI) is the technological development that incorporates scientific and engineering principles into intelligent machines, especially computer programs that reflect human neurological processes. AI computer programs include problem-solving algorithms that include decision procedures. To the extent possible, the algorithms are supposed to reflect human problem-solving processes, but since the neurological processes that underlie human thinking and learning are not fully understood, the best currently available decision processes are used in the programs.

> *Computers could be programmed to mimic the emotional processes of the human brain from which many wild-and-crazy ideas could be generated.*

Creative idea generation is just one task for which AI programs can be designed and used. Some neurologists have predicted that by 2050 the processes of the human brain that are responsible for thinking will be known. With templates of human intelligence available, machines with creative thinking abilities may be capable of generating a wider array of ideas than could be produced by humans, as the computers should be able to function faster and have a greater storage capacity than the individual human brain. With the capacity to combine unrelated ideas, AI algorithms of 2050 should be able to more efficiently solve water resource problems that require political compromises, incorporate economic criteria, assess ecological consequences, and evaluate risk and uncertainties. The creative component of the AI machine will be responsible for forming unique alternative solutions and then evaluate each of them using the political, economic, ecological/environmental, and risk criteria.

According to the well known futurist, Ray Kurzweil, a growth in machine intelligence will occur over the next millennium (Pohl 2008). The synergism between human intelligence and machine intelligence should enable greater efficiency in solving the complex water problems of 2050. Machine intelligence at its highest level will have four properties (Tweedale et al. 2008): (1) autonomy – the ability to operate without direct human intervention; (2) social ability – the capacity to interact with humans or other machines; (3) reactivity – the ability to perceive its surroundings and be responsive to changes in it; and (4) pro-activeness – the ability to independently behave in a goal directed manner. For this partnership to achieve a level of success that goes beyond that achievable through human intelligence alone, the partners must be willing to rely on each other's strengths: communication, conceptualization, and intuition of the human and information accumulation, emotionless problem analysis, and solution evaluation of the machine (Pohl 2008). While rules of conduct may be built into the machine agent, the human-machine team will need to rely on the conscience of the human (Pitrat 2009) when making decisions where values are involved. The basic rules of conduct will be adequate to allow the artificial being to be creative, but as the rules of conduct become more complex, the machine will be capable of greater creativity.

PERSONALITY, EMOTIONS, AND CREATIVITY

Is the engineering personality a limitation to creative thinking? Personality studies suggest that engineers are practical, analytical, and nonemotional and their interests are centered on mechanical-technical matters (Florman 1976). This characterization does not imply that the engineering personality type cannot be creative. An engineer can be just as creative as an artist. However, a person who has the engineering personality can increase his or her creative efficiency by having broader divergent thinking skills and allowing psycho-physiological emotional arousal. Allowing the emotions to trigger and guide cognitive processes at times when creative solutions are necessary is central to divergent thinking. Divergent thinking skills include the ability to form uncommon associations, to structure original thoughts, and to propose new outcomes from seemingly unrelated facts. Divergent thinking skills are influenced by emotions. Since emotions can be controlled and improved (Ross 1972), someone who has the engineering personality type can become more creative by enhancing his or her constructive emotional capacity. Innovation is one of the basic principles of emotional intelligence (EI). EI is enhanced by increasing a risk-taking attitude with flexibility and decreasing self-criticism (Cherniss and Caplan 2001).

If the traditional personality characterization of the nonemotional engineer will be the personality of 2050 water engineers, then the 2050 water resources problems that require creative solutions are unlikely to be solved. The lower-order skill of synthesis and a difficulty in incorporating emotions can limit engineers' creativity. Emotions help people organize, motivate, and sustain behavior, each of which is important in idea creation. Therefore, increasing one's sensitivity to the emotions can broaden the person's creative ability.

The idea of emotion is difficult to define, but emotions very often play a major role in creative idea generation. The four fundamental elements of emotion are (McCuen and Shah 2007): (1) an arousal or behavior change occurs; (2) an internal physiological response happens; (3) the internal response is accompanied by an external change (e.g., altered facial expression); and (4) the emotion can act as a behavior motivator (e.g., scream). Each of these four elements occurs when a person is participating in a creative activity. For example, in a brainstorming session, the participants generally have a heightened arousal, a flow of adrenalin, a change in facial expression as an outward sign of seriousness, and a raising of the voice when responding.

If the algorithms built into the computers of 2050 are to be effective in developing creative solutions to problems, they will need to model both the emotive and cognitive processes of the human brain. Limiting the algorithms to just cognitive processes will result in computers that creatively function much like the person who has the engineering personality where the emotions are covert and barely used. To achieve the goal of incorporating emotive ability into computer algorithms will require greater understanding of the way that emotional learning occurs. Shrader

(1972) indicated that a person's creativity efficiency can be increased by knowing the psychological process.

Education plays a vital role in developing a person's emotive ability and, therefore, the potential for creative efficiency (Bugliarello 1969). Most engineering and science courses do not focus on emotions. Instead, the material emphasizes cognitive reasoning. Therefore, if creativity will be important to the water engineers of 2050, then engineering education will need to heed the philosophy of ASCE's Body of Knowledge (BOK; ASCE 2008). The BOK indicates that engineers need to develop a better appreciation of human behavior, the humanities, and the social sciences. It is this part of the engineering student's education where creative skills would be enhanced. Courses in fantasy literature, sculpture, art, and philosophy emphasize greater appreciation for the role of emotions in life decisions. Since education can direct one's attitudes, it is important that those engineers who will be practicing in 2050 develop the attitudes that promote creative thinking. An education based on the BOK philosophy is likely to achieve this end.

> *If computers of 2050 are to be effective in developing creative solutions to problems, they will need to model both the emotive and cognitive processes of the human brain.*

EDUCATION IN THE INTERIM

Innovation, a child of creative thinking, is beginning to gain a footing in engineering education. Very often, programs that stress innovation are focused on manufacturing rather than innovation as a general problem solving tool, but if creative thinking is to become a standard part of engineering education, then we may have to accept that the emphasis will be on "applied" creativity. This is not a bad direction, as we will need applied creative decision making as 2050 is approached. The general principles of creativity will need to be introduced into engineering programs, and students can get the applications through their general education courses.

Just as improvements in hardware and software will be necessary for computers to play a major role in problem solving, water resources education will need to incorporate more open-ended problem-solving activities at the expense of lectures. Open-ended projects provide more opportunity for and require more use of the creative process. Freshmen project courses and senior-level capstone are examples of such requirements. Undergraduate research is a good opportunity for the application of the creative process.

THE FUTURE

The current water problems of today are more pronounced than the problems of previous generations. We should expect the complexity of problems to increase as we approach 2050. Increases in populations and the greater concentration of people in urban centers will be a primary factor in increased complexity of issues and conflicts between stakeholders. Solving societal problems, conflicts, and complex issues in 2050 will benefit from multiple creativity paradigms. Computer-assisted approaches to creative thinking that are based only on storage and retrieval will not be sufficient to meet the demands of the problems. Technology-assisted creativity where the creative ability of the technology is at a higher level than human creativity will be necessary to provide the array of solution alternatives needed to meet the demands. Computers will serve as both facilitators and participants, but just as the creative process of each human is different, the creative capacity of each computer will be different and based on a unique creativity algorithm. Creative problem-solving will need to mature through several generations of change before 2050, with the creative capacity increasing with each generation.

The advancements in creative thinking needed to achieve a creative professional level by 2050 will require new research, changes in education, and most significantly changes in attitude. With respect to research, neuroscientists will need to uncover the mental processes related to creative thought. Greater understanding of the role of emotions and cognition, as well as their interaction, during creative thought will be necessary to improve human creativity and design the intelligent machines that will be involved in solving the water problems.

To enhance the use of creativity in decision processes, new decision processes will be needed. These processes will allow for human-computer interaction in making decisions, not just having the computer in a subservient role. Current decision methods underplay the role of emotions, as existing decision processes have an underlying cognitive basis. Current decision processes also are biased against the independence of idea generation and evaluation. This bias must be overcome for emotive/creative ideas to mature into realistic solutions to complex problems. Computers will also likely be more capable in generating a large number of alternative ideas than humans generally do, so the part of the decision process that involves the evaluation of alternatives will need greater emphasis. A lack of advancement in the process of decision making will hinder the use of creativity.

Changes in attitude will be necessary to allow creative thinking to play a major role in solving the complex water problems of 2050. First, the benefits of improved creativity must be recognized. The attitude that creative thinking is fun, but unnecessary to solve today's problems, needs to be replaced with the attitude that creative thinking is an essential problem-solving tool for water resources. Second, as previously indicated, water resources engineers will need to embrace intelligent, thinking computers as a partner in developing optimum solutions to critical problems. Third, the common belief that emotions are destructive forces will need to be overcome. Changes in attitude will only occur if educational programs support creative thinking as a legitimate skill. Creativity will need to be recognized as a fundamental element of leadership.

REFERENCES

ASCE (2008). *The ASCE body of knowledge*, 2nd ed. ASCE Press, Inc. Reston, VA.

Bradshaw, G. F., Langley, P. W., and Simon, H. A. (1983). "Studying scientific discovery by computer simulation." *Science*, 22 (4627), 971-975.

Bugliarello, G. (1969). "Developing creativity in an engineering science course – Socrates revisited." *Eng. Educ.*, 59 (3), 877-880.

Cherniss, C., and Caplan, R. D. (2001). "Implementing emotional intelligence programs in organizations." *The emotionally intelligent workplace*, C. Cherniss and D. Goleman, eds., Jossey-Bass, San Francisco, CA, 286-304.

Florman, S. C. (1976). *The existential pleasures of engineering*. St. Martin's Press, New York, NY.

Lumsdaine, E., and Lumsdaine, M. (1995). *Creative problem solving*, McGraw-Hill Book Co., New York, NY.

McCuen, R. H. and Shah, G. (2007). "Implications to ethics education of recent neuroscience research on emotions." *J. Leadership Studies*, 1(3), 44-56.

Pitrat, J. (2009). *Artificial beings: the conscience of a conscious machine*. John Wiley & Sons, Inc., New York, NY.

Pohl, J. (2008). "Cognitive elements of human decision making." *Intelligent decision making: an AI based approach*, G. Phillips-Wren, N. Ichalkaranje, and L. C. Jain, eds., Springer-Verlag, Berlin, Germany, 41-78.

Ross, S. D. (1972). *Moral decision: an introduction to ethics*, Freeman, Cooper & Company, San Francisco, CA.

Schrader, S. R. (1972). "Professional education: the need for creativity." *J. Prof. Activities*, 98 (PLI): 85-95.

Tweedale, J., Sioutis, C., Phillips-Wren, G., Ichalkaranje, N., Urlings, P., and Jain, L C. (2008). "Future directions: building a decision making framework using agent teams." *Intelligent decision-making: an AI-based approach*, G. Phillips-Wren, N. Ichalkaranje, and L. C. Jain, eds., Springer-Verlag, Berlin, Germany, 387-410.

AUTHOR INFORMATION

Richard H. McCuen is the Ben Dyer Professor of Civil and Environmental Engineering at the University of Maryland, College Park, where he has taught since 1971. He has authored many articles and books on mathematical modeling, probability and statistics, and their applications to engineering, hydrologic sciences and water resources management. He has a BS from Carnegie-Mellon University and MS and PhD from the Georgia Institute of Technology. Email: rhmccuen@eng.umd.edu

Chapter 34

Reflections from a Water Resources Modeler and Planner in 2050

William Werick

ABSTRACT

Impact simulation and multi-criteria decision-making models are used together to support water resources decision-making. This essay, in the form of a short story, forecasts advancement in decision support systems based on the intertwined social change and technical progression in chip technology and bioengineering. Decision support models are portrayed as necessary but insufficient to produce good water management solutions today because the decisions in a democracy are driven by political factors far outside the domain of the decision models. The essay imagines a future in which politics has co-opted decision support algorithms for its own purposes, and asks whether those of us dismayed at our current inability to implement good new decisions would be happy in a world where all decision factors were optimized.

"Politicians and conflicts are like horses and hay -
the results are the same."

INTRODUCTION

Predicting technological progress forty years into the future is riskier now than it was in 1400 or even 1900; the impact of technology seems now to change as the cube of change in time. Forty years ago I took a BASIC programming course as an elective for my mathematics degree. Computers had been around for 25 years, and by 1970, thousands of people were using them through remote terminals even while electro-mechanical calculators shook the desks they were bolted to as they performed exponential calculations. We were confident that in another 25 years the use of computers would be commonplace among mathematicians for numerical solutions; we did not guess that they would be as popular in the art department.

In 2009, I was part of a workshop put on by the US Army Corps of Engineers' Institute of Water Resources, Sandia National Labs, the US Institute for Environmental Conflict Resolution, and the US Environmental Protection Agency. The collective goal was to improve methods of computer assisted negotiations, including decision support systems, by identifying their weaknesses and focusing future work on those weaknesses. We asked a handful of luminaries to first imagine it was 2040 and that water management issues were resolved quickly with good solutions, and then to tell us what had changed since 2010 to make it possible. The answers (alluded to in the text that follows) expanded our perspective and I felt I had to apply that broader view here. So I wrote a short story in which the great-granddaughter of a pioneer in the use of computers to support water decisions communicates with her mother about an encounter with Mark Lorie, a young practitioner in 2010, who is concerned about the way decision support systems have evolved. The story format helped me apply the lesson from my BASIC days that progress is synergistic, and that the future of decision support is not in our hands but will develop organically, influenced by advances that carom around all fields of scientific inquiry and social change. And it allowed me to apply the insight from the 2009 workshop. I inverted it to create a concern in the mind of the septuagenarian Mark Lorie, but the point is that power will speak to us more than we speak to power.

THE TRANSMISSION

Dear Mother,

I am linking you because of a recent anomaly in my data. I saw a charming old man yesterday who spoke to me (and I mean he actually spoke, he used his larynx!) about things that no search reveals. He was anxious, and that made me worried, even a little about great-grandfather. In fact, had we been linking, his transmission would have been routed through Calibration. Now I wonder if I am infected and should come home, but I can't know because there is no protocol for sound wave transmissions and I'm hoping you remember, perhaps, something from when you were young? An earlier version? Any rules on how to correct sound wave data? I see you are receiving my transmission – that's a good sign, I'm probably OK. Tell you what, I'll link what he told me; if you block me – well, then that would certainly answer my question.

He said his name was Mark Lorie and that he was born in North America in 1975. He insisted on speaking, which was strange for me, not just sound coming from a face but also the awful slowness of it. If he had not been speaking about your grandfather, I would have gone to sleep. It took over ten minutes for him to describe his life, a long time no matter if you were alive in the last century! Here, I'll tell you my capture of what he said:

"May I sit down? Thank you. Do you mind if we speak? I am old and still prefer it. Good. Your address caught my eye. I knew your great-grandfather, when he was totally carbonic. No, totally, not even a Depcon receiver. Back when he piloted airplanes. Yes, I can tell you about those days but I'd ask you not to link while you listen. OK? Good – you'll find this interesting."

"When I first met Pete – that's what we called him - we all spoke. I mean, there was email if you were in two different places, yes, but if you were face to face, it would have been considered rude – silly! - to communicate electronically. And sometimes, you just had to have a conversation, so to share ideas we would actually have to go to the same place. Very inefficient! Conferences! It makes me laugh when I think of the old days. Parallel tracks, yet. Travel all that distance and then not even receive!"

"Anyway, Pete had come of age when computing was done on silicon wafers and, except for certain cosmetic enhancements, no one then thought of inserting silicon into our bodies. Pete was among the first to be enhanced, as we called it then, and it took courage – the insertion process was barbaric. They had to actually cut open his head and put a module in there. The modules were safe, they had tested them first on football players to be sure, but you have the images, these things were huge, the size of an almond, and until he had it replaced years later, you could see a noticeable bulge above his right ear. It was quite the status symbol then, we called them 'Goicoccheas' and it showed you were quite something if you had a lump over your ear. But I'm getting noisy, let me filter."

"When Pete was a kid, there were no computers, and certainly no cognitive enhancements, so if you could figure out a cube root in your head you were considered powerful, 'smart' we'd say. He was a smart one, and when he grew up he created these quaint uses, he was part of a movement, really, dabbling in new uses for computers, but of course, everything was crude and disconnected. I won't bore you with the stories your great-grandfather and his kind bored me with when I was your age – they loved to remember the 80 column cards, and the cardboard boxes they kept them in, and it was the letter 'O' not a zero, and 'I left the cards and came back the next morning ...' I said I would not bore you, so let me wake you by saying, there are things that are not in your data that you should know, that trouble me. This is why I asked you to not link, and if you wish to block, I would understand. No? Good, that's a kindness to an old man."

Mother, I'm pausing his stream now to say that I listened because I didn't have an algorithm for not listening. I felt anxious, though. OK, here is Mr. Lorie again.

"Pete was a true believer, a systems man I would call him then, and I was of that faith, too. We wanted to model real life, real decision-making, but we painted life as stick figures, abstractions of much more complex and elusive decisions. It was our great disappointment that we so rarely influenced decisions, and we hoped that as we learned to do our work better, we would someday re-shape the world with communal, rational analysis. Seeing you – I've wanted to know for a long time - is Pete happy with the way things unfolded, the influence of our machines? Well, yes, of course, you're happy. It's because – well, if you would tolerate just two minutes more of speaking. You are kind; I can see your great-grandfather's twinkle in your eye."

"Well, if our models were simple, at least they were broad. Many in our field - we both worked in water management – had been trained to think in the narrowest abstractions. We worked with lawyers, for example, who thought of water only as property, and hydraulic engineers for whom water was fluid, period, climatologists who equated climate with climate models. As children they must have been able to feel the whole life of water, they must have yearned like normal people to roast on a beach and then plunge into cooling waves. They must have listened to the sound of struggle in the centuries of great river songs – Volga Boatmen, Ol' Man River. But in the academies, narrow distillation was a mark of honor. The worst were - but I can see you are starting to sleep again, so let me just say that your grandfather's early labors were in what we called decision support. There! I see a spark in your eye! What? Oh, sorry, sometimes I spit a little when I speak, I'm out of practice. Well, forgive an old man and let me continue."

> **Well, if our models were simple, at least they were broad.**

"So we thought, and your great-grandfather was among the first, we thought we could model decisions with numbers, in a computer. IBM had invented display scopes in the 1950s and by the 1980s regular people had the scopes, we called them monitors for a while, and this allowed people to communicate with computers in a primitive way. Your great-grandfather and others - there was a man named Palmer, another was Hobbs, of course, the original Goicocchea - they were all cousins in this same early systems cult, and they made these stick drawing representations of decision-making. There was Iris and there was Stella, no, these were not women - we were engineers, after all. But the point is that these old ones imagined a decision as a product sum, scores for each possible decision in each category - the reasons or criteria - times the weight, and then added up for all the criteria. Some of us built system simulation models to provide the scores; others built multi-criteria decision-making models – MCDMs we said - to mix the scores and criteria weights to rank alternative decisions."

"But there was no applause. Normal people, singing 'Wade in the Water' on the beach, didn't relate. And yet now, our machines are so influential! That is the part –

can you still hear me? I don't want this transmission to be picked up by others, nor do I want to spit on you again, so tell me if – OK, good. You see, real decision-makers – politicians – once scorned them. It made us sad, but we were believers and we persevered. Had we not been so persistent we might not have had what we have now. So we are really partly responsible. This is what I want you to ask your great-grandfather about."

"I remember being so frustrated – why were our models not more influential? And we wanted to figure this out, so, of course, we held a conference. We flew to Denver in 2009 and I asked people, imagine it's 40 years from now and we have been successful, the world is using our models, water is managed wisely and conflicts are resolved expeditiously. I asked them to tell me, 'what happened?' And of course, the idea was that whatever we imagined had happened, we would then try to do that."

"The answers would surprise you, because so many, especially the political scientists, believed decision support systems would never influence how decisions were made. Real power is never given, they said. If a decision is important, then the outcome will be decided by self-interested power, limited, to some extent, by legal constraints - the Magna Carta and subsequent. Worse, they told us, politicians need conflict like horses need hay – it keeps them alive, but you know what horses make of hay. For a new man to get elected he has to show that the old one isn't addressing a big, important problem. Kennedy's missile gap!"

> *Politicians need conflict like horses need hay – it keeps them alive, but you know what horses make of hay.*

"Well, these pessimistic critics were guys like Bill Lord and Len Shabman and Doug Kenney, but the engineers, as we used to say, 'assumed friction was zero,' and they engaged the question, trying to imagine the technical improvements that would take place. But the weird thing was, we assumed that change would continue inside parallel tubes. We didn't imagine the organic cross connections. Like the early computer geniuses thought that one day there would be dozens of computers and they would be used to solve mathematical problems. Yes, we presumed chips would be a thousand times faster and would cost a hundred times less, we forecast that, but we still pictured the chips in little boxes and we were still typing and staring. And we figured we would still be modeling but the models would be really cool, with three-dimensional holograms and Dolby Surround that we could impress governors with. We never thought the governors would control the models."

"It's not like we couldn't have seen that advances in genetics would accelerate because of advances in computing. We had already seen that, but we just didn't imagine the new ways that would happen. If you time traveled to our conferences in 2009 – I know, I'm just saying if that were possible - and told us that in our lifetime our children would be born with carbon processors grown from the genetic instructions passed on from their parents...we would have listened, we might not have said it was impossible. But we wouldn't think about it after you left. Honestly?

We would have bet on flying cars before inherited processors. We just couldn't imagine the interplay of innovation."

"And the social acceptability? I didn't complain when they started implanting MCDMs in sex offenders. I mean, all the alternatives were worse – castration, solitary confinement, recidivism - so I took that first step with everyone else, and instead of child abuse we had a lot of reformed sex offenders who considered all the alternatives, weighed the probable consequences and got sick to their stomachs from their aversion secretions. And I supported offering career criminals a choice - imprisonment or MCDM – although many in our public meetings of old would have chosen prison. No, that's an old man's joke. But, really, we had imprisoned so many by then, it saved us a fortune! And if you supported MCDMs for prisoners, then why not give addicts that choice, and then what about drunk drivers? Decision support chips could rationally analyze blood alcohol levels and the expected values of the consequences, then trigger secretions that left the drinker disgusted at the idea of his social recklessness! And after drunk drivers, compulsive buyers, the tardy, fat people and then good women who loved bad men."

"After that came luxury brand chips with foreign languages and the ability to read music, and pretty soon the costs were subsidized with thought ads and then the dream ads! The machines were now so cheap every child outside of France had one! Am I spitting again? OK, sorry, I was getting carried away."

"So where was I? Oh, yes – well, the designers were creating MCDMs that were driven by self-interest – that's what sold advertising neurons. The 'Heartless Bastard' model was the biggest selling Carbon MCDM from 2028 to 2034, seven years straight, until the government stepped in to save the life insurance industry – I mean the deaths among non-productive dependent adults shot up 711% in two years, and the murderers, of course, had figured out all the angles and had eluded conviction. People were making decisions based on a personal benefit-cost ratio."

"And then Quinn Edwards ran for President on the promise to control these machines, to re-program them for collaboration. She was elected by a landslide and the legislation was signed in the first year of her presidency, perhaps a little too hastily. It fell to EPA to select the new criteria and weights, and of course, there was a lengthy review process, where all the lobbyists weighed in. We started with the civic duty criteria and kept moving until we got to the appropriate taste criteria, and what young parent would want a child without a processor, given the tax incentives and the tremendous difference in learning levels? I have tried to link to Pete to ask him what he thinks of all this optimization, but I have not been able to, not since the beginning of Edwards' fourth term as President."

Mother, that's enough of his capture. He was nicer than this diatribe would suggest. He had a kindly manner. And I tried to lift his depression, comparing our times to great-grandfather's time. The wars, the hoarding of riches by a few, the crime, the political arguments, the unending stream of imperfect movies and novels, the confusion about what to wear. I thought about it mother, and was more than 99% certain that I was happy, and am glad to hear that you feel within a percentage point of the same way.

But where exactly is great-grandfather?

Your loving daughter.

AUTHOR INFORMATION

Bill Werick is a water resources planner. He retired from the US Army Corps of Engineers in 2004 after serving in the Buffalo district until 1987, and subsequently at the Corps' Institute for Water Resources (IWR). At IWR he met visionaries like Gilbert White, Arthur Maass, Mike Fiering, Ted Schad, Jim Wallis, and Nick Matalas who were able to tell him the history of using computers to study water resources issues first hand. Most notably, Bill Whipple, a retired Corps General, described his trip to Princeton with two senior Corps officials in the early-1950s where John von Neumann convinced the Corps it could use computers to do hydraulic calculations. In the early 1990s Bill and Rick Palmer developed their shared vision planning approach and have since applied it around the world, including the recent and ongoing studies of the Great Lakes sponsored by the International Joint Commission. He is currently a director of the Great Lakes Observing System. E-mail: bill@werick.com

Chapter 35

Future Prospects for Water Management and Adaptation to Change

Eugene Z. Stakhiv

ABSTRACT

Successful long-term adaptation to a changing environment over the next 40 years by the water sector will require considerable luck on the geopolitical front, coupled with a focused program of technology transfer from sectors that will be changing: defense, homeland security, biotechnology and communications. By 2050, there will be a convergence of nanotechnology, biotechnology, information technology and neurotechnology that will drive innovation in the future, and will profoundly advance water resources availability through an acceleration of more efficient, resilient and robust adaptation mechanisms for the water sector. The water sector needs to be better organized to seek and incorporate technology transfer opportunities with other related sectors. Adaptation to changing environments over the next 40 years requires a much more focused enterprise, akin to a "Manhattan project." Near-term (i.e., between 2010 and 2030) adaptation solutions are needed to bridge the time until new technologies come on line. Another "Harvard Water Program"-type effort is needed to devise a set of planning and evaluation principles that fall under the general rubric of "robust decision-making," designed specifically to deal with infrastructure planning and management under climate change and uncertainty. Federal initiatives currently underway are developing guidelines for moving in that direction.

"Now that's what I call robust!"

INTRODUCTION

We are living in a changing world, and these changes are apparent in many sectors of our economy and in many ways we carry out our daily activities. These changes are brought on by the growth and shifts in human populations to urban areas, to different age distributions, and to different standards of living, and the consequent changes in land use and the spatial and temporal patterns of water consumption. These changes, plus the impacts of climate change (IPCC 2007), all affect our water resource systems. The effects can be both beneficial in some regions of the world and adverse in other regions. In both cases we must adapt to these changes. In this chapter I attempt to identify some of these major changes and impacts, discuss what is taking place today to adapt to them, especially by the US government, and finally offer my view of what the future may be like, or should be like, some 40 years from now in order to identify and motivate actions we should be taking today to prepare for that future.

PAST AND PRESENT ISSUES

For the past 50 years, the US has followed a path of what could be termed "autonomous adaptation" to variability and change, which has proved to be reasonably effective with respect to water resources management (Lettenmaier et al. 1999; Lins and Stakhiv 1998; Olsen et al. 1999). There have been very few failures of the nation's water management infrastructure – i.e., where the infrastructure failed before its design capacity was exceeded. It should be remembered that most of the nation's large water infrastructure projects (locks, dams, levees, irrigation canals and conveyance tunnels) were built between the 1930s through the 1970s, well before the era of sophisticated modeling, risk and reliability analysis and an adequate database existed for determining risk and uncertainty associated with climate variability. However, the structures still stand and have performed effectively through a wide range of unanticipated events. In other words, they have been remarkably robust and resilient.

Though the science of hydrology, hydraulic engineering, watershed modeling and data collection has improved dramatically since the 1970s, especially with the advent of satellite-based data, the dominant changes that influence the design of contemporary hydraulic structures since 1970 have come from the multi-objective planning paradigm rather than from changes in engineering design standards and criteria. The basic standards used for designing hydraulic infrastructure – notions like the probable maximum flood (PMF) for spillway design or application of a 100-year return period as the basis for traditional levee design and the flood insurance program – are based on years of engineering experience and empirical analysis.

Planning and evaluation principles in the US have changed dramatically during the past 50 years, influenced largely by the ideas of the Harvard Water Program (Maass et al. 1962), and implemented through the planning guidance of the US Water Resources Council (WRC 1973, 1983). The principal purpose of planning, though, was not to design reliable, robust and resilient hydraulic structures, but to implement projects and programs that served a more diverse range of social needs, and adequately accounted for the direct and indirect economic, social and environmental costs by optimizing net economic benefits subject to environmental constraints. Thus, operational reliability, robustness and resiliency of projects was actually reduced by eliminating a range of engineering safety factors that typically accounted for the hydrologic uncertainties and unknowns, and ignorance associated with a highly variable climate, poor models, and inadequate databases.

Ironically, the focus on risk and uncertainty analysis, together with multi-objective optimization effectively reduced much of the engineered redundancy of many projects that were based on the original standards-based paradigm. Furthermore, the addition of numerous other social, cultural, and ecological requirements and constraints, along with a host of new project purposes that were never authorized by legislation (recreation, ecological flows, floodplain benefits, etc.) actually reduced the degrees of freedom that operators had to manage in emergencies, and further decreased the robustness and resiliency of each water management infrastructure system. Ironically, but not surprisingly, these social, cultural, ecological requirements and constraints that are to enhance sustainability have reduced the flexibility of water managers to operate and prepare for uncertainties, contingencies and emergencies.

> *Various social, cultural, and ecological requirements and constraints intended to enhance sustainability have reduced the flexibility of water managers to operate and prepare for uncertainties, contingencies and emergencies.*

As was demonstrated by the devastation of hurricane Katrina, today's water management systems are not designed to protect against the full range of possible expected events that could occur in the future; they are designed to minimize the combination of risks and costs of a wide range of hazards to society. This risk-cost balance is constantly being adjusted by societies. For example, the US has safety standards for floods based on a 100-year return period that assumes a historically determined risk-cost optimum for our systems. Of course, as population density in urban areas increases, these standards may have to change and begin to approach the risk-averse standards of the Netherlands and Japan. The setting of new design standards and planning criteria are probably the most important aspects of any adaptation strategy. With America's wealth, technology and institutional resilience, most of the worst predictions of impacts on our water systems anticipated through 2050 can be overcome *even if the nation proceeds on its current unfocused path of water resources management and adaptation.* All impacts, that is, except for climate change impacts on natural ecosystems. Ecosystems may have to largely adapt on their own to climate change, though there are ways to ameliorate some of the worst anticipated impacts through ecological engineering.

If we are to effectively deal with the mostly unknown uncertainties of change, one of the paths that may have to be considered is a return to the prior era when water engineers recognized that there was a great deal of risk, uncertainty and unknowns, and accommodated for this ignorance in the way they designed structures. This was, *de facto*, an early and unacknowledged form of applying what today is known as the "precautionary principle." Engineers knew that there was persistence in the hydrologic record with trends and multi-decadal fluctuations, and they understood that there were events that were much larger and more extensive than the short measured hydrologic records. They planned for the unknowns by designing system redundancy and adding safety factors. So many projects have functioned under a much wider range of conditions and purposes than designed for because of this inherent understanding about risk and uncertainty. These systems have repeatedly been adapted to a broader range of needs and conditions by sequential reallocation of storage and changes of operating rules, reflecting more resilience and robustness than anticipated (Fiering 1982; Rogers and Fiering 1986).

The formal risk-analytical protocols promoted in conjunction with economic optimization principles and existing stringent economic decision rules can neither account for the "unknowns" of change, nor can they easily accommodate the "precautionary principle" – i.e., designing projects in such a way as to anticipate even highly uncertain changes. The discount rate used to justify the economic viability of water projects is a major factor in discounting the impacts of future events beyond a 20-year time horizon. When a relatively high discount rate (6-10%) is coupled with the traditional "expected annual damages" approach of flood or drought events, a "double discount dilemma" is imposed that effectively cancels out any real application of the "precautionary principle." Current economic evaluation procedures used by most major water management agencies would not cover anticipated climate change impacts beyond the year 2030.

Adaptive management principles – i.e., progressively learning and incrementally adjusting water management as one moves forward in time – is the paradigm that has been practiced by the water management community *de facto* under the rubric of what the Intergovernmental Panel on Climate Change terms "autonomous adaptation" (Stakhiv and Pietrowsky 2009). Adaptive management may be the most effective way of dealing with future change impacts under the current evaluation procedures and high degree of uncertainty. To effectively accommodate a new version of the "precautionary principle," together with the broader aims of "sustainable development," there will have to be a paradigm shift from the deterministic view embodied in the "Principles and Guidelines" of the WRC (1973, 1983) to a much more flexible set of multi-objective evaluation principles and procedures that more appropriately account for the full range of social, environmental and regional economic dimensions of water infrastructure under a wide range of uncertain climate scenarios. It may require an end to the era of rational analytic optimization to one where robustness and resiliency features are built into water projects. However, the fundamental changes must come in the economic evaluation principles that are used for project justification, e.g., changing decision rules from "maximize net benefits" to "minimize risk-cost." The process has already begun in many federal agencies in order to accommodate the uncertainties associated with planning and designing infrastructure under change uncertainty.

A VISION FOR 2050

While I cannot pretend to be able to predict what the future in the US will be like in 2050 and how that will impact our water systems, I can tell you what I would like, and expect, to see when that time comes. On a more global scale, I would hope to see in 2050 considerably less social, political and economic instability, especially in the currently volatile regions of the Middle East, sub-Saharan Africa, Central Asia and southeast Asia, and the recognition that this happened, in part, because of the successful implementation of improved water management systems that have reduced to a large extent the poverty in those regions.

> *Sustainable development may require an end to the era of rational analytic optimization to one where robustness and resiliency features are built into water projects.*

What I expect to see by 2050 in the US are dramatic improvements in a wide range of existing tools and techniques centering on weather and climate forecasts and human behavior. I expect to see the water management community using greatly improved reliability in short-term, seasonal and intra- and inter-annual forecasts of all the basic climate characteristics of importance to reservoir management and agriculture. Nanotechnology and materials science breakthroughs make it possible to achieve a high degree of wastewater recycling and water conservation and cheaper membranes for desalinization. Furthermore, just as each household has its own self-contained heating and cooling systems, I expect that each home in 2050 will have their own treatment and recycling water units, with a dual pipe water system for drinking water and "gray water" for outdoor uses, all powered by solar and non-fossil fuel energy. Water management and large-scale storage and distribution and conveyance systems will be used to sustain critical aquatic ecosystems that are threatened by climate change and aridity in the southwestern regions of the US.

Energy will be relatively inexpensive because of advances in renewable energy sources (wind, solar and fusion energy), and desalting technology will be relatively inexpensive and provide most of the water supply for major coastal cities. The water supply systems of the US will be much more interconnected, so that sharing of water supplies and shortages will be more common and increase the overall robustness and resiliency of existing systems. Desalinized groundwater sources and irrigation return flows will be serving basic agricultural needs in arid regions.

GETTING TO 2050

The conventional contemporary water management wisdom or philosophy is that water resources cannot be managed effectively without several key components in place that are necessary but not sufficient prerequisites for integrated water resources management (IWRM). These are:

- National water policy that lays out roles, responsibilities and management objectives.
- National/regional/river basin water management plans that are consistent with national water policies.
- River basin commissions that implement and manage resources for entire watersheds according to plans that are updated periodically.
- Enabling regulatory and institutional regime, with enforcement mechanisms.
- Coordinated federal/state/local management.

The irony is that the US, which has most vigorously developed and promoted the IWRM paradigm for developing nations through its foreign aid programs and involvement in the World Bank and USAID, itself falls far short of applying these principles domestically. The reason is that the key aspect of what makes water management work effectively is the enabling institutional (legal, regulatory, and organizational mechanisms) environment and something that has often been left off the list – technological development and financing. Developing nations lack all three key prerequisites (financing, regulation and technology). The US has a very strong institutional infrastructure based on a federal system of distributed responsibilities, or the equivalent of the "subsidiarity" principle of governance. This system has been relatively successful by working from the bottom up through a broad framework of federally-based resource management and environmental protection regulations that are effectively enforced at the state and local levels. This includes federal subsidies and financing of projects that meet stringent technical, social, environmental and economic criteria, with a robust system of technological innovation and application.

Hence, there is a dual system of water infrastructure planning in the US that obviates the need for a highly coordinated vertical system of IWRM, although, in principle, it is still desirable to have a fully integrated system. The planning and design of federally sponsored projects, whether directly planned by the federal agencies or as a consequence of cost-shared grants to local entities (e.g., stormwater sewers, treatment plants, highway culverts, etc.) all reflect the accumulation of federal laws and regulations that represent an integration of resource management and environmental protection laws. The added fundamental factor is that the planning of federal projects serves as the most effective means for technology transfer and changes in standards and criteria. Federal agencies also regulate local public and private sector development through a variety of regulatory agencies and a plethora of water quality, floodplains, land use, and watershed and coastal zone management regulations and grant programs.

All of these agencies, regulations and programs are potential instruments for more rapid technology transfer. Technological innovation has to become an even more important component of future adaptation, and the pace of application of numerous technologies developed for other purposes needs to accelerate in the water sector. For example, the cell phone alone can be a ubiquitous tool for addressing many of the world's important water management problems. Already, mobile phone penetration throughout the world is expected to reach 75% by 2012. Imagine a network of cell phone-sized, hand-held environmental sensing devices for climatology, soil moisture and chemistry, water quality, streamflow, etc. that continuously transmits data via satellite linkages to data processing and modeling centers. These centers would monitor evolving storms and continuously update forecasts for communities downwind or downstream. Every remote village could be linked to an information center providing the following services:

- Best time for planting and harvesting various crops based on highly reliable short-term forecasts
- Hourly soil moisture and precipitation forecasts
- Commodity prices and options for crops best suited for forthcoming forecasted conditions (1-, 3-, 6-month forecasts)
- Real-time information on rainfall intensity, and accurate 5-, 10-, 30- day forecasts of rainfall, drought, etc.
- Specific alerts for storms, hail, tornados, and frost conditions

This should all be possible because of rapid advances in satellite-based global environmental monitoring. This monitoring, coupled with greatly improved models for forecasting conditions, will revolutionize farm-based agricultural practices, thereby reducing water demands in the future while increasing yields.

Oddly enough, most of our modern technological advances have come about from the "military-industrial complex" – the need to build better and smarter weapons to fight smarter wars (Friedman 2009). This includes the US space program, whose origins and major purpose was, and is, for defense (and offense). The Defense Advanced Research Projects Agency (DARPA) is a major creative technological enterprise, responsible for many modern innovations, including the Internet. Because the US is likely to be engaged in a perpetual state of warfare over the next 40 years, with ever-increasing demands for "smart" systems to provide the technological edge that will help the US in waging some form of warfare against an elusive and dispersed enemy, we can expect continued acceleration of technologies that will have direct application to water and natural resources management. The key will be to find a way to bridge the vast gap in technology transfer between those developments, and useful applications in the water sector.

> *The potential benefits to water resources management from advances in the space program are enormous.*

The near-term (10-20 years) potential benefits to water resources management from advances in the space program are enormous. But it's more than a matter of better sensors and more satellites. There need to be corresponding improvements in ground-based monitoring networks, and an integration of knowledge from all sources, including complementary airborne monitoring systems in order to improve water resources management, according to the US National Research Council (NRC 2007, 2008). Though the science agencies (NOAA, NASA, USGS, NSF) are working relatively closely together to realize these possibilities, there needs to be more engagement of the resource management agencies, and funding of joint pilot studies so the technologies are transferred more quickly to the entities responsible for decision-making. An ancillary development that would be required to enhance space-based analysis is a substantial upgrading of the cyber-infrastructure that would be required for more effective and quicker implementation of those advances. The most immediate payoff would be for improving real-time reservoir management, and management of large water-based ecosystems. The US Army Corps of Engineers, for example, already has instituted a comprehensive real-time reservoir management system in every Corps District (CWMS- Civil Works Water Management System). All that is lacking is reliable real-time information.

Current Trends
What are the basic trends that are most likely to affect the technological acceleration that will revolutionize water management? There is already occurring a convergence of several different lines of technology that will transform economics and society more profoundly and rapidly than ever before. Nanotechnology, biotechnology, infotechnology and neurotechnology are the converging technologies that will be melded to accelerate innovations in many different fields (Canton 2006). Biotechnology alone has the greatest potential for enhancing farm yields and feeding the world while using water that is currently unfit for irrigation use. Think of the rapidity of recent technological advances, and their impact on medicine, communications and energy production. These advances will increase and multiply exponentially, with applications ultimately finding their way, by about 2025, into water resources management in three of the biggest water use arenas: agriculture, municipal and industrial water supply and wastewater treatment.

The confluence of main technological trends and advances that are likely to benefit rapid and effective adaptation of the water sector to change are:

- Cybernetics, artificial intelligence and instantaneous information technology (smarter internet)
- Nanotechnology
- Cost-effective energy technology (solar, space-based energy, algae as fuel)
- Biotechnology (genetic engineering) to help feed the populace and save endangered species
- Space-based environmental monitoring systems and instantaneous feedback to predictive models even to remote areas of the globe
- Geoengineering to reverse global warming (e.g., giant reflectors in orbit; greening deserts; iron fertilization of the sea; aerosols in the stratosphere)
- Effective, reliable prediction of most weather and climate events
- Renewable energy replacing fossil fuel entirely – low carbon societies
- Desalinization (in conjunction with cheap fusion energy) becoming cost-effective and providing water for most large coastal urban areas and megacities

- Vastly improved sanitation and wastewater treatment technologies and recycling
- Biotech approaches to pest control for improved agricultural yields
- Ecological engineering to preserve habitats, reverse species extinctions and combat invasive species
- A wide array of "on-farm" agricultural management technologies that will increase yields and decrease pollution and water use

Algae are likely to become the surprising choice for future biofuel production. Not only can it provide a surprisingly high concentration of lipids, but it can fix a great deal of carbon dioxide. Furthermore, algae can be used to treat wastewater, while producing biofuels such as biodiesel, ethanol, biogas, and hydrogen. Organic waste from about 1,200 dairy cows, 5,000 pigs or 30,000 people would supply nutrients for 10 hectares (25 acres) of algae ponds. Approximately 65,000 liters per hectare (7,000 gallons per acre) of oil per year could be produced from algae ponds (McIntyre 2009). About 4,000 hectares (10,000 acres) of algal ponds would be required to remove the CO_2 released while producing biofuels with a 500 MW coal-fired power plant.

Imagine a simple technology for future energy that requires only three elements: sun, saltwater and algae. Algae are lipids, comprising 30-60% oil. Halophytic algae, cultivated correctly, could ameliorate the world's food and energy shortages. There exist more than 10,000 natural halophyte plant species, and some 250 of those are usable as staple food crops. A great deal more fuel per hectare can be obtained with algae than with ethanol crops like corn, and halophytes can be used as a petrochemical to make plastic or as a feedstock for animals. Currently the Chinese are producing genetically modified corn and rice that grow in saltwater marshes. Imagine instead of growing corn or rice, turning the Great Salt Lake into a giant algae pond that could produce up to $250B/yr of biofuels! Many deserts are near coasts and much of the irrigated return flows are saline in arid and semiarid areas. This water typically is diverted to the desert, and evaporates. If we could divert a portion of the Mediterranean's seawater to the Sahara Desert, irrigate it and grow algal biomass, one could conceive of replacing all the fossil carbon fuel that we currently use today. These ideas have been developed not by water resources specialists or agronomists, but scientists working for NASA (Bushnell 2009) who are exploring unconventional methods for human survival in hostile environments on different planets.

Robust Decision-Making
Even before the suite of emerging technologies start kicking in sometime about 2025, there are many improvements in existing conventional approaches that fall under the general rubric of "robust decision-making" (RDM). RDM is a framework for making decisions with a large number of highly imperfect forecasts of the future. RDM relies on many plausible futures (e.g., climate change models, historic information, tree-ring data, etc.), and then allows analysts and decision-makers to identify a series of near-term and long-term actions (options) that are robust across a very wide range of futures. Rather than rely exclusively on a single future or a probabilistic forecast of a possible future, the approach asks what can be done today to set the stage and shape a

more desirable future (Lempert et al. 2010). The strategy has three complementary components:

1. Seeking robust rather than optimal projects or strategies, which requires a substantial revision of current economic and optimization decision rules routinely used in water resources management
2. Employing adaptive strategies to achieve robustness such that near-term strategies are explicitly designed with the expectation that they will be revised as better information becomes available
3. Using computer-aided analysis for interactive exploration of hypotheses, options and possibilities

A practical version of RDM has been developed by water resources planners in the US Army Corps of Engineers and applied successfully under the label of "Shared Vision Planning" (Werick and Palmer 2008). It has been used most directly for change adaptation in two Great Lakes regulation studies for the Lake Ontario-St. Lawrence system (ILOSL 2006) and the Upper Great Lakes (IUGLS 2009). And it addresses the more flexible evaluation and decision-making approach of *satisficing and systematic analysis* advocated by Rogers and Fiering (1986). Before RDM can be used more routinely and across many federal agencies, the basic economic evaluation framework that underpins all water resources planning must be adjusted as well. Steps are being taken in that direction by two ongoing federal interagency efforts initiated and led by the White House. The first is the Council on Environmental Quality's (CEQ) Interagency Climate Adaptation Task Force and the second related initiative is the proposed revisions to the "Principles and Guidelines" (WRC 1983) for water resources planning, also led by CEQ. These new guidelines will require all agencies to apply the guidelines in a comparable and consistent manner.

CONCLUSIONS

There is reason to believe that there will be a quantum leap in technology that will greatly change the way water is managed and developed in the future. In water operations alone, there will be a quantum leap in much improved availability and use of resources in terms of operating existing infrastructure more efficiently. Future water development, coupled with technological adaptations, will add to the resources base. Population will likely stabilize at about 9 billion by 2050 according to a UN forecast, so there is reason to be hopeful about the future, despite the unknowns of global warming. For the near-term, there are rapid changes occurring in the manner in which water is being managed and biotechnology is being infused into the agricultural sector so that crops yields should keep pace with expanding populations through 2050.

REFERENCES

Bushnell, D. (2009). "Algae: a panacea crop?" *The Futurist,* 43(2), 29.

Canton, J. (2006). *The extreme future: the top ten trends that will reshape the world for the next 5, 10, and 20 years*, Dutton, New York, NY, 371 p.

Fiering, M. B. (1982). "Estimating resilience by canonical analysis." *Water Resour. Res.*, 18 (1), 51-57.

Friedman, G. (2009). *The next 100 years: a forecast for the 21st century*, Doubleday, New York, NY, 253 p.

Intergovernmental Panel on Climate Change (IPCC). (2007). *Climate change 2007: synthesis report. Contribution of working groups I, II and III to the fourth assessment report of the Intergovernmental Panel on Climate Change.* [Core Writing Team, Pauchauri, R. K., and Reisinger, A. (eds.)]. IPCC, Geneva, Switzerland, 104 p, <http://www.ipcc.ch/publications_and_data/publications_ipcc_fourth_assessment_report_synthesis_report.htm> (Oct, 2010).

International Lake Ontario-St. Lawrence River Study Board (ILOSL). (2006). *Options for managing Lake Ontario and St. Lawrence River water levels and flows*, Final report, International Joint Commission, Washington, DC, and Ottawa, Canada, 146 p.

International Upper Great Lakes Study Board (IUGLS). (2009). *The formulation and evaluation of Lake Superior regulation plans for the international upper Great Lakes levels study: a strategy document for IPR review*, International Joint Commission, Washington, DC, and Ottawa, Canada.

Lempert, R., Popper, S., and Banks, S. (2010). "Robust decision making: coping with uncertainty." *The Futurist*, 44(1), 47-48.

Lettenmaier, D. P., Wood, A. W., Palmer, R. N., Wood, E. F., and Stakhiv, E. Z. (1999). "Water resources implications of global warming: a U.S. regional perspective." Climatic Change, 43, 537-579.

Lins, H., and Stakhiv, E. (1998). "Managing the nation's water in a changing climate." *J. Am. Water Resour. As.*, 34 (6), 1255-64.

Maass, A., Hufschmidt, M. M., Dorfman, R., Thomas, Jr., H. A., Marglin, S. A., and Fair, G. M. (1962). *Design of water resources systems*, Harvard University Press, Cambridge, MA.

McIntyre, R. (2009). "Algae's powerful future." *The Futurist,* 43(2), 25-32.

National Research Council (NRC). (2007). *Earth science and applications from space: national imperatives for the next decade and beyond*, National Academies Press, Washington, DC.

National Research Council (NRC). (2008). *Integrating multiscale observations of U.S. waters*, National Academies Press, Washington, DC, 198 p.

Olsen, J. R., Stedinger, J. R., Matalas, N. C., and Stakhiv, E. Z. (1999). "Climate variability and flood frequency estimation for the upper Mississippi and lower Missouri Rivers." *J. Am. Water Resour. As.*, 35 (6), 1509-23.

Rogers, P., and Fiering, M. (1986). "Use of systems analysis in water management." *Water Resour. Res.*, 22(9), 146S-148S.

Stakhiv, E., and Pietrowsky, R. (2009). *Adapting to climate change in water resources and water services,* Perspectives on climate and water resources, no. 15, World Water Council, Marseilles, 12 p.

US Water Resources Council (WRC). (1973). *Water and related land resources: establishment of principles and standards for planning*, Federal Register, 36 R24778, September 10.

US Water Resources Council (WRC). (1983). *Economics and environmental principles and guidelines for water and related land resources implementation studies*, US Government Printing Office, Washington, DC.

Werick, W., and Palmer, R. (2008). "It's time for standards of practice in water resources planning." *J. Water Res. Planning and Management.-ASCE*, 134 (1), 1-2.

AUTHOR INFORMATION

Eugene Stakhiv has spent his entire professional career of 37 years with the US Army Corps of Engineers, and has served as study manager for several large river basin studies and metropolitan water supply studies in the US. Dr. Stakhiv has extensive international experience, primarily with the World Bank, serving as senior advisor to the water Ministries of Iraq, Bangladesh, Ukraine, Armenia and the Aral Sea Basin countries, and as Science Attaché to the US Ambassador to UNESCO. He has authored over 100 papers, and 150 technical reports. He earned a PhD in Water Resource Systems Engineering from the John Hopkins University. Email: Eugene.Z.Stakhiv@usace.army.mil

Chapter 36

Water Resource Management Modeling in 2050

Daniel P. Loucks

ABSTRACT

Water resources development projects inevitably have economic, environmental and social impacts. Impact prediction using computer modeling is a major activity of water resources systems planning and management today and will be no less so in 2050. Computer-based optimization and simulation models incorporated within interactive graphics-audio based decision support systems will continue to help us identify those plans, designs and policies that maximize the desired impacts and minimize the undesired ones as well as making clearer the tradeoffs between the two. By 2050 participants using these decision support systems should be able to embed themselves within and interact with these systems that provide a dynamic virtual reality environment in ways that facilitate and enhance the political process of planning and decision-making as well as provide the desired physical, socio-economic, environmental, ecological information.

INTRODUCTION

When design and management decisions are made about environmental and water resource systems, they are based on what the decision-makers believe, or perhaps hope, will take place as a result of their decisions. These predictions are based on very qualitative information and beliefs and on quantitative information provided by measured data and mathematical computer-based models. Today computer-based quantitative modeling is used to enhance mental models. These mathematical models are considered essential for carrying out economic, environmental, and social impact assessments. Mathematical simulation and optimization models packaged within interactive computer programs, together with judgment, provide a common way for planners and managers to predict the behavior or performance of any proposed water resources system development plan, design and/or management policy. Having some idea of the impacts of any plan, design and policy before irreversible commitments are made not only saves money (often a considerable amount of money), but also helps reduce, if not prevent, unwanted adverse environmental, social and political consequences as well.

It is hard to imagine any major water resources planning and management activity taking place in the world today without involving the application of computer databases coupled to some form of optimization and/or simulation modeling. Anyone associated with water resources planning and management today is surely being exposed to, and possibly assisted by, the use of computer models. The same will be true in 2050, but those models will be adapted to computer technologies not even imagined today. I'm going to try to imagine that future, realizing I will probably never know how far off the mark I was by the time 2050 occurs.

> *Anyone associated with water resources planning and management today is surely being exposed to, and possibly assisted by, the use of computer models.*

The past fifty years have witnessed what we consider major advances in our abilities to model the engineering, economical, ecological, hydrologic and sometimes even the institutional or political components of large, complex, multipurpose water resources systems. Applications of models to real systems have improved our understanding and hence have often contributed to improved system design, management and operation. They have also taught us how limited our modeling methods and skills remain in comparison to the multiple interdependent physical, biochemical, ecological, social, legal and political (human) processes that govern the performance of water resource systems. These processes are affected by uncertainties in things we can measure, such as water flows, volumes, constituent concentrations and demands. They are also affected by the unpredictable actions of individuals and institutions that are affected by what they get or do not get from the management and operation of such systems, as well as by other events having nothing directly to do with water.

Developing models of water systems is an art as well as a science. It requires knowledge of the system being modeled, the client's objectives, and goals and information needs (which are often changing), and also some analytical and programming skills. Models are always based on assumptions or approximations, and some of these may be at issue because of differences in opinion among model users. Applying these approximations of reality in ways that improve understanding and eventually lead to better decisions clearly requires not only modeling skills, but also the ability to communicate effectively.

The models we build to guide us in water resources systems planning and management produce information. They inform decision-makers; they do not produce decisions. With few exceptions (e.g., the closing of the Rotterdam gate to prevent flooding), I believe this will be true in 2050 as it is today. Computer-based modeling is not going to take the place of humans. What computer modeling analyses tell us may be ignored by those who requested such analyses. To know, for example, that there are less expensive alternatives than forcing every wastewater treatment plant to produce drinkable effluent that gets discharged into dirtier water bodies, or that cloud seeding may, on average, reduce the strength of hurricanes over a large region does not mean that cheaper treatment strategies or that such cloud-seeding activities should be undertaken. Managers or operators may know that not everyone will benefit from decisions they may make to say, save money or reduce damages, and those whose net benefits, however measured, are reduced will likely scream louder than those who gain. In addition, decision-makers may feel safer with inaction than action (Shapiro 1990; Simon 1998). There is a strong feeling in many cultures and legal systems that failure to act (nonfeasance) is more acceptable than acts that fail (misfeasance or malfeasance). We all feel greater responsibility for what we do (the sins of commission) than for what we do not do (the sins of omission).

However, our aversion to risk should not deter us from addressing sensitive issues in our models and communicating the results to those responsible for decision-making. Modeling efforts should be driven by the need for information and improved understanding. It is that improved understanding (not improved models *per se*) that may eventually lead to improved system design, management and/or operation. Models used to inform or aid water resources planners and managers are not intended to be, and rarely are (if ever), adequate to replace their judgment. This we have learned, if nothing else, in over fifty years of computer-based modeling experience. And I think it will be the case in the next 40 years, even though our modeling and communication capabilities will be much greater than they are today.

The remainder of this chapter presents a brief example to demonstrate how models can be used to address water management issues. Then some general thoughts on the major challenges facing water resources systems planners and managers are offered together with how those challenges might be met over the next four decades with the help of technology that has yet to be developed. We humans will certainly not evolve as fast as our technology, and it is the social-political aspects of decision-making that will continue to constrain and guide us and that will dictate what modelers or analysts must accomplish to provide the right amount and quality of information at the right time to those who can benefit from it. This chapter concludes with a discussion of the impact new computer technology will surely have on the development and use of models for water resources planning and management by 2050.

A VISION OF MODELING IN 2050

What I would like to see in 2050 is the ability of each of us to enter and interact with a virtual environment of what we are modeling. First of all we should be able to tell our computers, maybe even orally, what our planning and management problems or goals are and from that, and maybe after some additional vocal dialogue between the computer system and us, it should be able to automatically call upon all the associated databases of all the needed disciplines and create a virtual environment that we can enter and manipulate to learn what is best to do, for example, to enhance the welfare of shellfish and fish impacted by excessive nutrient concentrations in an estuary and at the same time mitigate against any hardship of the upstream farmers and residents that are the sources of the nutrients.

These options for displaying data, whether historic, obtained from environmental sensors, or the results of modeling, will be in 3-D on Google Earth's world-wide geographic database. This database will be a very high resolution one obtained, in part, from cameras that can take and process over one million pictures of the earth's geosphere, biosphere and cultural features per second and, again in part, from digitizing and assimilating the world's published literature, all resulting in a massive amount of spatially and temporally indexed physical, environmental, ecologic, economic, and social data needed for practically anyone's analyses. In 2050 we can look back and be amused at just how crude 2010's technology and databases were for creating tools we called decision support systems that could, and indeed did, help achieve shared visions among stakeholders.

> *In 2050 each of us should be able to enter and interact with a virtual environment of the system we are modeling.*

What I can't see in 2050, and what I really do not want to see then as I look up or down from where I'll be, is our ability to model and predict individual human behavior. I (unlike Simon (1998)) don't believe it is or will be possible, and it is a good thing it isn't. If we could predict human behavior it would be a boring world. We need surprises. We need the challenges of adapting to these surprises. We need to have reasons to keep learning, and among other things, keep improving our new "modeling" abilities to better understand and manage the physical, biological, social-economic and geopolitical world we live in. My virtual reality vision involves humans and their interactions among themselves and with the world's data and models. It does not see models substituting for humans when used for informing or even making planning and management decisions.

CHALLENGES ON THE ROAD TO 2050

Planners and managers of water resources systems will continue to be responsible for solving particular water-related problems or meeting special water resources needs. When they fail, they will hear about it. The public will let them know. What will continue to make their job particularly challenging is that the public will still consist of individuals with different needs and expectations. Furthermore, institutions where water resources planners and managers work (or hire consultants to work for them) will be like most institutions these days: they must do what they can with limited financial and human resources and authorities. Their clients will be everyone who uses water, or at least who are affected by the decisions they make when managing water.

The overall objective of these planners and managers and their institutions will be to continue to provide a service, such as a reliable supply of water, an assurance of water quality, the production of hydropower, protection from floods, the provision of commercial navigation and recreational opportunities, the preservation of wildlife and enhancement of ecosystems, or some combination of these or other purposes. Furthermore they will continue to be expected to do this at a cost no greater than what people are willing to pay. Meeting these goals (i.e., keeping everyone happy) will not get any easier if indeed it will be even possible. Simple or even sophisticated technical measures or procedures will not necessarily ensure a successful solution to any particular set of water resources management problems, at least not the types of interesting and complex problems of concern to so many who have insufficient water for even drinking and sanitation as exist today.

Everyone who has had any exposure to water resources planning and management knows that one cannot design or operate a water resources system without making compromises. In 2050 these compromises will continue to be over competing purposes (such as hydropower and flood control) or competing objectives (such as environmental enhancement versus economic efficiency, or who benefits and who pays, and by how much and where and when). After analysts with their models identify possible ways of achieving various objectives and provide estimates of associated economic, environmental, ecological and social impacts, it is the planners and managers who have the more difficult job. They have to decide what to do. This is true today and I predict it will be also true in 2050.

Planning and managing involves developing among all interested and influential individuals an understanding and consensus that legitimizes the decisions and enhances their successful implementation. Water resources planning and managing are processes that will continue to take place in a social or political environment. They involve leadership and communication among people and institutions, and the skills required are learned from working with people, not with computers or models. Moving an organization or institution into action to achieve specific goals involves a number of activities, including goal-setting, debating, coordinating, motivating, deciding, implementing and monitoring. Many of these activities must be done simultaneously and continuously, especially as conditions (objectives, water supplies, water demands, financial budgets) change over time.

These activities create a number of challenges that are relevant to modelers or analysts. They include how to identify creative alternatives for solving problems, finding out what each interest group wants to know in order to reach an understanding of the issues and a consensus on what to do, and developing and using modeling and computer technology to facilitate this "shared vision or understanding" among all stakeholders. By 2050 we will surely have a technology that far exceeds what today's analysts have available and can use to contribute to this stakeholder participatory process. Even if it includes being able to witness in virtual reality alternative model solutions that identify all associated impacts, the challenge will remain of incorporating all this into the largely political planning and management process so that everyone can effectively contribute to that largely qualitative socio-political processes. Research and development in this social science area coupled with improved technology is sorely needed if we are going to achieve an effective use of this new modeling environment and technology by 2050.

> *Regardless of available technology in 2050, water resources planning and managing will continue to take place in a social or political environment, i.e., an environment dominated by humans and their institutions*

This challenge underscores the continuing need for improved communication among the analysts, system planners, managers and operators, and policy-makers. Objectives stated at one point in time often change over time. Even those individuals participating as analysts and stakeholders may change over the course of a decision-making process. Communication should be made easier and more effective in this virtual environment that technology can provide, and we need to work towards making it happen. This virtual environment must include all interested stakeholders and decision-makers throughout the decision-making process in an effort to indeed achieve a shared vision of not only how a system works, but also how it should be developed and managed.

Over the next 40 years increasing developments in computer technology will motivate the concurrent development of an impressive set of new models, modeling methods and computer software that will improve our ability to identify creative alternative solutions to problems as well as facilitate interaction and communication between the analysts or modelers and their clients. Maybe we won't be talking to each other within interactive hologram environments (or maybe we will), but in any event these new technological developments in modeling and computer hardware and software will give planners and managers improved opportunities to increase their understanding of their real (not just modeled) water resources systems and at the same time reduce the costs of modeling.

Even if we have and can use virtual reality to our advantage, and as impressive as that may be, we should continue to have a healthy skepticism about what we see, hear, and read in such computer-generated environments, especially concerning what might happen in the future. If we are looking into the future via computer technology or crystal balls, we must admit that many of our assumptions, such as parameter values, cannot even be calibrated, let alone validated. Changes in our land cover and uses and climate make us question the use of what has traditionally been a backbone of all hydrologic modeling, the historical record. Our conclusions or estimates can be very sensitive to those assumptions. One of our major challenges is to deal with this so-called deep or severe uncertainty (where often we don't even know what we are uncertain about) and to communicate this uncertainty in understandable ways to those who ask about the uncertainty of our model predictions.

If there is truth in the expression "decision-makers don't know what they want until they know what they can get," how do modelers know what decision-makers will need before even they do? Obviously modelers cannot know this. Over the last two decades or so this challenge has been addressed by developing and implementing decision support systems (DSSs) (Fedra 1992; Georgakakos and Martin 1996; Jakeman et al. 2008; Loucks and da Costa 1991). It has not always been easy to involve all concerned stakeholders in the DSS development process in a way that they feel ownership and trust the model and software. Will it be any easier in the future if these DSSs are extended to include virtual environments? Maybe so, and maybe not, but the ability to interact with that (computer-generated) environment should and must foster trust and faith in the environment's responses. While there may be no agreement on the best of various assumptions to make, or objectives to achieve, stakeholders can learn by witnessing in this simulated 3D environment which of those assumptions matter and which do not for each considered objective. In addition, just the process of interacting in this virtual environment by stakeholders will create discussions among stakeholders that can lead toward a better understanding of everyone's interests and concerns and just maybe to more widely acceptable decisions.

The year 2050 may not be that far away for those needing to make informed decisions about parts of our environment that could be better understood by witnessing and reacting to them within a virtual hologram environment. Consider for example the possible increase in temperatures in parts of Asia due to carbon emissions and how it could impact millions, if not billions, of people. In my visualized virtual environment you could travel in real time to where you could witness about 12 million people and assets worth over 2 trillion dollars being exposed to coastal flooding from sea level rise, and other regions being flooded due to much higher frequencies and amounts of rainfall. These regions have been painted red, an indication of the possible devastation. In other regions agricultural production is dropping due to ozone levels that interfere with plant photosynthesis. You could see large areas colored light brown showing increased risk of drought. And if you keep looking you could see where moist and dry savannah forests are declining by one-third, as well as areas where tropical seasonal forest cover would increase by the same level. However, loss of evergreen forests would mean loss of biodiversity and extinction of many species. Finally, or maybe not, the melting glacial zone in the Himalayas could also be highlighted, indicating concern over projected ecological devastation and the regions where there is an increase in the malaria season due to the rise in temperature and humidity. If anyone thinks this vision is too far-fetched, you can observe this now, if not in virtual reality, on maps provided by Google Earth. It cannot help but make one think about how and at what cost such adverse impacts might be avoided.

CONCLUSION

The users of water resource system models are typically the planners and managers who have problems to solve and who could benefit from a better understanding of what options they have and what impacts may result. They want advice on what to do and why, what will happen as a result of what they do, and who will care and how much. Modelers need to provide planners and managers with meaningful (understandable), useful, accurate and timely information. This information serves to help them better understand their system, its problems, and alternative ways to address them.

In recent years both the state of the science and the state of practice of water resources systems modeling has noticeably advanced. The tools available to professionals have become increasingly easier to use, and those trained in universities in the subject area are increasingly being employed in international and national governmental organizations and consulting firms that are dealing with complex integrated water resources planning projects. Furthermore, as water resource systems are increasingly stressed due to the growth of demand accompanied by increasing uncertainty and variability of supply, and increased pollution, the economic and social benefits of using these modeling approaches has become more pronounced. Improved decision support software and shared vision modeling together with increasing stakeholder involvement in the planning and management processes provide additional evidence that we are indeed witnessing a renaissance in the use of the systems approach to water resources planning and management.

Models, including ones that create virtual realities, developed and used to assist in the planning and management of complex water resource systems, even if based on real-time data from the actual system, are by design simplifications of the real system. Model predictions of how real systems may function or will perform under alternative designs and management policies or practices may therefore be controversial or uncertain. Future events and conditions are always unknown and of course any assumptions incorporated within models may affect their predictions. While modeling has become and will continue to be a necessary part of any planning activity in this field, the results of any quantitative analysis are always only a part, albeit a key part, of the information that must be considered by those involved in the overall planning and management decision-making process. That, I believe, will apply in 2050 just as it does today.

The challenge for us today is to create a decision support environment where we are not only able to generate useful physical, environmental, ecological, economical and perhaps even social information relevant to the system being studied, planned or managed, but also the right level of information useful to decision-makers when they need it. We also need to have a technology-based environment that facilitates and enhances the political planning and decision making process itself. With the help of those now creating new computer technology, and creating applications such as Google Earth for example, we can all work towards achieving this modeling capability for water resources planning and management by 2050.

REFERENCES

Fedra, K. (1992). "Advanced computer applications." *Options*, International Institute for Applied Systems Analysis, Laxenburg, Austria, December.

Georgakakos, A. P., and Martin, Q. W., eds. (1996). "An international review of decision support systems in river basin operation." *Proc. of the Fifth Water Resources Operations Management Workshop*, ASCE, Arlington, VA.

Jakeman, A. J., Voinov, A. A., Rizzoli, A. E., and Chen, S. H. (2008). *Environmental modeling, software, and decision support*, Elsevier, The Netherlands.

Loucks, D. P., and Da Costa, J. R., eds. (1991). *Decision support systems*, NATO Series G, Vol. 26, Springer-Verlag, Berlin.

Shapiro, H. T. (1990). "The willingness to risk failure." *Science*, 250 (4981), 609.

Simon, H. A. (1998). "Prediction and prescription in system modeling." *Proc., 15th Anniversary of IIASA*, International Institute for Applied Systems Analysis, Laxenburg, Austria.

AUTHOR INFORMATION

Daniel P. Loucks obtained his formal education at Pennsylvania State University; Yale University, and Cornell University. Since 1965 he has been on the faculty of the School of Civil and Environmental Engineering at Cornell where he teaches and conducts research in the development and application of economics, ecology, environmental engineering and systems analysis methods to the solution of environmental and regional water resources problems. He has been a consultant to various international and national agencies and organizations and private firms and has taught at various universities in North America and abroad. Email: loucks@cornell.edu

Chapter 37

Hydromorphologic Scientific and Engineering Challenges for 2050

Richard M. Vogel

ABSTRACT

By the year 2050, the hydrologic cycle will be influenced by changes in climate, water use, land use, and water infrastructure at nearly all spatial and temporal scales. It may be impossible to find a "pristine" or "research" watershed subject only to natural or virgin hydrologic conditions. Nearly every hydrologic method introduced prior to 2050 will have been adapted to account for the increased uncertainty and nonstationarity which have become the central challenges of our profession. A new subfield of hydrology termed hydromorphology will emerge to describe the structure, evolution and dynamic morphology of watershed systems over time (e.g., years, decades and centuries). The need for this new field will arise due to the enormous societal challenges and demands resulting from human impacts on environmental and water resource systems. The science of hydromorphology will develop a conceptual basis for improving our understanding of the impact of humans on the hydrosphere. Hydromorphologic engineers will introduce methods for the detection, attribution, design, management and prediction of water resources in a hydrosphere which by 2050 will be dominated by an extremely complex coupling between human and hydrologic systems.

"Hydromorphology - trying to find a home."

HYDROMORPHOLOGY: THE EVOLUTION AND STRUCTURE OF HYDROLOGIC SYSTEMS

In the 21st century, it became apparent that a wide range of environmental damages are linked to urbanization including, but not limited to: decreases in biodiversity, increased flooding, degradation of human health, decreases in evapotranspiration (due to replacement of vegetation by impervious surfaces) and a general decrease in the overall quality of our air, water and soil resources. The hydrologic effects of urbanization are primarily a result of both continuous and abrupt land-use and infrastructure changes that lead to changes in the land and the atmospheric component of the hydrologic cycle as well as changes in the water use cycle. Urbanization leads to the construction of water distribution systems, as well as an infrastructure to accommodate storm water and sewage. All of these modifications to the landscape result in changes to the hydrologic cycle and watershed processes. There has been a wide range of initiatives relating to watershed management to ameliorate past damages and/or prevent future environmental damages resulting from the urbanization of watersheds. Regardless, watershed systems evolve due to changes in land-use, climate, and an array of other anthropogenic influences. The evolution of a watershed system in response to such influences at the scale of years to centuries is termed its hydromorphological response (Dressler et al. 2006).

Traditional hydrologic approaches assume stationarity (Milly et al. 2008) and such approaches omit the influence of humans on the structure and evolution of hydrologic processes. By the year 2050, traditional approaches which focus primarily upon natural physical hydrologic processes will become obsolete. Humans and hydrologic processes are coupled and models and methods which do not account for that coupling will lead to unrealistic results, and thus become outdated.

By the year 2050 the science of hydrology will merge with many other fields outside the realm of the traditional sciences. During the late twentieth century, hydrology merged with several traditional scientific fields resulting in the fields of ecohydrology, geohydrology and hydrometeorology. During the first half of the 21st century, hydrology will merge with numerous disciplines within the social and medical sciences. In due course, the need for hydromorphology will arise as described below.

Geomorphology is to Geology as Hydromorphology is to Hydrology

Geology is that branch of science dealing with the study of the Earth, the materials of which it is made, the structure of those materials, and the processes upon them.
Hydrology is that branch of science dealing with the study of water on earth, including its occurrence, distribution, movement, and its relationship to all aspects of the environment with which it interacts.
Geomorphology is that subfield of Geology dealing with the structure and evolution of the surface of the earth, including the origin and dynamic morphology (changing structure and form) of the earth's land surfaces.

By analogy: *Hydromorphology* is a subfield of Hydrology dealing with the structure, evolution, origins and dynamic morphology of the earth's water resources due to both natural and anthropogenic influences.

> *Hydromorphology deals with problems relating to the structure, evolution and dynamic morphology of hydrologic systems over time.*

HUMANS WILL HAVE TRANSFORMED THE HYDROSPHERE BY 2050

As predicted recently by numerous investigators (Röckström et al. 2009; Vörösmarty et al. 2010, and many others), by 2050, the hydrosphere will be almost completely transformed by humans. Approaches addressing the nonstationarity of hydrologic processes will become the norm and stationary approaches which were dominant during the twentieth century, will be generally outdated in 2050. In 2050 it will be difficult to find a hydrology or other water resource textbook which ignores human impacts due to urbanization, agriculture and other land use modifications.

As a result of the profound transformations of the hydrosphere, new scientific and engineering disciplines will arise to meet the societal challenges posed by those transformations. A science of hydromorphology will develop to improve our conceptual understanding of the impacts of the multiple interacting, coupled and pervasive human and natural influences on the behavior of hydrologic systems. An engineering discipline of hydromorphology will emerge to develop improved methods to operate, plan and manage our water resources to accommodate the increased uncertainty and nonstationarity which result from the multiple interacting, coupled and pervasive human and natural influences which have led to ecosystem degradation, biodiversity losses, and global climate change.

A Scientific View of Hydrologic Systems and Watershed Models in 2050

By 2050, the hydromorphological response of watersheds will be paramount to hydrologists, due to the then pervasive impacts of population growth, urbanization, ecosystem degradation, biodiversity losses, and global climate change. Those pervasive human influences combined with our improved awareness and ability to detect and attribute hydromorphological impacts will make the notion of a pristine or virgin watershed only a distant abstraction or vestige of the pre-industrial era. In 2010, we usually define a *scientific* or *research* watershed as a pristine or virgin watershed without human impacts. In 2050, *scientific* or *research* watersheds will exhibit a wide range of anthropogenic influences, ranging from forested and agricultural watersheds to highly urbanized watersheds all dominated by water infrastructure. Consequently, in the year 2050, nearly all scientific watershed models will by necessity, include mathematical or conceptual models of a wide range of human processes in addition to traditional natural hydrologic processes such as infiltration, evaporation, and groundwater outflow included in current models. At present, most conceptual formulations of human influences such as residential and industrial water use, "best management practices," and irrigation and stormwater systems were developed by engineers and incorporated in engineering models useful for design of infrastructure and operating complex water resource systems. In 2050, scientific hydrologists will be studying what is now, in 2010, under the purview of engineering hydrologists, because their focus will evolve to improving our understanding of the coupling and interactions among human and natural processes.

> *In 2050 nearly all scientific watershed models will include a wide range of human processes in addition to traditional natural hydrologic processes.*

An Engineering View of Hydrologic Systems and Watershed Models in 2050
Analogous to the developments in scientific watershed models described above, by 2050, engineering-oriented watershed models will also have evolved to meet the new and emerging challenges of hydromorphology. Concerns over watershed damages due to population growth, urbanization, ecosystem degradation, biodiversity losses, and global climate change will lead engineers to develop fully integrated and modular modeling systems. The new generation of hydrologic and watershed models described in the previous section will be routinely integrated with climatic, demographic, geographic, ecologic, economic and decision oriented systems models to solve a new class of engineering problems. Engineers will no longer be designing water resource infrastructure in isolation, such as an individual culvert, dam, well or recharge basin. Instead, such infrastructure will be designed using integrated systems models, so that for example, flood control objectives and water supply objectives are not in competition with one another, but rather, a recharge basin may be chosen because it serves to both reduce flood flows and increase groundwater supplies, while simultaneously improving water quality goals and ecosystem services. It will become common practice for engineers to use the type of generalized watershed management modeling systems envisioned by Zoltay et al. (2010) when they attempted to develop an integrated decision support system for selecting the optimal combination of management alternatives from a much wider class of land, ground and surface water, recycling, wastewater, and best management practices than had been considered previously.

CONCLUSIONS

By the year 2050, the field of hydromorphology will be a rich and fertile young discipline dealing with the myriad of scientific and engineering challenges created by the wide range of natural and anthropogenic influences which have literally "morphed" the hydrologic cycle at all spatial and temporal scales. Hydrologic or watershed systems will evolve due to a variety of both natural and anthropogenic influences such as changes in land use and water use due to urbanization, and agriculture, climate change, modifications to water infrastructure and water use and a variety of other factors. By 2050, a major transition will have occurred in the development, management, and use of our water resources on local, regional, and global scales (Röckström et al. 2009; Vörösmarty et al. 2004, 2010). Hydrologic scientists and engineers have always been concerned with how to plan under nonstationary and uncertain conditions. What will be different in 2050 is that anthropogenic modifications to the hydrosphere will be so profound and pervasive that the central challenge facing hydrologists will be how to manage our water resources in an uncertain and nonstationary environment while simultaneously responding effectively to ecosystem degradation, biodiversity losses, and global climate change.

REFERENCES

Dressler, K., Duffy, C., Lall, U., Salas, J., Sivapalan, M., Stedinger, J. R., and Vogel, R.M. (2006). "Hydromorphology: structure and evolution of hydrologic systems at the scale of years to centuries." *Borland lecture by Upmanu Lall*, Colorado State University, Fort Collins, CO, March 20, 2006.

Milly, P. C. D., Betancourt, J., Falkenmark, M., Hirsch, R. M., Kundzewicz, Z. W., Lettenmaier, D. P., and Stouffer, R. J. (2008). "Stationarity is dead: whither water management?" *Science*, 319, 573-574.

Röckström et al. (2009). A safe operating space for humanity. *Nature*, 461. 472-475, DOI:10.1038/461472a.

Vörösmarty C., Lettenmaier, D., Leveque, C., Meybeck, M., Pahl-Wostl, C., Alcamo, J., Cosgrove, W., Grassl, H., Hoff, H., Kabat, P., Lansigan, F., Lawford, R., and Naiman, R. (2004). "Humans transforming the global water system." *EOS*, 85 (48), 509-520.

Vörösmarty, C. J., McIntyre, P. B., Gessner, M. O., Dudgeon, D., Prusevich, A., Green, P., Glidden, S., Bunn, S.E., Sullivan, C. A., Liermann, C. R., and Davies, P. M. (2010). "Global threats to human water security and river biodiversity." *Nature*, 467 (7315). 555-561, DOI: 10.1038/nature09440.

Zoltay, V., Vogel, R. M., and Kirshen, P. H. (2010). "Integrated watershed management modeling: optimal decision-making for human and natural components." *J. Water Res. Pl.-ASCE*, 136 (5), 566-575.

AUTHOR INFORMATION

Richard M. Vogel has been a professor of civil and environmental engineering at Tufts University since 1984. He received a BS and MS degree from the University of Virginia in the areas of engineering science and environmental science, respectively, and a PhD in Water Resource Systems Engineering from Cornell University. He is the director of an interdisciplinary graduate education and research program in Water: Systems, Science and Society. His research program focuses upon the areas of hydrologic and environmental statistics, water allocation, regional hydrology, regional water assessment, flood and drought management, climate change impacts, natural hazards as well as watershed modeling and management. He was awarded the 1995 Walter L. Huber Prize in Civil Engineering and the 2009 Julian Hinds Award, both from ASCE. He has published over 93 refereed journal articles. Email: Richard.Vogel@tufts.edu

Chapter 38

Dendrohydrology in 2050: Challenges and Opportunities

Franco Biondi and Scotty Strachan

ABSTRACT

Most existing water infrastructure and allocation policies rely on relatively short (<200 years) instrumental records. While it has been recognized for some time that multi-century time series of hydrological variables with annual to seasonal resolution can be obtained from tree-ring chronologies, in the next few decades it will become increasingly clear that such records allow water managers to plan for a wider spectrum of extreme conditions in individual watersheds, especially in the western US. Such a longer historical perspective can reduce the uncertainty associated with regional modeling and operational forecasts because the past is rich with episodes that are outside the modern envelope of variability. By the year 2050 dendrohydrologists will have obtained a more mechanistic understanding of the processes that link wood formation to the hydrologic cycle, and will have designed more sophisticated reconstruction tools by improving numerical methods used for producing tree-ring chronologies and by integrating dendrochronological records into mechanistic simulation models of small and large watersheds.

"Let me tell you about that terrible drought 500 years ago."

INTRODUCTION

Dendrohydrology is the analysis and application of tree-ring records for hydrological studies. As a subdiscipline of modern tree-ring science, dendrohydrology started in western North America with an emphasis on using ring-width time series to extend gage records of river runoff (Hardman and Reil 1936; Schulman 1946). Because insight on variability of freshwater resources is critical for sustainable water management, growth records obtained from long-lived tree species have been used to extend the relatively short (< 200 years) instrumental time series of, for instance, streamflow (Meko et al. 2001), precipitation (Gray et al. 2004), soil moisture (Yin et al. 2008), snow water equivalent (Woodhouse 2003), Palmer Drought Severity Index (Cook et al. 2004), standardized precipitation index (Touchan et al. 2005), flood events (St. George and Nielsen 2003), and lake levels (Bégin 2001). Sophisticated statistical methods (e.g., Meko 1997) have been very effective in producing dendrohydrological records one to two orders of magnitude longer than existing instrumental data, thereby generating a range of scenarios previously unavailable to water managers. In addition, these long time series provide a large enough sample of dry and wet episodes that multivariate stochastic models can be fit to estimate the likelihood of severe events with specific duration, magnitude, peak, or their mutual combination (Biondi et al. 2008).

An extensive review of dendrohydrology, as was done by Loaiciga et al. (1993), is outside the scope of this chapter. However, we emphasize that conceptual underpinnings are best described at the watershed level. At this scale, wood formation can be linked to type, amount, and timing of precipitation, timing and amount of temperature threshold exceedance, and timing and amplitude of evapotranspiration (ET) rates, all interacting within the bounds of local soil characteristics, topography, and stand dynamics.

Until now, the parameter most often reconstructed from tree-ring records has been river runoff (Meko and Woodhouse 2011). Although streamflow is not directly related to tree growth, it is an indicator of the upstream water budget, which in turn influences wood growth, especially in semi-arid environments (Fritts 1976). Furthermore, river gage records are relatively abundant and long compared to instrumental measurements of other variables (such as soil moisture), and tree-ring chronologies tend to have higher correlations with river runoff than with other local hydrological parameters (such as precipitation).

All tree-ring proxy records track the presence/absence of a combination of limiting factors, which in turn are filtered and identified through numerical correlation analysis with concurrently recorded data (Cook and Kairiukstis 1990). A major challenge in any type of dendrochronological reconstruction is to properly identify the eco-physiological mechanisms that are behind observed statistical relationships. Often the identification of limiting processes becomes impossible due to the absence of sufficient data or because the correlation between tree-ring indices and hydrological variables (streamflow volume, drought index, etc.) involves multiple species and sites over a large geographical area (e.g., Woodhouse et al. 2006, Zhang et al. 2004).

When proxy records are used to augment time series of hydrological parameters, reconstruction methods are based on assuming that statistical relationships observed in recent times remain valid over the entire length of the reconstruction (National Research Council 2006). A similar assumption is used in reservoir operation and water allocation when considering instrumental data to be unaffected by variability on time scales longer than the record length (Redmond et al. 2002; US Water Resources Council 1981). Recently, such stationarity assumptions have been challenged under the hypothesis of impending future climate change associated with human activities (Milly et al. 2008). While nonstationary probabilistic models of relevant environmental variables could be best for water planning decisions, information from long-term historical knowledge can still satisfy the immediate needs of water managers, because the past is rich with episodes that are outside the modern envelope of variability (Biondi et al. 2001). In the next few decades, however, dendrohydrology will need to evolve rapidly to remain a viable subdiscipline of hydrologic science, and to continue providing usable information to water managers.

DENDROHYDROLOGY IN THE NEXT 40 YEARS

The most obvious future challenge to (and opportunity for) dendrohydrology is geographical: trees suitable for reconstructing past processes are not uniformly distributed. Identifying new sampling sites and developing additional records will remain an ongoing activity. In fact, despite a number of threats to old-growth forests (natural decay, disease, wildfire, logging, exurban sprawl, etc.), the number of supra-long tree-ring chronologies has kept increasing in recent years, even in the highly populated areas of Europe (e.g., Friedrich et al. 2004; Nicolussi et al. 2009).

Numerical methods will also improve, both for producing tree-ring chronologies and for statistical reconstructions. For the former, theory-based approaches to ring-width standardization have recently been proposed (Biondi and Qeadan 2008; Melvin and Briffa 2008), and some of them are becoming easily accessible through their incorporation in public-domain, widely used software packages, such as R (Bunn 2008). For the latter, statistical reconstructions, which already incorporate noise and autoregressive terms in Monte Carlo simulations (e.g., Meko et al. 2001), will also implement non-parametric and/or Bayesian approaches.

> *The greatest advancements during the next few decades will derive from focusing on the small watershed scale, where localized results can be of immediate use to land managers and stakeholders.*

The greatest advancements during the next few decades will derive from focusing on the small watershed scale, where localized results can be of immediate use to land managers and stakeholders. In mountainous, topographically complex terrain and water-limited environments where dendrohydrology can be practiced, basin-scale climate variability, and its downstream ecological effects, may overshadow regional-scale patterns. For instance, in the Great Basin of North America, locations less than 100 km apart experience seasonal differences in precipitation regime linked to winter *vs.* summer circulation (Bradley 2009). While actual precipitation amounts in this region are relatively small, varying warm-season thunderstorm activity can have a disproportionate effect on watersheds through lightning strike frequency, which in turn regulates wildfire regime (Dilts et al. 2008).

Future eco-hydrological models for small watersheds will unravel how landscape-scale factors such as land use changes, wildfires, species invasions, or geomorphic processes (e.g., landslides) can lead to changes in hydrological variables, particularly stream runoff, independently of climate. Different scenarios can be simulated in a water balance model that uses proxy-derived precipitation and/or temperature from annually or seasonally resolved paleorecords (such as tree-rings), and also includes parameters to account for changes in the water cycle that occur due to modifications in fire regime, grazing, vegetation cover, topographic features, etc. (Saito et al. 2008). This approach is also capable of using tree-ring records to reconstruct more than one hydrologic variable at a time, since it can simultaneously estimate multiple components of the water cycle (Solander et al. 2010). Finally, use of process-driven dendrohydrology at the small watershed scale would facilitate information transfer between climate scientists and water managers.

Individual tree-ring sites may be capable of recording seasonal-specific processes related to evapotranspiration rates and water supply (e.g., Biondi 1993). In the next few decades, the eco-physiological basis for using tree growth as a measure of hydrometeorological conditions will become properly established. Intensive field measurements of hydrologic, atmospheric, ecologic, lithologic, and pedologic variables for identification of the specific process(es) recorded by wood formation will clarify the interactions between mechanisms that control tree-ring records (Downes et al. 2009). Analysis of stable isotope ratios found in components of the hydrologic cycle, including tree xylem and foliage, will further explain how trees utilize water for radial growth (Hartsough et al. 2008; Loader et al. 2007).

Once process-level relationships have been identified, further testing will be necessary to determine their uniformity over the four dimensions of space and time. As conditions move progressively away from a four-dimensional origin where stationarity and linearity exist, these assumptions become progressively weaker. For instance, while modern calibration studies can reveal the main hydroclimatic signals embedded in tree-ring records, there is always the possibility that such signals were weakened in the past if environmental conditions exceeded certain thresholds. Results obtained from examining uniformity over space in fixed timeframes will be used to evaluate changes in uniformity over time at fixed locations. Debate on the "death" of stationarity could then circumvent the arduous search for all-encompassing, nonstationary solutions, and focus instead on quantifying a "rate of applicability decay" over time and/or space, to examine how it affects scientific knowledge and real-world policy making.

CONCLUSION

In the next few decades, improved knowledge on eco-physiological controls of wood growth and new methods of tree-ring chronology development will allow dendrochronological records to become part of small-watershed models used to manage water resources. As dendrohydrology reaches its full value and recognition in the next 40 years, water managers will realize that historical information can be used to define an expected range of variability, including worst-case scenarios, to guide operational strategies in the face of extreme future uncertainty. In general, by 2050 it will have become clear in multiple fields of applied science that the past is a legacy to elicit and embrace, not a corpse to forsake and disregard.

REFERENCES

Bégin, Y. (2001). "Tree-ring dating of extreme lake levels at the Subarctic–Boreal interface." *Quaternary Res.*, 55, 133–139.

Biondi, F. (1993). "Climatic signals in tree-rings of Fagus sylvatica L. from the central Apennines, Italy." *Acta Oecol.*, 14, 57-71.

Biondi, F., Kozubowski, T. J., and Panorska, A. K. (2001). "A probability model for analyzing regime shifts over time." *EOS Transactions of the American Geophysical Union*, 82(47), Abstract GC22A-0270.

Biondi, F., Kozubowski, T. J., Panorska, A. K., and Saito, L. (2008). "A new stochastic model of episode peak and duration for eco-hydro-climatic applications." *Ecol. Model.*, 211, 383-395.

Biondi, F., and Qeadan, F. (2008). "A theory-driven approach to tree-ring standardization: defining the biological trend from expected basal area increment." *Tree-Ring Res.*, 64(2), 81–96.

Bradley, M. L. (2009). "Pre- and post-settlement stand development of woodland ecosystems in Lincoln County, Nevada." M.S. thesis, University of Nevada, Reno, Reno, NV.

Bunn, A. G. (2008). "A dendrochronology program library in R (dplR)." *Dendrochronologia*, 26, 115–124.

Cook, E. R., and Kairiukstis, L. A. (1990). *Methods of dendrochronology*, Kluwer, Dordrecht, The Netherlands, 408 p.

Cook, E. R., Woodhouse, C. A., Eakin, C. M., Meko, D. M., and Stahle, D. W. (2004). "Long-term aridity changes in the western United States." *Science*, 306, 1015-1018.

Dilts, T. E., Sibold, J. S., and Biondi, F. (2008). "A weights-of-evidence model for mapping the probability of fire occurrence in Lincoln County, Nevada." *Proc., 2008 Annual Meeting of the Association of American Geographers*, Boston, MA.

Downes, G. M., Drew, D., Battaglia, M., and Schulze, D. (2009). "Measuring and modelling stem growth and wood formation: An overview." *Dendrochronologia*, 27(2), 147-157.

Friedrich, M., Remmele, S., Kromer, B., Hofmann, J., Spurk, M., Kaiser, K. F., Orcel, C., and Küppers, M. (2004). "The 12,460-year Hohenheim oak and pine tree-ring chronology from central Europe - a unique annual record for radiocarbon calibration and paleoenvironment reconstructions." *Radiocarbon*, 46(3), 1111-1122.

Fritts, H. C. (1976). *Tree rings and climate*, Academic Press, London.

Gray, S. T., Fastie, C. L., Jackson, S. T., and Betancourt, J. L. (2004). "Tree-ring-based reconstruction of precipitation in the Bighorn Basin, Wyoming, since 1260 A.D." *J. Climate*, 17(19), 3855-3865.

Hardman, G., and Reil, O. E. (1936). *The relationship between tree growth and stream runoff in the Truckee River Basin, California-Nevada*, Bulletin No. 141, Agricultural Experiment Station, University of Nevada, Reno, NV.

Hartsough, P. C., Poulson, S. R., Biondi, F., and Galindo Estrada, I. (2008). "Stable isotope characterization of the ecohydrological cycle at a tropical treeline site." *Arct. Antarct. Alp. Res.*, 40(2), 343–354.

Loader, N. J., McCarroll, D., Gagen, M., Robertson, I., and Jalkanen, R. E. (2007). "Extracting climatic information from stable isotopes in tree rings." *Stable isotopes as indicators of ecological change*, T. E. Dawson and R. T. W. Siegwolf, eds., Elsevier, 27-48.

Loaiciga, H. A., Haston, L., and Michaelsen, J. (1993). "Dendrohydrology and long-term hydrological phenomena." *Rev. Geophys.*, 31(2), 151-171.

Meko, D. M. (1997). "Dendroclimatic reconstruction with time varying predictor subsets of tree indices." *J. Climate*, 19(4), 687-696.

Meko, D. M., Therrell, M. D., Baisan, C. H., and Hughes, M. K. (2001). "Sacramento River flow reconstructed to A.D. 869 from tree rings." *J. Am. Water Resour. As.*, 37(4), 1029-1039.

Meko, D. M., and Woodhouse, C. A. (2011). "Application of streamflow reconstruction to water resources management." *Dendroclimatology: progress and prospects*, M. K. Hughes, T. W. Swetnam, and H. F. Diaz, eds., Springer.

Melvin, T. M., and Briffa, K. R. (2008). "A 'signal-free' approach to dendroclimatic standardisation." *Dendrochronologia*, 26(2), 71–86.

Milly, P. C. D., Betancourt, J. L., Falkenmark, M., Hirsch, R. M., Kundzewicz, Z. W., Lettenmaier, D. P., and Stouffer, R. J. (2008). "Stationarity is dead: whither water management?" Science, 319, 573-574.

National Research Council. (2006). *Surface temperature reconstructions for the last 2,000 years*, Committee on Surface Temperature Reconstructions for the Last 2,000 Years, The National Academies Press, Washington, D.C.

Nicolussi, K., Kaufmann, M., Melvin, T. M., van der Plicht, J., Schießling, P., and Thurner, A. (2009). "A 9111 year long conifer tree-ring chronology for the European Alps: a base for environmental and climatic investigations." *Holocene*, 19(6), 909–920.

Redmond, K. T., Enzel, Y., House, K. P., and Biondi, F. (2002). "Climate variability and flood frequency at decadal to millennial time scales." *Ancient floods, modern hazards: principles and applications of paleoflood hydrology*, K. P. House, R. H. Webb, V. R. Baker, and D. R. Levish, eds., American Geophysical Union, 21-45.

Saito, L., Biondi, F., Salas, J. D., Panorska, A. K., and Kozubowski, T. J. (2008). "A watershed modeling approach to streamflow reconstruction from tree-ring records." *Environ. Res. Lett.*, 3(2), 024006 (doi:10.1088/1748-9326/3/2/024006).

Schulman, E. (1946). "Tree-ring hydrology of the Colorado River basin." *University of Arizona Bulletin*, 16(4) / *Laboratory of Tree-Ring Research*, Bulletin No. 2, University of Arizona, Tucson, AZ.

Solander, K., Saito, L., and Biondi, F. (2010). "Streamflow simulation using a water-balance model with annually-resolved inputs." *J. Hydrol.*, 387(1-2), 46-53, doi:10.1016/j.jhydrol.2010.03.028.

St. George, S., and Nielsen, E. (2003). "Palaeoflood records for the Red River, Manitoba, Canada, derived from anatomical tree-ring signatures." *Holocene*, 13(4), 547–555.

Touchan, R., Funkhouser, G. S., Hughes, M. K., and Erkan, N. (2005). "Standardized precipitation index reconstructed from Turkish tree-ring widths." *Climatic Change*, 72, 339–353.

US Water Resources Council. (1981). *Guidelines for determining flood flow frequency*, Bulletin 17B, Hydrology Committee, Washington, D.C.

Woodhouse, C. A. (2003). "A 431-yr reconstruction of western Colorado snowpack from tree rings." *J. Climate*, 16, 1551-1561.

Woodhouse, C. A., Gray, S. T., and Meko, D. M. (2006). "Updated streamflow reconstructions for the Upper Colorado River Basin." *Water Resour. Res.*, 42(5), W05415, doi:10.1029/2005WR004455.

Yin, Z.-Y., Shao, X., Qin, N., and Liang, E. (2008). "Reconstruction of a 1436-year soil moisture and vegetation water use history based on tree-ring widths from Qilian junipers in northeastern Qaidam Basin, northwestern China." *Int. J. Climatol.*, 28, 37–53.

Zhang, Z., Mann, M. E., and Cook, E. R. (2004). "Alternative methods of proxy-based climate field reconstruction: application to summer drought over the conterminous United States back to AD 1700 from tree-ring data." *Holocene*, 14(4), 502-516.

AUTHOR INFORMATION

Franco Biondi is Geography Associate Professor and DendroLab Director at the University of Nevada, Reno, where he is also a member of four interdisciplinary graduate programs: Hydrologic Sciences, Environmental Sciences, Atmospheric Sciences, and Ecology, Evolution, and Conservation Biology. He received a Laurea (Italian Doctorate) in forestry from the Università di Firenze, and MS and PhD in watershed management and geosciences from the University of Arizona in Tucson. He has authored or co-authored over 50 peer-reviewed articles on climate and forest dynamics, ecohydrological changes, and spatial processes. Email: fbiondi@unr.edu

Scotty Strachan is a DendroLab Research Associate and Geography Graduate Student at the University of Nevada, Reno, where he has been participating in dendrochronological investigations since 2002. Along with Dr. Biondi, he has identified, sampled, and crossdated over 40 climatically-sensitive tree-ring chronologies in the western United States, the majority of which exceed 500 years in length. His current research is focused on applying tree-ring records to studies that benefit local stakeholders in the Great Basin, ranging from archaeology to water supply issues. Email: strachan@unr.edu

V CONCLUSIONS

Chapter 39

Our Collective Vision

ABSTRACT

This chapter summarizes the visions of the authors who have contributed to this book and explores what is needed to make these visions happen. Several themes are pervasive in this collection of visions for 2050: 1) the inherent variability of water resources is being compounded by non-stationarity issues; 2) the need to provide adequate and reliable water, food, and sanitation to expanding populations, especially in urban areas, will continue to drive management decisions; 3) technological advances will proceed at a rapid pace to provide new options for addressing water and environmental management issues; and 4) adaptable, robust and integrated approaches will dominate water and environmental resources planning and management as we proceed toward achieving our visions for 2050.

"So, it is likely to be up and down until 2050,
but I doubt you will have to abandon the planet."

OVERVIEW

Creating this book has been an adventure. It has forced us to think about just what we would like to observe when we get to the year 2050 (a heroic assumption for some of us), and just what we might do to make that vision a reality. We who have contributed to this book are all involved in some way with the environment and water. Our chapters are focused on issues and aspects related to environmental and water resources planning, policy and management, but at the same time we have recognized the influence of broader economic, educational, institutional, social and technical factors that will surely influence the environment and water resources that will exist in 2050 and how they are managed.

We are not the first to develop future visions for the 21st century. The American Society of Civil Engineers (ASCE) held a Summit on the Future of Civil Engineering (ASCE 2007) to articulate a future vision for the year 2025 for all levels and facets of the civil engineering community. Cosgrove and Rijsberman (2000) presented a water vision for 2025 as a result of a vision development exercise by the World Water Council. As of 2010, some of their visions related to building new water storage facilities and increased investments in rehabilitation of water bodies have occurred, but many of their visions related to full-cost recovery of water supplies, removal of water subsidies for agriculture, and biotechnology and scientific developments are not yet evident. A business vision for 2050 put forth by the World Business Council for Sustainable Development (2010) emphasizes the need to double agricultural output by 2050, but not increase the amount of land or water required. A recent assessment of sustainability for the 21st century completed by the Tellus Institute demonstrated that proactive reforms of policy and technology could lead to a sustainable future in 2100, with a leveling off of water stress and total demand by 2050 (Raskin et al. 2010). Taking a primarily economic approach, the 2030 Water Resources Group, a consortium of business interests, also advocates policy reforms and technological advances to close the gap between water demand and supply in 2030 (2030 Water Resources Group 2009).

In our first introductory chapter, we discussed futurology and visioning, concepts that are inherent in looking at where our field may be in 2050. We also took the opportunity to briefly reflect on the current state of our environment and water resource systems and at the issues making headlines in today's world: the uniqueness of water as a resource (there are no substitutes and everything that lives or is made requires it), issues stemming from the increasing uncertainties and risks associated with water quantity and quality, water's role in conflicts, and managing water in an increasingly urban environment.

In our second chapter, we looked 40 years back in time (approximately the equivalent length of time between now and 2050) and examined what was going on in the field of environmental and water management in the 1960s and 1970s and how successful those professionals were in thinking about a future 40 years later. In that era, water management and environmental management were separate fields, with water managers, scientists, and engineers predominantly focused on water resources development projects to address water supply, hydropower, and flood control needs. Environmental management was in its infancy, with the recent publication of *Silent Spring* by Rachel Carson and the first Earth Day in 1970. Some of our predecessors like Gilbert White did indeed foresee some of the challenges we are addressing today, and advocated approaches for meeting those challenges. Although today we benefit from some of the decisions made 40 years ago, other decisions were not as fortuitous. For example, we are far more concerned about ecosystem rehabilitation and environmental quality than were those making decisions 40 to 50 years ago. The examination of past conditions and assessments impresses upon us that while the future is ill-defined and hard to predict, our actions today can surely influence it.

Much of what we do in all aspects of our lives is in some way influenced by the various stressors or drivers of change. Our third chapter in the introductory section of our book identified and discussed six such stressors that affect decisions we make in managing our environment and water resources. These include: natural and climate-related stressors; demographic and social stressors; economic stressors; technological stressors (including infrastructure and security); governance stressors (institutions, policies, laws and finance); and environmental stressors, including public health, pollution and sustainability. The interactions among these six components pose real challenges for decision-makers as they try to identify and implement plans and policies that will lead to beneficial outcomes with respect to all six aspects of our collective welfare.

FUTURE VISIONS

This book presents future visions - the visions of a variety of prominent people in the field of the environment and water resources of what the desired condition of this water world should be like in 2050. In this concluding chapter we are going to attempt to meld these individual visions into a more global vision for 2050. So, let's now jump into a time capsule and travel to the year 2050 to see what the ideal water world of the future looks like. We have grouped the visions expressed in this book into three broad categories: Planning and Policy; Education; and Science and Technology. Though most of the visions cross two or even all three of these general categories we found it useful to use this grouping to organize the book and its conclusions.

> *Let's now jump into a time capsule and travel to the year 2050 to see what the ideal water world of the future looks like.*

Planning and Policy

It's 2050 and space travel is now affordable and routine. We'll take advantage of this to see what the ideal state of the world's water resources and their management looks like from an orbital spacecraft as we circle the globe. Looking down we see a planet that is in harmony with the use of its environmental resources.

International issues

Viewing the whole world, the percentage of its people without safe water for drinking, cooking, washing, and hygiene, is now one tenth of what it was some 40 years ago in spite of 3 billion more people. Finally the world has achieved sustainable sanitation that involves not only access to basic sanitation and hygiene, but also the safe disposal of human waste, proper attention to pollution and environmental degradation, and a commitment to sustainability (Lenton and Lane, Ch.6). Achieving this goal required both a significant ratcheting up of political commitment and an unleashing of energy and innovation – institutional, financial and technical – at all levels. This effort had to dovetail with the larger societal concerns for environmental sustainability.

> *The world has achieved not only access to basic sanitation and hygiene, but also the safe disposal of human waste, proper attention to pollution and environmental degradation, and a commitment to sustainability.*

Agriculture remains the largest water consumer in the world. Over the past 40 years scientists and engineers have figured out how to produce more and safer food, on less land, with less freshwater, using less energy, fertilizers, and pesticides (Walter, Ch. 16) while at the same time sharply reducing the level of greenhouse gas emissions. The water supply and wastewater systems that serve the majority of the world's population are integrated into the entire infrastructure of numerous megacities where most people live (Heaney and Sansalone, Ch. 17 and Daigger, Ch. 18). They are being managed adaptively in the face of a more variable supply – both in quantity and duration – that the world is now experiencing. Science and technology has conquered most of the water quality problems of some 40 years ago and can quickly adapt to the water quality challenges introduced by new technology and emerging chemicals and drugs. The challenge for adaptive management remains one of timing, i.e. being able to recognize changes sufficiently in advance so as to gain the political, and hence the financial support needed to adapt in time to prevent crises when it is often the event of a crisis that motivates the political system to pay attention and respond (Shamir and Howard, Ch. 4). While generating the financial resources needed to address long-term problems is still a challenge, local, national and international water resource management agencies are now working together as appropriate to address water management issues over a range of spatial and temporal scales including those pertaining to coastal zone management and sea pollution.

> *The challenge for adaptive management is to adapt in time to prevent crises rather than adapting in response to them.*

As we observe the world in 2050 we see that it hasn't stopped changing. But unlike 40 years ago, water managers have overcome the old challenge of convincing the public that we can easily adapt to those changes in time to avoid greater future costs and damages or to realize greater future benefits. The recognition of climate change impacts is one example of this. Now no one doubts that the climate is changing in ways that have not been observed in hundreds of years. Adaptation includes modifying or inventing new technologies, rules, regulations, and/or institutional and political arrangements as needed.

Transboundary water agreements are common in 2050 especially in water scarce regions. International development agencies (such as the UN family and the international development banks) are increasingly effective in facilitating international transboundary agreements where needed. There now exist many cooperative management agreements among governmental, quasi-governmental, private, and non-state actors for achieving equitable and effective water allocations. The creation, implementation, and enforcement of effective water sharing agreements between and among riparian governments are central to stakeholder consensus (Draper, Ch. 5).

Integrated river basin management and legal issues
As we glide down towards earth from space we can view entire river basins and see that they are being managed as whole entities in an integrated way (Grigg, Ch. 7). Integrated water resources management is the common framework for planning, organizing, and operating water systems and to unify and balance the relevant views and goals of multiple stakeholders. Advances in technology and our understanding of human behavior over the last 40 years have resulted in better ways of reaching stakeholder consensus and of conflict resolution. There is increased transparency and accountability. Communication among professionals in different disciplines and between professionals and the public has become more effective. Integrated water management is viewed as critical for democracy in the complex world of 2050, and water managers, engineers, and scientists have a lead role in promoting it.

> *Integrated water management is viewed as critical for democracy in 2050, and water managers, engineers, and scientists have a lead role in promoting it.*

Many of the problems of 40 years ago that were the principal barriers to achieving integrated river basin management, namely the "silo" nature of the many legislative statutes to address environmental stewardship goals, the absence of facilitating provisions in legislation, and the lack of institutional mechanisms in place in most river basins and watersheds, have been overcome (Vicory and Tennant, Ch. 8). All basins have management plans that are comprised of sub-plans for local watersheds. These plans are facilitated by well-coordinated legislative mandates and policies that are informed by available scientific data. Advances in technologies and tools have facilitated integrated approaches, and financial resources are available to support a full range of monitoring. Appropriate institutions guide planning and programs across political jurisdictions as well as the planning process to insure that impacted stakeholders and citizens participate as equal partners in decision-making.

Forty years ago legal regimes for managing surface waters were stressed by technological change, population growth, and climate change. These stresses led to major reforms to water law at the local, national, and international levels over the past forty years (Dellapenna, Ch. 9). Security of investment capital and incentives to promote the best use of water were necessary, as well as the protection and enhancement of the public and ecological dimensions of water management. Water law has now, in 2050, become a major, functioning tool for accomplishing these objectives rather than merely serving to perpetuate an increasingly dysfunctional status quo.

Well-functioning water markets each provide the flexibility needed for water re-allocation under increasing demands and possible climate change (Howe, Ch. 10). On a broader geographical scale, these markets have taken planning and management back to the river basin level. Water resources planning and policy has become more efficient, integrated, sustainable, and transparent (Viessman and Perez, Ch. 11). Some 40 years ago water resources policy was at a critical tipping point in which environmental and water resource planners and managers were faced with more complex financing and stakeholder expectations, climate change, and the need to adopt more sustainable approaches to water resources planning. Now it is common to perform integrated analyses and planning involving all environmental resources, not just water.

Now that we have landed our space capsule back on earth, we can look more specifically at how water is managed at local levels.

Water utilities
Water utilities are much more integrated and much more responsive to the challenges of a changing and uncertain source of supply (Mulroy, Ch. 12). We now have a much better understanding of climate change and adaptation, including mitigation policies and programs to cope with climate change. Understanding climate change and enacting the appropriate adaptation and mitigation measures will continue to be critical to weathering unprecedented future challenges that loom on the horizon.

> *Greater consolidation and regional collaboration, new technologies and sources of supply, and conservation options now shape core water supply strategies of water utilities.*

Water utilities played a major institutional role in achieving the mid-21st century provision of adequate supplies of safe drinking water for much of the population of the world (Means, Ch. 13). Demographics, water supply constraints, rising water costs, growing energy/water nexus, required changes over the past 40 years in infrastructure, finance, environment, and regional collaboration. While the societal mandate for water utilities remains the same as in 2010, namely to provide high quality and adequate supplies to sustain quality of life, there is now much greater consolidation and regional collaboration, new technologies and sources of supply, and conservation options that shape core water supply strategies for all utilities regardless of location.

Flooding issues and options
In 2050, floods still occur, but finally we see that flood damages are showing decreasing trends in spite of increased population, property values, and climate-induced changes that seem to cause more extreme peak flows and durations, and sea level rise. This is the result of learning how to better manage flood risks. It is also the result of increased personal responsibility on the part of individuals subject to flooding. Civil engineers, governments and the public at large are taking on the challenge of ensuring that all floodplains are sustainably developed and managed in ways that recognize that floodplains are for floods as well as for economic development activities (Galloway, Ch. 14).

Coastal city flooding due to sea level rise, storm surges, inland flooding from intense precipitation events, and increased frequency and duration of droughts forecasted some 40 years ago is in evidence today (Major, Ch. 15). Every coastal city now has the ability to effectively adapt to climate change and its impacts. However, the cost of this adaptation has been and will continue to be substantial. In cases of severe drought, various demand management measures are now available, including improved desalination technology powered by cheaper renewable energy. And while everyone seems to want to carry a biodegradable water bottle with them, they now purchase them without water and then fill them with tap water. Treated tap water is preferred where it is available and increasingly it is available wherever people live, even in the less developed regions of the world.

> *Civil engineers, governments and the public ensure that floodplains are sustainably developed and managed so that floodplains are for floods as well as for economic development activities.*

Irrigated agriculture
Because of the recognition that irrigated agriculture as practiced in most countries some 40 years ago could not be sustained without better water management and use of new technologies, these needed changes have occurred. The yields of rain-fed crops have also increased (Walter, Ch. 16). In addition to achieving more diversified and intense cropping systems, there is now increased emphasis on protecting the environment and maintaining healthy aquatic ecosystems. This aspect of water management continues to grow in importance. Increased international trade and meeting target levels of national food security continue to motivate more efficient use of the world's land and water resources devoted to agriculture production.

Urban water management
More than 70% of the human race – over 6 billion people – now live in urban areas, and most of these cities are near the coasts. Over the past 40 years the equivalent of seven New York Cities were added to the planet every year. Cities continue to bring together the systems by which our world works: education, transportation, public

safety, and health care, and they continue to generate the bulk of carbon dioxide emissions and account for 60% of all human water use. Managing urban infrastructure systems has increasingly involved managing people and institutions. It includes demand management and the sustainable use of water resources (Palmisano 2010).

> *In 2050, over 70% of us live in urban areas. Managing urban infrastructure now involves managing people and institutions.*

During the past 40 years, urban stormwater management has evolved from a focus on drainage and flood control to inclusion of stormwater quality associated with nonpoint pollution (Heaney and Sansalone, Ch. 17). Today stormwater is being used for a variety of low impact development alternatives. Key drivers of the changing attitudes concerning stormwater use are the greatly increasing relative costs of providing water and energy; greater development of more sustainable green materials and infrastructure systems; and technological advances that allow proactive management of urban stormwater systems using real time control and including source controls.

Population growth, coupled with increased standards of living and growing resource limitations required changes in the historical urban water management approach. New approaches and enabling technologies now allow integrated 21st century urban water management systems to be assembled (Daigger, Ch. 18). Such systems require the removal of much less water from the natural environment, achieve energy neutrality and provide significant nutrient recovery. These approaches are more efficient, use local water resources, incorporate greater recovery and recycling and include advantages such as easier expansion, reduced urban heat island effects, and dramatically increased urban aesthetics. Education and professional practice has broken down historical barriers between drinking, storm, and wastewater systems design and operation, allowing a more integrated systems perspective.

> *Urban water management systems now remove very little water from the natural environment, achieve energy neutrality and provide significant nutrient recovery.*

Ecosystem management
There has been a shift in the approach now used to maintain biodiverse, fully functioning aquatic ecosystems compared to that used some 40 years ago. At that time, failure to include the goods and services provided by freshwater ecosystems in the design, development and operation of water infrastructure resulted in the degradation of these ecosystems (Poff and Richter, Ch. 19). Now human societies and governments incorporate robust principles of ecosystem science into planning and management of freshwater resources to ensure long-term sustainability of freshwater ecosystems. Four major pathways now exist for maintaining viable and robust freshwater ecosystems: 1) active incorporation of ecosystem principles into water resource systems planning and management; 2) integration of social and

ecological sciences into sustainability criteria; 3) coordination of regulatory and management authorities over water; and 4) interdisciplinary education and research. Implementation of these pathways continue to require substantial political will and sustained efforts from the technical community to devise water management strategies that meet both human and ecosystem needs.

Education

The education of water resources planners, engineers and economists has changed over the past 40 years. These changes in how we educate tomorrow's professional and technical workforce has happened because of changes in our natural and man-made environment, the evolution of the fields of environmental and water resources engineering, economics and law, changes in society and what it expects from professionals, and changes in technology (Wright, Ch. 20). Compared to the educational environment 40 years ago, students and faculty in 2050 enjoy many advances in technology, an increased public awareness of water issues and increased public pressure for water sustainability. There is universal technical general education and the technical workforce is much more diverse than it was some four decades ago. Most undergraduate engineering programs in the US routinely include global learning communities and lifeline learning.

> *Advances in educational technology have transformed learning to an "open learning movement" that uses inter-institutional collaboration to make education available anywhere in the world at any time.*

Graduate education in water resources planning and management is now much more interdisciplinary than in the past. The management of environmental- and water-related issues requires an interdisciplinary scientific and engineering background and approach. Universities acknowledge this and have adapted their graduate programs to meet this need (Saito et al., Ch. 21). Different universities have different interdisciplinary graduate programs but each required changes in the traditional structure of higher education. These structural changes and the development of popular interdisciplinary programs that involve interdisciplinary research as well as teaching happened because interested graduate students became the next generation of faculty that promoted interdisciplinary efforts and because funding agencies and organizations that ultimately hired other graduates emphasized the need for interdisciplinary education and skills.

Compared to 2010, advances in educational technology have fundamentally transformed learning (Cohon, Ch. 22). This includes an "open learning movement" with greatly increased inter-institutional and international collaboration to make education available anywhere and at anytime. There has also been an emergence of the three-year residential bachelor's degree program in which four years of material are crammed into three by using online courses. There has also been a real disassociation of the traditional university structure. In some cases "faculty" have become independent contractors, selling their content to universities, online publishers or directly to students, and their research skills to clients that include universities.

Science and Technology

Valuing water
The notion of the value of water and the natural environment and how we measure it has shifted significantly over the past 40 years (Cohon, Ch. 22). The implications for society and water systems planning and management have been profound, making the achievement of sustainability considerably easier because of the fundamental changes that have occurred in the basic economic development model and how we quantify the economic value of our natural and environmental resources.

Non-stationarity impacts
Four water resources issues have dominated the research agenda over the past 40 years: 1) hydrologic variability, hazards, water supply and ecosystem preservation; 2) urban landscape design; 3) non-point water quality issues, and 4) climate change, resiliency, and non-stationarity (Hirsch, Ch. 23). The paradigms that are now driving water resource management include managing watershed or stream systems for desirable ecological outcomes, keeping water on the landscape in urban environments, and incorporating uncertainty in water resource strategies through adaptation and robust designs and institutions. There is a continuing need to collect and analyze long-term data to learn about the evolving state of the system, understand ecosystem processes in the water and on the landscape, and find innovative ways to manage water as a shared resource.

> *Water management now includes managing waters for desirable ecological outcomes, keeping water on the landscape in urban environments, and allowing for future uncertainty through adaptation and robust designs and institutions.*

Those using models and data to address the non-stationarity issues and study other water management issues are benefiting from the considerable improvements in these tools and in the quantity and quality of data over the past 40 years (McCuen, Ch. 24). Human-induced changes can be monitored better due to improved measurement approaches and sensor technologies. The studies of non-stationarity issues have required coupled modeling approaches, longer return periods for design, novel calibration methods, and broader educational backgrounds with more exposure to statistical methods, physical hydrology, and decision theory.

Hydropower production
There has been little change in today's hydropower plant technology compared to a century ago (Howard and Stedinger, Ch. 25), yet today power generation is highly integrated, and the availability of extensive real-time monitoring has enabled more effective reservoir management. Resolution of relicensing and rate issues is quicker

now due in part to virtual meetings coupled with computer systems that integrate factual data and scientific issues with personal and group preferences. Overall, advances in related technologies, anticipated increases in demand and thermal generation, constraints on transmission systems, and the intermittent character of green energy generation facilities has caused hydropower to be more valued today than it has been in the past.

> *Today's water distribution system is fully monitored, tracked and controlled from the treatment plant to the customer's tap.*

Urban water infrastructure
Advances in water distribution system technology have resulted in both structural changes in distribution systems and significant advances in operations and water quality control in distribution systems (Grayman et al., Ch. 26). Today distribution system water is fully monitored, tracked and controlled from the treatment plant to the customer. New pipe technologies extend the life of distribution infrastructure. Dual or multiple water systems are commonplace, smart pipe sensor technologies continuously assess water quality and hydraulic conditions, and asset management systems track the history, condition, and operation of individual components of water distribution systems. These advances have been a result of an increased research and investment strategy, a longer-term view of needs by the water industry and an acceptance by customers of the need to invest in upgrading the aging infrastructure.

Urban water and wastewater infrastructure are now able to self-monitor, adapt to changing conditions, and self-repair and regenerate. Integration of water infrastructure sensor technology and networks with signal and data handling, processing and analysis systems are critical for the operation of the sensed water infrastructure existing today, in 2050. The sensed water infrastructure provides increased efficiency in inspection and maintenance, rapid detection and response, macro-level trend analysis and compliance testing, and efficient prediction of system performance (Dzombak et al., Ch. 27).

Today engineers and planners take a more comprehensive, integrated systems approach to urban infrastructure development that incorporates green technologies through holistic systems approaches (Struck, Ch. 28). These technologies are no longer considered "green" but are simply "technologies" that are widely recognized to have environmental benefits. The integrated systems and holistic total resource management approach of 2050 includes the explicit consideration of air, amenities, energy, solid waste, transportation, urban development, and integrated water management involving quantity and quality, and evolved by forcing integration between formerly separate departments and developing completely new roles for these integrated departments as circumstances dictated.

Irrigation technology
Advances in engineering and irrigation technology have provided extraordinary opportunities for improved irrigation management, such as the adoption of deficit

irrigation strategies and greater reliance on wastewater reuse to counteract decreases in available water supplies in comparison to the demands (English, Ch. 29). Ecological engineering has enabled the routine incorporation of ecosystem processes into irrigation designs, so that, for example, return flows are of higher quality than the original diversions. Irrigation management now considers a wider range of impacts, including public health. Coordinated institutional partnerships are now commonplace because of their utility in effectively implementing improved irrigation management technologies.

Groundwater management modeling
Groundwater resources remain critical for meeting water supply reliability targets and flow requirements for the maintenance of aquatic ecosystems. Informed husbanding of groundwater resources continues to be essential for the survival of people in many parts of the world. The unsustainable groundwater management practices of the past have been replaced with sustainable conjunctive use of groundwater (Pinder, Ch. 30). Over the past 40 years groundwater flow and transport models have been increasingly used to address issues related to geothermal energy, carbon sequestration, and long-term storage of high-level radioactive material from nuclear power plants and other sources. New occurrences of groundwater contamination are now rare.

Information technology
Geographic information systems (GIS) continue to be important tools for analyzing as well as displaying and understanding spatial data, and in its dynamic mode, time series data as well (Wallace, Ch. 31). Continued and combined advances in web-based mapping, community map collaboration, global positioning systems, wireless data communications, display technologies, and parallelization of computing devices, have all contributed to today's state-of-the-art GIS. Truly revolutionary ideas have been applied over the past 40 years and will continue to emerge for water resource applications. Today GIS is a mainstream "must-have" tool and it is hard to find any decision support system for river basin studies that does not use GIS.

> *We use and benefit today from the continued increase in computational capability, improved interoperability, expanded storage capability and connectivity, as well as a profound evolution of software and data norms .*

Information technology (IT) has had a major impact on how we are able to manage our environment and water resources (Rowney et al., Ch. 32). The continued increase in computational capability, improved interoperability, expanding storage capability and extending connectivity, as well as a profound evolution of software and data norms have given us what we use and benefit from today. This includes the ability to represent the real world more perfectly in analysis and simulation tools, revolutionizing engineering practice by enabling fine-grained representation of physical problems. Additionally, there have been shifts in the notion of information accreditation, a drive towards formal accreditation of common engineering tools, changes in fundamental engineering education, and a paradigm shift of the notion of professionalism in IT services sectors that have resulted in changes in practice, not just in speed and scale, but in kind.

To deal with complex water problems, more creative problem-solving has become necessary (McCuen, Ch. 33). This is now facilitated by computers that exhibit the creative processes of inspiration, preparation, illumination, and actualization. Advancements in computer technology, especially algorithms in the form of artificial intelligence based on the neurological processes of discovery, have been developed. Today's engineers are using emotions for creative idea generation. Engineering education has required attitude changes and broader thinking skills such as those emphasized in the 25th edition of the ASCE Body of Knowledge (ASCE 2008).

> *More creative problem-solving is facilitated by computers that exhibit the creative processes of inspiration, preparation, illumination, and actualization.*

Werick (Ch. 34) writes to us in 2050 using advanced human-machine interface technology similar to that discussed by McCuen. Werick tells us about decision support systems based on the intertwining of social change and technical progression in chip technology and bioengineering. Multi-criteria decision-making models have been placed on implantable chips, and these implants have been programmed to enable true collaboration where all decision factors, even political ones, are optimized in the minds of all. Their full implementation has led to societal changes that permit community decision-making based on personal benefit-cost analyses.

Transformative developments in nanotechnology, biotechnology, information technology, and neurotechnology have led to more efficient, resilient and robust adaptation mechanisms for the water sector (Stakhiv, Ch. 35). Over the past forty years, the water resources/environmental field has focused their efforts through major enterprises akin to the "Manhattan Project" and the "Harvard Water Program" to adapt to the changing environments that has enabled water resources infrastructure planning and management to deal more effectively with change and uncertainty.

Just as they were 40 years ago, models are still needed to assist planners and managers making water resources development decisions to estimate the economic, environmental and social impacts of those potential decisions (Loucks, Ch. 36). However, today computer-based optimization and simulation models incorporated within interactive graphics-audio based decision support systems are better able to identify plans, designs and policies that maximize desired impacts, minimize undesired ones, and clearly describe tradeoffs between the two types. It is also common today to observe stakeholders actively leading the planning and management processes within a dynamic virtual/holographic reality environment.

> *It is now common to observe stakeholders actively leading the planning and management processes within a dynamic virtual/holographic reality environment.*

Evolution of new disciplines

Today the subfield of hydrology called hydromorphology is no longer a new concept (Vogel, Ch. 37). It continues to focus on the structure, evolution and changing morphology of hydrologic systems over time, especially those impacted by humans. Multiple and interacting sources of uncertainty and nonstationarity dominates approaches used by hydromorphologic engineers to detect, attribute, design, manage, and predict the performance of water resource systems.

Water managers are now using multi-century time series of hydrological variables derived from tree-ring chronologies to plan for a wider spectrum of extreme conditions in individual watersheds, especially in the western US (Biondi and Strachan. Ch. 38). Because the past is rich with episodes outside the modern envelope of variability, these longer historical perspectives have reduced the uncertainty associated with regional modeling and operational forecasts. A more mechanistic understanding of the processes that link wood formation to the hydrologic cycle and more sophisticated reconstruction tools to produce tree-ring chronologies have enabled dendrohydrologists to integrate dendrochronological records into mechanistic simulation models of small and large watersheds.

ACHIEVING THESE VISIONS

Creating visions of an ideal 2050, and even thinking about how to achieve them, is relatively easy. Getting our society to accept such visions, and to be willing to meet the challenges of achieving them, is harder. We today tend to be way too focused on satisfying short-run goals to the exclusion of longer-term ones, even when we know it will be to our, and our children's, detriment in the long-run.

> *We tend to be way too focused on satisfying short-run goals to the exclusion of longer-term ones, even when we know it will be to our, and our children's, detriment in the long-run.*

Consider, for example, the needs of, and associated costs for, bringing our water resources infrastructure up to a reasonable level of repair and performance. In the US, aging, broken or under-designed wastewater collection and treatment systems discharge billions of liters of untreated wastewater into surface waters each year. The US Environmental Protection Agency estimates that $390 billion (today's dollars) will be needed over the next 20 years to update or replace existing systems and build new ones to meet increasing demands (ASCE 2010).

Just where is this amount of money going to come from? How will the necessary political support be created and sustained over the next 40 years? Do we need to wait until the failure rate and associated inconveniences exceed some threshold before people say enough? Perhaps we need to market this gaping long-standing need in infrastructure (and not just water-related infrastructure) as a "war" on infrastructure decay and, in the US, let the US Army Corps of Engineers take charge. Even if this flippant suggestion were implemented, its successful outcome is doubtful.

These infrastructure cost estimates are based on the assumption that we will have to dig up old sewers and replace them with similar systems. Further, they are based on the assumption that both sewage and stormwater runoff loads must be treated. But do we need systems of such capacities? What we need first is a vision of alternatives to sewers. Engineers of the telecommunication industry today are no longer installing telephone wires to and from each phone in every house, apartment and office desk because wireless technology is eliminating this past need. Can we develop and implement a sewerless technology? Can we eliminate the use of sewers and the use of treated high quality water to transport wastewater from our toilets to wastewater treatment plants? Can wastewaters from urban apartments and office buildings be "treated" on site, eliminating, in a cost-effective way, the need for sewers in urban areas? Can we think of cities that are green with vegetation that effectively and substantially reduces the need for stormwater sewers and instead promotes runoff infiltration into the ground? As a vision for 2050, why not? Indeed steps in this direction are already being taken in various cities of the world.

The Erie Canal, Hoover Dam, New York City's water supply reservoirs and aqueducts, and the California Aqueduct that brings water from northern California to southern California are all examples of visionary projects. Visionary projects are an engineering tradition, and have been major drivers of economic development. With some exceptions, such grand projects as these involving substantial amounts of concrete may not be possible or even desirable today, but other grand projects that involve structural and non-structural components, and that serve multiple purposes, objectives, stakeholders and institutions, are no less challenging and will require no less vision and leadership from both professionals and politicians. Who will show and articulate that vision? And who will lead all of us in fulfilling that vision?

The sorry state of our infrastructure and the unwillingness of the public to want to pay for its upkeep is a symbol of how we may have lost our way. By refusing to pay for essential investments, the public and its politicians are sacrificing long-term growth (as well as employment opportunities). And why not? After all, this seems to be a winning electoral strategy. Have we become a society whose leaders compete over who can show the least vision, the least concern about the future and the greatest willingness to pander to short-term, self interests?

We have some four decades to achieve these visions of an ideal 2050. The extent to which we succeed will depend on how well professionals from a range of disciplines can effectively work together to show the public, and its decision-makers, this vision and how it can be achieved. It no doubt will require making tradeoffs between expenditures that yield immediate modest short-term benefits and expenditures that yield far larger long-term benefits. It will involve dealing with risks and uncertainties. It will involve adapting our visions and strategies to changing environments and social goals. Rather than being intimidated by all of these challenges, we should seize the opportunity to contribute as much as we can toward conquering them. What could be more useful as well as enjoyable?

Given the substantial uncertainties associated with the future, robust planning and decision-making methods are worth exploring. Substantial uncertainty also favors the implementation of a flexible or adaptive development and management strategy, making incremental adaptive decisions, rather than undertaking large-scale changes, when possible. Adaptive measures as part of a sequence of responses allow for incremental or directional change in the future, as considerations of reliability, vulnerability, knowledge, experience and technology dictate. This may also include delaying implementation of specific (potentially harmful) measures while exploring options and building the necessary standards and regulatory environment.

The long-term future may be dominated by factors that are very different from current ones and hard to imagine based on today's experiences. Meaningful long-term planning must confront the potential for surprise. Any policy carefully tuned to address a "best guess" forecast or well-understood risks may fail in the face of inevitable surprise. Narratives about the future, whether fictional or historical, can help humans imagine futures different from the present. Scenario planning provides a framework for *what if–ing* that stresses the importance of multiple views of the future together with their uncertainties. However, despite the advantages of using scenario analyses, they all suffer from ultimately being wrong. We really cannot put our feet into the shoes of those living some 40 to 50 years from now and observe their environment, needs, objectives or goals, and beliefs. What we *can* do is seek robust strategies that perform reasonably well for a wide range of plausible scenarios and that allow adaptation over time to a changing environment.

> *It is important for all of us to have our visions, and as a community strive for a consensus vision, and then work hard to achieve it.*

An important component of any attempt to delve into and improve the future is forward-looking thinking. All too often within the water and environmental field, this forward-looking vision is missing. We often hear of supposed medical breakthroughs that will result in significant health improvements 20, 30, or even 50 years in the future. The same cannot be said for the water and environmental field where most of our research and development is expected to provide paybacks within periods of a few years or maybe a decade at most. What is required to establish such forward-looking research and development programs? Three elements of such programs include: 1) governmental and private investments that value work that does not necessarily result in immediate gains; 2) academic acceptance of research that is far more speculative; and 3) increased emphasis on creativity at all levels of education and research.

And finally a jab at ourselves. As a profession, we are not very successful in obtaining the support for, and accepting the risks of, taking on really forward-looking research. This should be the task of our academic institutions, especially the more prestigious ones that can attract and train our most gifted graduates. Their job is not only to teach knowledge, but to create it as well. With noted exceptions, much of the research efforts in these institutions consist of marginal improvements on some otherwise well-established process or algorithm or planning procedure. It is safe, it is fundable, it can be completed in the "normal" time for a master's or doctorate degree, and it can be published. If we cannot increase our efforts to work with leading industries, government research laboratories, and universities on more risky projects aimed at achieving advances in the physical, chemical, biological, and social sciences, and in engineering technology, envisioned in that ideal vision of the future, that vision will not happen. It is our job. We are the researchers, whether in academia or industry or government service, and we are the peer reviewers of research proposals, and the members of advisory panels of funding agencies. Let's have the courage to at least begin to make a significant change in the types of research we engage in today.

We as professionals in environmental and water resources management can certainly adopt adaptive, robust and forward-looking development plans and policies as we proceed on this journey into the future. However, without visions of where we want to go, such plans and policies may not lead us to a state we would like to observe when we get there. We hope this visioning exercise motivates each of us to think more about what we would like to see in the future, and then work towards that ideal. Our visions of what we wish to see in 2050 may differ and certainly they will evolve. That's okay. We believe what is important is for all of us to have our visions, and as a community strive for a consensus vision, and then work hard to achieve it.

REFERENCES

2030 Water Resources Group. (2009). *Charting our water future: economic frameworks to inform decision-making*, 2030 Water Resources Group, <http://www.mckinsey.com/clientservice/water/charting_our_water_future.as px> (Oct, 2010).

American Society of Civil Engineers (ASCE). (2010). 2009 *report card for America's infrastructure*, <http://www.infrastructurereportcard.org/>(8 December 2010).

American Society of Civil Engineers (ASCE). (2008). *The ASCE body of knowledge*, 2nd ed., ASCE Press, Inc., Reston, VA.

American Society of Civil Engineers (ASCE). (2007). *The vision for civil engineering in 2025*, prepared by the ASCE Steering Committee to Plan a Summit on the Future of the Civil Engineering Profession in 2025, American Society of Civil Engineers, Reston, VA.

Cosgrove, W. J., and Rijsberman, F. R. (2000). *World water vision*, Earthscan Publications, Ltd., London, UK, <http://www.worldwatercouncil.org/index.php?id=961> (Dec, 2010).

Palmisano, S. (2010). *The Future of the city*, Newsweek, Jan 25, 2010-05-14

Raskin, P. D., Electris, C., and Rosen, R. A. (2010). "The century ahead: searching for sustainability." *Sustainability*, 2, 2626-2651.

World Business Council for Sustainable Development. (2010). *Vision 2050: the new agenda for business*, World Business Council for Sustainable Development, Geneva, Switzerland, <http://www.wbcsd.org/templates/TemplateWBCSD5/layout.asp?type=p&MenuId=MTYxNg&doOpen=1&ClickMenu=LeftMenu> (Oct, 2010).

Index

Page numbers followed by _t_ indicate a table.